Britain and Germany in Europe 1949–1990

STUDIES OF THE GERMAN
HISTORICAL INSTITUTE LONDON

GENERAL EDITOR: Peter Wende

Britain and Germany in Europe 1949–1990

EDITED BY
JEREMY NOAKES, PETER WENDE,
AND
JONATHAN WRIGHT

THE GERMAN HISTORICAL
INSTITUTE LONDON

OXFORD
UNIVERSITY PRESS

OXFORD

UNIVERSITY PRESS

Great Clarendon Street, Oxford ox2 6DP

Oxford University Press is a department of the University of Oxford.
It furthers the University's objective of excellence in research, scholarship,
and education by publishing worldwide in

Oxford New York

Athens Auckland Bangkok Bogotá Buenos Aires Cape Town
Chennai Dar es Salaam Delhi Florence Hong Kong Istanbul Karachi
Kolkata Kuala Lumpur Madrid Melbourne Mexico City Mumbai Nairobi
Paris São Paulo Shanghai Singapore Taipei Tokyo Toronto Warsaw

with associated companies in Berlin Ibadan

Oxford is a registered trade mark of Oxford University Press
in the UK and in certain other countries

Published in the United States
by Oxford University Press Inc., New York

British Library Cataloguing in Publication Data

Data available

Library of Congress Cataloging in Publication Data

Data applied for

ISBN 0–19–924841–9

1 3 5 7 9 10 8 6 4 2

Typeset in Baskerville
by Hope Services (Abingdon) Ltd.
Printed in Great Britain
on acid-free paper by
Biddles Ltd., Guildford and King's Lynn

Foreword

This volume grew out of a Medlicott Symposium held at the University of Exeter in March 1998. The Medlicott symposia were established by the Department of History at the University of Exeter in memory of Professor W. N. Medlicott who held the chair and was head of the Department during the post-war years. The topics selected for the symposia reflect the research interests of Professor Medlicott and central to these were international history and, more specifically, German diplomatic history of the nineteenth and twentieth centuries. In the light of this, a symposium on the relations between Britain and Germany between 1949 and 1990 appeared highly appropriate. The Department approached the German Historical Institute in London, who very kindly agreed to become joint organizers of the symposium. The organizers then brought together leading scholars from both countries.

Quite apart from the requirements imposed by the format of the Medlicott series, the topic of Anglo-German relations during this period recommended itself as a subject of major importance. Moreover, the timing of the symposium, nearly a decade after the reunification of Germany in 1989, seemed very appropriate, with the intervening years facilitating a nuanced picture of what could now be regarded as a discrete period of British–German relations. Since Britain was one of the former occupying powers with residual responsibilities, particularly in Berlin, and also a key member of NATO at a time when Germany was at the heart of the Cold War, and with West Germany as a leading member of the EEC and a growing economic power during a period when Britain was conducting an agonized courtship of the Common Market, diplomatic, defence, and economic relations between the two countries inevitably provided the main focus for the symposium. However, relations between Britain and the two Germanies were by no means confined to high politics and trade, and the organizers of the symposium were anxious to explore broader cultural influences both at the élite and the popular levels. Thus, for Britain throughout much of the period relations with Germany, particularly at the popular level, were fraught with tensions of various kinds. It could be argued that one reason for this emotionally charged atmosphere was that the British people's attitude to Germany was, in part at any rate, an aspect of their response to a post-war era of reduced international status and relative economic decline. In Germany, by contrast, attitudes to Britain were more balanced because less central to the nation's self-image. Here, at any rate in the Federal Republic, Britain's main influence was arguably in the role it played in helping to provide models for the post-war Western orientation of German intellectual and cultural life both at the élite and popular levels.

We would like to take this opportunity to thank a number of individuals who helped to make our symposium a success. Professor Kathleen Burk, Professor Harald Husemann, Professor Charlie Jeffery, Professor Roger Morgan, Professor Peter Pulzer, and Professor Marie-Luise Recker made invaluable contributions to the discussion and/or in chairing the sessions with tact and efficiency. Dr Lothar Kettenacker played an invaluable role as a member of the steering group. Last, but by no means least, we owe a great debt to Dr Angela Davies for her careful preparation of the manuscript for publication.

Jeremy Noakes
Peter Wende
Jonathan Wright

Contents

Illustrations

(between pp. 214–215)

1. Peter Brookes (*The Spectator*, 24 Feb. 1990). 'One Fatherland'
2. Bernard Cookson (*Sun*, London, 7 Apr. 1987). 'Ve vill occupy ze sunbeds here at precisely 5 a.m. . . . !'
3. Bill Caldwell (*Daily Star*, 5 June 1992). 'At least there's a guaranteed sunbed.'
4. Bill Caldwell (*Daily Star*, 4 July 1990). 'Please don't get so excited, Mein Fuhrer—it's only a game of football.'
5. *Private Eye*, cover, 'Anglo-German Relations' (No. 90, 28 May 1965).

Acknowledgements

We are grateful to the following for permission to reproduce material used in this volume:

The Goethe-Institut London for excerpts from the exhibition catalogue *Coping with the Relations: Anglo-German Cartoons from the Fifties to the Nineties*, edited by Karin Herrmann, Harald Husemann, and Lachlan Moyle (Osnabrück: secolo verlag, 1993).

Express Newspapers, the *Sun*, London, and *The Spectator* for cartoons. Cartoons by Bill Caldwell: © Express Newspapers; cartoon by Bernard Cookson: © Bernard Cookson/News International Newspapers Limited (7 April 1987); cartoon by Peter Brookes: © *The Spectator* (24 February 1990).

Private Eye for kind permission to reproduce its cover, No. 90, 28 May 1965.

Frau Hella Wolter for the cartoon by Jupp Wolter on the jacket of this volume.

Introduction
Britain and Germany in Europe, 1949–1990

Jonathan Wright

The subject of Anglo-German relations since the foundation of the Federal Republic in 1949 has, until recently, been comparatively neglected by historians.[1] This is in striking contrast to the attention devoted to the relationship in the first half of the century: the growing hostility before 1914,[2] the attempts at European reconstruction in the 1920s,[3] the ever-absorbing topic of appeasement,[4] wartime planning for post-war Germany,[5] the early history of the Cold

I should like to thank my co-editors and my colleagues Anne Deighton, Anthony Glees, and Peter Oppenheimer for their very helpful comments. They are not, of course, responsible for any errors that remain or the opinions expressed here.

[1] Exceptions include D. C. Watt, *Britain Looks to Germany: British Opinion and Policy towards Germany since 1945* (London: Oswald Wolff, 1965); Karl Kaiser and Roger Morgan (eds.), *Britain and West Germany: Changing Societies and the Future of Foreign Policy* (Oxford: Oxford University Press, 1971); Karl Kaiser and John Roper (eds.), *Die Stille Allianz: Deutsch-Britische Sicherheitskooperation* (Bonn: Europa Union, 1987); and the series of the *Arbeitskreis Deutsche England-Forschung*, edited by Gustav Schmidt. A new study concentrating on the post-Cold War period is Klaus Larres and Elizabeth Meehan (eds.), *Uneasy Allies: British–German Relations and European Integration Since 1945* (Oxford: Oxford University Press, 2000).

[2] Paul M. Kennedy, *The Rise of the Anglo-German Antagonism, 1860–1914* (London: Allen & Unwin, 1980).

[3] For example, Douglas Newton, *British Policy and the Weimar Republic 1918–1919* (Oxford: Clarendon Press, 1997); F. L. Carsten, *Britain and the Weimar Republic: The British Documents* (London: Batsford, 1984); Anne Orde, *British Policy and European Reconstruction after the First World War* (Cambridge: Cambridge University Press, 1990); Constanze Baumgart, *Stresemann und England* (Cologne: Böhlau, 1996).

[4] For example, R. A. C. Parker, *Chamberlain and Appeasement: British Policy and the Coming of the Second World War* (London: Macmillan, 1993); Gustav Schmidt, *The Politics and Economics of Appeasement: British Foreign Policy in the 1930s* (Engl. edn., Leamington Spa: Berg, 1986); David Dilks, ' "We must hope for the best and prepare for the worst": The Prime Minister, the Cabinet and Hitler's Germany, 1937–1939', *Proceedings of the British Academy*, 73 (1987), 309–52.

[5] Albrecht Tyrell, *Großbritannien und die Deutschlandplanung der Alliierten, 1941–1945* (Frankfurt am Main: Metzner, 1987); Lothar Kettenacker, *Krieg zur Friedenssicherung: Die Deutschlandplanung der britischen Regierung während des Zweiten Weltkrieges* (Göttingen: Vandenhoeck & Ruprecht, 1989).

War,[6] and military government to 1949.[7] Of course, there are some good reasons for this difference: relations between Britain and the Federal Republic were less central to either side than they had been earlier in the century; the decline of British power meant that for both their relationship with the United States took priority;[8] in addition, partly as a consequence of British hesitation and obstruction, the Federal Republic developed a unique relationship with France as its primary partner in European integration.[9] Nevertheless, Anglo-German relations remained important both directly to each side and as part of the Western alliance system as a whole during the Cold War. Britain and the Federal Republic were partners in NATO; indeed, the Federal Republic's admission into NATO had been contrived by British diplomacy after the plan for a separate European Defence Community had failed to find a majority in the French National Assembly.[10] Britain and the Federal Republic rapidly became important markets for each other; their bilateral trade grew faster than the overall export growth of either in the whole period 1950–86, and since then they have become more closely integrated by a sharp bilateral increase in investment (albeit from a very low base).[11] In contrast to earlier periods of Anglo-German relations, Britain and the Federal Republic shared a democratic political culture, though a different

[6] Anne Deighton, *The Impossible Peace: Britain, the Division of Germany and the Origins of the Cold War* (Oxford: Clarendon Press, 1990).

[7] J. Foschepoth and R. Steininger (eds.), *Britische Deutschland- und Besatzungspolitik 1945–49* (Paderborn: Schöningh, 1985); Ulrich Reusch, *Deutsches Berufsbeamtentum und britische Besatzung: Planung und Politik 1943–1947* (Stuttgart: Klett Cotta, 1985); Barbara Marshall, *The Origins of Post-War German Politics* (London: Croom Helm, 1988). See also the contribution by Peter Alter in this volume.

[8] Roger Morgan, *The United States and West Germany 1945–1973: A Study in Alliance Politics* (London: Oxford University Press, 1974); Wolfram F. Hanrieder, *Germany, America, Europe: Forty Years of German Foreign Policy* (New Haven: Yale University Press, 1989); Wm. Roger Louis and Hedley Bull (eds.), *The Special Relationship: Anglo-American Relations since 1945* (Oxford: Clarendon Press, 1986); Gustav Schmidt (ed.), *Zwischen Bündnissicherung und privilegierter Partnerschaft: Die deutsch-britischen Beziehungen und die Vereinigten Staaten von Amerika, 1955–1963* (Bochum: Universitätsverlag Dr. N. Brockmeyer, 1995).

[9] Haig Simonian, *The Privileged Partnership: Franco-German Relations in the European Community, 1969–1984* (Oxford: Clarendon Press, 1985).

[10] Saki Dockrill, *Britain's Policy for West German Rearmament 1950–1955* (Cambridge: Cambridge University Press, 1991), 133–50; Anne Deighton, 'Britain and the Creation of Western European Union, 1954', in Anne Deighton (ed.), *Western European Union 1954–1997: Defence, Security, Integration* (Oxford: European Interdependence Research Unit, St Antony's College, 1997), 11–27.

[11] Jens Hölscher and Henry Loewendahl, 'Anglo-German Post-War Economic Relations and Comparative Performance', Ch. 11 below.

pattern of political institutions. This facilitated the renewal and strengthening of contact between the two societies at many levels, for example the far-sighted support by German educational foundations for foreign graduates to study in Germany, as well as an increasing number of German students at British universities.[12]

Unsurprisingly, for most of the post-1949 period, Anglo-German relations have been cordial and constructive. There have, however, also been significant conflicts: notably when Harold Macmillan, as Prime Minister, tried to bully Konrad Adenauer into supporting Britain against France over the form of the European Community[13] and later when Margaret Thatcher tried to hold up the process of German unification.[14] These conflicts revealed an underlying tension, which was the more surprising as good relations became the norm. Both arose at root from British fears of German 'dominance'.[15] This was, and is, a complex phenomenon—a compound of national stereotypes,[16] collective memories of two world wars, resentment at the change in power relationships between Britain and Germany over the last fifty years, and anxiety for the future of distinctive features of British politics in a European 'super-state', whose institutions resemble those of the Basic Law rather than the Westminster model.[17] The

[12] See the contribution by Peter Alter in this volume.

[13] John P. S. Gearson, *Harold Macmillan and the Berlin Wall Crisis, 1958–62: The Limits of Interests and Force* (London: Macmillan, 1998); Martin P. C. Schaad, *Bullying Bonn: Anglo-German Diplomacy on European Integration, 1955–61* (London: Macmillan, 2000).

[14] Margaret Thatcher, *The Downing Street Years* (London: Harper Collins, 1993), 790–99, 813–15. Philip Zelikow and Condoleezza Rice, *Germany Unified and Europe Transformed* (Cambridge, Mass.: Harvard University Press, 1995).

[15] For a discussion of this fear in its historical and contemporary contexts see Lothar Kettenacker, 'Großbritannien—Furcht vor deutscher Hegemonie: Englische Spekulationen über die Deutschen', in Günter Trautmann (ed.), *Die hässlichen Deutschen? Deutschland im Spiegel der westlichen und östlichen Nachbarn* (Darmstadt: Wissenschaftliche Buchgesellschaft, 1991), 194–207; id., 'Zwangsläufige deutsche Dominanz?—Über Konstanten britischer Europaperzeptionen', *Tel Aviver Jahrbuch für deutsche Geschichte*, 26 (1997), 235–49.

[16] For the earlier history of these stereotypes, see Peter Pulzer, 'Der deutsche Michel in John Bulls Spiegel: Das britische Deutschlandbild im 19. Jahrhundert', in *Jahrbuch des Historischen Kollegs 1998* (Munich: Oldenbourg, 1999), 3–19.

[17] On discussion of the Westminster model in the early years of the FRG, see Marie-Luise Recker, 'Westminster als Modell? Der Deutsche Bundestag und das britische Regierungssystem', in Gerhard A. Ritter and Peter Wende (eds.), *Rivalität und Partnerschaft: Studien zu den deutsch-britischen Beziehungen im 19. und 20. Jahrhundert. Festschrift für Anthony J. Nicholls* (Paderborn: Schöningh, 1999), 313–35. For the correspondence between the institutions of the FRG and the European Union, Simon J. Bulmer, 'Shaping the Rules? The Constitutive Politics of the European Union and German Power', in Peter J. Katzenstein (ed.), *Tamed Power: Germany in Europe* (Ithaca: Cornell University Press, 1997), 49–79.

aim of this volume is to contribute towards an understanding of the evolution of Anglo-German relations, both at the level of high politics and at the no less important level of the interaction of two societies and cultures.[18] The volume is the outcome of a conference of British and German historians, sponsored jointly by the University of Exeter as part of a series in memory of W. N. Medlicott, who as the senior editor of *Documents on British Foreign Policy 1919–1939* was a leading authority on Anglo-German diplomatic history, and the German Historical Institute in London.

The first theme considered is the way in which Anglo-German relations have affected and been affected by the process of European integration. Clemens Wurm discusses British policy in the first phase from 1948 to 1955. He points out that in 1948–9, with the intensification of the Cold War, Britain's priority shifted from Western Europe to the United States as the ultimate guarantor of survival. The preservation of Britain's world role, and the political and economic arrangements that underpinned it, were seen as essential to maintain Britain's standing in the United States and American willingness to invest in the Atlantic alliance. The Schuman Plan of 1950, however, showed both that Britain and France had different conceptions of the future of Europe and that Britain could not exercise a veto over the supranational plans of the West Europeans, particularly since they enjoyed American support. British governments of both parties failed to reassess Britain's long-term interests in the light of this reverse. This was understandable, given Britain's distinctive position, but it was nevertheless a decisive failure, reflected in the detached position Britain again took in the negotiations for the European Economic Community in 1955–6.

Harold Macmillan is an interesting example in this context. As Alan Milward shows, he had a keen sense from the early 1950s of the importance to Britain of European integration. Indeed, among political leaders of his generation he was unusually sensitive to the danger of a supranational European Community, seeing in it a threat to British trade and Britain's international standing. Macmillan consistently advocated an active policy towards Europe but with the aim of preventing supranational institutions emerging.

---

[18] On the difficulty of establishing the links between them, Roger Morgan, *Britain and Germany since 1945: Two Societies and Two Foreign Policies*, The 1988 Annual Lecture (London: German Historical Institute, 1989).

He failed to understand the power of the forces driving the process of integration and discovered too late that Britain lacked the means to control them. The application to join the Community in 1961 was his last desperate attempt to change its character. Of particular interest to this volume is the way in which Macmillan constantly portrayed the danger of a united Europe in terms of German domination. He drew on his sense of history, on the tradition of British opposition to any single power controlling the continent, on his experience of both wars and the 1930s, on the perils for the British economy of a world with American tariffs, a German-dominated European customs union, and a declining Commonwealth unit. In this way he showed the power that historical analogy can exercise over policy-makers and the way it can mislead, when it is not balanced by an equal sense for the importance of change. Macmillan does not appear to have reflected on the significance of the Federal Republic becoming a successful democracy or why it was that European states that had, unlike Britain, been occupied by Germany in the war saw a supranational Europe as a solution to the problem of German power.

In a wide-ranging contribution, Martin Schaad considers the complications for the Federal Republic of being caught between the rival British and French concepts of European integration. In the case of the British attempt to attach the Free Trade Area to the Common Market, he points out that this failed not simply because of an emerging Adenauer–de Gaulle axis, encouraged by Adenauer's suspicions of Macmillan's willingness to appease the Soviet Union over Berlin, but because of Bonn's priority of the political union of Europe. The British proposals found support on economic grounds in Ludwig Erhard's Ministry of Economics but their fate was sealed by the (correct) suspicion of the *Auswärtiges Amt*, shared by Adenauer, that they were (at least in part) a ploy to keep Europe divided.[19] In a second example, Schaad considers the way in which Anglo-German relations became enmeshed in the political alignments that had been formed in Bonn in the late Adenauer period. In particular, he shows how in 1964–5

[19] See also Sabine Lee, 'German Decision-Making Elites and European Integration: German "Europolitik" during the Years of the EEC and Free Trade Area Negotiations', in Anne Deighton (ed.), *Building Postwar Europe: National Decision-Makers and European Institutions, 1948–63* (London: Macmillan, 1995), and Sabine Lee, *An Uneasy Partnership: British–German Relations between 1955 and 1961* (Bochum: Universitätsverlag Dr. N. Brockmeyer, 1996).

Chancellor Erhard and his Foreign Minister, Gerhard Schröder, concerned at President de Gaulle's increasingly headstrong policies towards NATO, the European Economic Community, and German unification, looked (in vain) for support from London against the Gaullist wing of the Christian Democrats, which was spurred on by Adenauer. In a concluding example, Schaad considers the role of the Franco-German axis and the place of Britain in the post-Cold War European Union, as it contemplates enlargement beyond the dreams of its founding fathers. Could it be that the British model of looser integration, in the form of different degrees of integration for different member states, or 'variable geometry' as it is called, will shape the future after all?

Despite the differences between the British and German concepts, European integration was not solely or even mainly a source of conflict in Anglo-German relations. Piers Ludlow assesses the importance of German support for British entry to the Community from 1961 to 1972. He points out that German officials disliked the division between the six members of the European Community and the seven members of the Free Trade Area, both for economic reasons and because a divided Western Europe was a source of weakness in relation to the Soviet Union. The Federal Republic therefore welcomed British initiatives to join the Community and offered its support, subject only to the constraints set by maintaining Germany's *rapprochement* with France and the integrity of the Community itself. Germany could not force its views on France but its attitude helped to moderate and ultimately to overcome the division caused by Britain's exclusion.

In contrast to differences over European integration, which persisted after Britain became a member of the Community in 1973, the relationship between the two states in the area of security—the second theme of this volume—remained close. Both states were loyal members of NATO, despite opposition from the SPD in the 1950s and the Labour Party in the 1980s and despite the flirtation with Gaullism of a wing of the CDU in the early 1960s.[20] In each state, governments of different parties accepted the overriding imperative that defence against the Warsaw Pact was possible only with the United States. The singular power in this respect was

---

[20] On the West German aspect of the relationship, see Emil J. Kirchner and James Sperling (eds.), *The Federal Republic of Germany and NATO: 40 Years After* (London: Macmillan, 1992).

France under President de Gaulle and his successors, which complicated the Franco-German relationship.[21] Despite the common ground between Britain and Germany, however, there were some differences of perspective. For Britain, as for other European powers, the American guarantee through NATO also served a secondary purpose, namely the containment of German power within the alliance and therefore a tacit guarantee that Germany would never again threaten the peace of Europe. This was also consciously willed by Adenauer and silently accepted by his successors as part of the wider purpose of Western integration. However, it obviously left unresolved the awkward question of the priority to be put on German reunification by German governments and their NATO partners. It also left open the sensitive question of whether Germany would ever have equal status in NATO, particularly with regard to strategy and nuclear weapons. As the natural first theatre if conventional war were to break out, this was clearly a matter on which Germans had reason to feel strongly. However, the British were in practice scarcely less at risk and this led to a shared concern to represent European interests to the United States, as American strategy developed in ways which made the Europeans feel uncomfortable.[22]

Gustav Schmidt sets the scene with a discussion of the complexities of Germany's place in Western strategy in the early 1950s, from the negotiations for the abortive European Defence Community to the Federal Republic's entry into NATO. He explores the conflicts between the goals of the major participants: the United States, Britain, France, the Federal Republic, and the NATO command. In particular, he stresses the ways in which nuclear strategy influenced policy. From 1952, Britain moved towards a policy of nuclear deterrence and keeping open the possibility of détente with the Soviet Union, while Adenauer's priority was to achieve a security guarantee from the United States in return for Western integration and German rearmament. After some discussion the United States also put the priority on Western integration before détente (and therefore before German reunification), partly because NATO

---

[21] Georges-Henri Soutou, *L'Alliance incertaine: les rapports politico-stratégiques franco-allemands, 1954–1996* (Paris: Fayard, 1996).

[22] Christoph Bluth, *Britain, Germany and Western Nuclear Strategy* (Oxford: Clarendon Press, 1995); Beatrice Heuser, *NATO, Britain, France and the FRG: Nuclear Strategies and Forces for Europe, 1949–2000* (London: Macmillan, 1997).

strategy required forward bases to allow for the deployment of nuclear weapons. The control and command of these weapons and the question of the Federal Republic's status as a non-nuclear power within the alliance raised further difficult issues.

Beatrice Heuser reviews the whole period of Anglo-German relations within NATO. She shows that despite the differences over how German interests were to be accommodated, solutions were found and co-operation remained the dominant key until the storms of the Thatcher era. The idea of German participation in a European multinational force, disliked by the British as a substitute for their independent nuclear force, was abandoned in favour of German membership in a Nuclear Planning Group in 1965. Here the two Defence Ministers, Denis Healey and Gerhard Schröder (and subsequently Helmut Schmidt), established an influential partnership and formulated the policy guidelines which were adopted by the alliance in 1969. The partnership continued into the 1980s with agreement by both governments on the stationing of Intermediate Nuclear Forces, despite public opposition, to maintain the balance of threat in Europe and to prompt negotiations for arms control beyond the superpower agreements on strategic weapons. It is a disturbing reflection on the antagonism generated by Thatcher and German unification that what appeared to be a well-established area of Anglo-German co-operation swiftly became a source of conflict and rivalry instead. Heuser suggests two explanations. First, the co-operation remained secret and its importance was therefore never recognized by a wide public. Second, there was a residual core of hostility among British attitudes towards Germany, which revealed itself in a desire to keep control of German strategy, and more generally in outbursts of anti-German sentiment fed, perhaps, by a sense of malaise at the decline of Britain.

The city of Berlin occupied a unique place in the post-war settlement. By reason of its four-power occupation, and being surrounded by the Soviet zone and, after 1949, the GDR, Berlin became the fulcrum for the two great trials of strength in 1948–9 and 1958–63 of the Cold War in Europe. As such, Berlin provided the supreme test of the commitment of the Western allies to uphold their ideals, and the rights of Germans under their protection, against Soviet pressure and threats. At the same time, the Berlin crises also provided a powerful argument for the Western allies to seek détente with the Soviet Union to find a lasting solution to the

Berlin problem. Anglo-German relations were caught up in both aspects of Berlin's role and displayed distinctive features in each.

Lothar Kettenacker reviews the impact of Berlin on British policy from 1944, when Britain proposed a special scheme for Berlin, to 1989–90 when Thatcher tried to use the status of an occupying power to delay German unification. With respect to the two Berlin crises, he contrasts the stout resistance of Ernest Bevin (as Foreign Secretary) and General Robertson (as the British Military Governor) in 1948 with the ambiguity and weakness of Macmillan in 1958–63. This reflected a wider shift in the British attitude to the Soviet threat between the immediate post-war period and a decade later. Whereas in the 1940s parallels were drawn between Stalin and Hitler,[23] a decade later Macmillan saw the Berlin crisis in terms of the 1914 analogy: 'Above all, we must not slip into the 1914 position—mobilisation sliding into war.'[24] Macmillan and his Foreign Secretary, Selwyn Lloyd, were prepared to offer *de facto* recognition of the German Democratic Republic in return for Soviet guarantees for the status of West Berlin. Adenauer also saw the danger of the crisis escalating out of control, but he was both contemptuous of Macmillan's attempts to play an independent role as a mediator and suspicious of his willingness to placate Khrushchev at the expense of the Federal Republic and its policy on unification.

Klaus Larres places the second Berlin crisis in the wider context of British policy towards the GDR in the 1950s and 1960s.[25] He shows in detail how, with the exception of the second Berlin crisis, British governments of both parties placed good relations with the Federal Republic and maintaining the cohesion of the Western alliance above the possible benefits to be derived from closer ties with the GDR. The GDR's main bait for recognition was trade. The ostensible opportunities for exports were attractive to British businessmen and officials at the Board of Trade in a period when

---

[23] Beatrice Heuser, 'Stalin as Hitler's Successor: Western Interpretations of the Soviet Threat', in Beatrice Heuser and Robert O'Neill (eds.), *Securing Peace in Europe, 1945–62* (London: Macmillan, 1992), 17–40.

[24] Macmillan diary entry, 4 Feb. 1959, quoted in Harold Macmillan, *Riding the Storm: 1956–1959* (London, Macmillan, 1971), 587–8.

[25] The history of Britain's relations with the GDR offers a case study in the politics of seeking and refusing recognition. The relationship is well described by Bert Becker, *Die DDR und Großbritannien 1945/49 bis 1973: Politische, wirtschaftliche und kulturelle Kontakte im Zeichen der Nichtanerkennungspolitik* (Bochum: Universitätsverlag Dr. N. Brockmeyer, 1991).

Britain's economic performance was sluggish compared to its major competitors. Another seductive argument was that the Federal Republic had a much larger volume of trade than Britain with the GDR. Despite the temptations, however, British governments were careful to maintain an official distance from the private business organizations involved from both the British and (supposedly) the East German side and refused requests for long-term credit guarantees. Only in November 1969 did Britain follow other Western states in allowing a three-year trade agreement to be signed. By that time, with Brandt as Chancellor and *Ostpolitik* ascendant in Bonn, there was little danger that this concession would be politically divisive.

The problem of Berlin and the issue of what attitude to adopt towards the GDR were bound up with British policy on German unification, the third theme of this volume. In the 1950s Churchill had a vision of a unified Germany at the centre of a European security system, with mutual guarantees on the model of the Locarno Pact, but this time involving the Western powers and the Soviet Union.[26] His ideas met with a hostile reception both in his own administration and in the United States. Thereafter, it became increasingly accepted by British governments that despite their public support for German reunification, the reality of two German states was likely to last as long as the Cold War. Both Anthony Eden, as Foreign Secretary and Prime Minister, and Macmillan were attracted towards schemes for reducing the tension between the two sides by military 'disengagement'. These proposals came to nothing before the second Berlin crisis and were subsequently replaced by attempts to limit nuclear testing and nuclear proliferation, followed by arms control agreements between the superpowers. Macmillan played a significant role in promoting the first Test Ban Treaty in 1963, with the support of President Kennedy.[27] As Larres points out, neither the Americans nor the British were sympathetic to West German attempts to exclude the GDR from the Treaty, an indication that détente now had priority over maintaining the pariah status of the GDR. This

---

[26] Klaus Larres, *Politik der Illusionen: Churchill, Eisenhower und die deutsche Frage 1945–1955* (Göttingen: Vandenhoeck & Ruprecht, 1995).

[27] Brian White, *Britain, Détente and Changing East–West Relations* (London: Routledge, 1992), 95–105.

stance was repeated by President Johnson in negotiating the Non-Proliferation Treaty in 1968 over Bonn's objections.[28]

The Federal Republic was thus forced to accommodate itself to American-led détente rather than merely British 'disengagement' plans or solo deviations over Berlin. The *Ostpolitik* of the Great Coalition of 1966–9 and its dramatic development once Willy Brandt became Chancellor in October 1969 was, in part, Bonn's response to this new situation. *Ostpolitik*, in turn, provoked a variety of reactions in London.[29]

In the main, Britain welcomed the Federal Republic's new policy, which was after all in line with Britain's own long-standing efforts to reduce tension in central Europe. Harold Wilson strongly supported Brandt in talks with President Nixon.[30] The same position was maintained, though more cautiously, by the Conservative government of Edward Heath, with Sir Alec Douglas-Home as Foreign Secretary, which took office in June 1970. Behind the scenes in the Foreign Office, however, more doubts were expressed.

These can be found in an interesting exchange of views which took place as Brandt's policy started to achieve a positive response from the Soviet Union in the summer of 1970.[31] The British ambassador in Bonn, Sir Roger Jackling, urged firm support for *Ostpolitik* 'because it appears to coincide with our own aim of reducing tensions in Europe, and because we need close bilateral relations with the Federal Republic'. The ambassador in Moscow, Sir Duncan Wilson, agreed. He interpreted Soviet policy as working actively 'for a *de facto* accommodation in Central Europe' with a view to influencing the 'future development of Europe as a whole', particularly in face of the negotiations for the enlargement of the European Community.[32] In a comment on this dispatch,

---

[28] Hanrieder, *Germany, America, Europe*, 91–5.

[29] See the recently published balanced and informative assessment by Roger Morgan, 'Willy Brandt's "Neue Ostpolitik": British Perceptions and Positions, 1969–1975', in Adolf M. Birke, Magnus Brechtken, and Alaric Searle (eds.), *An Anglo-German Dialogue: The Munich Lectures on International Relations* (Munich, 2000), 179–200.

[30] Michael Clarke, 'A British View', in Richard Davy (ed.), *European Detente: A Reappraisal* (London: Royal Institute of International Affairs, 1992), 93; Henry Kissinger, *The White House Years* (London: Weidenfeld & Nicolson, 1979), 416.

[31] G. Bennett and K. A. Hamilton (eds.), *Documents on British Policy Overseas*, Series III, Vol. 1, *Britain and the Soviet Union, 1968–72* (London: The Stationery Office, 1997), 243–6, 250–8. See the review by Anne Deighton, '*Ostpolitik* or *Westpolitik*? British Foreign Policy, 1968–75', *International Affairs*, 74/4 (Oct. 1998), 893–901.

[32] Sir D. Wilson to Mr Bendall, 3 July 1970; *Documents on British Policy Overseas*, Series III, 1, No. 48.

Sir Alec Douglas-Home added a cautionary note: 'But is there not a possible alternative that if the Europeans get together and America begins to withdraw her military presence the Soviet Union might have a better chance to manipulate the European scene and penetrate by showing herself co-operative and friendly?'

The relevant Deputy Under-Secretary in the Foreign Office, Sir Thomas Brimelow, summarized the results of subsequent internal discussion in a major dispatch sent to the principal embassies on 14 August 1970, immediately after the signature of the Treaty between the Soviet Union and the Federal Republic.[33] The dispatch carefully assessed the advantages and risks of recent developments. It interpreted the Treaty as 'a success for Soviet diplomacy' although not all its traditional demands had been achieved, including that of full diplomatic recognition of the GDR. However, the Soviet success 'is not necessarily a criticism of the Soviet–Federal German Treaty. Herr Brandt's long term calculation has been that only by recognizing realities can the Federal German Government create a situation in which the future reunification of Germany may become possible. . . . But whether the long term advantages for which Herr Brandt hopes will ever be achieved is an open question.' The danger of the Soviet Union acquiring influence over the discussions for an enlargement of the European Community was not rated highly, but in the longer term it might be able to complicate 'the intrinsically difficult policy of developing political and military cooperation in Western Europe' especially as 'there is a fairly widespread propensity to indulge in wishful thinking about *détente* in relations with the USSR, while few European Ministries of Finance are willing to authorise adequate defence expenditure'.

On the other hand, Brimelow continued, although in the past they had enjoyed 'trying to make our flesh creep' with the idea, the danger of the Soviet Union trying a new Rapallo policy was discounted. They might, however, encourage the FRG to greater independence of the West and hope 'one day they may be able to impose a radical change on the balance of power in Europe by playing the card of German reunification'. The greater danger in the medium term was that the Soviet Union would try to exploit 'détente' through their campaign for a European security conference to

---

[33] Sir T. Brimelow to Mr Edmonds, 14 Aug. 1970; ibid., no. 50.

extend their influence over Western Europe. This did not mean that the Soviet–German Treaty was 'in any sense unwelcome'. Brandt's policies were making it harder to sustain propaganda about German *revanchisme*. They might also 'make possible an easing and an increase in the scale of East–West relations'. This might, in turn, contribute 'to the internal evolution of the Communist systems in Eastern Europe', though equally their leaders would seek to contain the process. Indeed, if Western European co-operation developed, the Soviet leadership might tighten control over Eastern Europe and 'prevent the gradual process of *rapprochement* on which Herr Brandt seems to be pinning his hopes'. The conclusion was that 'our priorities in Europe should continue to be the collective security of Western Europe and Western European integration'. Until these were achieved, 'we must expect that Warsaw Pact propaganda regarding European security and *détente* will be designed to change the balance of power in Europe to our disadvantage. So long as this remains the case, the need for wariness and caution is not likely to diminish.'

This dispatch is a classic statement of the Foreign Office's traditional policy of seeking a balance between détente and security.[34] In the 1950s and early 1960s, Britain sought to complement the hard line of its NATO allies by finding ways to defuse tension. As the United States embarked on détente and the Federal Republic took the lead in Europe, British officials reverted to a more cautious policy which emphasized security. The four-power agreement on Berlin of September 1971, the main benefit of *Ostpolitik* for the Western occupying powers, was accepted without enthusiasm as the best that could be achieved in the circumstances.[35] Underlying this reserve, there was also an understanding of the decline in British influence. If the superpowers were engaged in accommodation, there was no role for Britain as mediator. The priority for British policy by the 1970s was to secure admission to the European Community, not to play an independent role on the global stage. Sir Duncan Wilson, for instance, argued that Britain should present itself to the Russians as having more to offer 'as a compact European power in the 1970s than as a declining world

[34] White, *Britain, Détente and Changing East–West Relations*, 162–87; Clarke, 'A British View', 86–113.
[35] See the exchange between Sir Alec Douglas-Home and Edward Heath, 1 Sept. 1971; *Documents on British Policy Overseas*, Series III, 1, 377.

power in the 1960s'.[36] Britain was content to support *Ostpolitik*, without either high hopes or serious objections. In any case, there was not much else it could do. An additional motive was the desire to maintain the co-operation of the Federal Republic for its renewed application to join the European Community, in the favourable climate created by President de Gaulle's resignation.

The contrast with British policy twenty years later, when German unification suddenly became a real issue, could hardly have been greater. In the early 1970s, unification seemed a remote possibility, part of a distant accommodation with the Soviet Union or, alternatively, a card which the Soviet Union might play to lure the Federal Republic from the Western alliance. When it happened in 1989–90, it came about in exactly the opposite way, through the erosion of Soviet power and a deliberate shift in Soviet priorities, allowing the conditions set by the West in the 1950s to be met—free elections and the right of the new state to remain in NATO. It is all the more surprising that this astonishing success for Western policy should have met with such a muted, and even hostile, British response.

An important part of the explanation was, of course, Margaret Thatcher. She had taken a prominent stand on behalf of East European dissidents, particularly 'Solidarity' during her visit to Poland in November 1988. As was to be expected, she welcomed the end of the Cold War and the triumph of democracy as, in part, a personal victory. But her pleasure was diluted by the return of an old anxiety, perhaps dating from her wartime childhood, of German domination.[37] In her own words:

This welcome revolution of freedom which swept eastern Europe raised great strategic issues, above all in the West's relations with the Soviet Union . . . But I also saw at once that it had profound implications for the balance of power in Europe where a reunified Germany would be

[36] In his Annual Review of the Soviet Union, 1 Jan. 1970, summarized in *Documents on British Policy Overseas*, Series III, 1, 206–7. Britain was indeed able to develop a new role in the 1970s and 1980s in the organization to co-ordinate the foreign policies of the members of the European Community, European Political Co-operation, and in the pan-European Conference on Security and Co-operation in Europe (the 'Helsinki process'). Clarke, 'A British View', 96–101. For an informative account of Britain's role in the Helsinki process from the Foreign Office documents, see Keith Hamilton, *The Last Cold Warriors: Britain, Détente and the CSCE, 1972–1975* (Oxford: European Interdependence Research Unit, St Antony's College, 1999).

[37] See the entry for 19 Dec. 1989 in the diaries of George Urban, *Diplomacy and Disillusion at the Court of Margaret Thatcher: An Insider's View* (London: I. B. Tauris, 1996), 133.

dominant. There was a new and different kind of 'German Question' which had to be addressed openly and formally: I did so.[38]

The way in which she did is well-known and has coloured perceptions of the British attitude to unification ever since. How far Thatcher's fears were, in fact, typical is much more doubtful. Polls showed considerable volatility, with the percentage in favour of unification between October 1989 and December 1990 varying between 45 and 72 per cent.[39] Of the broadsheet press, the *Guardian*, the *Observer*, the *Independent*, and the *Financial Times* were strongly critical of Thatcher's policy, while she received support from *The Times*, and with reservations from the *Daily Telegraph* and *The Economist*.[40] Nevertheless, because of the power a determined Prime Minister can wield in the Westminster system, British policy on unification carried the stamp of Thatcher's personal mission. Unsurprisingly, she failed to halt the process of unification. The time when Britain could resist, even with half-hearted French support, the combined weight of Germany and the United States was long past. The Foreign Office, as we have seen, had already accepted this fact in the early 1970s. Mrs Thatcher tried to reverse the trend by the power of argument but, on this occasion, she had to acknowledge that her policy met with 'unambiguous failure'.[41]

Sir Julian Bullard, British ambassador in Bonn in 1984–8, puts this dramatic story in perspective. He shows that although Mrs Thatcher was not alone in her fears, British policy was made in response to a wider agenda, including a range of issues raised by the Prime Minister herself. There was the danger that German unification might upset the process of reform initiated by

[38] Thatcher, *The Downing Street Years*, 769.

[39] A poll for *The Economist* in January 1990, which registered the lowest percentage support, also showed that 'Predictably the British young are more in favour of unification and less fearful of Germany than the old'. Ines Lehmann, *Die deutsche Vereinigung von außen gesehen: Angst, Bedenken und Erwartungen in der ausländischen Presse*, vol. i: *Die Presse der Vereinigten Staaten, Großbritanniens und Frankreichs* (Frankfurt am Main: Peter Lang, 1996), 289–91.

[40] Ibid. 292–430. Lehmann does not include the *Daily Telegraph* in her analysis but it is represented in the files of press cuttings of the German Embassy in London. These show that the *Daily Telegraph* was initially doubtful about unification (editorial, 19 Oct. 1989) but was later supportive of Kohl's leadership (editorial, 30 Nov. 1989) and by implication critical of Thatcher's unwillingness to accept the inevitable (editorial, 5 Feb. 1990). (I am grateful to the press department of the German Embassy for giving me access to this collection.)

[41] Thatcher, *The Downing Street Years*, 813. See also Lothar Kettenacker, 'Britain and German Unification', in Larres and Meehan (eds.), *Uneasy Allies*, 99–123.

Mikhail Gorbachev, as General Secretary, and indeed undermine Gorbachev himself. There was also the complexity of the issues raised by unification—legal, financial, political, the impact on European security and the European Community, Berlin, even the question of Germany's future frontiers. These were complex questions and there was a strong argument for taking them slowly to avoid mistakes that would be difficult to put right. Together with the Foreign Secretary, Douglas Hurd, British officials co-operated in helping to formulate solutions, though in practice this process was facilitated by the fact that Soviet leaders were ultimately willing to accept Western terms in their desire for a settlement. However, British policy was not made by Mrs Thatcher alone and, Sir Julian suggests, when the full story is known it will be seen in a better light.[42]

The context in which political decisions are made is formed not only by the immediate issue and the preferences of policy-makers but also by the political, economic, and social systems of the states they represent. The second half of this volume explores this broader context, highlighting both the contrasts between the two societies and the links which have been established since 1949. Together they help to shape the mutual perceptions and misperceptions which make up Anglo-German relations.

The economic success of the Federal Republic has been one of the *forces profondes* of the post-war period, helping to sustain ambitious political goals from European integration to German unification. It has also provided a ready measure of Britain's failure to maintain its leading position as an industrial power. The difference in achievement suggests more fundamental differences. Relative economic decline may be attributed to inconsistent policy-making, arising from the Westminster system of adversarial politics; to poor management and industrial relations, springing from ingrained class divisions not improved by the educational system; to the dominance of the City of London seeking short-term profits for shareholders at the expense of long-term investment; or simply to a sustained attempt to provide a generous welfare state and full employment which proved too heavy a burden on the public finances, aggravated by governments who preferred inflation to

---

[42] This conclusion is anticipated by Yvonne Klein, 'Obstructive or Promoting? British Views on German Unification 1989/90', *German Politics*, 5/3 (Dec. 1996), 404–31.

the political costs of cutting public spending.[43] It is beyond the scope of this volume to evaluate these or other theories about 'the decline of Britain'.[44] What is of interest for our theme is the degree to which in each case the Federal Republic supplies a counter-example: a consensual political system with decentralized powers, a meritocratic society without an educational divide by privilege, a consistent record of capital investment, the 'social market' model of the welfare state, and an independent central bank to maintain the value of the currency.[45] A symbolic moment, exemplifying the humiliation of Britain and the strength of the Federal Republic, was the British application for a conditional loan from the International Monetary Fund in September 1976 and Prime Minister James Callaghan's appeal to Chancellor Helmut Schmidt to support this request in Washington.[46]

Of course, the contrast between conditions in Britain and the Federal Republic may be overdrawn and the evidence does not all point in the same direction. The reversal of British economic policy, which started with Callaghan and Healey and became a crusade under Thatcher, altered the terms of the comparison. It became respectable (even in some quarters in Germany) to laud the Anglo-Saxon model of a deregulated economy, and the Westminster system which made possible a sharp change of direction, in comparison to the supposedly over-regulated Rhineland model and the political system in Bonn which blocked change and produced only 'Reformstau'. Although the terms of the debate changed, however, the perceived contrast between Britain and the

[43] See for instance, S. E. Finer (ed.), *Adversary Politics and Electoral Reform* (London: Anthony Wigram, 1975); Samuel H. Beer, *Britain Against Itself: The Political Contradictions of Collectivism* (London: Faber & Faber, 1982); Will Hutton, *The State We're In*, rev. edn. (London: Vintage, 1996).

[44] On the complexity of the concept and a critical discussion of rival theories, see Barry Supple, 'British Economic Decline since 1945' and Charles Feinstein, 'Success and Failure: British Economic Growth since 1948', in Roderick Floud and Donald McCloskey (eds.), *The Economic History of Britain since 1700*, 2nd edn., vol. iii: *1939–1992* (Cambridge: Cambridge University Press, 1994), 318–46, 95–122.

[45] See, for example, the comparative essays on the economy and political culture in Karl Rohe, Gustav Schmidt, and Hartmut Pogge von Strandmann (eds.), *Deutschland—Groß-britannien—Europa: Politische Traditionen, Partnerschaft und Rivalität* (Bochum: Universitätsverlag Dr. N. Brockmeyer, 1992).

[46] Kathleen Burk, 'The Americans, the Germans and the British: The 1976 IMF Crisis', *Twentieth Century British History*, 5/3 (1994), 351–69. Denis Healey, the Chancellor of the Exchequer, describes the crisis, during which he admits that 'For the first and last time in my life, for about twelve hours I was close to demoralisation', in Denis Healey, *The Time of my Life* (Harmondsworth: Penguin, 1989), 428–33.

Federal Republic remains at its centre, only slightly modified by a degree of convergence between Tony Blair's 'Third Way' and Gerhard Schröder's 'Neue Mitte'.[47]

Jens Hölscher and Henry Loewendahl chart the success of the German economy and the ways in which it outperformed Britain from the 1950s to the mid-1980s. In terms of Anglo-German trade, they highlight the significant difference as Germany's superiority in the road vehicles industry, leading to the acquisition (and subsequent disposal) of Rover by BMW and of Rolls-Royce by Volkswagen. Despite the improvement of key aspects of Britain's performance since the mid-1980s, it still lags behind Germany in per capita incomes and, perhaps more important, in the fraction of GNP devoted to capital investment and research and development. This suggests that the Rhineland model will be in a better position to shape its future than a British economy increasingly dependent on decisions taken elsewhere. Benedikt Koehler complements the picture with a survey of the City of London. He shows that the financial services industry has indeed been a British success story in the post-war period, even if sometimes for whimsical reasons such as the effect of United States' regulations in facilitating the Eurodollar market and the success of the German émigré, Sigmund Warburg, in exploiting the Eurobond market. Although sterling lost its importance as a reserve currency to the Deutschmark, the City of London preserved its position as a financial centre, inter alia responding to the growth of a global financial market with the deregulation of 'Big Bang'. The rapid increase in the number of German banks represented in London is evidence of the City's continuing success and of the new degree of integration of international financial markets.

The differences between the political and economic systems of Britain and the Federal Republic help to sustain a more or less constant public debate about differences in history, culture, and national characteristics. As the caricatures reproduced in this volume show, images of Germany in the British press vary from the unflattering to the offensive. Nor is this stereotyping the preserve

---

[47] Ralf Dahrendorf, 'Es lebe der Unterschied! Deutschland und Großbritannien in Europa', in Ritter and Wende (eds.), *Rivalität und Partnerschaft*, 363–70. The most notable example of convergence is perhaps the decision by the Chancellor of the Exchequer, Gordon Brown, in 1997 to restore to the Bank of England the responsibility for setting interest rates to achieve a target for inflation.

of tabloid journalism alone. It can be found equally on the left wing of the Labour Party and the Eurosceptics in the Conservative Party. For Lady Thatcher, a believer in 'national character', history warns that since unification under Bismarck, 'Germany has veered unpredictably between aggression and self-doubt'.[48] This might be described as a British élite image, captured in Churchill's reported aphorism that 'the Germans are either at your throat or at your feet'.[49] A more widespread critical view would depict Germans as efficient, highly organized, determined, humourless, unimaginative, and liable to bullying and racism. And from the German side, unattractive characteristics of the English would include arrogance, amateurishness, loutishness, xenophobia, and an inability to grow out of the Second World War. There is a significant difference, however, between the role which these images play for each side. The British media frequently express anti-German sentiments with no equivalent on the German side. Even a liberal newspaper, the *Guardian*, was prepared to carry an article by admittedly a professional controversialist, Julie Burchill, during the Kosovo crisis which contained the phrase 'scratch a Croat, find a Kraut' and concluded that, in contrast to the Second World War, 'by reducing Serbia to rubble, side by side with our buddies, the Luftwaffe, we're the Fascists'.[50] It is hard to imagine that similar language would have been tolerated about any other nation. Periodic controversies arise when a German Minister, as recently Michael Naumann, has the temerity to protest.[51] Judging by the press, anti-German sentiment has much greater resonance in Britain than the other way round. The Major Government even succumbed to the temptation of making Germany the scapegoat

---

[48] Thatcher, *The Downing Street Years*, 791.

[49] Quoted by D. C. Watt, *Britain Looks to Germany*, 114. Similar sentiments were expressed in the memorandum on the meeting at Chequers on 24 March 1990 between Mrs Thatcher and a group of British and American historians of Germany to discuss the potential dangers of German unification; the *Independent on Sunday*, 15 July 1990, reprinted in Harold James and Marla Stone (eds.), *When the Wall Came Down: Reactions to German Unification* (New York and London: Routledge, 1992), 233–9 . For a rounded view of Churchill's attitude to Germany, see Gordon A. Craig, 'Churchill and Germany', in Robert Blake and Wm. Roger Louis (eds.), *Churchill* (Oxford: Oxford University Press, 1993), 21–40.

[50] Julie Burchill, 'The Age of Reason', the *Guardian* (3 Apr. 1999). Another example of this genre is the diatribe by A. A. Gill, 'Hunforgiven', in the *Sunday Times* (11 July 1999).

[51] See, for instance, the report in *The Times* (15 Feb. 1999) quoting British historians' opposition to Naumann's remarks.

for Britain's withdrawal from the exchange rate mechanism in 1992.[52]

It is natural, of course, that the Second World War should still exert a powerful hold on the British imagination. It also serves the purposes of that section of the British press that is opposed to European integration to play on fears of German dominance.[53] However, one may speculate that the heroic symbolism of 1940 also provides psychological respite from a sense of failure in the post-war period and this helps to keep the anti-German stereotype alive.[54] If so, it might explain why British policy towards European integration has been prey to bouts of unreasoning angst about German domination, so at odds with the habitual British claim to pragmatism. There is an intriguing parallel with German Anglophobia before the First World War, which was more a reflection of domestic political and social divisions than of contact with Britain.[55] In any event, this is essentially a British problem, but in so far as anti-German sentiment is an accepted, if vulgar, part of British discourse, it is not only a tedious joke. It damages Anglo-German relations and, like any prejudice, it obstructs accurate perception.[56]

An interesting example of the influence of public opinion on policy-makers is provided by Anthony Glees in his account of the visits of President Heuss to Britain in 1958 and of the Queen to the Federal Republic in 1965. Visits by heads of state, who are not also heads of government, are seldom of much political consequence. In this instance, however, because of the recent past and the sensitivities of British governments and the monarch to public and press opinion, the visits acquired an unusual emotional charge. Heuss was welcomed with care and decorum but without warmth. Oxford University's Hebdomadal Council accepted the Theodor

[52] Anthony Glees, 'The Diplomacy of Anglo-German Relations: A Study of the ERM Crisis of September 1992', *German Politics*, 3/1 (Apr. 1994), 75–90.

[53] Peter J. Anderson and Tony Weymouth, *Insulting the Public? The British Press and the European Union* (London: Longman, 1999), 60–92.

[54] See, for instance, Richard Davy, 'Großbritannien und die Deutsche Frage', *Europa Archiv*, 45/4 (25 Feb. 1990), 139–45, and the discussion of public attitudes under the Major Government in Anthony Glees, 'Building a New Europe: Britain, Germany and the Problem of Russia', *German Politics*, 8/1 (Apr. 1999), 163–8.

[55] Wolfgang J. Mommsen, *Two Centuries of Anglo-German Relations: A Reappraisal* (London: German Historical Institute, 1984), 18–22.

[56] Hugo Young, 'Germano-phobia still grips us as the British refuse to forget the war', the *Guardian* (16 Feb. 1999).

Heuss Research Fellowship but declined the Foreign Office's request for an honorary degree for the Federal President. The Queen's return visit was postponed with various excuses (some genuine), as Macmillan concluded that the political risk in terms of British public reaction was not worth the goodwill to be gained in Germany. In the end, the repeated postponement threatened to become an issue between the two governments—a snub to the dignity of the Federal Republic. The extraordinary welcome the Germans gave the Queen, when the visit finally took place, both showed its significance as a symbol of recognition and acceptance that the post-war era was over and, in turn, helped to carry the British media and public opinion in its wake. Glees suggests that it opened the way to the most fruitful period of co-operation between the two countries until old fears were revived by unification.

It is the task of intellectuals to question national myths as well as sometimes to create them. Anthony Nicholls shows in his study of modern and contemporary historians how actively British and German historians have been engaged in the nineteenth and twentieth centuries in both endeavours. He demonstrates a convincing trend since 1945 away from patriotic history among historians of Germany in both countries. In the 1950s and 1960s Germany's liberal intelligentsia largely adopted the view that Germany had followed a disastrous course from the eighteenth century, which distinguished it from the classic democracies of Britain, France, and the United States. This view both reflected, and perhaps assisted, the process of building a democratic political culture in the Federal Republic. It was left to British historians to attack the *Sonderweg* thesis in the 1980s, pointing out that the model made favourable assumptions about Britain which were far from self-evident. In the great controversies about German history in the post-war period, British and German historians have been found on both sides of the debates. In this instance, at least, one can point to the emergence of a genuinely international community.

As Peter Alter points out in his survey of Anglo-German cultural relations after 1945, this achievement did not happen in a vacuum. One happy consequence of the military occupation of Germany, unlike 1919, was the growth of cultural links starting from the 're-education' policy of military government. The British Council in Germany was soon complemented by the German Academic Exchange Service and the Goethe Institute in Britain.

The Königswinter Conferences developed into a uniquely successful forum for debate between élites from both sides. One measure
of the importance of this institutional framework is the research it
has generated in both Britain and Germany. Another is the
absence of any comparable relationship in the inter-war period.

Ease of communication depends upon language. One of the
developments since the Second World War, so taken for granted that
it is often unremarked, is the way in which English has established
itself as the first foreign language in the Federal Republic. Klaus
Reichert subjects this development to a close, critical examination.
He shows the dangers of impoverishment in the humanities that
exist from the adoption of a media—and computer—based form of
English monoculture, that destroys the thought patterns of German
and which, in fact, makes it harder to understand Shakespeare or
Milton than if Latin or French were acquired first. On the other
hand, he also suggests that the decline of exclusive national languages may have advantages—in the case of German borrowing
from English, a wittier, more playful, and more agile German influenced among other sources by pop music and rap.

One arena of Anglo-German confrontation which it is impossible to ignore is football. Andreas Helle reviews the coverage in the
British and German press of the matches between the two national
teams since 1966. He shows the degree to which these encounters
have become charged with emotion on the British side, as a clash
between two cultures, with Germany replacing Scotland from 1970
as 'the old enemy'. The belligerent language of the English
tabloids, especially in the European championships of 1996, suggests that victory and (more often since 1966) defeat are seen as
symptoms of national revival and decline. The Germans are seen
as playing a 'modern' Continental style of game, efficient and
methodical, whereas the English have (or lack) heart. On the
German side, metaphors of war are a cultural taboo and while
there is some introspection about German stereotypes, there is also
a greater tendency to treat England as simply one respected opponent among others.

It is not the task of an introduction to draw conclusions and,
given the range of the essays in this volume, conclusions could in
any case be only tentative and impressionistic. Certain themes,
however, recur. For most of the post-war period, the interests of
Britain and the Federal Republic have been congruent though their

bilateral relationship has not been of primary importance to either. Anglo-German relations have accordingly been generally good within a multilateral framework, formed most obviously by the United States, France, the other West European powers, and, at a distance, the Soviet Union and its allies.[57] Nevertheless, there have been times of tension. Adenauer and his successors frequently found the British arrogant and unhelpful, while British governments at times resented the privileged relationship between Bonn and Paris or, more recently, Bonn and Washington. Underlying this tension have been the fears, evoked by Macmillan and paraded by Thatcher, that European integration would lead to German 'domination' of the continent. This fear, in turn, became entangled in some quarters with 'the decline of Britain' question from the 1960s. It was perhaps inevitable that this so-called decline should be instinctively measured against the success of the Federal Republic, given the Second World War and the very different starting points afterwards. That instinct was enhanced by the differences between the political, economic, and social systems of the two countries, which made comparison natural and instructive.[58] In the 1940s and 1950s, British policy-makers could not conceive of their future as part of a European Community organized on supranational lines. As the perception of decline became general in the 1960s and 1970s, by contrast, entry into the European Community was widely seen as necessary to reinvigorate the economy and maintain Britain's political standing.[59] This process was, however, also opposed by powerful minorities in each of the main parties and even by some of those who regarded it as inevitable. This opposition resurfaced in 1989–90 in a new fit of fear at German unification. It remains to be seen whether this will prove a temporary spasm or become an enduring feature of the British political landscape.

[57] For a concise summary of the interactions within NATO, see Gustav Schmidt, 'Introduction' to 'Changing Perspectives on European Security and NATO's Search for a New Role: From the 1960s to the Present', *Contemporary European History*, 7/3 (Nov. 1998), 287–310.

[58] This represents only the latest phase of a long history of comparing Britain with the German territorial states, and particularly Prussia, as representing different types in the history of the modern state. John Brewer and Eckhart Hellmuth (eds.), *Rethinking Leviathan: The Eighteenth-Century State in Britain and Germany* (Oxford: Oxford University Press for the German Historical Institute London, 1999), 1–21.

[59] Not all supporters were moved by purely pragmatic motives. One who can claim to have identified with the movement for European integration is Edward Heath. See Edward Heath, *The Course of My Life: My Autobiography* (London: Hodder & Stoughton, 1998), 721–26.

Although it is understandable that British attitudes to Germany since 1949 have been influenced by perceptions of British decline, there is an irrational element in this comparison. Economic historians are doubtful about how far, if at all, the British economy has suffered a decline, other than that which was inevitable as a result of the century-long reversion from being the first industrial power and a global imperial power, a reversion only hastened by the Second World War. The same could be said of Britain's political influence. The perception or misperception of British decline and the way it has affected some British attitudes to Germany and to European integration is thus richly ironic. The fear of 'German dominance' and 'loss of sovereignty' is a defensive reflex, and shows a refusal to question the assumptions on which it is based—notably that power shared is power lost. An unprejudiced study of the success of the Federal Republic since 1949 demonstrates the opposite. But the inherited norms of British politics—single majority-party government at home and the balance of power on the European continent—have made this hard to accept. Perhaps membership of the European Union will yet help to modify these norms. Perhaps, on the other hand, Germany's European identity will be weakened by the challenges which now face the European Union. At the very least, it seems safe to conclude that the history of Britain and Germany in Europe since 1949 is too interesting and serious a subject to be neglected by historians.

Part I

EUROPEAN INTEGRATION

2

Britain and West European Integration, 1948–9 to 1955
Politics and Economics

CLEMENS A. WURM

This essay examines the British government's attitude towards European integration from 1948–9 to 1955. It identifies the domestic and international forces that shaped Britain's European and integration policies. Combining political and economic approaches, the analysis includes forms of economic integration which are too often left out in the literature. Their inclusion considerably modifies the conventional assessment of Britain's policy towards European integration.

The essay deals first with underlying reasons for British reticence towards integration, describes the main lines of Britain's European policy, and looks at the years 1948–9 when the government defined its policy towards European integration. The second and central part investigates the government's attitude towards the main continental European initiatives for integration. The third part summarizes the argument and briefly turns to the question of how successful Britain was in its European and integration policies until 1955.

Why concentrate on the period from 1948 to 1955? In 1948–9 the British government defined its attitude towards European integration. In 1955, the foreign ministers of the six Schuman Plan countries took a fresh initiative for integration at Messina. From 1948–9 to 1955, despite differences of emphasis, there was a large measure of agreement in London on the basic lines of Britain's European and integration policies. The search for a new policy began in 1955–6 when a range of external and domestic factors caused the government to redefine the relative weight of the Commonwealth, the USA, and Europe in Britain's political priorities.

The term 'integration' also needs to be examined. There is no agreed definition of integration. Very generally speaking, we can take it to mean the amalgamation of, or the formation and maintenance of, close patterns of interaction between previously autonomous units. These patterns can be of a political, economic, or social nature.[1] For the purpose of this study, integration means the process of creating political communities with binding commitments (that is, the supranational dimension). In the period under discussion Britain, in the name of autonomy, rejected the contractual renunciation of sovereignty and membership in a politically integrated Western Europe.

I

Britain's European and integration policies differed from those of continental European countries, and in order to see the British government's policy on European integration in a proper perspective one has to keep in mind three aspects which can only briefly be touched upon here. Britain had won the war and did not regard itself as 'just another European country'. Belief that Britain was a world power was part of the mental world of its political leaders. The relationship between the United States, the Soviet Union, and Great Britain—'the crucial triangle'[2]—was the point of reference for Britain's post-war policy, and British attitudes towards Western Europe and European integration were developed in this framework. The main goal was to maintain Britain's world role in an international system increasingly dominated by the United States and the Soviet Union.

Britain's foreign trade and finance were concentrated on the world outside Europe. The sterling area was the world's second most important monetary subsystem and the pound sterling was, with the dollar, the leading international currency. In the late 1940s around 40 per cent of the world's trade was transacted in sterling.

---

[1] William Wallace, 'Introduction: The Dynamics of European Integration', in id. (ed.), *The Dynamics of European Integration* (London: Pinter Publishers, 1990), ch. 1; id., *The Transformation of Western Europe* (London: Pinter Publishers, 1990).

[2] Avi Shlaim, *Britain and the Origins of European Unity 1940–1951* (Reading: The University of Reading, 1978), 104–14.

Britain was 'the world's second biggest international trader'.[3] Almost 50 per cent of its exports and 40 per cent of imports were with the Commonwealth. In 1950 only a quarter of Britain's exports went to Western Europe, just over 10 per cent to the six Schuman Plan countries. Not until the mid-1950s was the direction of the flow of trade reversed, coinciding with Britain's gradual turn towards the EEC. An even more pronounced concentration on the world outside Europe can be seen in British foreign investments.

There were, third, strong mental barriers to close ties with Europe and to European integration. The ambivalence towards Europe was deeply rooted in history and had been reinforced by the impact of the war.[4] British membership of supranational European institutions was ruled out by both political parties. The advocates of active and direct participation in European integration were a small group and had little influence in the House of Commons. In the harsh words of Donald Watt they were 'outsiders, distinguished outsiders and distinguished nobodies'.[5] In his famous Zurich speech of 19 September 1946 Winston S. Churchill, as leader of the opposition, had called for the formation of 'a kind of United States of Europe' under Franco-German leadership. Yet, in his view Britain should 'sponsor' and support the New Europe, but not become a part of it. When in November 1951 Churchill became Prime Minister of the Conservative government, he continued the European and integration policies of the Labour governments. The 'Conservative Europeanists'—more European in outlook than the mainstream of the Conservative Party—favoured closer British co-operation with Europe in confederal or intergovernmental arrangements. The group of 'Tory Strasburgers'— the Conservative delegates to the Strasburg Assembly of the

[3] Alan S. Milward and George Brennan, *Britain's Place in the World: A Historical Enquiry into Import Controls 1945–60* (London: Routledge, 1996), p. xiv.

[4] Jill Stephenson, 'Britain and Europe in the Later Twentieth Century: Identity, Sovereignty, Peculiarity', in Mary Fulbrook (ed.), *National Histories and European History* (London: UCL Press, 1993), 230–54; Kenneth O. Morgan, 'The Second World War and British Culture', in Brian Brivati and Harriet Jones (eds.), *From Reconstruction to Integration: Britain and Europe since 1945* (Leicester: Leicester University Press, 1993), 33–46; id., 'England, Britain and the Audit of War', *Transactions of the Royal Historical Society*, 6th ser., 7 (1997), 131–53.

[5] Cited by Hans-Peter Schwarz, 'Die Strassburger Anfänge multinationaler Integrations-Historiographie', in Raymond Poidevin (ed.), *Histoire des débuts de la construction européenne (Mars 1948–Mai 1950) / Origins of the European Integration (March 1948–May 1950)* (Brussels: Bruylant, 1986), 453.

Council of Europe which included Boothby, Macmillan, Maxwell-Fyfe, and Sandys—wrongly believed that Britain could 'lead' Western Europe on Britain's terms.[6]

Yet Western Europe was a vital area of British interests. Recent research has shown that the British government kept a close watch on the situation on the European continent and, if necessary, actively intervened to shape European developments. In March 1947 Britain concluded the Treaty of Dunkirk with France. The British government played a leading role in implementing the Marshall Plan, initiated the Brussels Pact of March 1948, and was a driving force behind the founding of NATO. In January 1948, Foreign Secretary Ernest Bevin pleaded for a 'Western Union' including the overseas territories of Britain, France, and other colonial powers.[7]

Political stability, economic recovery, and military security were the goals Britain strove to attain in Western Europe. European co-operation was seen as a means of containing Communism, of enhancing Britain's prestige, and of reasserting Britain's world power. Yet to what extent would Britain be prepared to tie its fortunes to those of Western Europe? Would Britain move beyond its traditional attitude towards the European continent? Did Britain see itself as a European power and share the ambitions of those on the European continent who envisaged binding institutions and a common European future?

For the reasons set out above the limitations on Britain taking part in any European association had been narrow right from the beginning. They were set even more narrowly in 1948–9 when the British government, in a slow and gradual process, reappraised its global policy, defined its attitude towards European integration, and determined the limits of its commitment to Europe. The process was characterized by a marked shift away from Europe towards reliance on the USA. The explanation for this shift is complex and, as yet, incomplete. The reappraisal occurred against the background of increasing Cold War tensions, America's commitment to the defence of Europe, growing continental European

---

[6] Sue Onslow, *Backbench Debate within the Conservative Party and its Influence on British Foreign Policy, 1948–57* (Basingstoke: Macmillan, 1997), chs. 2–5.

[7] For surveys (with the literature) see Sean Greenwood, *Britain and European Cooperation since 1945* (Oxford: Blackwell, 1992), chs. 2–3; John W. Young, *Britain and European Unity, 1945–1992* (Basingstoke: Macmillan, 1993), ch. 1. 'Western Union' meant different things to different people and Bevin's ideas remained vague.

pressure for European integration, and increasing doubts in Whitehall about the stability of Western Europe and the economic and political benefits for Britain of close European co-operation. It coincided with the transformation of the Labour Left's attitude towards the USA initiated by the Marshall Plan and its abandonment of the Third Force vision.[8] The outstanding events accompanying the reappraisal were the signing of the Atlantic Treaty in April 1949 and the devaluation of the pound sterling from $4.03 to $2.80 in September 1949.

Britain turned to the vision of an 'Atlantic Union' and to closer co-operation with the United States and the Commonwealth. As the Chancellor of the Exchequer and the Foreign Secretary set out in an important policy paper of October 1949: 'Our relations with these areas take priority over our relations with Europe and for that reason alone there is a limit to the part we can play in European union.'[9] The 'special relationship' and the Atlantic alliance became the centre of British policy. Bevin saw the creation of NATO as his most significant achievement as Foreign Secretary. Viewed from London, Britain had established a 'new relationship' with the United States.[10] For political, military, and economic reasons the closest association with the USA was deemed indispensable. Britain must be America's principal ally. It had 'to remain willing to sustain a world position so that the United States would continue to find it a useful investment'.[11] Everything had to be done to maintain the role of sterling, the sterling area, and Commonwealth trade because leadership of the Commonwealth would strengthen Britain's status in Washington as the major partner of the United States.

In Britain's order of political priorities Europe had occupied the third place since the war, after the Commonwealth and the USA; it now came to be seen as 'the residual arena' in the three circles.[12]

---

[8] Jonathan Schneer, *Labour's Conscience: The Labour Left 1945–51* (Boston: Unwin Hyman, 1988); id., 'Hopes Deferred or Shattered: The British Labour Left and the Third Force Movement, 1945–49', *Journal of Modern History*, 56 (1984), 197–226.

[9] 'Proposals for the Economic Unification of Europe', Memorandum by the Secretary of State for Foreign Affairs and the Chancellor of the Exchequer, 25 Oct. 1949; PRO, CAB 129/37—C.P. (49) 203.

[10] 'Council of Europe', Memorandum by the Secretary of State for Foreign Affairs, 24 Oct. 1949; CAB 129/37—C.P. (49) 204.

[11] Peter Weiler, *Ernest Bevin* (Manchester: Manchester University Press, 1993), 182.

[12] Christopher Lord, *Absent at the Creation: Britain and the Formation of the European Community, 1950–2* (Aldershot: Dartmouth Publishing Company, 1996), 85.

European economic co-operation was not completely dismissed but the commitment to Western Europe had to be limited. Above all, Britain's economic structure had to be kept intact. 'We must not run risks which would jeopardise our chance of survival if the attempt to restore Western Europe should fail.'[13] When Western Europe broke down or was overrun by the Soviet Union, Britain, in co-operation with the USA and the Commonwealth, must be able to restore Western Europe. Close economic integration with Europe was ruled out because this would damage the British economy, undermine the resources of the sterling area, and hurt Commonwealth trade. 'On merits, there is no attraction for us in long-term economic co-operation with Europe. At best, it will be a drain on our resources. At worst, it can seriously damage our economy',[14] concluded a crucial meeting of senior Whitehall officials in January 1949. The 'basic premise'[15] of Britain's policy towards European integration is summarized in Bevin's statement of October 1949: 'Our relationship with the rest of the Commonwealth and, almost equally important, our new relationship with the United States ensure that we must remain, as we have always been in the past, different in character from other European nations and fundamentally incapable of wholehearted integration with them.'[16]

Charles S. Maier and Gustav Schmidt have rightly argued that Britain's attitude towards Western Europe after 1949 rested on a delicate balance between political and economic factors.[17] Whereas West Germany made economic concessions for political

[13] 'Our Policy to O.E.E.C. and our Proposals for its Structure', Memorandum by the Secretary of State for Foreign Affairs and Chancellor of Exchequer, 25 Jan. 1949; CAB 134/221—E.P.C. (49) 6.

[14] Minute of a meeting of Whitehall officials held on 5 Jan. 1949, reproduced in Richard Clarke, *Anglo-American Economic Collaboration in War and Peace 1942–1949*, ed. Alec Cairncross (Oxford: Clarendon Press, 1982), 209.

[15] Sally Dore, 'Britain and the European Payments Union: British Policy and American Influence', in Francis H. Heller and John R. Gillingham (eds.), *The United States and the Integration of Europe: Legacies of the Postwar Era* (New York: St Martin's Press, 1996), 167–97, 176.

[16] 'Council of Europe', Memorandum by the Secretary of State for Foreign Affairs, 24 Oct. 1949; PRO, CAB 129/37—C.P. (49) 204.

[17] Charles S. Maier, 'Alliance and Autonomy: European Identity and U.S. Foreign Policy Objectives in the Truman Years', in Michael J. Lacey (ed.), *The Truman Presidency* (Cambridge: Cambridge University Press, 1989), 273–98; Gustav Schmidt, ' "Tying" (West) Germany into the West—But to What? NATO? WEU? The European Community?', in Clemens A. Wurm (ed.), *Western Europe and Germany: The Beginnings of European Integration* (Oxford: Berg Publishers, 1995–6), 137–74.

gains in its integration and European policies, London pursued the opposite strategy. Economic integration with Europe was ruled out because this would damage the British economy and hurt the sterling area and Commonwealth trade. But Britain would help to provide military security for Western Europe, assure America's commitment in Europe, and play the traditional role of a balance between Germany and France. Britain's political importance combined with its prestige—its perceived role as trans-Atlantic mediator and intermediary between the rest of Europe and the United States and as a security provider—would guarantee Britain's political influence on the Continent, help contain integrationist schemes, and prevent things there from developing in a way prejudicial to Britain's interests.

II

Throughout the post-war years the British government firmly rejected European federalism and federalist solutions. The Labour Party was convinced that a federal Europe would be anti-socialist, dominated by conservative or 'reactionary' forces.[18] Britain, it was argued, was different from other European nations. It had a long, independent history as a nation-state which formed the legitimate framework for political action. Britain was a global, not just a European power. It had no written constitution favouring the informal relationship characteristic of the Commonwealth. The British government's view was clearly revealed in its reactions to the plans to set up a European Assembly put forward by the European Movement after the Hague Congress of May 1948. Bevin in particular was upset. He rejected the notion that the Consultative Assembly of the Council of Europe could or should become a European Parliament. In the negotiations over the plan the British government made sure that the Council of Europe would be based on intergovernmental co-operation and that its

---

[18] Michael Newman, *Socialism and European Unity: The Dilemma of the Left in Britain and France* (London: Junction Books, 1983), 121 ff.; Eleonora Guasconi, 'Il Labour Party, il Trade Union Congress e il processo di integrazione europea dal 1945 al 1957', in Andrea Ciampani (a cura di), *L'altra via per l'Europa: Forze sociali e organizzazione degli interessi nell'integrazione europea (1947–1957)* (Milan: Francoangeli, 1995), 112–26.

functions would remain limited.[19] The Council of Europe was formed in May 1949. It had only consultative powers. Defence issues were excluded from its agenda since they would be covered by NATO. Policy would have to remain national and co-operative. For federalists the Council of Europe was a great disappointment.

Like federalism, schemes for European regional economic integration found no favour with British governments. The Americans and the Economic Co-operation Administration (ECA) strongly encouraged 'economic integration' as a key to Europe's economic recovery and as a step towards political union. Among the West European countries France in particular flirted with the idea of customs unions or economic unions and up to 1950 discussed proposals with its immediate neighbours, mainly in order to contain Germany.

When discussing Britain's attitude towards customs unions it is important to distinguish between British membership in a European customs union and a European customs union without Britain. In 1947–8 there had been support in the Foreign Office for British participation in a European customs union. The idea was, however, rejected by the Board of Trade and the Treasury, though for different reasons. The Board of Trade, which was highly protectionist, feared the dissolution of imperial trading arrangements, whereas the Treasury regarded a European customs union as a threat to the sterling area. Bevin, who in 1947–8 seems to have been in favour of British involvement in a European customs union for political reasons, wavered over the issue and in the middle of 1948 came out against the idea.[20] Since then—and until Britain's application for accession to the EEC in 1961—British membership in a European customs union was ruled out.

Though the case against customs unions was, fundamentally, a political one, the economic arguments should not be underestimated. In any case, political motives were not separable from economic or social ones and some of the arguments changed over time. One major obstacle was the dollar shortage. A European customs union would not solve the dollar problem, an important consideration in the late 1940s. Another obstacle was the idea of

[19] Marie-Thérèse Bitsch, 'Le Rôle de la France dans la naissance du Conseil de l'Europe', in Poidevin (ed.), *Histoire des débuts*, 165–98; John W. Young, *Britain, France and the Unity of Europe 1945–51* (Leicester: Leicester University Press, 1984), 108 ff.

[20] Alan S. Milward, *The Reconstruction of Western Europe 1945–51* (London: Methuen, 1984), ch. 7; Michael Hogan, *The Marshall Plan: America, Britain, and the Reconstruction of Western Europe, 1947–1952* (Cambridge: Cambridge University Press, 1987), ch. 3.

'economic sovereignty'. A major policy paper by Cripps and Bevin set out that Britain could not accept proposals for European 'economic unification' which involved (*a*) the loss of the government's responsibility for budgetary and credit policy or the management of reserves, (*b*) hindrance of British attempts to earn dollars, (*c*) European influence on the size of British dollar-earning or dollar-saving UK industries, and (*d*) any weakening of imperial preference.[21] The Labour Party and the Labour governments had an ambiguous attitude towards competition[22] and there was little belief in the potential economic benefits of customs unions. Though accepting in principle some of the standard arguments in favour of economic unions such as increased productivity or economic modernization, the emphasis was on the difficulties and risks involved. Denis Healey and Hugh Dalton from the International Department of the Labour Party strongly and aggressively argued that, in the short term, economic unions would cause dislocation, unemployment, loss of production, and social convulsion.[23] Customs unions, it was believed, would lead inevitably to political union. This was ruled out. For the government the objective was the one-world system, not integration with the regional or limited area of Western Europe. 'Complementary trade' with the Commonwealth underpinned by imperial preference seemed more attractive than 'competitive trade' with the economies of Western Europe.[24]

[21] 'Proposals for the Economic Unification of Europe', Memorandum by the Secretary of State for Foreign Affairs and the Chancellor of the Exchequer, 25 Oct. 1949; PRO, CAB 129/37—C.P. (49) 203; Jim Tomlinson, *Democratic Socialism and Economic Policy: The Attlee Years, 1945–1951* (Cambridge: Cambridge University Press, 1997), ch. 2.

[22] Helen Mercer, *Constructing a Competitive Order: The Hidden History of British Antitrust Policies* (Cambridge: Cambridge University Press, 1995); ead., 'Anti-Monopoly Policy', in Helen Mercer, Neil Rollings, and Jim D. Tomlinson (eds.), *Labour Governments and Private Industry* (Edinburgh: Edinburgh University Press, 1992), 55–73.

[23] On the attitude of the Labour Party, Healey, and Dalton see the documents reprinted in Walter Lipgens and Wilfried Loth (eds.), *Documents on the History of European Integration*, iii: *The Struggle for European Union by Political Parties and Pressure Groups in Western European Countries 1945–1950* (Berlin: Walter de Gruyter, 1988), esp. nos. 223 and 227. Dalton and Healey were sharply criticized by Labour MP Ronald W. G. Mackay who advocated British membership in a federal Europe. 'I cannot approve of this persistent denigration of the possible value of a single market. . . . To my mind such a market must, in the end, be an advantage.' Letter to Dalton, 9 Nov. 1949; LSE archives, Mackay papers 13/7b.

[24] Edmund Dell has rightly remarked that the preference for complementary as against competitive economies was 'inconsistent with Britain's multilateral professions, redolent of the most primitive mercantilism'; see Edmund Dell, *The Schuman Plan and the British Abdication of Leadership in Europe* (Oxford: Oxford University Press, 1995), 85.

The British government's attitude has been sharply criticized in
the literature. Yet there was a good economic rationale behind its
attitude and the policy is quite understandable under short-term
considerations, as even its critics admit. Membership in a
European customs union 'had nothing immediately to offer to the
process of economic reconstruction in Britain'.[25] There were practical problems to overcome which, however, were never put to
the test. Would a Western European customs union including the
colonies of the member states have been feasible? Could the
Commonwealth and a Western European customs union have
been co-ordinated and combined? Would a European customs
union including Britain in which the member states would have
received some form of preference have been acceptable to the
Americans? This remains unclear. On the other hand it has been
rightly argued that in the long run the Commonwealth provided
but a precarious substitute for Britain's involvement in Western
Europe, that Western Europe would have provided a better framework for growth, productivity, and national income than the
Commonwealth, and that there was evidence of this at the time.[26]
   The British policy towards European customs unions or economic unions without Britain is difficult to describe in detail,
though the general attitude seems clear. Both political and economic reasons militated against the idea. Continental European
customs unions would affect Britain's political role in Europe. By
according preferences to its members a customs union would dis-
criminate in tariffs against Britain's trade and damage its economic
and commercial interests. 'There were episodes when London's
policy was prepared to tolerate the formation of a European customs union excluding Britain, or at least to say in Washington that
it tolerated it. But economically, even when the political opposition
was muted, the conclusion was always firm that such a development could only hurt the United Kingdom.'[27]
   Among West European countries France was the main advocate
of a European customs union, and France approached Italy and
the Benelux countries even before the Marshall Plan. Named after
the countries involved, the proposed schemes became known as

---

[25] Milward, *The Reconstruction of Western Europe*, 248.
[26] Ibid., ch. 11; Lord, *Absent at the Creation*, 71 ff.
[27] Milward and Brennan, *Britain's Place in the World*, 41.

Fritalux and later as Finebel, a grouping of France, Italy, the Netherlands, Belgium, and Luxembourg. European economic integration was strongly supported by the Americans as a key to economic recovery and a step towards political union. Paul Hoffman, the head of the Economic Co-operation Administration (ECA), gave enthusiastic encouragement to economic integration in an address to the OEEC on 31 October 1949. The British, however, opposed Finebel, which was finally buried in early 1950. The British government favoured economic co-operation in a broader framework and put pressure on the Dutch, who insisted on Britain's prior consent and West Germany's inclusion in the scheme—something the French would not accept at the time. Yet it would be wrong to conclude that Finebel primarily foundered on Britain. Opposition and scepticism were widespread in all the countries involved, even in France.[28]

With the Schuman Plan and the foundation of the European Coal and Steel Community (ECSC) the idea of a European customs union receded into the background for a while. The project was, however, taken up by the Dutch in the Beyen Plan of September 1952,[29] and the Benelux governments returned to the idea in May 1955. The foreign ministers of the six member countries of the ECSC accepted the project at their meeting in Messina in June 1955 and invited Britain to join in the Spaak committee, whose work was to lead to the creation of the Rome treaties in March 1957. The British government after some deliberation accepted the invitation and at the end of June 1955 sent a 'representative' (Russell Bretherton from the Board of Trade) to the committee. When it became clear later in the year that

[28] On the French customs union proposals see Richard T. Griffiths and Frances Lynch, 'L'Échec de la "petite Europe": les négociations Fritalux/Finebel, 1949–1950', *Revue Historique*, 274/1 (1985), 159–93; Pierre Guillen, 'Le Projet d'union économique entre la France, l'Italie et le Benelux', in Poidevin (ed.), *Histoire des débuts*, 143–64 (Guillen maintains that the British initiative of 8 March 1950 for some form of European monetary union finally killed Finebel); Bruna Bagnato, *Storia di una illusione europea: Il progetto di unione doganale italo-francese*, with a foreword by Ennio di Nolfo (London: Lothian Foundation, 1995).

[29] Richard T. Griffiths and Alan S. Milward, 'The Beyen Plan and the European Political Community', in Werner Maihofer (ed.), *Noi si mura: Selected Working Papers of the European University Institute* (Florence: European University Institute, 1986), 595–621; Richard T. Griffiths, 'The Beyen Plan', in id. (ed.), *The Netherlands and the Integration of Europe 1945–1957* (Amsterdam: Neha, 1990), ch. 8.

Britain would not be able to 'steer' the talks and to dissuade the
Six from the customs union proposals the British withdrew from
the negotiations.[30] The reaction was in line with the government's previous views on European customs unions and in so far
could not come as a surprise. It is more surprising that Britain
had accepted the invitation to the Spaak committee at all. In a
way, even the government's misguided attempt of December 1955
to undermine the customs unions proposals of the Six and to
redirect their negotiations into OEEC may be seen as in line with
Britain's previous attitude.[31]

The approach Britain pursued in its policy on European trade
and commerce was trade liberalization within the OEEC. The
OEEC was largely under British control and was regarded in
Britain as the main forum for economic co-operation and policy
co-ordination. From 1949 onwards Britain was the leading force in
the OEEC Trade Liberalization Programme. Alan Milward and
George Brennan have argued that the motives behind Britain's
support for trade liberalization were largely political. Britain
wanted to take the lead in Europe, impress the Americans, and
lead the West Europeans away from Continental economic union
proposals towards the one-world system and offer a rival policy.[32]
Trade liberalization was not conceived as a step towards European
integration.

The OEEC Trade Liberalization Programme relaxed and
removed quotas on trade between Western European countries. It
did not include tariffs. Tariffs would be negotiated down in GATT
(and not much happened on this issue during the 1950s). The
exclusion of tariffs from trade liberalization allowed Britain to
retain imperial preference. As a result Britain was, in the 1950s, a
member of two discriminating trade blocs. In a way, it had 'the best
of both worlds'. It combined intra-European trade liberalization
with imperial preferences while maintaining its tariffs and its tariff
autonomy against the outside world.

[30] Simon Burgess and Geoffrey Edwards, 'The Six plus One: British Policy-Making and
the Question of European Economic Integration, 1955', *International Affairs*, 64 (1988),
393–413; John W. Young, ' "The Parting of the Ways?" Britain, the Messina Conference
and the Spaak Committee, June–December 1955', in Michael Dockrill and John W. Young
(eds.), *British Foreign Policy, 1945–56* (London: Macmillan, 1989), 197–224.
[31] Martin Schaad, 'Plan G—A "Counterblast"? British Policy Towards the Messina
Countries, 1956', *Contemporary European History*, 7 (1998), 39–60, 44–6.
[32] See Milward and Brennan, *Britain's Place in the World*.

What about monetary integration? Britain was a crucial member of the European Payments Union (EPU) founded in September 1950. The EPU is little known and has been badly neglected by research. Its aim was to liberalize trade and foreign exchanges in Western Europe, replacing the network of bilateral agreements on which intra-European trade had rested since 1945. Scholars such as Volker Hentschel see the EPU as 'perhaps the most important, most effective and most beneficial arrangement of European economic integration' since the war.[33] In British eyes, however, the EPU had nothing to do with European integration. The EPU was not regarded as a European solution but as a temporary device to finish in 1952 with the end of Marshall Aid. In London the EPU was considered as a purely technical or financial device, devoid of any political ambition.

There were fundamental differences between Britain and its EPU partners. The British wanted to make sterling convertible. By 'setting the pound free' and by re-establishing the full convertibility of sterling into the US dollar the British hoped to protect sterling's status as an international currency and to restore the City to its previous role in the international financial system. Neither the famous 'Robot' plan of 1951–2 nor the 'collective approach' took account of the EPU and the plans of the continental Europeans.[34] 'Operation Robot' had been devised by the Bank of England, and was 'supported enthusiastically'[35] by the Overseas Finance Division of the Treasury; in the end it was not accepted by the government as official policy. 'Robot' called for an early return to the external convertibility of the pound into the US dollar. The convertibility would apply to non-resident sterling earnings; the great majority of the sterling balances held in London would be blocked. 'Robot' envisaged a floating exchange rate for sterling. The EPU, however, was based on fixed exchange rates. The UK would have

---

[33] Volker Hentschel, 'Zwischen Zahlungsunfähigkeit und Konvertibilität. Frankreich und Deutschland in der europäischen Zahlungsunion', in Andreas Wilkens (ed.), *Die deutsch-französischen Wirtschaftsbeziehungen 1945–1960* (Sigmaringen: Jan Thorbecke Verlag, 1997), 101–33; 101. On the EPU see Jacob J. Kaplan and Günther Schleiminger, *The European Payments Union: Financial Diplomacy in the 1950s* (Oxford: Clarendon Press, 1989); Barry Eichengreen, *Reconstructing Europe's Trade and Payments: The European Payments Union* (Manchester: Manchester University Press, 1993).

[34] Alan S. Milward, *The European Rescue of the Nation-State* (London: Routledge, 1992), 367 ff.

[35] Comment by Alec Cairncross in id. (ed.), *The Robert Hall Diaries 1947–53* (London: Unwin Hyman, 1989), 202.

to pull out of the EPU, 'probably causing its dissolution and the reversal of Europe's trade liberalisation policies'.[36]

The 'collective approach' which succeeded 'Robot' in 1952 envisaged the return to convertibility for sterling contemporaneously with a small number of European currencies. The Europeans were expected to follow the UK and would be informed of Britain's policy after American support had been secured in bilateral negotiations. However, the British approach was based on unrealistic assumptions. The Europeans were hostile to floating exchange rates and were not prepared to dispense with the EPU. More importantly, the 'collective approach' depended on dollar support for the sterling reserves and on American co-operation to an extent that was not forthcoming. Convertibility at a fixed exchange rate came about at the end of 1958 and the step was finally taken by agreement with the other member states of the EPU. In the meantime, however, the weakness of sterling, Britain's gradual turn towards Europe since 1956, the setting up of the EEC, and the negotiations over Britain's free trade area proposal meant that conditions in Britain and Western Europe had changed considerably.[37]

In many ways the British attitude towards the Schuman Plan can be seen as the application of principles defined by the government in 1948–9. As is well known, the Schuman Plan of 9 May 1950 proposed to place the coal and steel industries of France and West Germany under a High Authority with sovereign powers as the basis for a wider European integration. Though the plan did not require British participation, Britain was asked to take part in the negotiations. After the famous French 'ultimatum' the government rejected the invitation on 2 June 1950. Recent research has shown that the Schuman Plan was thoroughly examined in

[36] Catherine R. Schenk, *Britain and the Sterling Area: From Devaluation to Convertibility in the 1950s* (London: Routledge, 1994), 119. On the history of the 'Robot' plan see Alec Cairncross, *Years of Recovery: British Economic Policy 1945–51* (London: Methuen, 1985), 234–71; Stephen J. Procter, 'Floating Convertibility: The Emergence of the Robot Plan, 1951–52', *Contemporary Record*, 7 (1993), 24–43; on the policy of the Bank of England and its pressure for convertibility see John Fforde, *The Bank of England and Public Policy 1941–1958* (Cambridge: Cambridge University Press, 1992).

[37] Sylvia Schwaag, 'Monetary Cooperation and Exchange Rate Management in the 1950s: Britain, Germany and France in the Return to Currency Convertibility' (Ph.D. thesis, University of London, 1997); ead., 'Die Wiederherstellung der Währungskonvertierbarkeit 1958 als Beginn einer neuen wirtschaftspolitischen Zielrichtung in Westeuropa', *Zeitgeschichte*, 24 (1997), 85–102.

London and regarded as inconsistent with the basic lines of British domestic and foreign policy. The surrender of sovereignty inherent in the French proposal, economic policy considerations, and Britain's perceived role in the world, in the view of the Attlee government, made British participation impossible. The negotiations over the French plan led to the creation of the European Coal and Steel Community by France, West Germany, Italy, Belgium, the Netherlands, and Luxembourg. In December 1954 Britain concluded an association agreement with the ECSC.

The Attlee government's policy over the Schuman Plan has been assessed in opposite ways by the literature. Alan Bullock and John Young have defended Bevin. Britain, they argue, had a positive European policy. No British government could have made any decision other than to refuse to join in the negotiations, given the nature of the French proposal, Britain's perceived global role, the Empire, and the state of public opinion.[38] Other scholars firmly contradict this view. They regard the refusal to take part in the negotiations as a big mistake and as the crucial opportunity when Britain 'missed the European bus' or 'abdicated leadership in Europe' (these, by the way, are not identical). Recent studies by Edmund Dell (a former Labour Minister) and Christopher Lord both give a highly critical account of the government's policy.[39] Both authors confirm the view developed by Alan Milward that by remaining absent from the Plan the British government, instead of serving the national interest, in the long run damaged it. Sovereignty was not strengthened but weakened. Dell in particular emphatically and convincingly argues that Britain had too many illusions about its place in the world, and that there was much complacency, arrogance, and prejudice in London against France, European integration, and the European continent.

Yet the case against the government can be overstated. Dell maintains that participation in the Schuman Plan 'was consistent with Britain's view of itself. It could be a global power, and at the centre of the Commonwealth and the sterling area, and still participate in the Schuman Plan. It could persist with its intergovernmental model

[38] Alan Bullock, *Ernest Bevin: Foreign Secretary 1945–1951* (Oxford: Oxford University Press, 1985); Young, *Britain and European Unity*, 28 ff., 52 ff.

[39] The titles of the two books are instructive: Edmund Dell, *The Schuman Plan and the British Abdication of Leadership in Europe* (Oxford: Oxford University Press, 1995); Christopher Lord, *Absent at the Creation: Britain and the Formation of the European Community, 1950–2* (Aldershot: Dartmouth, 1996).

of European cooperation and still participate in the Schuman plan.'[40] It seems doubtful whether things could have been reconciled as easily as Dell seems to believe, whether Britain's European policy and its view of itself could have been made consistent with the French or the continental European vision of Europe. Seen from a comparative perspective, Britain and France were the proponents and the representatives of different models of European integration and co-operation and champions of conflicting ideas on Europe and its role in the world.[41]

The claim that the Schuman Plan 'decided the course of post-war European history', as Dell maintains,[42] is debatable and probably exaggerated. On the other hand, there can be little doubt that the Schuman Plan was crucial. It was a watershed and had important consequences not only for West European integration but also for Britain's position in Europe. Until the Schuman Plan Britain was thought to have an implicit veto on further integration. The US ambassador to Paris, David Bruce, summed this up well on 25 April 1950: '(1) there will be no real European integration without whole-hearted participation by the UK, (2) the UK will not whole-heartedly participate . . . , (3) ergo, there will be no purely European integration'.[43] This changed two weeks later. France decided to move without Britain. The West European countries— or, more exactly, six of them—were no longer prepared to make integration and the character of the European institutions dependent on Britain's consent. They proceeded without Britain. The ECSC marked the institutional beginning of the Community of the Six which was to set up the European Economic Community in 1957. It created a framework for Franco-German reconciliation. It was (ironically enough) America's support that encouraged and made continental European integration possible irrespective of Britain's views. In any case, American endorsement of the Schuman Plan and of European integration more than compensated for Britain's absence.

The next important proposal for integration was the French government's plan to create a European army, as proposed by the

---

[40] Dell, *The Schuman Plan*, 3 f.

[41] Clemens A. Wurm, 'Two Paths to Europe: Great Britain and France from a Comparative Perspective' in id. (ed.), *Western Europe and Germany*, 175–200.

[42] Dell, *The Schuman Plan*, 4.

[43] *Foreign Relations of the United States 1950*, iii: *Western Europe* (Washington: United States Government Printing Office, 1977), 64.

French Prime Minister René Pleven in a speech in October 1950. The outbreak of the Korean war in June 1950 had heightened existing fears of the Soviet military threat to Western Europe and made demands for German rearmament more pressing, especially in the United States. Like the Schuman Plan, the Pleven Plan for a European army was devised by Monnet. For the French this was the only way to make German rearmament acceptable to the French people. The British government was sceptical towards the plan and doubted the military value of a European army, while neither the Labour nor the Conservative governments intended Britain to join a European army. Politically, a European army conflicted with Britain's aim of creating an Atlantic rather than a European community. Bevin regarded a European army under French leadership as 'a sort of cancer in the Atlantic body'.[44] Churchill, who himself had called for the creation of a European army in a speech made at the Consultative Assembly of the Council of Europe in August 1950, described the proposed army as a 'sludgy amalgam'[45]—sweeping aside what he had seemed to imply when in opposition.

Yet neither the Labour nor the Conservative governments openly rejected the French proposal. There were several reasons for this. The French were not prepared to discuss German rearmament other than in the framework of the Pleven Plan. A European army thus seemed the only device to allow West Germany to rearm. The Germans, after initial scepticism, accepted participation in a European army and became increasingly keen about the European Defence Community (EDC). The crucial argument, however, was that the Americans changed their minds and became supporters of the project. Under the circumstances the British government had no choice but to support the French proposal and promised the closest possible association with the EDC.[46]

---

[44] Bevin minute, 24 Nov. 1950; see Saki Dockrill, *Britain's Policy for West German Rearmament 1950–1955* (Cambridge: Cambridge University Press, 1991), 49.

[45] Cabinet Memorandum on 'United Europe', 29 Nov. 1951; PRO, CAB 129/48—CP (51)32.

[46] Saki Dockrill, 'The Tortuous Path to Western European Military Unity: 1950–1955', in Michael Dockrill (ed.), *Europe within the Global System 1938–1960: Great Britain, France, Italy and Germany: from Great Powers to Regional Powers* (Bochum: Universitätsverlag Dr. N. Brockmeyer, 1995), 101–18; 110. Britain's absence from the negotiations meant that the British were not involved in the debate over a European political community and a customs union which became attached to the EDC project.

In spite of British undertakings, including the intention to retain troops on the Continent, the French National Assembly rejected the EDC project on 30 August 1954. Different reasons have been advanced in the literature for the death of the EDC and recent research has shed new light on the attitude of the French and of the French Prime Minister, Pierre Mendès France, who publicly refused to support the project. Nationalism, mistrust of Germany, hostility to a supranational Europe, anti-Americanism, regard for the Soviet Union, the wish to keep open the nuclear option, and a determination to keep the French army as the symbol of national sovereignty and independence intact: a heterogeneous mix of motives accounts for the vote of the French National Assembly.[47] The rejection of the EDC was primarily the result of a 'querelle franco-française', of an internal-French controversy. The long-held view that the EDC collapsed because of Britain's absence or its lukewarm attitude towards the EDC[48] is, it seems, no longer upheld in the recent literature.

The alternative solution for West Germany's rearmament—the transformation of the Brussels pact into the Western European Union (WEU) and the incorporation of the Federal Republic of Germany into NATO—was largely devised by Eden and his government.[49] At the time this did much to shore up Britain's prestige on the European continent. And it may well be that the British move has not received the praise in the literature it has deserved. But the WEU was conceived as an instrument for the solution of an important, yet clearly defined and circumscribed problem—German rearmament. It was not intended as a potential basis for further integration. Saki Dockrill and Anne Deighton have pointed out that by separating the question of West Germany's rearmament from the ideal of European integration and by creating, through

[47] Jacques Bariéty, 'Frankreich und das Scheitern der EVG', in Rolf Steininger et al. (eds.), Die doppelte Eindämmung: Europäische Sicherheit und deutsche Frage in den Fünfzigern (Munich: v. Hase & Koehler Verlag, 1993), 99–131; Elisabeth du Réau, L'Idée d'Europe au XXe siècle: Des mythes au réalités (Brussels: Editions Complexe, 1996), 203–15; Marie-Thérèse Bitsch, Histoire de la construction européenne de 1945 à nos jours (Brussels: Editions Complexe, 1996), 81–93.

[48] This was the view of, for instance, Paul Noack, Das Scheitern der Europäischen Verteidigungsgemeinschaft: Entscheidungsprozesse vor und nach dem 30. August 1954 (Düsseldorf: Droste Verlag, 1977).

[49] Hans-Heinrich Jansen, Großbritannien, das Scheitern der EVG und der NATO-Beitritt der Bundesrepublik Deutschland (Bochum: Universitätsverlag Dr. N. Brockmeyer, 1992); Olaf Mager, Die Stationierung der britischen Rheinarmee—Großbritanniens EVG-Alternative (Baden-Baden: Nomos Verlagsgesellschaft, 1990).

the completion of the Western bloc in 1954–5, 'a psychological atmosphere of security', Eden made further moves towards European unity easier.[50] That may well be the case and if so, this was certainly not Eden's intention. Further integration was not in Eden's or Britain's perceived interest, as is shown by the events following the meeting of the ECSC foreign ministers in Messina in June 1955.

III

From 1948–9 to 1955, despite differences of emphasis, there was a large measure of agreement on the basic lines of British European and integration policies. Britain's self-interest was seen to lie in its world role, not in building a united Europe. NATO and the Atlantic Alliance were at the centre of British policy. Britain favoured loose forms of intergovernmental European co-operation, but rejected supranational integration. With the creation of the OEEC and the Council of Europe, the structure for European co-operation had been established. There seemed to be no need for further institutions. Britain welcomed Franco-German *rapprochement* (up to a point), but rejected close ties to the continental European powers and did not share their belief in the potential of European integration to bring about peace, growth, and security. European integration was a subordinate and peripheral issue. It was regarded not as an opportunity, but rather as a problem or a threat. Governments were convinced that Britain could shape Western Europe to its own wishes.

Although the substance of British policy was consistent, it should be pointed out that policy was not uniform. It varied according to issue areas and forms of integration. The view upheld in the literature that Britain rejected membership but was prepared to associate with European integration[51] has to be qualified

---

[50] Dockrill, *Britain's Policy for West German Rearmament*, 150; Anne Deighton, 'Britain and the Creation of Western European Union, 1954', in ead. (ed.), *Western European Union 1954–1997: Defence, Security, Integration* (Reading: The University of Reading, 1997), 11–25, 11; ead., 'The Last Piece of the Jigsaw: Britain and the Creation of the Western European Union, 1954', *Contemporary European History*, 7 (1998), 181–96; 182.

[51] Roger Bullen, 'Britain and Europe, 1950–1957', in Ennio di Nolfo (ed.), *Power in Europe?*, ii: *Great Britain, France, Germany and Italy and the Origins of the EEC, 1952–1957* (Berlin: Walter de Gruyter, 1992), 499–504; Young, *Britain and European Unity*.

and omits European economic integration. In matters of security and defence Britain aimed for a strong and united Europe to withstand and contain Soviet Communism, albeit in an Atlantic, not in a European framework. Western European economic integration in the form of customs unions was regarded as a threat because it would hurt British interests. Where British interests were threatened Britain's concern was 'effectively to prevent things from happening to which it was opposed, or to generate change in a way which would work in its interests without a concern for what other European states thought'.[52] Monetary integration with Europe was ruled out. As the pound sterling was the symbol of Britain's greatness, autonomy, and sovereignty, in monetary matters the scope even for co-operation with Europe was strictly limited. The fact that Britain finally returned to convertibility at the end of 1958 by agreement with the other member states of the EPU does not contradict this view.

A number of authors have argued that Britain's West European policy was highly successful in the first decade after the war. With the exception of the Schuman Plan and the ECSC, the divisions between continental European countries and the UK's relative strength prevented integrationist solutions and allowed Britain to shape outcomes in accordance with its perceived national interest. At the end of 1954, a 'British Europe', led by London, based on defence, organized along intergovernmental lines, and restricted to trade liberalization, seemed secure.[53] The failure of the EDC (amounting, in British eyes, to 'a crushing defeat'[54] of the 'Europeans'), Britain's diplomatic success over the Western European Union, and West Germany's entry to NATO all seemed to confirm Britain in its view of itself and its long-held view of the European continent.

Yet the impression was based on short-term considerations, adopts the view from Britain (not from the European continent), and reflects the perspective of Britain's political leaders at the time.

---

[52] Brian Girvin, 'The United Kingdom and the Green Pool: The Primacy of Interdependency over Integration', in Richard T. Griffiths and Brian Girvin (eds.), *The Green Pool and the Origins of the Common Agricultural Policy* (London: Lothian Press, 1995), 91–113; 104.

[53] Wolfram Kaiser, *Using Europe, Abusing the Europeans: Britain and European Integration, 1945–63* (Basingstoke: Macmillan, 1996), ch. 1.

[54] Roy Denman, *Missed Chances. Britain and Europe in the Twentieth Century* (London: Indigo, 1997), 194.

Since 1948–9 the gulf between the European continent and Britain over integration had widened.[55] Britain had been unable to identify the nature of European integration and the forces behind it. The diplomatic triumph of 1954 was to be short-lived and proved a Pyrrhic victory. Between 1955 and 1961 the British government made 'a slow one hundred and eighty degree turn' in its European policy and in 1961 applied for membership of the European Community it had rejected a couple of years before.[56]

[55] Clemens A. Wurm, 'Britain, Western Europe and European Integration 1945–1957: The View from the Continent', *European Review of History. Revue Européenne d'Histoire*, 6 (1999), 235–49; N. Piers Ludlow, *Dealing with Britain: The Six and the First UK Application to the EEC* (Cambridge: Cambridge University Press, 1997), ch. 1, esp. p. 17.

[56] Richard T. Griffiths, 'A Slow One Hundred and Eighty Degree Turn: British Policy towards the Common Market, 1955–61', in George Wilkes (ed.), *Britain's Failure to Enter the European Community 1961–63: The Enlargement Negotiations and Crises in European, Atlantic and Commonwealth Relations* (London: Frank Cass, 1997), 35–50; Wolfram Kaiser, *Großbritannien und die Europäische Wirtschaftsgemeinschaft 1955–1961: Von Messina nach Canossa* (Berlin: Akademie Verlag, 1996).

3

Childe Harold's Pilgrimage

Alan S. Milward

> *Coquettish in ambition, still he aim'd*
> *At what?*
> Canto IV, xci

Writers on the life and times of Harold Macmillan have commented on the paradox of a politician who spent almost twenty years of obscurity pursuing programmes of domestic economic reform and who then was to be remembered for a prime ministership dominated by his leadership on great issues of foreign policy.[1] Such little prominence as he had in the public eye in the inter-war period came, it is true, partly from his opposition to the foreign policy of the Chamberlain government from the Hoare–Laval pact onwards, but in the small group which so energetically campaigned against appeasement he was completely overshadowed by men like Churchill and Eden who had held great office. Furthermore, as Turner correctly argues,[2] his views at that time on foreign policy were in many respects derivative from his published opinions on the need for some form of domestic economic reorganization.[3]

While it is certainly the case that such ideas as Macmillan had on domestic policy fell on a much more receptive soil after 1945, it is also the case that his pamphleteering in the 1930s was based on much too bland a view of the possibilities of a social and economic consensus in British society. The outcome of five essays and two books on economic and social policy was that at the outbreak of the Second World War Macmillan had reached the age of 45 and served thirteen years as an MP without attaining any office.

---

[1] The point is made forcefully by R. Davenport-Hines, *The Macmillans* (London: Routledge, 1992), and with finer accuracy by J. Turner, *Macmillan* (London: Longman, 1994).

[2] Turner, *Macmillan*, 44–6.

[3] L. P. Carpenter, 'Corporatism in Britain, 1930–1945', *Journal of Contemporary History*, 11 (1976). A. Marwick, 'Middle Opinion in the 1930s: Planning, Progress and Political Agreement', *English Historical Review*, 79 (1964).

The paradox is that he is now remembered for the complete change he is alleged to have made in British foreign policy by forcing through his government the 1961 decision to apply for membership of the European Economic Community (EEC). Although that application failed in January 1963, it can be accepted that the change of policy was permanent. It remained after 1963 the policy of successive governments to enter the European Communities on acceptable terms as soon as it was possible, whereas before 1961 policy had been that membership of any European organization which had a supranational federation as its ultimate goal was impossible for the United Kingdom.

Macmillan himself presented that decision as a fundamental change of direction. The tendency of historical discussion has been to agree with him. Lee, for example, refers to it as a 'U-turn taken after an even more agonising and more controversial reappraisal by Cabinet, parliamentarians and public'.[4] How to explain it has puzzled most authors. It took a long time for Macmillan to persuade his fellow ministers and the Conservative Party that an application for membership was the correct step to take, and even then he was constrained by his ministers to accept that it should be an application made to discover the terms for entry. Macmillan was distinguished for his engagement with Europe rather than for any love of it, and the tone of many commentaries is that for him, as for Byron's hero, it was the nearest place where something might be found to relieve the spleen of his administration and the national economy.

Most typically, however, the application is explained as an act to which there was no alternative given the continuing grand ambitions of British foreign policy, and thus not so much a drastic change as a resigned acceptance, which gradually grew after 1956, of the inevitable. Macmillan is given only the credit for recognizing earlier than others the need to make an application which, the earlier it was made, would mean, he mistakenly hoped, changes in the condition of Britain less drastic than would otherwise be the case.[5] No one, however, presents Macmillan's pilgrimage, to

    [4] S. Lee, 'Staying in the Game? Coming into the Game?', in R. Aldous and S. Lee (eds.), *Harold Macmillan and Britain's World Role* (London: Macmillan, 1996), 136.
    [5] This is essentially the argument of the fullest study of the application: W. Kaiser, *Using Europe, Abusing the Europeans: Britain and European Integration, 1945–63* (London: Macmillan, 1996).

Canossa as Kaiser has it, as the consistent path involving neither U-turns nor retreats that it actually was.[6]

In opposition before 1951 and in office afterwards as minister for housing and local government, it was on the question of western European unity that Macmillan advanced his claims to higher office and it is from his immediate post-war concern with that issue that the eventual application to join the EEC sprang in a logical tactical progression.

Using the European Movement as an instrument of influence and the Consultative Assembly of the Council of Europe as a stage, he carried on a campaign against the first post-war Labour governments' refusal to participate in the Schuman Plan negotiations and later, when in office, against his own government's pursuit of a European policy no different from that of the two Labour governments. The mistaken assumptions of this long campaign were the mistaken assumptions which led to the failure of his later policies towards the European Community when he became Prime Minister, and which ultimately led him so inopportunely to the application for membership and to its rejection.

In July 1950 we find him telling the Conservative Inter-Parliamentary Committee of the Council of Europe that he did not think constitution-making would figure very prominently in the Consultative Assembly's activities. 'He believed', the records of the group record, 'that the Federal conception was not really strong among the serious Parliamentarians of Europe; and that discussion would largely rest on improving functional methods of cooperation'.[7] In fact the Strasbourg Assembly did little else but discuss federal constitutions for Europe over the next five years, even though in most of its member states the idea of a federal Europe did not indeed have much national parliamentary support. Three months later, in October 1950, we find Macmillan telling the same group that he 'considered the Conservative view, that British influence could be the determining factor between a good or a bad Schuman Plan, was being proved entirely right'.[8]

---

[6] Id., *Großbritannien und die Europäische Wirtschaftsgemeinschaft 1955–1961: Von Messina nach Canossa* (Frankfurt am Main, 1994).

[7] Duncan Sandys Papers, Report of the 6th Meeting of the Conservative Parliamentary Inter-Committee Group of the Council of Europe, 25 July 1950.

[8] Ibid., Report of the 7th Meeting of the Conservative Parliamentary Inter-Committee Group of the Council of Europe, 19 Oct. 1950.

What seemed to be evolving in western Europe out of post-war reconstruction, a federal political union inspired by Britain's military ally France, could be averted by more positive British leadership in Europe. From this position, which events on several occasions proved wrong, Macmillan did not swerve. This was to make him the most prominent critic in the Conservative Party of Foreign Secretary Anthony Eden's policy towards attempts at federation. With other leading conservative figures in the European movement, Macmillan argued for an assertion of Britain's leadership of Europe away from integration through surrenders of sovereignty and towards the intergovernmental association of sovereign nations.

Eden saw no purpose in going in either of these directions. To participate in integration was voluntarily to give away bargaining advantages which Britain still held. To suppose that France would change the path chosen in May 1950 in favour of British-led intergovernmentalism was, he argued, an illusion as long as centrist coalitions held sway in Paris. He was not, however, ready to oppose a European federation without Britain. Any land-based defence of the United Kingdom had to be staged in Germany and for that a German army was needed. From summer 1951, there seemed no other route to arming the German Federal Republic than through the European Defence Community (EDC), even if the price of that included the European Political Community. Without any thought of British membership and with no interest in the details of Europe's new constitution, Eden was ready to fight against his own Prime Minister and many of his ministerial colleagues to maintain public support for EDC as a contribution to the United Kingdom's national security. It is some measure of Macmillan's great ambitions that the Foreign Secretary's chief critic in this should have been the minister for housing and local government.

Two weeks after Eden became foreign minister Macmillan sent him a copy of a letter from his son-in-law, Julian Amery, one of Churchill's original placemen in the Strasbourg Assembly. Neither the Schuman nor the Pleven plans would come to much, Amery thought, having spoken to their opponents in France. 'We could still save them,' he wrote, 'it is a question of going in and making them work. Guy Mollet said he hoped we would ask for a special conference to discuss the terms on which we would go in. In his view it would not now be difficult to get both Plans amended to meet our particular requirements.'[9]

Sending to Eden Amery's letter was the opening shot of a persistent campaign against the Foreign Secretary's policy. The object of that campaign was unambiguously described afterwards in Macmillan's memoirs. He was an opponent of EDC because a European army would be of little military value. To invent a supranational authority in order to create such a force was an even greater mistake; 'I urged with all the strength I could command that the French government should abandon all the complicated constitution with which the French Foreign Secretary had tried to surround this simple conception.'[10] The Coal and Steel Community, too, was a danger:

While I could not argue against the view that the coal and steel and the defence structures, as now devised, were unacceptable to us, I frankly hoped and believed that they would break down. If they were successful, it might be a short-term advantage, especially if it facilitated immediate German rearmament. But the long-term future would be grim indeed. There would be a European Community, from which we should be excluded, and which would effectively control Europe. This was the historic struggle in which we had been engaged first against Louis XIV, then against Napoleon, and twice in our lifetime against Germany. Germany was weak now; in the long run she would be stronger than France, and so we might be bringing about in twenty years' time that domination of Europe by Germany to prevent which we had made such terrible sacrifice twice within a single generation. It should, therefore, be our hope that the Schuman Plan and—more important—EDC would fail.[11]

It followed that the United Kingdom should state its own view of the kind of European union it would join. There were various acceptable possibilities, Macmillan argued: a confederation based on continuous consultation between governments; a European Consultative Assembly which would gradually form a European public opinion; linking European currencies to sterling or to each other; a European preferential area linked to the imperial preference system; specialized, but not supranational, authorities to control defence production and heavy industry; participation in a

---

[9] R. Bullen and M.-E. Pelly (eds.), *Documents on British Policy Overseas*, series II, vol. 1 (London: HMSO, 1986), Amery to Macmillan, 12 Nov. 1951.

[10] H. Macmillan, *Tides of Fortune, 1945–55* (London: Macmillan, 1969), 223.

[11] Ibid. 466.

European Army made up of national components of at least divisional strength responsible to a co-operative international command structure like NATO. Only if these ideas failed should association with, but not membership in, the Communities, become policy, and only to mitigate the danger.

The so-called Eden Plan, whose intention was to allow the Consultative Assembly in Strasbourg to function, differently constituted, on the different occasions, as the common parliamentary body for the OEEC, the ECSC, and the EDC, was in part a response to Macmillan's criticism. Indeed, one of Macmillan's sympathizers, Anthony Nutting, minister of state at the Foreign Office, claimed with some exaggeration to be its true author. But Macmillan thought the Eden Plan a concession too far. It would still leave the federal constitution in place. The larger sessions of the Consultative Assembly would be larger only by virtue of the addition of members from 'associated' countries, of which, as things stood, the United Kingdom appeared likely to be the sole example, and they would be entirely without influence or significance. He wrote to Eden on 12 December 1951 criticizing it because it accepted the existence of the Six as a separate federal unit. 'Britain needs a united Europe', he argued, 'to fill the vacuum between the Iron Curtain and the Atlantic, and to attract Germany permanently to the West. It is essential, however, to British political and economic interests that a United Europe should not be dominated by Germany.' This could only be avoided by British partnership in the enterprise.

Britain's ties with the Commonwealth and with the United States make it impossible for her to join a Federation. She could, however, become a full member of a Confederation, organised on Commonwealth lines. For these purposes her relations with the other countries of the British Commonwealth would have to be considered as a domestic concern. By associating the economies of the Commonwealth and the continent it might stimulate the increase in production which we must have if we are to avert bankruptcy and continue as a World Power.[12]

Macmillan's remark that British imperial preferences should remain a matter of domestic concern only was not casual; he was

[12] Bullen and Pelly (eds.), *Documents*, no. 424, 'European Integration', Memorandum by Macmillan, 16 Jan. 1952. Although sent officially only to Eden, copies of the memorandum were made available to some of Macmillan's fellow members of the United Europe Movement.

to maintain the same position in 1956–7 when the United Kingdom made its Free Trade Area proposals. Preferences were a prop to the world power threatened by Germany's position in Europe. 'We shall have grave difficulties, even with full Commonwealth support, in the face of high American tariffs and growing German competition. If, on top of that, we are to see Western Europe and its colonial possessions pass into a German-dominated Customs Union and our own overseas markets threatened, the outlook will be dark indeed.'[13] From the start of his prime ministership he was not prepared to let a Continental common market and a completely separate United Kingdom coexist as commercial entities.

Should EDC and the Political Community come into being, he argued in 1952, the United Kingdom must ensure the subordination of the federation to the Council of Europe as it existed, rather than the other way round. If EDC failed, that would be the moment for Britain to retake the lead in Europe with proposals to link it to the Commonwealth in a structure of continuous consultation between independent nations. European currencies could, he argued, be linked individually or collectively to sterling. The supranational authorities of the Communities could then be replaced by specialized agencies where power still rested with national governments. Such an agency would be able to create and control a European Army in which the national units remained national and into which British units could thus be integrated. Only if all else failed should British leadership in Europe be established by association with, but not membership of, the Six.

When the Eden Plan was accepted by Cabinet on 13 March 1952, Macmillan, so he relates, contemplated resignation.[14] It would not have been long a matter for much public attention that the head of a minor ministry should resign over a question of foreign policy. He could only keep his peace until his position would be more powerful, although he tried unsuccessfully to win Churchill's support against Eden's decision.

---

[13] Ibid.   [14] Macmillan, *Tides of Fortune*, 472.

> *But where is Harold? Shall I then forget*
> *To urge the gloomy wanderer o'er the wave.*
>
> Canto II, xvi

The eventual rejection of EDC and with it the European Political Community was 'a good result for us', Macmillan recorded,[15] albeit one that he observed only from the touchline. Three months later he became minister of defence. When Eden became Prime Minister in April 1955 he made Macmillan Foreign Secretary, although only as his second choice. In that office he remained only until the end of the year, when Eden, who had tried to remove him in September, finally was able to do so. He was Foreign Secretary when the United Kingdom participated in the Spaak Committee but decided against membership of the common market. After the demanding and complicated intricacies of defence policy he was free, as far as Eden allowed it, to practise what before he had had unavailingly to preach.

When the invitation to participate in the Spaak Committee was issued the new Foreign Secretary was attending a United Nations meeting in San Francisco. There was considerable hesitation at first in London over accepting it, and had it not been for Macmillan, there might have been only a British observer rather than a representative on the Committee. Returning, he treated his officials to an exposition of his views which followed closely his submission to the Cabinet in February 1952. The federal future for Europe was fading, he told them, partly because of the conflicting opinions of its supporters about Germany's future. 'We had always been inclined to say rather loosely that we did not mind other European Powers federating if they wished, but in fact if they did so and became really strong it might be very embarrassing for us. Europe would be handed over to the Germans, a state of affairs which we had fought two world wars to prevent.' Because OEEC would become less important as its tasks were completed, influencing the efforts to relaunch Europe meant that we 'should go in at the beginning and try to keep as many of the initiatives as possible in a form in which we could join'.[16] The next day he pressed in Cabinet for a full representative to be sent, against R. A. Butler's wish to send only an observer.[17]

---

[15] Macmillan, *Tides of Fortune*, 480.

[16] FO 371/116042, Record of a meeting between the Secretary of State and officials, 29 June 1955.

[17] CAB 128/29, Cabinet conclusions, 30 June 1955.

The indications which Spaak gave to the Steering Committee of his *ad hoc* organization in November 1955, the last occasion on which the British representative was present, of what the proposals in his report were likely to be, showed how illusory Macmillan's belief in the possibilities of British influence was. Macmillan had little choice but to go along with the policy of self-exclusion and hope that proposals for a common market would prove unacceptable to France. The situation was the more galling for him because Eden so closely supervised his activities and because self-exclusion was the outcome of the pursuit of the one-world policy in which he had altogether less faith than his fellow ministers. He sought a firm assurance in late September that the representative would not be withdrawn before there had been full consultations.[18]

Six weeks later, without consultation with or even communication to the other participants, the tacit decision was taken that there was no point in his being there any longer. The Foreign Secretary had no plan on which to base a pro-active policy in Europe and was bound in those circumstances to accept what happened. Sir Harold Caccia, one of the three Under-Secretaries in the Department, was nevertheless closely representing Macmillan's views when he exercised pressure on Burke Trend, chairman of the unofficial Common Market Working Party which was preparing a report to serve as the basis of advice to ministers. Caccia insisted that it was so improbable that the Six would go ahead without Britain that it was unnecessary to report, as Trend had intended to do, on what the political consequences of such a development would be.[19] Macmillan, with support from Peter Thorneycroft, the President of the Board of Trade, was committed to thwarting the Six's project by some new British initiative in OEEC which would prevent, as he saw it, the division of the West and would guard Britain's future against German economic domination in Europe. It was in November that the official search for such a change of policy began, but two days before Christmas Macmillan was moved to the Exchequer. His voyage towards Europe was, nevertheless, not abandoned.

It emerged as 'Plan G'. 'What then are we to do?', Macmillan wrote to the Treasury Permanent Under-Secretary Sir Edward Bridges in February 1956. 'Are we to just sit back and hope for the best? If we do that it may be very dangerous for us; for perhaps

[18] FO 371/116048, Macmillan to Butler, 23 Sept. 1955.
[19] FO 371/116050, Caccia to Edden, 17 Oct. 1955.

Messina will come off after all and that will mean Western Europe dominated in fact by Germany and used as an instrument of the revival of power through economic means. It is really giving them on a plate what we fought two wars to prevent.' His answer was still the same, 'to reconcile our position as head of the sterling area and as head of the Commonwealth with some degree of European co-operation'.[20] Plan G, which became the Free Trade Area proposal, showed no awareness of the adaptation which observation of European aspirations should have shown to be necessary. Agricultural trade was excluded from the Free Trade Area proposals and Commonwealth preferences would remain, two of the principal reasons for France's eventual rejection of them.

> *Long-absent Harold reappears at last;*
> *He of the breast which fain no more would feel,*
> *Wrung with the wounds which kill not, but ne'er heal.*
>
> Canto III, viii

Once he had claimed the prime ministership in January 1957 Macmillan was captain of the voyage, with no new navigation charts, but, as he thought, with weapons that he was prepared to use.

We must not be bullied by the activities of the Six. We could, if we were driven to it, fight their movement if it were to take the form of anything that was prejudicial to our interests. Economically, with the Commonwealth and other friends, including the Scandinavians, we could stand aside from a narrow Common Market. We also have some politico-military weapons.

With these weapons supposedly available, he concluded that 'We must take the lead in widening their project, or, if they will not cooperate with us, in opposing it.'[21] His uncertainty about the direction in which to fire, however, was reflected in his note to his Secretary, F. A. Bishop, about political governance of the proposed Free Trade area. 'In my view, agreement to some kind of managing board and abide by a majority vote on decisions which come within the general fabric would be a very good offer from us. We could call it supranational and they would like this. If they behaved badly we would resign from the whole affair.'[22] 'They', however,

---

[20] T 234/100, Macmillan to Bridges, 1 Feb. 1956.
[21] PREM 11/2133, Macmillan to Thorneycroft, 15 July 1957.
[22] Ibid., Macmillan to Bishop, 16 July 1957.

showed no interest in the constitutional governance of a Free Trade Area which offered them, economically, so little.

When this became clear in May 1958 the blame inevitably fell on France. The Prime Minister's first reaction was to fire in all directions by threatening a reversion to protectionism. 'We should certainly put on highly protective tariffs and quotas to counteract what Little Europe was doing to us.'[23] But would not the Six be as strong in any trade war as the United Kingdom? And was not such a reaction, as alarmed officials minuted, self-defeating? The EEC had to be gradually dissolved into a wider, non-supranational, non-discriminatory, international commercial framework within which, if British foreign policy was to remain as it had been since 1948, the USA and the Commonwealth were also present. France's decision to sign the Treaty of Rome had proved decisive in Europe's rejection of British leadership towards the one-world policy; its implementation of the terms of that Treaty would make that rejection a fixed element of the international economic and political order. That was why such a small degree of tariff discrimination against British exports to the Six as would be present from the initiation of the first round of EEC tariff reduction and the initiation of the common external tariff, events which in themselves could have had little effect on British trade, was seen as a decisive political moment. The Prime Minister's hopes and ambitions became fixed on influencing President de Gaulle, a man whom he had known in many moods in ill-fortune and in good throughout the struggles of the World War.

> Look on that part which sacred doth remain
> For the lone Chieftain, who majestic stalks,
> Silent and fear'd by all: not oft he talks
> With aught beneath him . . .

> Canto II, xix

Macmillan was direct in his first official meeting with the Chieftain. 'If France were traditionally protectionist, Great Britain was traditionally isolationist. It had been a great effort and departure from tradition for us to keep four divisions on the continent. If we were to be threatened by a trade war by the Six we would be driven back on ourselves and would have to seek our friends elsewhere.'[24]

[23] PREM 11/2315, Macmillan to Lloyd, 24 June 1958.
[24] PREM 11/2531, Record of conversation at Hôtel Matignon, 29 June 1958.

De Gaulle had many more pressing problems than relations between the United Kingdom and the EEC to solve. He committed France to the Treaty of Rome, in spite of his many harsh earlier opinions on it, because of the immediate economic benefits it promised. His determination to strip out of it its inherent momentum towards a supranational federation did not mean that he would not implement its commercial core. Threats to withdraw militarily from the Continent were only likely to increase German dependence on France. Threats to break up NATO would be seen by de Gaulle as offering interesting possibilities. Threats of isolationism gainsaid all that was supposed to be the objective of British policy. They could scarcely be taken seriously. They reduced confidence, already low, in the consistency and trustworthiness of British policy. They were not truly realizable. 'What remedies have we?', Macmillan asked Selwyn Lloyd. 'Can we take action on the economic plane, in GATT by a tariff war, or by some other forms of discrimination to counter their discrimination against us? . . . I have already said something pretty stiff to de Gaulle but then he will have forgotten it by now.'[25]

In December 1958 the Free Trade Area proposal was rejected beyond retrieval by France. A fortnight after winning the 1959 election the Prime Minister made it clear to his new Cabinet that, nevertheless, Europe would be the first and main focus of his new government's attention. 'For better or worse', he wrote to Lloyd, 'the Common Market looks like being here to stay at least for the foreseeable future. Furthermore, if we tried to disrupt it we should unite against us all the Europeans who have felt humiliated during the past decade by the weakness of Europe. We should also upset the United States, as well as playing into the hands of the Russians. And, of course, the Common Market has certain advantages in bringing greater cohesion to Europe. The question is how to live with the Common Market economically and turn its political effects into channels harmless to us.' The new government should thus at once begin a thorough study of 'the sort of price which it would be worth paying in order to be economically associated with it (something more in fact than just the concept of the Free Trade Area)'.[26]

[25] Free Trade Area Office files (FTA/102), Macmillan to Lloyd, 15 Oct. 1958.
[26] PREM 11/2985, Macmillan to Lloyd, 22 Oct. 1959.

It was from a weekend discussion at Chequers with his Cabinet at the end of November 1959 that the new tactic of 'near-identification' emerged. 'Near-identification' was a way of tracking the external commercial policy of the EEC, so as to minimize the commercial policy distinctions between the EEC and the United Kingdom and so make the persistence of the Six in remaining a separate unit appear in American eyes strategically divisive, while holding firmly before the eyes of the other five member states the image of a France arbitrarily excluding the United Kingdom from a set of politico-economic arrangements within which its membership would other-wise benefit them. By this point the failure to understand the electoral power of the economic forces which held the Six together in a complex pattern of allegiance had evolved into an almost wilful blindness. European preferences brought them continued prosper-ity and the stability of that pattern could only be guaranteed by the automatic implementation in the specified timetable of the pro-gramme of the Treaty of Rome. For the smaller member states the supranational structure was their guarantee that the terms of the Treaty could be enforced on France. The hopes which de Gaulle's alternative vision of a 'Europe of the nations' awoke in Macmillan's breast were dupes. De Gaulle was forced to take the Treaty as a package. 'Why is it difficult', Macmillan wrote to Lloyd in December, 'to make the United States realise that the Six, which they support for the sake of European political unity, is in fact (because of the economic threat to the United Kingdom and others) a threat to European unity?'[27]

In his search for an EFTA–EEC agreement in 1960 Macmillan frequently returned to the idea of some form of non-commercial bargain with de Gaulle's France to gain his purpose, as well as to his 1930s protectionism in his readiness to override GATT rules or to abandon the commitments of earlier governments to the one-world system. His occasional petulant threats to withdraw from Europe into Fortress Britain were discounted by officials as dead ends. Should all pressures on the EEC fail, Macmillan's position, clearly set out while Eden was still Foreign Secretary, remained unaltered. The United Kingdom must not be excluded from the centre of political decision-making in Europe, because the result of that exclusion would be the loss of its position in Washington as the

[27] PREM 11/2985, Macmillan to Lloyd, 11 Dec. 1959.

first among European allies. and an economic handicap which would result in the loss of Commonwealth leadership. These anxieties were much greater in 1960–1 than when he had first defined his policy in the early 1950s. If the Six could not be stopped or broken, he had then argued, and only then, was the government's position of association, but not membership, acceptable. They had not been stopped. Britain was excluded. Association had got nowhere. 'Near-identification' was accepted by de Gaulle without interest or concession as a policy which the United Kingdom was constrained to pursue. The logical culmination was membership, because it was the only way in which the European Communities could be changed and the United Kingdom's international status maintained.

Writing in 1964, Con O'Neill, who in 1963 became the United Kingdom representative to the EEC, put on paper a truth which could scarcely be uttered in the course of the unsuccessful negotiations for membership in 1961–3. 'Probably the only way', he wrote, 'by which we could effectively change the character of the Community in order to convert it to something less dangerous to our interest is by getting inside it. A large, if unavowable, part of our objective in negotiating for membership from 1961–3 was precisely that of changing the character of the Community. Our entry would have changed it. That is why we were kept out.'[28]

Stop! for thy tread is on an Empire's dust!

Canto III, xvii

Had Britain obtained membership on the terms negotiated by January 1963, bearing in mind that several important issues were still unsettled, the only leverage it would have had to change the EEC commercially was a generalized commitment of the Six to tariff reduction in the GATT framework, as desired by the Eisenhower and Kennedy Administrations, and to an international conference to regulate world commodity markets for agricultural products. Prices of Community agricultural products were, however, already fixed at a level far higher than Britain wished. Free entry into Britain for Commonwealth products would be ended. An exception for New Zealand was under discussion, but even that was uncertain because the French were

[28] T 232/1011, O'Neill to Butler, 25 July 1964.

already denying, before de Gaulle's January 1963 veto, that that was something they had agreed to. At the end, when no further concessions in favour of United Kingdom–Commonwealth trade could be hoped for, even Macmillan's earlier close associate in the European Movement at Strasbourg in the days of opposition to Labour policy, Duncan Sandys, who had been brought into the Cabinet to support membership, doubted whether the terms were acceptable.

The experience of the negotiations turned Commonwealth economies towards other markets. Canada accepted what no doubt was inescapable, that its commercial privileges with the United Kingdom could never be such as substantially to modify its trade and capital dependence on the USA. Prime Minister Diefenbaker as the leader of a Commonwealth loyalist movement received only sentimental approval from Prime Minister Menzies. Menzies had his eyes set on Australia's longer-term future, in its own continent its own manifest destiny. South Africa was no longer in the Commonwealth by the conclusion of the negotiations. India and Pakistan got better terms out of the negotiations mainly because of shifts in industrial policy inside some EEC member states away from textiles, which benefited their exports. In any case, India did not disguise that its motivation for such close attention to the details of the commercial negotiations was that the Continental market for its goods was one way to reduce the weight of the commercial connection with the United Kingdom on its manufactured exports. New Zealand, while pleading a powerful case for special treatment, was nevertheless engaged in the longer-term study of how to reorientate the dominant agricultural sector of its economy to Asian markets.

In the face of strident Commonwealth demands to maintain trade privileges for agricultural exports to the United Kingdom the government understood it was in many cases being black-mailed. In the Australian case, it was being blackmailed by the federal government so that Menzies could keep the Country Party with its farming community support in his coalition. In the Canadian case, it was being blackmailed into long arguments over tinned salmon and other foodstuffs whose values were insignificant in the total volume of Anglo-Canadian trade in order to prop up a disastrously failing Conservative Party government in Ottawa. But Commonwealth governments for their part saw that Britain had been ready to sacrifice the imperial preference system in the summer of 1962 in order to enter the EEC. Acceptance of the Common Agricultural Policy meant a future regime in which greater British food output would reduce Commonwealth food exports to the United Kingdom. Officials had not wanted to open negotiations from the position that as many Commonwealth preferences as possible should be maintained. They could see no real chance of such a position being acceptable to the Six. It was a late relief to them and to Edward Heath when in autumn 1962 they were finally allowed to abandon that position and get down to what they thought of as real negotiations. It was a decision accepted only with great reluctance by Macmillan.

> *Childe Harold bask'd him in the noon tide sun,*
> *Disporting there like any other fly,*
> *Nor dream'd before his little day was done*
> *One blast might chill him into misery.*
>
> Canto I, iv

It is unlikely, but not impossible, that the support given for so long to the Commonwealth demands to maintain the preferential structure of trade may have contributed to the dismal outcome, if only by prolonging the negotiations to a date by which de Gaulle was secure enough to pronounce a unilateral veto. They certainly underlined the force of some of the argumentation of the President's fateful speech in January 1963 which finally swatted all Macmillan's hopes.

> *A thousand years scarce serve to form a state;*
> *An hour may lay it in the dust . . .*
>
> Canto II, lxxiv

The whole negotiation for entry into the European Communities was conducted under the illusion fostered by Macmillan, that because de Gaulle was so scathing in his views of the inflated ambitions of the European Commission, British membership would mean that the EEC would come to resemble the Anglo-French commercial and political unions which had been explored by both countries before 1948. Supranationality and a European federation would disappear as any threat to the Continent's two ancient and powerful nation-states. But de Gaulle had been forced to accept the defeat of his project to reform the constitutional arrangements of the Communities before 'real negotiations' on Britain's application began. Officials were much less influenced by Macmillan's illusory vision, but few understood the allegiances that held the Communities together. When the imperialist Gaitskell committed the Labour Party at its 1962 annual conference to opposition to membership in the EEC and called it the end of 'a thousand years of history' the dramatic exaggeration hit home, because Macmillan's government had never accepted that if the Six did stay together there would be a central enforcement mechanism the acceptance of which was a surrender of some area of national sovereignty. Nor did it accept, in spite of Macmillan's preoccupation with the threat of a future German domination of western Europe, that maintaining the control over Germany which the Community institutions implied might also imply further surrenders of sovereignty of a more drastic kind in the future.

The impact of the Treaty of Rome on parliamentary sovereignty and British law, accurately presented to Cabinet in Lord Kilmuir's report on it, was later minimized by a second report, upon which the government imposed narrow restrictions, by Lord Dilhorne. Macmillan treated the problem of diminished sovereignty as one which would be resolved by British entry itself. It was a remarkable feat of sleight of hand for a government to conduct a debate about the national future and convince so many that there was no question that the future would be national. It could only have been achieved through the interplay of mutual ignorance.

That perspective bestows an extra emphasis on the logical continuity of Macmillan's policies and actions, from his role as a minister in the Conservative Party's delegation to the first meetings of the Assembly of the Council of Europe to that as the Prime Minister who presided over the British application to join the European Communities. That application was made by the most conspicuously persistent and consistent enemy of the European Communities in the British political system.

> . . . t'was a foolish quest,
> The which to gain and keep he sacrificed all rest.

Canto III, lxxvi

4

Bonn between London and Paris?

MARTIN P. C. SCHAAD

1. Introduction

Ever since the beginnings of the Federal Republic of Germany, relations between Bonn and Paris are said to have been closer than those between Bonn and London. It is not only that successive German administrations accorded higher priority to *rapprochement* with France than to accommodating British interests. The fruits of these efforts are also readily identifiable, for example, in the Treaty of Franco-German Co-operation of 1963, and in the creation of European institutions and communities. The pivotal role played by German and French politicians and diplomats in searching for the compromises necessary to secure the establishment of the ECSC and the EEC has led to the emergence of what is frequently termed the *Bonn–Paris axis*.[1] Moreover, the understanding thus developed has not been confined to the creation of the said communities, but has characterized their operation and development ever since. From early attempts at political integration originating in the Fouchet plans, to the Union agreed at Maastricht; from tentative steps towards monetary integration during the 1970s and 1980s, to the decision to introduce a single currency by 1999—Franco-German co-operation and good relations between their leaders was of paramount importance to the success, as its absence was to the failure, of any given initiative.

By contrast, post-war Anglo-German relations have not rendered similarly tangible results. There is little positive to report aside from Anthony Eden's diplomatic feat of integrating Germany into the Western Alliance after the failure of the EDC. Instead, bilateral relations as well as multilateral co-operation

---

[1] See e.g. R. T. Griffiths, 'Die deutsch-französische Achse und der Ursprung der europäischen Integration', *Historicum* (Spring 1994), 18–23.

appeared marred by disagreement: from the familiar history of British attempts to prevent the establishment of the EEC, to Margaret Thatcher's 'we want our money back', to the unfortunate wrangle over German unification, and finally to the various opt-outs secured at Maastricht. On issues of European integration in particular, a certain continuity can be observed with London being generally seen as non-committal, reluctant or—at worst—as hindering the process.

It would be over-ambitious here to seek to evaluate comparatively the Federal Republic's relations to London and Paris for the entire period since the 1950s. Instead, this essay will discuss three episodes, which to some extent confronted Bonn with a choice between the two capitals. The selection may appear arbitrary, and no claim is made for its representative value for the entire period, as the ups and downs of diplomatic relations provide ample counter-evidence to any generalization based on such isolated cases. Nor does the choice of episodes follow a rationale of *the most significant*—hence there is no discussion of the first British application, and no in-depth assessment of the French empty chair policy. Less momentous episodes may, indeed, be more helpful in examining the tenets, the mode, and the climate of foreign policy decision-making in Bonn. Thus the following pages will discuss the end of the Free Trade Area negotiations in 1958, the implications of a minor scandal in the *Auswärtige Amt* in 1965, and highlight the changed co-ordinates of foreign policy-making in reunified Germany as witnessed during the negotiations towards the Amsterdam Treaty of 1997.

2. Free Traders and Francophiles

The first episode taken to examine Bonn's relations to London and Paris refers to what in effect was the first French veto—the unilateral breaking-off of the negotiations towards the British-inspired all-European Free Trade Area (FTA) at the end of 1958.

The British had first proposed the FTA in 1956, following the realization that the creation of a Continental customs union would harm their exports by imposing an external tariff. The solution to this problem envisaged an area free of tariffs comprising all seventeen European OEEC members, including the six signatories of the Treaty of Rome. It was to be a complement to, not a substitute for, the common market. The essential difference, however, was that it gave non-members of the European Community free market access without requiring them to take part in supranational integration. Moreover, it left Britain and the other non-members of the Community free to determine their own tariff levels *vis-à-vis* third countries—an essential requirement for preserving British preferential commercial relations to the Commonwealth.

What appeared to be an exceptionally good deal for Britain was not without attraction for other European countries, notably Germany and Holland, whose foreign trade with non-members of the European Community was substantial in volume. The share of German exports to these markets was even greater than its exports to Community countries, so that the proposed tariff-free access had great appeal. It was public knowledge at the time that a sizeable minority within the German government even preferred the Free Trade Area over the customs union of the Six. Not surprisingly, therefore, British hopes for German support ran high, and throughout the negotiations, London sought to capitalize on Bonn's assistance.

2.1. De Gaulle and the end of the Free Trade Area

None the less, the negotiations for the Free Trade Area were marred by numerous difficulties and dragged on for nearly two years. Partly, these difficulties were organizational (Community members always had to co-ordinate their position before real bargaining could take place, and even when it did, it was difficult to keep an orderly discussion going with seventeen delegations assembling nearly 200 negotiators in a room). Partly, the difficulties were of a technical nature (relating above all to *origin control*, that is, criteria to determine if a product has been produced within the FTA, or whether it is merely a re-export).

However, the most important factor preventing a swift and successful conclusion to the negotiations was the simple fact that the French government entertained little enthusiasm for the scheme. Its opposition was partly based on economic arguments: with the British government insisting that agriculture was to be excluded from free trade treatment, the French saw little reason to support the scheme. They had already reluctantly accepted that the many benefits they derived from the common market had to be paid for by opening up their hitherto protected industrial markets. At least, the other five members of the Community had agreed in principle to a common agricultural policy which was expected to compensate for allowing competition, not to mention the substantial financial support French overseas territories could expect from the newly established Community. No such deal was inherent in the British FTA plan. In essence, it meant exposing France's weak industrial base to yet more competition while receiving little by way of compensation.

Of course, 1958 also witnessed the return of General de Gaulle to the political arena. His support for European integration in any form was doubtful—not just a reputation he was to acquire in the following decade of his presidency. Given that he assumed power before the first tariff cuts agreed in the Treaty of Rome were to be implemented in January 1959, the newly established Community seemed in great danger.

Yet even greater than his dislike of supranational integration was his mistrust of *Anglo-Saxons*. If European integration was acceptable only as a vehicle for restoring France to its former status of *la grande nation*, the participation of Britain certainly was not. Hence, in addition to the numerous objections raised against the FTA on economic grounds, the French disapproval of the scheme assumed a distinctly political character in the summer of 1958.

Indeed, it did not take the new French President long to put an end to the negotiations. On 14 November 1958 he had his Information Minister, Jacques Soustelle, declare that it was impossible to form a Free Trade Area 'as wished by the British'.[2]

---

[2] See Chancellor's Office report to Adenauer, 17 Nov. 1958, in B 136/2597 (Files of the Bundeskanzleramt, Bundesarchiv, Koblenz. Subsequent references to the Chancellor's Office (BuKa), the Ministry for Economics (BMWi), and the private papers of Herbert Blankenhorn (Nachlaß Blankenhorn, NL 351), are also to documents held in Koblenz). Initially, the announcement was not interpreted as the definite end of the FTA negotiations: see report by the German OEEC representative Karl Werkmeister to *Auswärtige Amt* (AA) and BMWi, 17 Nov. 1958, in B 102/11159 (BMWi), noting that Soustelle belonged to a small new party (Union de la nouvelle Republique), which sought to attract not only votes, but also financial help from French industrial federations. A very similar interpretation was offered by the British representative Sir Hugh Ellis-Rees, 17 Nov. 1958, in FO 371/134514 (Foreign Office Papers, Public Record Office, London. All subsequent references to the Foreign Office (FO), the Prime Minister's Office (PREM) and the Cabinet (CAB) are also to files held here). See also AA report to Adenauer, 19 Nov. 1958, in AA: West I 200/150 and the report by German embassy, Paris, 15 Nov. 1958, in AA: West I 200/351 (all in Political Archive of the German Foreign Ministry, Berlin. All subsequent references to the AA are also to the Political Archive in Berlin).

Instantly, this innocuous announcement threw the negotiations into turmoil, with the British chairman, Paymaster-General Reginald Maudling, suspending the meeting and postponing planned sessions.[3]

2.2. Having to choose?

Faced with the breakdown, the British government took rather drastic measures to bring the French back to the negotiating table. It sought to apply economic pressure to the Six by threatening retaliatory tariffs and by attempting to organize non-members of the Community into forming a preferential trade bloc of their own, which was later to become the European Free Trade Association.[4] Clearly, such economic pressure was largely lost on France as its exports to Britain and the other prospective FTA countries were marginal. The addressees of this economic stick were the other five members of the Community, and, among them, the German government in particular. If the five were to fail to convince France, then the issue would have to be resolved by the Germans alone. The occasion on which British hopes rested in this regard was the forthcoming meeting between Chancellor Konrad Adenauer and President Charles de Gaulle at Bad Kreuznach in November 1958.[5]

The meeting between the two statesmen has attracted much attention, for it saw not only General de Gaulle's anxiously awaited commitment to honouring the Treaty of Rome, but it also marked the end of any hope for a comprehensive all-European Free Trade Area.[6] This simultaneity of decisions suggested to many a commentator that Bonn had made a choice in favour of Paris and against London. It could even be argued that if the Bonn–Paris axis was formed by co-operation during the negotiations towards the

[3] According to the BMWi's chief negotiator, Alfred Müller-Armack, Maudling had 'lost his nerve' over what was merely a 'philological problem' by prematurely declaring an indefinite postponement of further committee meetings, as cited in the Bundeskanzleramt report to Adenauer, 17 Nov. 1958, in B 136/2597 (BuKa).

[4] For the formulation of these tactics, see ES (58) 36, 21 Nov. 1958, in CAB 134/1837, discussed in ES (58) 14th meeting, 20 Nov. 1958, in CAB 134/1837.

[5] See e.g. leader comment in *The Times*, 18 Nov. 1958, entitled 'France the Wrecker'.

[6] See 'Agreement at Bad Kreuznach', 26 Nov. 1958, in B 102/10912 (BMWi), also in AA: West I 200/1. See also note by Ambassador Herbert Blankenhorn, Paris, 26 Nov. 1958, in NL 351, vol. 92a, pp. 243–4.

European Coal and Steel Community, it was cemented by exclusion with the end of the FTA. The interpretations offered for Adenauer's decision to abandon the British usually emphasize three interlinked factors.

First, it is argued that de Gaulle quite explicitly forced the choice upon the Chancellor by declaring French acceptance of the Treaty of Rome to be conditional upon putting an end to the FTA.[7] The ease with which Adenauer apparently agreed can be explained by the fact that since European integration represented a central plank of his foreign policy, it appeared wise to hang on to a successfully concluded Treaty with substantial supranational elements, while sacrificing the wider and much looser arrangement of the FTA, which was, after all, still at the planning stage. Moreover, the British Free Trade Area proposal had always been regarded as a consequence of the creation of the European Community, rather than as an integration effort in its own right. Thus a failure of the Community was expected also to mean the end of the FTA.[8]

The second factor contributing to the Bad Kreuznach decision is seen in the internal divisions within the German Cabinet. Adenauer is said to have consistently favoured Franco-German *rapprochement* and political integration over mere trading arrangements. Consequently, he had never been wedded to the idea of the FTA and, instead, it was the Ministry for Economics under Ludwig Erhard which had given the misleading impression of solid German support. The British government is said to have, in a sense, backed the wrong horse by trusting Erhard to deliver on his promises.[9]

A third and final factor cited in connection with the Bad Kreuznach meeting is the mounting Berlin crisis following Khrushchev's speech of 12 November, which triggered off the second Berlin crisis.[10] General de Gaulle's promise to adopt an uncompromising stance against Soviet tactics of division struck a

[7] See de Gaulle's comments, as recorded by Blankenhorn, 24 Nov. 1958, NL 351, vol. 92b, pp. 7–8.

[8] See, for example, Vice-Präsident of the ECSC High Authority Franz Etzel to Erhard (copies to Adenauer and Brentano), 17 Nov. 1956, AA: MB vol. 48.

[9] See e.g. the reference to this hope for Erhard as being 'Britain's basic miscalculation', in Miriam Camps, *Britain and the European Community, 1955–1963* (London: Oxford University Press, 1964), 155.

[10] See e.g. Hans-Peter Schwarz, *Adenauer: Der Staatsmann, 1952–1967* (Stuttgart: Deutsche Verlagsanstalt, 1991), 466–7, and Sabine Lee, *An Uneasy Partnership: British–German Relations between 1955 and 1961* (Bochum: Universitätsverlag Dr. N. Brockmeyer, 1996), esp. ch. 6.

chord with a German Chancellor plagued by uncertainty about the reaction of the Western Alliance. Underlining the reliability of Paris as a security partner, the Soviet threat is thus said to have contributed to the decision to abandon the FTA.

2.3. For Paris, against London, or both?

There is no reason to doubt the validity of the central argument: confronted with the choice, Germany's foreign policy interests would cause it to lean towards the European Community which was to come into effect within weeks. This contained at least a promise of political integration, and, it must not be forgotten, was strongly supported by the United States government.[11] The much looser plans for European free trade, on which an agreement was not even in sight, and which was supported by neither France nor the United States, simply did not qualify as an alternative.[12]

So far, so good, it seems. However, other factors offered in accounting for the results of the Bad Kreuznach meeting tend to give a misleading impression. In combination, they suggest two elements. First, Adenauer's decision is depicted as a solitary one, as an *ad hoc* response to de Gaulle's two carrots and stick—the two carrots being the fulfilment of EEC commitments and solid support over Berlin, the stick being the threat of withholding these if the FTA was not abandoned. By implication, this also seems to suggests that the decision had little if anything to do with London—Adenauer explicitly opting for Paris, for the EEC, or for security, while sacrificing London by default, or because of the incompatibility of the two. It is with regard to these two implicit elements that the above explanation for Adenauer's acquiescence at Bad Kreuznach is questionable.

Far from being *ad hoc* in character, the Chancellor's response can be shown to have been meticulously prepared by the *Auswärtige Amt*. In fact, those passages of the communiqué which confirmed the commitment to the Community while at the same time sealing the fate of the FTA had been drafted jointly by the state secretaries of

---

[11] For the lack of US support in this crucial phase, see Pascaline Winand, *Eisenhower, Kennedy and the United States of Europe* (London: Macmillan, 1993), 119.

[12] During the final phase of the FTA negotiations, the US government was increasingly concerned about the increased tension between Paris and Bonn. See AA Sub-Department 'Peaceful use of atomic energy' to the Head of the AA's Sub-Department 'European political integration', Wilhelm Hartlieb, about an intervention of the US embassy, 6 Nov. 1958, AA: West I 200/351.

the French and German Foreign Ministries. The drafting meeting between Hilgar van Scherpenberg and Couve de Murville took place on 19 November, five days after Soustelle's announcement and no less than a week before the Kreuznach meeting itself.[13] In the light of the meeting, the emphasis on Khrushchev's speech cannot be fully maintained either. Admittedly, the mounting crisis had been discussed at Bad Kreuznach, yet the idea of Adenauer spontaneously and single-handedly abandoning the FTA in return for French support over Berlin clearly cannot be sustained in view of the preparatory meeting between the state secretaries. Security concerns are not detectable in the records of the latter meeting.

More credible is the idea of Bad Kreuznach representing the outcome of a prolonged internal division, in which the free trade convictions of Ludwig Erhard were pitched against the long-standing preference for supranational integration that characterized the *Bundeskanzleramt* and the *Auswärtige Amt*. Erhard and others had indeed sought to use the FTA negotiations to undermine the common market.[14] Moreover, just as the negotiations were heading for a crisis, Adenauer had sent Erhard on a prolonged tour of Asia, in order to avoid undue interference.[15] But again: do these circumstances indicate that Bad Kreuznach was a conscious decision in favour of Paris, and only by default one against London? Had London, by trusting Erhard, really lobbied the wrong side in this internal debate?

In fact, this is highly doubtful. The British government can be shown to have been acutely aware of Erhard's lack of influence with regard to European integration. While he was certainly helpful in moderating French demands, the ultimate decision was known to rest with the Chancellor.[16] In this respect, the British

[13] See record of the meeting between van Scherpenberg and Couve de Murville, including the agreed formula identical to the communiqué, 19 Nov. 1958, in NL 351, vol. 94, pp. 7–14.

[14] For a more detailed account of such attempts by Erhard, see Martin Schaad, 'Plan G—A "Counterblast"?', *Contemporary European History*, 44 (1998), 39–60. For the AA's suspicion that Erhard would 'sacrifice the EEC', see Hartlieb to Karl Carstens (Head of the AA's Political Department 2, responsible for European integration and co-operation as well as relations to the countries of Western Europe), 22 Mar. 1958, in AA: PA 200/149.

[15] See Schwarz, *Adenauer: Der Staatsmann*, 465.

[16] Well aware that the Ministry for Economics did not represent the majority view, the Treasury, for example, had advised British lobbying efforts to be directed at the Chancellor and the Foreign Ministry as early as April 1957: see Frank Figgures (then Under-Secretary at the Treasury) to Russell Bretherton (Under-Secretary at the Board of Trade, former British representative at the Spaak committee discussions of the Messina Six), 23 Apr. 1957, in FO 371/128343.

government was under no illusions: European integration was regarded as an essentially political issue in Germany.

Recognizing that Adenauer himself—and perhaps also Foreign Minister Heinrich von Brentano—was the key to securing German support for the FTA, British officials, and, in particular, Prime Minister Harold Macmillan himself, had not missed an opportunity to lobby them. Yet the British government faced a serious problem in selling their scheme to a German Chancellor who had little interest in economic issues, let alone possessed the rather technical knowledge necessary to follow disputes such as that regarding origin control.

Nor was it obvious how to promote the FTA on its political merits. This is not to say that British diplomats and politicians did not try to do just that. However, given that the institutions and decision-making procedures envisaged for the FTA were not at all comparable to those of the EEC, British emphasis on the political character of the scheme quickly turned into stressing the negative political consequences of a failure of the scheme. Indicative of this approach was Harold Macmillan's famous memorandum to Peter Thorneycroft, in which he outlined British reactions if the FTA negotiations were to break down:

if Little Europe is formed without a parallel development of a Free Trade Area we shall have to reconsider the whole of our political and economic attitude towards Europe. I doubt if we could remain in NATO. We should certainly put on highly protective tariffs and quotas to counteract what Little Europe was doing to us. In other words, we should not allow ourselves to be destroyed little by little. We would fight back with every weapon in our armoury. We would take our troops out of Europe. We would withdraw from NATO. We would adopt a policy of isolationism. We would surround ourselves with rockets and we would say to the Germans, the French and all the rest of them: 'Look after yourselves with your own forces. Look after yourselves when the Russians overrun your countries.'[17]

This was, of course, an internal communication (and one that was swiftly swept under the carpet by more level-headed officials).[18] Yet Whitehall was not able to prevent Macmillan from

---

[17] Macmillan to Foreign Secretary Selwyn Lloyd, 24 June 1958, in PREM 11/2315.

[18] Some officials had warned against this approach at an early stage. See e.g. a report of HM Ambassador to Bonn, Sir Christopher Steel: 'Adenauer was not convinced of our sincerity, either in defence matters or in European Economic Co-operation', Steel to FO, 6 May 1957, in PREM 11/1829A.

openly threatening Adenauer during state visits.[19] In doing so, the Prime Minister did not shy away from attempts to disrupt Franco-German relations. At their meeting of October 1958, for example, a skilful scheduling of topics ensured that the exchange on FTA issues was preceded by a discussion of NATO matters. Macmillan first gave Adenauer a summary of the tripartite proposals for NATO, which de Gaulle had made to the US and British administrations without informing the Germans.[20] Having thus dealt a blow to the Chancellor's confidence in the General and Germany's security arrangements at large, Macmillan then quite openly threatened Adenauer not to let the FTA negotiations fail: 'No British Government could continue to take part in the military defence of a continent which had declared economic war upon her. The United Kingdom would become isolationist. We could not have a Europe which was militarily united and economically divided.'[21]

Such admonitions were not favourably received within the German government, though Macmillan's threats were not given much credibility.[22] Instead, utterances to this effect were usually interpreted as over-anxiousness on the part of a declining power. None the less, in a situation in which foreign and security policy concerns were mounting simultaneously—first complications within NATO, increasing East–West tension, and renewed doubts about the realization of the EEC—Macmillan's tactics of 'playing the Germans off against the French in this matter'[23] left the

[19] See e.g. Macmillan to Adenauer, 25 Oct. 1958, in PREM 11/2706. For one of the rare secondary sources acknowledging the consequences of Macmillan's threats of late 1958, see Jonathan Wright, 'The Role of Britain in West German Policy since 1949', *German Politics*, 5 (1996), 26–42.

[20] See record of the meetings between Adenauer and Macmillan, 8–9 Oct. 1958, in PREM 11/2328. See also Macmillan's letter to Adenauer, 25 Oct. 1958, in PREM 11/2706.

[21] Record of the Adenauer/Macmillan meetings, 8–9 Oct. 1958, in PREM 11/2328. Not all British officials agreed with the line taken by Macmillan. Paul Gore-Booth, Deputy Under-Secretary at the FO, for example, rather poetically asked 'to threaten or not to threaten: that is the question'. See Gore-Booth's reply to Harold Caccia (HM Ambassador to Washington), 14 Nov. 1958, in FO 371/134513. The Foreign Secretary politely but firmly stated that 'in terms of modern warfare our own defence as well as that of continental Europe is at stake. If our troops began to leave Europe the American troops would soon follow them.' See his letter to Macmillan, 31 Oct. 1958, in PREM 11/2352.

[22] For an assessment of the political and economic importance of Britain and the sterling area, see van Scherpenberg to the BMWi's State Secretary Alfred Müller-Armack, 17 Oct. 1958, in AA: West I 200/150.

[23] The Prime Minister's private secretary Philip de Zulueta to Macmillan, 20 June 1958, in PREM 11/2531.

impression that Britain was an awkward as well as unreliable partner. This assessment contributed to an atmosphere which considerably eased Bonn's decision to abandon the FTA project in favour
of closer relations with Paris (and the Community).

Of course, none of this should be overestimated. As long as the
FTA proposal was a complement to the EEC, it was in Germany's
economic interest to support it. In November 1958, the French
President had transformed this complement into a question of
alternatives. Perhaps the best illustration of the German position
on the Free Trade Area was the characterization by an *Auswärtige
Amt* official at the time: 'We are standing in between the British and
the French; our sympathies lie largely with the former, but we are
contractually bound to the latter in a framework which in the long
term is a political concept.'[24]

It was the said contractual obligation which, as early as 1958,
restricted Germany's foreign policy options. Yet this episode serves
to highlight that it was not only de Gaulle who forced the German
government to choose between London and Paris. Internal divisions in Bonn, as well as British tactics, both also contributed to the
impression that good relations with one capital would always be to
the detriment of relations with the other. Set against an even more
complex backdrop of actors and interests, this impression also
characterized the second episode chosen to illustrate the relative
weight Bonn attached to its relations to Paris and London.

3. Gaullists and Atlanticists

Seven years after the FTA failure and, of course, two years after de
Gaulle had vetoed British entry into the Community,[25] relations
with Paris and London were once again hotly debated in Bonn.
This section will examine the domestic consequences of an effort to
improve Anglo-German relations by institutionalizing consultation

---

[24] Hartlieb to Carstens, 5 Dec. 1958, in AA: West I 200/150: 'Wir stehen zwischen Briten
und Franzosen; ersteren gehören überwiegend unsere Sympathien, an letztere sind wir ver-
traglich gebunden und das im Rahmen einer auf lange Sicht angelegten politischen
Konzeption.'

[25] For an insightful account of the negotiations on the first application, see N. Piers
Ludlow, *Dealing with Britain: The Six and the First UK Application to the EEC* (Cambridge:
Cambridge University Press, 1997); of particular interest here, pp. 219–23, entitled 'A
German rescue?'

procedures in the summer and autumn of 1965. However, before delving deeper into the issues at stake here, it may be helpful briefly to allude to the wider political context, that is, to the state of Germany's foreign relations in the mid-1960s.

3.1. Multiple foreign policy dilemmas

By the mid-1960s, Germany was facing a number of difficulties with regard to its security policy. While NATO remained the central plank in any meaningful defence, a certain divergence of interests began to emerge between the Federal Republic and its partners. With a slight thaw in East–West relations, the Alliance was taking a less confrontational stance towards the Warsaw Pact, entering into negotiations towards disarmament, and discussing a first treaty on non-proliferation of nuclear weapons. In principle, the German Foreign Minister, Gerhard Schröder, welcomed improved relations, having himself initiated a cautious policy review with the Moscow visit of his state secretary Karl Carstens and with the opening of trade missions in Poland, Romania, and Bulgaria.[26]

On the other hand, the improved climate threatened to undermine Bonn's *Deutschlandpolitik* in a number of respects. There was a latent fear that Alliance partners would be tempted to accept compromises at Germany's expense. The efforts of the French government to improve relations with Poland, for example, raised German anxieties about the possibility of a deal being struck over their heads. Bonn's efforts to have a reference to the Oder–Neiße border deleted from the final communiqué of the Paris visit of the Polish Prime Minister Cyrankiewicz led to agitated speculation in the German press.[27] Though Konrad Adenauer's infamous reference

[26] For Schröder's views, see his article 'Germany Looks at Eastern Europe', *Foreign Affairs*, 44 (Oct. 1965), 15–25. For Carstens' visit to Moscow, see Karl Carstens, *Erinnerungen und Erfahrungen* (Boppard: Boldt, 1993), 294–5. For a more general discussion about the difficult reorientation of Germany's foreign policy in this regard, see Wolfram F. Hanrieder, *Germany, America, Europe* (New Haven and London: Yale University Press, 1989), 176–82.

[27] See e.g. *Frankfurter Allgemeine Zeitung*, 13 and 16 Sept. 1965. For the diplomatic effort to prevent any official French reference to the Oder–Neiße Line see report by the German embassy, Paris, sent to AA, 3 Sept. 1965, in *Akten zur Auswärtigen Politik 1965*, ii (Munich: Oldenbourg, 1996), no. 342 (*AAPD 1965*). Ignoring the German request, the French government did not issue an official refutation: see Horst Osterheld, *Außenpolitik unter Bundeskanzler Ludwig Erhard, 1963–1966* (Düsseldorf: Droste, 1992), 234.

to Germany being once again 'encircled' may have been exaggerated, it did capture the prevailing feeling of insecurity.[28]

The envisaged non-proliferation treaty was particularly problematic because of its implicit international recognition of East Germany.[29] Admittedly, the Hallstein doctrine of severing diplomatic links with any country recognizing the GDR had already crumbled, and had become untenable after Walter Ulbricht's visit to Cairo in spring 1965. Yet if East Berlin were now also to be a signatory of an international treaty alongside the Federal Republic and most of its allies, the division of Germany would have been cemented in a way deemed irreconcilable with the Basic Law.

Perhaps even more importantly, non-proliferation threatened to end Schröder's hopes for a successful conclusion to the so-called MLF project, a NATO plan for a (surface-ship based) multilateral nuclear force.[30] In addition to fulfilling long-standing nuclear ambitions, the MLF had promised to counter German insecurities regarding East–West relations by giving Bonn a say with regard to the deterrent. In December 1964, however, the project had suffered a serious setback with the US government officially denying Chancellor Erhard's claim that they were prepared to conclude the project on a bilateral basis, if necessary.[31] With this bold statement, the Chancellor had sought to rekindle the waning support of other prospective members, notably the British.[32] Most importantly, though, it was meant to overcome what had by then turned into active opposition by the French government. The gamble did not pay off—and though the German government remained

---

[28] Adenauer first voiced his fear of 'encirclement' after de Gaulle had spoken warmly about Franco-Soviet relations when bidding farewell to the outgoing Soviet ambassador to France in March 1965. He repeated his warning in an interview in *Bild*, 9 Oct. 1965, in which he put the blame for the situation squarely on Schröder's neglect of relations to Paris. See also *Die Zeit*, 19 Oct. 1965.

[29] See the official reaction of the AA to the British and Canadian treaty drafts, as sent by Carstens to Germany's permanent representation at NATO, 14 July 1965, in *AAPD 1965*, ii, no. 281.

[30] See Carstens' memo to Germany's permanent representation at NATO, 14 July 1965, in *AAPD 1965*, ii, no. 281.

[31] See President Lyndon B. Johnson's speech at Georgetown University, as reported in *Europa-Archiv*, no. 24 (1964), p. D626. On the decision-making process within the US administration, see Adrian W. Schertz, *Die Deutschlandpolitik Kennedys und Johnsons* (Cologne: Böhlau, 1992), 282–6.

[32] See *Die Welt*, 7 Oct. 1964.

officially committed to the MLF, most commentators now deemed the chances of the project negligible at best.[33]

Finally, the Alliance itself appeared threatened as an institution.[34] Having called for a reform of NATO for some time, General de Gaulle finally announced that the French would withdraw from its integrated command structure in 1966 (which also raised the question as to whether French troops would remain in Germany thereafter).[35]

Thus Germany's security policy appeared increasingly out of step with those of its partners. Disintegrative tendencies, the fear of an East–West compromise, and the continuing exclusion from any participation in nuclear defence all contributed to the impression that the Alliance no longer served German interests to the extent to which it had during the height of Cold War confrontation. The prevailing mood in the mid-1960s formed, therefore, a stark contrast to the successes of institution-building and West Germany's integration which had characterized the previous decade.

A similar feeling of insecurity also prevailed with regard to the project of European integration, the second pillar of Germany's *Westbindung*. Here, the problems which had emerged concerned both the political development of the Community as well as the Common Agricultural Policy as its most ambitious, and, of course, its most costly, experiment at creating a common market.

With regard to political integration, Chancellor Erhard had sought to breathe new life into the proceedings after the failure of the Fouchet plans. In November 1964 he had proposed further intergovernmental co-operation in the fields of foreign policy, defence, cultural policy, and general economic and trade policy (the latter to be organized within the institutional framework of the existing Community, the former to be established around regular ministerial and summit meetings).[36] Whereas the plan

[33] See, for example, leader comment of the *Frankfurter Allgemeine Zeitung*, 30 Oct. 1965, referring to 'the MLF (or whatever is left of the crumpled-up paper it was written on)' (my translation).

[34] In the summer of 1965, Washington was becoming increasingly 'displeased' with Paris over the issue of NATO reform: see report by Wilhelm Grewe, Ambassador to NATO, to AA, 8 June 1965, in *AAPD 1965*, ii, no. 237.

[35] See *Frankfurter Allgemeine Zeitung*, 10 Sept. 1965, 15 Oct. 1965, on his proposals for NATO reform. See also *Der Spiegel*, 15 Sept. 1965.

[36] See Herbert Müller-Roschach, *Die deutsche Europapolitik* (Baden-Baden: Nomos, 1974), 83–6.

received immediate support from the Italian government, the French President appeared reserved.[37] For his government, the issue of setting agricultural prices, in particular for cereals, was the more pressing, not least because of the favourable income effect which a rise in German price levels would have on French farmers. In Germany, conversely, the rise in prices was, of course, less popular.

When Erhard signalled in December 1964 that Germany was finally ready to agree to raise its cereal prices, he linked his gesture of good will to the issue of political integration. As he made clear to the *Bundestag*, he expected France to respond in kind when it came to his political initiative.[38] However, Erhard's announcement did not have the desired effect.[39] While debating the remaining technical issues concerning the final shape of the Common Agricultural Policy (CAP), its financing, and the level of agricultural tariffs *vis-à-vis* non-members, Commission President Walter Hallstein came forward with a far-reaching proposal which envisaged the European Community treating agricultural levies as its own resources.[40] The financial independence which the Commission would thus be granted was to be balanced by giving the European Parliament a greater say in budgetary matters. In essence, the Commission thereby sought significantly to increase the supranational room for manœuvre independent of national governments. Not surprisingly, the intrepid move of the Commission infuriated the French President, as it was so obviously designed to undermine the French vision of a *Europe des Patries*.[41] The long-running feud between Commission President Hallstein and the General was thus brought to a head.[42] Although the German and other governments distanced themselves from the Commission proposals, both issues, CAP financing and further

[37] Ibid. 90–1.   [38] See *Stenographische Berichte des Bundestages*, 2 Dec. 1964, 7300–2.

[39] The subsequent Rambouillet meeting between Erhard and de Gaulle on 19–20 January revealed French reservations concerning the choice of an appropriate forum in which the Six were to organize their consultations. See Müller-Roschach, *Deutsche Europapolitik*, 89.

[40] A short appreciation of the Commission's proposals is contained in Müller-Roschach, *Deutsche Europapolitik*, 91–2.

[41] For the French government's immediate reaction to the Commission's proposals, see the comments of its speaker, as reported in Heinrich Siegler, *Europäische politische Einigung 1949–1968: Dokumentation* (Bonn: Siegler, 1968), 333.

[42] In a press interview, Charles de Gaulle referred to anyone who still envisaged a supranational Europe as a *Jean-foutre*. See *Le Monde*, 10 July 1965.

political integration, were now in doubt.[43] When the Ministerial Council failed to reach a CAP compromise on 1 July 1965, the General had its representative declare that they would not accept the planned introduction of limited majority voting, and that instead, the French representative would no longer take part in Council meetings.[44] The infamous *policy of the empty chair* had begun.

3.2. A French alternative?

The question widely debated at the time was, of course, whether there was a *European* alternative to the MLF, or, in the wider context, whether the idea of a Franco-German Union could be revived as a counterweight to disintegrative tendencies within NATO and the European Community.

With the *Bundestag*'s debate on the Franco-German Treaty of 1963, an uneasy middle course had been steered between the idea of a political union with Paris, and continuing close relations with the United States and other partners within the Alliance. The ratification law had been given a preamble reaffirming the Atlantic dimension of Germany's foreign policy. However, by the mid-1960s the domestic debate about a missed opportunity for Franco-German Union had not lost any of its acrimony. On the contrary, the simultaneity of the French challenge to a weakened NATO and European Community in the summer and autumn of 1965 renewed the persuasive power of this presumed remedy.

Following the French withdrawal from the Ministerial Council, some within the ruling coalition in the *Bundestag* were now openly calling for a Franco-German Union as a solution to the mounting constitutional crisis. Embracing de Gaulle's vision of Europe would put an end to the wrangling over the future direction of integration policy and stabilize the Community. Yet this certainly did not represent the views of the *Auswärtige Amt*. Nor did it please the Ministries for Economics or Agriculture, who would have had to pay the price in terms of a French-designed Common Agricultural

---

[43] The General had apparently turned Erhard's *Junktim* of Dec. 1964 against the Chancellor's proposal, by now linking the disagreement on the financing of agriculture to his refusal to start contemplating Erhard's political proposal. See Siegler, *Europäische politische Einigung*, 341, on a working meeting between the two in Bonn, 11–12 June 1965.

[44] See *Archiv der Gegenwart*, 2 July 1965, pp. 11933–4, and Müller-Roschach, *Deutsche Europapolitik*, 94–6.

Policy. Indeed, the existence and nature of any such French offer remained unclear. Upon being pressed by the leader of the CDU/CSU parliamentary party, Rainer Barzel, Erhard apparently confirmed that in the summer of 1964 the General had offered: 'If we, France and Germany, were to come together, we would determine the course of European policy, and the other four [EEC member states] . . . would have to adapt or subordinate themselves to what we decide.'

The German Chancellor claimed to have 'rejected the offer with indignation, as . . . [he] . . . regarded it as immoral'.[45] While Erhard may thus not have considered it an adequate response to the crisis of integration policy, the advocates of Franco-German Union drew additional strength from a combination of their European argument with a security argument. Not only designed to overcome the empty chair crisis, Franco-German Union was also portrayed as offering an alternative route to nuclear defence, replacing the ailing MLF policy. There is indeed continuing uncertainty as to whether the French President did or did not offer participation in the *Force de Frappe* in return for the German government abandoning the MLF plan. Karl Carstens, at least, claimed to remember the offer, but himself judged it insincere after consulting the protocols of de Gaulle's visit to Bonn of July 1964.[46] With de Gaulle's announcement of the French withdrawal from NATO's integrated command structure, the issue of having to choose between Paris and Washington resurfaced in autumn 1965. Some circles within the CDU/CSU parliamentary party were now even more forceful in calling for closer political and security ties with Paris, much to the annoyance of Ludwig Erhard and his Foreign Minister, who both viewed any weakening of the Atlantic Alliance as damaging Germany's essential foreign policy interests.[47]

---

[45] Both quotations represent Franz-Josef Strauß's recollection of a meeting of Oct. 1965. See Franz-Josef Strauß, *Erinnerungen* (Berlin: Siedler, 1989), 434 (my translation).

[46] See *Akten zur Auswärtigen Politik 1964*, ii (Munich: Oldenbourg, 1995), no. 186 (*AAPD 1964*).

[47] The question of choosing between Paris and Washington in regard to the MLF was, of course, not only a question of whether or not to accept a French offer. Forcing the MLF clearly meant annoying the General. By 1965, the AA was becoming very concerned about possible French reactions to a successful conclusion of the project, which in their view might also include official recognition of the GDR by France. See *AAPD 1965*, ii, no. 389.

3.3. British assistance?

Of course, this essay has to address the question of whether closer co-operation with the Wilson administration promised to alleviate Germany's foreign policy difficulties. On the face of it, there seemed little hope for any support from London. Harold Wilson's unfortunate remark that his government did not want to see a 'German finger on the trigger' clearly indicated that the MLF was not high on the list of priorities there.[48] Yet with the MLF becoming increasingly doubtful, the British alternative proposal for an Atlantic Nuclear Force (ANF) began to be viewed as a credible fallback position.

With regard to the wider question of East–West relations, London's record was equally mixed. While generally regarded as a reliable partner in the Alliance, Britain at times seemed to undermine the solidarity of the West. For example, when the German government reacted to friendly pressure to abandon the sale of wide-diameter pipes to the Soviet Union as part of a strategic goods embargo, British firms quickly stepped in to take the order.[49] British plans for reorganizing the Rhine Army raised additional concern.[50] At a different level, though no less symbolic, the English Football Association announced that Vorwärts Ost-Berlin would be allowed to play Manchester United at Old Trafford—the first time an East German side was to play in any NATO country.[51]

London's reliability was also in doubt when it came to the crisis in Brussels. Though Britain was unaffected as a non-member of the Community, German papers noted the relaxed, and even amused reaction with which the disintegration of the Six was viewed there.[52] Yet German perceptions of likely British reactions were a curious and ambiguous mixture of concern and expectations. De

---

[48] See Carstens, *Erinnerungen und Erfahrungen*, 293–4, and the discussion in Wright, 'The Role of Britain', 26–42.

[49] See record of the meeting between Foreign Minister Gerhard Schröder and his British counterpart Lord Home, 10 Apr. 1963, in *Akten zur Auswärtigen Politik 1963*, i (Munich: Oldenbourg, 1995), no. 144 (*AAPD 1963*).

[50] See e.g. Herbert Blankenhorn, *Verständnis und Verständigung* (Frankfurt am Main: Propyläen, 1980), 485.

[51] See *Frankfurter Allgemeine Zeitung*, 19 Oct. 1965.

[52] The *Frankfurter Allgemeine Zeitung* even suggested that Prime Minister Wilson and the majority of the Labour Party continued to be 'grateful' to de Gaulle for his veto on British entry, and that 'nowhere did de Gaulle's views on Europe receive as much understanding as among British Socialists', 11 Sept. 1965.

Gaulle's vision of a Europe of nations was, of course, closer to what the British could agree to; on the other hand, there was some hope in Germany that if the worst came to the worst, a Community of five would allow for the swift entry of Britain and other EFTA countries.[53]

All in all, Britain could not be said to offer an alternative to France as Germany's main European partner. Nor did it present much of an alternative route to a nuclear defence policy. Instead, London appeared detached from Bonn's main foreign-policy concerns.

3.4. A means to an end or a pawn in a game?

So far, it has been argued that much of the debate in Bonn centred on an alleged choice to be made between Paris and Washington, with London playing a subordinate role, if any. Indeed, the CDU/CSU was split between Atlanticists and Gaullists, the former group comprising, among others, Chancellor Erhard, Foreign Minister Schröder, Defence Minister Kai-Uwe von Hassel, and the CDU foreign policy expert Kurt Birrenbach, while the latter were led by the ambitious ex-defence minister Franz-Josef Strauß.[54] The two camps argued vehemently about the necessity of compromise with France, or of strengthening of ties (including nuclear co-operation) with the United States.[55]

However, it is important to bear in mind that in the summer of 1965, neither side in this debate had a credible foreign policy concept to offer. The Gaullists were in no position to refer to a concrete French offer of political integration, let alone nuclear defence integration (which did not prevent them from arguing that this option did exist). The Atlanticists, on the other hand, slowly had to accept the waning support for MLF and a severe crisis in Brussels.

In this complicated situation, the idea of intensifying Anglo-German bilateral relations carried some appeal for Foreign Minister Gerhard Schröder. Though by no means of major importance in themselves, improved Anglo-German relations

---

[53] See e.g. Blankenhorn, *Verständnis und Verständigung*, 492, and Robert L. Pfaltzgraff, Jr., 'Britain and the European Community 1963–1967', *Orbis*, 12 (1968), 87–120, at 90.

[54] See Carstens, *Erinnerungen und Erfahrungen*, 258.

[55] A perceptive account of the divisions within the German government is found in *Frankfurter Allgemeine Zeitung*, 30 Oct. 1965, in which the leader comment also contains a passionate plea not to force the government into a corner by reducing complex foreign policy dilemmas to this seemingly simple choice.

could help in bringing pressure to bear on France (Community affairs), whilst also assisting in the search for a solution to the MLF problem (ANF).

The success of the Queen's visit to Germany in May 1965 was taken as an opportunity to seek to improve Anglo-German relations.[56] Following the favourable reception the idea had received during these talks, the *Auswärtige Amt* formulated a concept of regular bilateral consultations regarding all major concerns of foreign policy. However, it was clear to German diplomats that any such procedure would have to be informal and that no treaty would be signed.[57]

The preparations of the *Auswärtige Amt* for the bilateral consultation plan were thus well under way, when a major government crisis broke out after the CDU/CSU-FDP coalition won the elections of September 1965.[58] The process of forming a new Cabinet was protracted for an unprecedented six weeks, which were characterized by an intense conflict about Erhard's plan to retain Gerhard Schröder as Foreign Minister. It was an extraordinary conflict rooted as much in personal animosities and ambitions as in disputes about foreign policy orientation and party-political calculations.[59] The Gaullist opposition to Schröder was formidable, including not only Franz-Josef Strauß, but also ex-Chancellor Adenauer and even Federal President Heinrich Lübke, who now combined their efforts to remove the Foreign Minister. At the height of the conflict, Adenauer and Lübke went as far as to seek to override the constitutional authority of Erhard by arguing that the Federal President could simply refuse to appoint Schröder—

---

[56] For a report on the visit, and the suggestion to establish bilateral consultations, not least in order to put pressure on Paris and to counteract 'disintegrative tendencies' within the Western Alliance, see Blankenhorn to AA, 9 June 1965, in *AAPD 1965*, ii, no. 239.

[57] Indeed, the German Minister for Economic Co-operation, Walter Scheel, had openly asked Foreign Minister Michael Stewart for his reaction to a proposal by the British Liberal Party for an Anglo-German Treaty similar to the Franco-German arrangement. Stewart is reported to have reacted 'evasively': see report on the meeting sent by German Embassy, London to AA, 2 June 1965, in *AAPD 1965*, ii, no. 230.

[58] For a first draft of the concept, see AA memorandum, 23 June 1965, in *AAPD 1965*, ii, no. 260.

[59] For an in-depth account of the conflict, see *Der Spiegel*, 6 Oct. 1965. For long-standing personal animosities towards Schröder, see Strauß, *Erinnerungen*, in which he held the Foreign Minister personally responsible not only for 'destroying' Adenauer's achievements of Franco-German *rapprochement* (p. 416), but also for having been instrumental in forcing his own resignation as Defence Minister (p. 417).

unprecedented in the constitutional history of the young Federal Republic.[60]

Whilst this conflict was raging, a leak had opened in the *Auswärtige Amt*.[61] A junior diplomat, a certain Hans Graf Huyn, had 'misunderstood' the comments of his superior during a departmental conference, at which the latter had supposedly said that 'the time of integration policies had to be over', that 'bilateral relations with all European states had to be intensified', and, finally, that consultations had already been mutually agreed with London.[62] Huyn later claimed that his conscience had forced him to pass on this information to Karl Theodor Freiherr von Guttenberg, a CSU member of parliament and one of the most outspoken among the Gaullists.[63] This provided Schröder's adversaries with the opportunity for which they had been waiting. Guttenberg seized it, himself passing the information on to Adenauer, who in turn raised a hue and cry at the *Bundeskanzleramt*. Claiming that Schröder was secretly seeking to kill the Franco-German Treaty by preparing a similar contractual arrangement with Britain, as one of the two countries President de Gaulle disliked most, Adenauer also sought to convince the leader of the CDU parliamentary party, Rainer Barzel, to resist Erhard's Cabinet nominations. By implication, the charge included the sabotage of what was left of the European Community. In essence, Erhard and Schröder were accused of throwing overboard one of the tenets of Germany's post-war foreign policy.

In a stormy meeting at the *Bundeskanzleramt*, the fall of a government which had not even been formed was only averted by Erhard denying all knowledge of the plans for Anglo-German consultations (a palpable lie, as later became apparent during an Erhard–Schröder confrontation).[64] The Huyn affair, as it became

---

[60] Adenauer's proposal prompted the *Frankfurter Allgemeine Zeitung* to print a lengthy article about constitutional provisions, which severely criticized the ex-Chancellor, 14 Oct. 1965. In an earlier issue, the paper pointed to the selective amnesia which had allowed Adenauer to question the role of the Chancellor in determining policy, while he himself insisted on his *Richtlinienkompetenz* while in office, 11 Oct. 1965. See also *Der Spiegel*, 13 Oct. 1965.

[61] For the official position of the *Auswärtige Amt* on the Huyn affair, see memorandum by Carstens, dated 18 Nov. 1965, in *AAPD 1965*, ii, no. 420. See also Osterheld, *Außenpolitik unter Bundeskanzler Ludwig Erhard*, 252–3 and 263–4; Carstens, *Erinnerungen und Erfahrungen*, 259–60; and Volker Hentschel, *Ludwig Erhard: Ein Politikerleben* (Munich: Olzog, 1996), 586–8.

[62] See Hans Graf Huyn, *Die Sackgasse* (Stuttgart: Seewald, 1966), 400 (my translation).

[63] See e.g. Guttenberg's interview in *Der Spiegel*, 17 Nov. 1965.

[64] See Osterheld, *Außenpolitik unter Bundeskanzler Ludwig Erhard*, 252.

known, dragged on for some months. It was discussed in the *Bundestag*, received extensive coverage in the national press, and even made international news.[65] This was mainly due to some unfortunate remarks attributed to Huyn's superior, and to Schröder seeking to take disciplinary action against the young diplomat. Huyn resigned, taking up employment as an assistant to Franz-Josef Strauß—conscience or partisan conviction?[66] Be that as it may, the details of the Huyn affair are, of course, of marginal interest here. More interesting is the light which the affair casts on the role and weight of Britain in German official thinking at the time. Three conclusions can be drawn.

First, improving relations with London was not an end in itself. Even as a means of attaining other foreign policy goals, the German proposals were not as sincere as they may have seemed. They could easily be sacrificed, as demonstrated by Erhard's swift denial.

Secondly, the Huyn affair revealed the readiness with which relations with London were publicly misused for personal ambitions. Tactical considerations about the long-term impact on Anglo-German relations were of secondary importance if a Cabinet post was at stake.

Thirdly, and in contrast to the 1950s, London no longer had to threaten or offer anything—in Bonn, a mere mention of closer Anglo-German ties was enough to do the damage. It was not least the continued presence of Adenauer which ensured that the Franco-German *rapprochement* took precedence. His real influence was certainly exceeded by his symbolic value. Any initiative which the Gaullists could depict as undermining the achievements of the Federal Republic's first Chancellor attracted public attention which could be turned against its advocates. Improving Anglo-German relations was of that ilk. In this sense, London was but a pawn in the internal power struggle within the coalition.

[65] Examples include: 'Kleine Anfrage' of the SPD, in *Bundestag-Drucksache*, 5. Wahlperiode, no. 113, 9 Dec. 1965, and Schröder's reply of 6 Jan. 1966, in *Bundestags-Drucksache*, 5. Wahlperiode, no. 160; *Der Spiegel*, 17 Nov., 15 Dec. 1965, and 24 Jan. 1966; *Frankfurter Allgemeine Zeitung*, 26 Nov. 1965. In his book, Huyn himself cites a number of international press reports, including *The Times*: see Huyn, *Die Sackgasse*, 389–442.

[66] For the opposing recollections of the meeting and the ensuing affair, see the memoirs of the superior, Paul Frank, *Entschlüsselte Botschaft: Ein Diplomat macht Inventur* (Stuttgart: Deutsche Verlagsanstalt, 1981), ch. 10, entitled *Das trojanische Pferd*, pp. 129–36, and Huyn, *Die Sackgasse*, 389–442. The book written immediately after the affair was significantly subtitled *Deutschlands Weg in die Isolierung*.

4. Economic or Political Union?

The collapse of Communism in 1989 and 1990 clearly raised one simple, yet essential question regarding Germany's involvement in, and commitment to, the European Community as one of the central elements of the policy of *Westbindung*. To what extent did Bonn's willingness to integrate depend on the historical contingencies of the post-1945 order and its specific place therein? How directly was the Federal Republic's unquestioned loyalty to the institutional arrangement of the 1950s the result of its status as a semi-sovereign and divided country, situated at the East–West line of confrontation?

Clearly, the two episodes discussed above have highlighted the importance of these factors. However, their continued relevance may now have to be reassessed, given German reunification and the effective end of East–West confrontation. By extension, the relative weight of London and Paris may also be reviewed. A brief analysis of the negotiations leading to the Amsterdam Treaty of 1997 may thus serve as a third and final episode to illustrate the complexities of Bonn's foreign policy preferences and options.

4.1. Negotiating the Treaty

Without attempting to recapitulate the negotiations towards the Amsterdam Treaty in full, it may suffice to emphasize that the successful conclusion (and the swift German ratification) of this treaty was made possible by two essential compromises, in both of which Paris and Bonn had played the leading roles. The first of these compromises had become necessary in order to overcome the impasse reached with regard to the furtherance of integration beyond the scope of the Maastricht Treaty. While many a member-state government did accept the idea of a moderate extension of qualified majority voting in existing policy areas, there was little hope that the addition of further policy areas would be possible— in fact, this was ruled outside the remit of the Intergovernmental Conference (IGC) at an early stage. Yet with enlargement looming, the likelihood of securing agreement on the deepening of integration at a later stage appeared slim indeed. As all substantive extensions of EU powers require unanimously agreed Treaty revision, the idea of reconciling the divergent interests of more than twenty member states indeed appears remote (on the Continent these difficulties were, incidentally, suspected to be the negative motivation behind the vocal British support for widening over deepening). The Franco-German compromise proposal involved the reintroduction of a modified version of the CDU-proposal of *Kerneuropa*, now presented as a much more positively termed *flexible integration* or *enhanced co-operation* arrangement.[67] A joint initiative of Foreign Ministers Klaus Kinkel and Hervé de Charette ensured that the idea of sub-groups of member states progressing faster and further than others towards unification found its way into the negotiations.[68] One may argue, of course, that the compromise eventually reached on this issue at the Amsterdam summit owed much to the change of government in London. Still, there is no escaping the fact that the stimulus for further integration had once again been provided by the Paris–Bonn axis.

A further, yet somewhat different example underlining the continued centrality of the Paris–Bonn axis in furthering (or halting) integration initiatives is provided by the Amsterdam summit meeting itself. Different, because rather than suggesting a solution to a problem faced by all member states, the meeting witnessed a barter type of negotiation between the interests of the two governments. Germany's insistence on the so-called *stability pact*—not least to be seen against the background of growing concern about the Euro in domestic public opinion—was pitched against French demands for EU powers in fighting unemployment. Here, the incoming Socialist government needed to be seen to deliver on pledges made during the election campaign. Only when the apparently irreconcilable traditions of restrictive fiscal policy and an active employment policy had both been agreed after two days of negotiations, could the original agenda of the IGC be pushed through in one single 'night of the long knives'.

---

[67] See CDU/CSU Bundestagsfraktion; *Neuer Schwung für Europa: Überlegungen zur europäischen Politik* (Bonn: Pressebüro der Fraktion, 1 Sept. 1994), reprinted in English as W. Schäuble and K. Lamers, 'Reflections on European Policy', in *A German Agenda for the European Union*, ed. by Federal Trust for Education and Research and the Konrad Adenauer Foundation (London: Federal Trust, 1994).

[68] See memorandum *Agence Europe: Bulletin Quotidien Europe*, Europe Documents no. 2009, 29 Oct. 1996.

4.2. Out in the wilderness

It seems that the interventions of the two governments were thus not only crucial to overcoming a bottleneck in negotiations, but also successful in securing their interests in tandem. The same cannot be said for London's influence, its negotiating position being constantly undermined by the divisions within the ruling Conservative Party. Of course, this had been a feature of Anglo-European relations for some time—some would argue ever since the referendum of 1975 had shown the deep uncertainty about Britain's place in the European Community. The approach of the Major government in the intergovernmental negotiations can perhaps best be illustrated by the work of the Reflection Group. Its report of December 1995 is a noteworthy document, as its main purpose was not to present solutions, but disinterestedly to record different opinions, while at times indicating the minority/majority proportions. Given that the experts gathered in the Reflection Group were not to commit their governments in what was a preparatory exercise, the report did not identify the member states with any of the positions it noted. None the less, it did not take much guesswork to identify the British position in laconic sentences such as: 'One member, in principle, opposes any extension [of majority voting]', or 'one member thought issues of human rights were best dealt with at the national level'.[69] John Major's claim to be 'at the heart of Europe' amounted to little more than an attempt to steady the heartbeat at a rate suitable for hibernation only.[70]

The change of government seemed to promise a new approach, at least in the metaphors chosen. No longer aiming at 'the heart', the new Foreign Secretary announced in his first policy statement on the EU that his government aimed for Britain to take its 'rightful place in the driving seat of Europe'.[71] This was, however, before the Amsterdam summit. After the meeting, Prime Minister Tony Blair presented the Amsterdam results to the House of Commons

[69] See 'A Strategy for Europe', Final Report of the Reflection Group on the 1996 Intergovernmental Conference (5 Dec. 1995, SN 520/95).

[70] Prime Minister Major's promise to the German Chancellor Helmut Kohl in March 1991 as quoted in John W. Young, *Britain and European Unity, 1945–1992* (London: Macmillan, 1993), 162.

[71] Robin Cook's first policy statement as Foreign Secretary, 2 May 1997, on the Foreign Office's Internet site: http://www.fco.gov.uk/keythemes/europe.

as a great negotiation success for Britain. He took great pride in having won a hard fight to retain border controls (a fight that never was), in having secured opt-outs on the Justice and Home Affairs integration at large, in having preserved the national veto on Foreign and Security Policy, and, finally, in having turned the French proposal for an interventionist employment policy into a measure to increase the flexibility of labour markets.[72] Considering these comments one may wonder, driving seat or braking system?

4.3. Same as it ever was?

It may, therefore, be tempting to argue that Britain is continuing to play the part of seeking to hinder or stall the integration process. The Bonn–Paris axis, by contrast, appears to function even after East–West confrontation and German *Westbindung* or *Einbindung* have ceased to provide the European Community with an external stimulus.

Yet this reading of the Amsterdam Treaty would be misleading, given that the failure to overhaul the institutional system weighs heavily on the Union set to accept new members. Moreover, even with regard to what has found its way into the new Treaty, the semblance of progressive integration can no longer be maintained. It has emerged that the stability pact has no teeth, that the employment chapter will not provide additional funds, and that there is no agreement on how a common security policy will develop in the future. With regard to the flexibility clause, there is great uncertainty as to what this instrument is meant to achieve. The General Secretariat of the Council, for example, thinks of it merely as a threatening device to overcome the unanimity requirement for Treaty changes.[73] Even the much hailed part transferral of justice and home affairs to the first pillar of Community competence— billed as the main progress achieved at Amsterdam—is effectively little more than a postponement, given that in five years the Council once again has to agree unanimously to accept majority voting in this area.

It is interesting to note that this latter provision was inserted on Bonn's insistence. Similarly, the reform of voting procedures was

---

[72] See his comments on 18 June 1997, in *Hansard Parliamentary Debates*, col. 316, also found on www.parliament.the-stationery-office.co.uk.

[73] Private information.

also limited by Chancellor Kohl, prompting the British Foreign Secretary, Robin Cook, to voice unprecedented criticism of Germany's integration policy. Speaking in Hamburg, he told his audience that 'on the issue of qualified majority voting we found we took a position that was a little bit more advanced than that of Germany'.[74] While the positions of London and Paris appear closer in this instance, a Bonn–London coalition can be held responsible for watering down the French proposals on the employment chapter.

All in all, the picture that emerges with regard to the latest round of negotiations on European integration is one of confusion about goals, disputes about means, and changing coalitions on detail. The external threat has evidently disappeared as an integration motive, being replaced, perhaps, by that of managing Germany's new-found economic and political strength at the centre of Europe or the strengthening of the Continent's position in the age of globalization. Unlike *Westbindung*, these new motives do not suggest any specific institutional arrangement, particularly if viewed from Bonn. Germany's overall loyalty to the project of European integration is certainly unbroken. Yet increasingly, attention (public and political) is focused on detail, judging each initiative on its economic merits, as well as measuring it against the new-found sovereignty.

The experience of the negotiations towards the Amsterdam Treaty demonstrate, if anything, that economic and political interests no longer point Bonn as obviously to Paris as *Westbindung* did in the past. Conversely, London's current vision of Europe no longer seems to conflict with the tenets of German foreign policy. Eventually, the European enterprise may well come full circle in so far as a loose free trade arrangement with weak institutions may turn out to be Bonn's (Berlin's) preferred answer—the FTA plan of 1956 might just resurface in disguise.

[74] Speech by the Foreign Secretary to the Overseas Club and the Senate, City Hall, Hamburg, 9 Sept. 1997.

5

Constancy and Flirtation
Germany, Britain, and the EEC, 1956–1972

N. Piers Ludlow

Few bilateral relationships better illustrate both the pace of change in post-war Europe, and also, paradoxically, the enduring legacy of the past, than that between Britain and the Federal Republic of Germany. The speed of evolution is perhaps the more striking: less than a decade after the Federal Republic's creation, Britain, one of the four former occupying powers, was beating a path to Bonn in order to solicit German help in sorting out its problematic relationship with the European Community. The divergent fortunes—economic and political—of the two countries could scarcely have been more clearly demonstrated: the former occupant was now a *demandeur*, the defeated power the target of Britain's appeals for assistance. And yet amidst all this change, many of the attitudes created by the recent past persisted. British approaches to Bonn were still marked by a degree of haughtiness or even arrogance that seemed to suggest that little had altered since 1949, while the German response, so often characterized by an almost excessive desire to help and please, and by a strong aversion to leadership, was still that of a country haunted by its recent past. A brief investigation of Anglo-German relations in the period between 1956 and Britain's belated entry into the EEC thus throws light not just on the fraught tale of Britain's slow and painful adaptation to the realities of European integration, but also on the wider picture of evolution and change in Western Europe's first three post-war decades.

The decade and a half on which this chapter focuses is, in policy terms, a period characterized by the contrast between German constancy and British change. For the Federal Republic a key foreign policy objective—shared by the Adenauer, Erhard, Kiesinger, and Brandt governments alike—was to bring Britain closer to, and if at all possible into full membership of, the EEC. And if the objective remained all but unchanged, so too did the tactics adopted to this end. Similarly, the limitations of the German approach were much the same in 1971–2 as they had been in 1956–8. British policy, by contrast, shifted rapidly. In 1956–8, British policy towards the EEC was characterized by the advocacy of the free trade area scheme intended to complement the nascent Community with a wider zone of tariff liberalization comprising Britain, Scandinavia, and the Alpine countries as well as the Six. By 1961, however, this idea had been superseded by the quest for full, albeit conditional, membership. During Harold Wilson's first term this objective had been to all intents and purposes abandoned, only to be revived, this time without explicit preconditions, in the wake of Labour's second election victory and the sterling crisis of 1966. As in 1963, however, British plans had been derailed by General de Gaulle. It was thus only in 1971–2, after de Gaulle's departure from the Elysée, that the UK's lengthy courtship with the European Community was brought to an end with a successful membership negotiation. Britain's attitudes towards Germany, moreover, also changed considerably during the period—both in the arguments employed to win German backing and, more fundamentally, in the importance attached to such German support. This essay will therefore first examine the reasons for, and characteristics of, German support for Community enlargement, and then assess the use to which Britain put this support. It will conclude by trying to determine how important the Anglo-German dimension was in the overall saga of Britain's relations with Europe. Throughout the article will draw upon archival evidence from Germany, Britain, and the Community institutions in Brussels.[1]

Trade and Balance—the Determinants of German Constancy

German support for close British involvement with, and if possible membership of, the European Communities was remarkable in its solidity. Britain's own policy towards Europe varied so much in the course of the 1950s and 1960s that any of the Six might have been

[1] The author would like to thank the archivists in Bonn, Koblenz, Brussels, and London for their help. Thanks are also due to James Ellison, Sylke Skär, Katharina Böhmer, and Jonathan Hollowell.

forgiven for giving up on London. After all, such an uncertain and spasmodic courtship might well have been interpreted as the precursor to an equally unsatisfactory marriage. Furthermore, support for Britain frequently placed Bonn in a position highly exposed to the crossfire on the issue between its two principal foreign policy partners, the United States and France. Self-preservation alone might thus have suggested that the best course was for Germany to let the issue lie or, at least, to allow others to lead the campaign for British membership. And yet Germany persisted in its advocacy of enlargement. It is therefore necessary to begin this survey by investigating why the embrace of such a hesitant suitor was so ardently desired by Bonn.

Part of the answer, unromantically, was money, or economics at least, for West German trade with Britain was highly valuable (see Table 5.1). In 1960 Britain was Germany's ninth most important export market, buying 5.4 per cent of Germany's exports. By 1964 the figure had fallen slightly to 4.9 per cent, while in 1971 it was down to 4.5 per cent.[2] For imports, too, Britain was a major supplier: in 1960 Germany imported more from the UK than from any other country bar the USA—a full 12 per cent of its total. By 1964 this had fallen to 11 per cent and by 1971 it was a mere 8 per cent, Britain having been overtaken as a source of imports by the Netherlands, France, Italy, and Belgium.[3] Nevertheless the level of trade remained highly significant, and the fact that Britain was being outperformed by four of Germany's Community partners only seemed to reinforce the message that in order to preserve its valuable trade links and if possible to reverse their relative downward trend, Germany needed to get the UK inside the EEC.

There was much more, however, than simply UK–German trade at stake. Tied up with the whole issue of Britain's relations with Europe was the wider question of the relations between the EEC and the British-led European Free Trade Association (EFTA). While Britain remained outside the EEC, no end to the Six/Seven split was feasible; conversely a solution of the British problem would, of necessity, entail a resolution of Western Europe's commercial divide. West Germany's trade with Scandinavia, Austria,

---

[2] *Statistisches Jahrbuch für die Bundesrepublik Deutschland 1965* (Wiesbaden: Statistisches Bundesamt, 1966), 338, and *Statistisches Jahrbuch für die Bundesrepublik Deutschland 1972* (Wiesbaden: Statistisches Bundesamt, 1973), 308.

[3] *Statistisches Jahrbuch 1965*, 336, and *Statistisches Jahrbuch 1972*, 307.

TABLE 5.1. German trade with Britain, 1960–1971.

Trade with Britain (%)	1960	1964	1971
German exports	5.4	4.9	4.5
German imports	12	11	8

Switzerland, and Portugal as well as with the UK was likely to be significantly affected by the UK's accession to the Community. As Table 5.2 shows, this was of crucial importance. Prior to the Community's creation, Germany had actually exported marginally more to the EFTA nations added together than to its five prospective EEC partners.[4] By 1960 this was no longer the case. Despite a small drop in relative importance, however, the EFTA member states were still markets which Germany could ill afford to lose. Switzerland remained Germany's fourth largest export market, buying 7 per cent of total German exports, Sweden the seventh with 5.4 per cent of German exports, Austria the tenth with 5.1 per cent, Denmark the eleventh, Norway the twelfth, and Finland (an EFTA associate) the thirteenth.[5] Even without including Britain, EFTA was thus the destination of exactly a quarter of all German exports. Similarly in 1971, while all of the EFTA countries had declined in relative importance (and had lost out particularly to the countries inside the EEC), Switzerland, Austria, Sweden, and Denmark all remained among Germany's twelve most important export markets, with Norway and Finland not far outside in fourteenth and eighteenth places respectively.[6] Just under 20 per cent of German exports still went to the four Nordic and two Alpine countries. EFTA as a whole therefore remained a rich prize.

The value of Germany's economic links with the Seven resulted in a steady pressure on the government from two particular sources. The first was industry and especially the *Bundesverband der Deutschen Industrie* (BDI). Thus, for example, Fritz Berg, the association's long-standing President, regularly lobbied both the Chancellor and the

---

[4] For a much more detailed analysis of Germany's trade with EFTA see Markus Schulte, 'Challenging the Common Market Project: German Industry, Britain and Europe 1956–63', in Anne Deighton and Alan Milward (eds.), *Widening, Deepening and Acceleration: The European Economic Community, 1957–63* (Baden-Baden: Nomos, 1999), 167–83.

[5] *Statistisches Jahrbuch 1965*, 338.   [6] *Statistisches Jahrbuch 1972*, 308.

TABLE 5.2. German trade with EFTA members, 1958–1971.

German exports to (%)	1960	1971
Switzerland	7	6.8
Sweden	5.4	3.4
Austria	5.1	4.7
Denmark	3.5	2.2
Norway	2.3	1.4
Finland	1.7	1.1

Foreign Minister while a succession of BDI reports emphasized the need to end the Six/Seven split. As one 1967 study leaked to the British put it: 'The problem of Britain's accession can not be considered in isolation. Britain is rather the key to the general solution of the EEC/EFTA problem. The inclusion of the remaining countries of EFTA in the Common Market is for the German economy at least as important as, if not even more important than, the accession of Britain . . . The whole German trade surplus is achieved almost exclusively in commerce with EFTA.'[7] A second source of pressure on the Federal government were the northern German *Länder*, which had traditionally enjoyed strong ties with Britain and Scandinavia. In November 1959, for instance, the Senates of Hamburg, Bremen, Niedersachsen, and Schleswig-Holstein wrote to Konrad Adenauer pointing out that in 1958, 33 per cent of their exports had gone to the countries which were soon to form EFTA compared to a mere 17 per cent sold to the rest of the EEC. They therefore urged the Federal Chancellor to act urgently to prevent this commerce being impeded by tariff barriers.[8] Likewise, in the course of the crisis of January 1963 the mayor of Hamburg, Dr Engelhardt, wrote to Schröder asking that Germany do its utmost to safeguard the 800-year-old commerce between northern Germany and Scandinavia.[9] There were thus no shortage of voices within Germany ready to underline the importance of these

[7] PRO. EW 5/8, translation of a BDI report, 27 Jan. 1967.

[8] BAK. BKA, B-136, vol. 2553, Verhältnis zwischen der EWG und der EFTA. Letter from the Senates of Hamburg, Bremen, Niedersachsen, and Schleswig-Holstein, 7 Nov. 1959.

[9] AAA, Bestand B-150, Bestellnummer 2, Ref. 200 (IA2), vol. 1236, Engelhardt to Schröder, 23 Jan. 1963.

economic ties, should Bonn ever seem to waver in its support for EEC enlargement.

Alongside such economic factors, there were also a variety of political reasons which made closer British links with Europe an attractive prospect. From a geo-strategic point of view, it was widely hoped that the enlargement of the Community and the ending of the EEC/EFTA divide would strengthen Western unity in the face of the Soviet threat.[10] Conversely, many in Bonn feared that Western division over the issue of British membership might undermine European solidarity *vis-à-vis* the East. In 1963 the Economics Ministry assessment of de Gaulle's veto concluded: 'If, instead of that, the old split between the EEC and EFTA re-emerges and, in addition, a new split develops between the EEC-Europe and America, then there can only be one person who gains from the whole situation: Khrushchev.'[11] Similarly, there were many who hoped that British membership would strengthen and improve the Community. At a most basic level such expectations centred on the qualities and values which it was hoped the British would bring into the Community. A good example of such thinking was provided by Karl Schiller, the Minister of Economics, who commented in December 1966 that 'British pragmatism, common sense and readiness to compromise were all needed there [in Brussels]'. Slightly more Machiavellian were tactical hopes that once Britain joined it would side with Germany in pressing for a commercially open Community, unburdened by too costly a Common Agricultural Policy. These were clearly expressed, for example, by a 1962 report on the implications of enlargement, prepared by the Federal Ministry for Agriculture.[12] Most important of all were calculations of Community balance. In early 1966, for instance, Kurt Schmücker, the Minister of Economic Affairs, had a long talk with the British Ambassador, Sir Frank Roberts:

---

[10] See e.g. AAA, Ref. 200, vol. 48, Jansen memo, 26 Jan. 1961.

[11] 'Wenn statt dessen der alte Riß zwischen EWG und EFTA neu entsteht und ein neuer Riß zwischen EWG-Europa und Amerika hinzukommt, kann es aus der ganzen Situation heraus nur einen einzigen Gewinner geben: Chruschtschow.' AAA. Bestand B-150, Bestellnummer 2, Ref. 200 (IA2), vol. 1236, Sprechzettel für Herrn Minister zur Kabinettsitzung am 25.1.1963, EA3—905 883, 22 Jan. 1963.

[12] BAK, BKA, Bestand B-136, vol. 2560, Bundesministerium für Ernährung, Landwirtschaft und Forsten, VII A 3, Zwischenbericht über den Stand der Verhandlungen mit Großbritannien über den Beitritt zu den drei Europäischen Gemeinschaften, 25 June 1962.

He said that his own personal conviction was that if a favourable decision on British membership had not been reached by the end of 1967 the EEC would probably break up or fade away. The reason he gave for this was the state of Franco-German relations and the impact on other members. During the short period when France and Germany had played a duet within the EEC this had disturbed the others. Now that Franco-German relations were more like a duel and likely to remain so this was even more fatal. Although resistance had to be made to the French and Germany was the only EEC country strong enough for this purpose it was politically undesirable in the wider sense that Germany should take such a lead. During last year's EEC crisis she had been able to work through the Belgians, the Italians and the Dutch in turn but this could not go on for ever. The EEC needed the UK as the essential balancing factor.[13]

And finally there were also party political reasons in Bonn for wishing to settle the issue of British membership. The enforced separation between the Seven and the Six had resulted in some very public disputes within the CDU in particular. In 1959, for instance, Ludwig Erhard had underlined his personal annoyance at Adenauer's seeming acceptance of the divide by sponsoring a poster campaign with a pithy, if mathematically dubious, slogan of '6 + 7 + 5 = 1'—Europe, in other words, could only be truly united once the six EEC members, the seven countries of EFTA, and the five western states which belonged to neither economic grouping were gathered together within a single economic unit.[14] An end to open quarrelling of this sort could not but be welcomed by Germany's Christian Democrats.

Economics and politics thus combined to ensure that Germany was well aware that Britain's entry into the Community should be a foreign policy priority, regardless of the political make-up of the German government or the personal rapport between the Chancellor and the Prime Minister. Individual Chancellors and ministers could and did affect the energy with which Germany pursued its goal. Adenauer's personal ambivalence about Community enlargement is thus of some significance.[15] Fundamentally, however,

[13] PRO. EW 5/8. Roberts to FO, no. 95 Saving, 2 May 1966.

[14] Miriam Camps, *Britain and the European Community 1955–1963* (Oxford: Oxford University Press, 1964), 200–1.

[15] For a discussion of Adenauer's attitude see Hans-Peter Schwarz, *Adenauer: Der Staatsmann, 1952–1967* (Stuttgart: Deutsche Verlags-Anstalt, 1991), 747–53 and 762–9; Sabine Lee, 'The Federal Republic and the Enlargement Negotiations', in Anne Deighton and Alan Milward (eds.), *Widening, Deepening and Acceleration: The European Economic Community, 1957–63* (Baden-Baden: Nomos, 1999); N. Piers Ludlow, *Dealing with Britain: The Six and the First UK Application to the EEC* (Cambridge: Cambridge University Press, 1997), 174–9.

Germany had too much at stake for even the most powerful of leaders to reverse its support for British membership. As Willy Brandt
put it in early 1967: 'This was not after all purely a sentimental question of friendship between two countries, although this was important, but it was a vital German national interest to widen the EEC
and for this Britain was the key.'[16]

Ally, Adviser, and Advocate—German Policy
Towards Britain

In practical terms, this German conviction that enlargement was
in its national interest had several important effects. The first and
most obvious was that it ensured that all British approaches to the
Community described were given a warm rhetorical welcome by
Bonn. In 1961, for instance, the German draft for the opening
statement of the membership negotiations noted: 'We have always
been aware of the fact that Europe without Great Britain cannot
be a complete Europe. We are, therefore, particularly pleased to
receive news of the British decision to enter into negotiations with
a view to joining the EEC.'[17] Similarly, both the Federal
Government spokesman and the SPD leadership gave a warm
welcome to Wilson's November 1966 announcement that 'sound-
ings' were to begin on the possibility of a new British approach.[18]

Warm words, moreover, were normally flanked by useful practical assistance and advice. In 1960 it was Bonn that responded first
to British feelers about possible bilateral pre-negotiations, and
three rounds of official level meetings were held between
November 1960 and the application itself in the summer of 1961.[19]
In the course of these, and other less formal Anglo-German
encounters, a great deal of invaluable advice was passed on to the
British: the warm pro-European language of Edward Heath's

[16] PRO. EW 5/8. Roberts to FO, no. 77, 12 Jan. 1967.
[17] 'Nous avons toujours été conscients du fait qu'une Europe sans la Grande-Bretagne ne
peut constituer une Europe complète. C'est avec autant plus de satisfaction que nous
accueillons maintenant la décision britannique d'entamer des négociations en vue de son
adhésion à la CEE.' Council of Ministers Archives, Brussels, 07.151. Préparation par le
Conseil de la réunion ministérielle entre les états membres et le Royaume-Uni, ainsi que la
déclaration commune des six devant être prononcée par le président du conseil CEE lors de
cette réunion, tenue les 8/9 novembre. First German draft S/555/61 (RU15), 3 Nov. 1961.
[18] PRO. EW 5/8. Roberts to FO, no. 1630, 12 Nov. 1966 and no. 1642, 15 Nov. 1966.
[19] Ludlow, *Dealing with Britain*, 33–4 and 39.

opening statement in Paris in October 1961—a speech which was widely praised by Community representatives—was largely attributable to German advice that Britain make a positive 'political' commitment to the Community, in order to dispel any lingering doubts about the sincerity of the UK application. Equally well-intentioned, if less fruitful, were German efforts in 1960–1 to sound out the French and discover what position they were likely to adopt in any eventual negotiation. German hopes of setting up a trilateral meeting were to come to naught, but it was typical that an attempt had been made.

Likewise in 1966 Erhard used the Anglo-German summit in May to recommend that any new British approach to the Community begin by sounding out the Five on the matter and then forcing de Gaulle to make a clear statement on enlargement—advice that Wilson tried to follow from November onwards.[20] At much the same time the German government had put in hand both its own internal study of the likely practical problems that enlargement might entail and encouraged the British 'quietly and unobtrusively' to begin bilateral discussions with a team of German experts. On this occasion, the Labour government steered clear of any pre-negotiations. Once again, however, the German instinct had been to offer the maximum possible assistance.

It must be added that German behaviour of this sort, while undeniably well-intentioned, was not always totally helpful. In the run-up to the 1961 application, the flexibility which Germany displayed in the course of the pre-negotiations may have contributed to Britain's delusion that more would be on offer in Brussels than was actually to be the case. In particular, German predictions that Britain might be permitted to participate in the ongoing CAP negotiations even before it had formally entered the Community, were too easily taken at face-value in London. There was therefore considerable disappointment in Whitehall when the French ensured that no would-be members were included in the discussions.[21] And as late as 1966 *Auswärtiges Amt* officials were engaging in rather improbable wishful thinking about the possibility of Britain being invited, as a prospective member, to join in on the

---

[20] *Akten zur Auswärtigen Politik der Bundesrepublik Deutschland 1966* (Munich: R. Oldenbourg Verlag, 1997), i, doc. 158.

[21] Ludlow, *Dealing with Britain*, 65.

renegotiation of the Treaty of Rome necessitated by the fusion of the three Communities.[22] By this last occasion, however, British officials had learnt from their earlier mistakes and treated this suggestion with the suspicion that it fully deserved.[23] Despite the potential for misunderstanding, however, German willingness to help prepare the British for each approach to the Community was of significant utility to the UK government.

Of still greater value to Britain were many of the negotiating positions adopted by the Germans, when, in 1961–3 and again in 1970–2, actual substantive talks were allowed to begin. Throughout the summer of 1962, for instance, German representatives such as Rolf Lahr and Günther Harkort pressed hard for the Community to be as generous as possible towards Britain, and in particular to adopt a sympathetic approach towards Commonwealth agricultural imports. When, in late July, the French complained that a proposal put forward by Britain represented so retrograde a step that it should immediately be withdrawn, it was Lahr who led the counter-attack, reminding his colleagues that what was under way was not a mere commercial negotiation, in which the pursuit of national interest was the norm, but instead a negotiation intended to open the door of the Community to a new member state. As a result a totally different spirit and approach was needed.[24] A few days later, moreover, the German representatives were once again at the forefront of an abortive effort to devise a special package of measures designed to meet the particular requirements of New Zealand—the Commonwealth country most likely to be adversely affected by British membership of the EEC.[25] In the light of these and numerous other similar interventions, it is not surprising that Harkort, the chief German representative at official level, was described by the British as 'almost invariably the most useful of the Deputies' while Lahr, his counterpart among the ministers, was adjudged 'helpful'.[26]

Finally, the Germans also did their utmost to mitigate Britain's isolation during those periods when through French opposition or British vacillation an actual British approach to the Community was impossible. Thus in the aftermath of 1963, it was the Germans, together with the Belgians, who were most active in putting forward schemes for some form of free trade area linking Britain to the Six. The scheme failed to get off the ground—that it was made

---

[22] PRO. EW 5/8, Galsworthy to Statham, 19 Apr. 1966 and 1 June 1966.   [23] Ibid.
[24] Ludlow, *Dealing with Britain*, 146.   [25] Ibid. 151.   [26] Ibid. 161.

at all, however, testifies to Germany's desire to avoid too sharp a Six/Seven divide. At the same time, the Germans gave serious thought to ways in which some type of multilateral consultation machinery might be established so as to allow a degree of British influence over Community decision-making. Again the plans came to naught—but it was a revealing episode none the less.[27] And during the years of seeming Labour lack of interest in joining the Community, visiting German politicians did their utmost to inform Britain about what was happening in Brussels, to establish how the Community might avoid disrupting British interests or make a new membership bid more problematical, and within the Community to keep the issue of enlargement alive. A revealing French cartoon from late 1963 depicts Erhard and de Gaulle, with the former smoking one of his trade-mark cigars and emitting a pall of smoke in the shape of the British Isles which hangs irritatingly in front of the General's face.[28] Due in large part to German persistence, de Gaulle was never able to exclude the issue of enlargement altogether from the Community's agenda.

The consistency with which Germany tried, by these various means, to bring closer their goal of an enlarged Community should not, however, be allowed to conceal two very important limitations to German Anglophilia. The first and most remarked upon was Germany's reluctance to pursue British membership to the extent of damaging the Federal Republic's relations with France. This tendency is, of course, primarily associated with the Adenauer period and the ageing Chancellor's seemingly desperate pursuit of Franco-German *rapprochement*. His determination to secure good relations between France and Germany at virtually any cost was first apparent in 1958 when, at the Bad Kreuznach meeting with de Gaulle, the German Chancellor acquiesced in the controversial French decision to bring to an end the free trade area negotiations.[29] Four years later it had become still more marked,

---

[27] Both episodes are discussed in Oliver Bange, 'Picking Up the Pieces: Schröder's Working Programme for the European Communities and the Solution of the 1963 Crisis' (Ph.D. thesis, London School of Economics, 1997), 91–108, and 121–32.

[28] Reproduced in Edmond Jouve, *Le Général de Gaulle et la construction de l'Europe* (Paris: Librairie générale de droit et de jurisprudence, 1967), ii. 843.

[29] Gérard Bossuat, 'The Choice of "La Petite Europe" by France, 1957–1963: An Ambition for France and for Europe', in R. Griffiths and S. Ward, *Courting the Common Market: The First Attempt to Enlarge the European Community 1961–3* (London: Lothian Foundation Press, 1996), 65–6.

leading in particular to Adenauer's August 1962 clash with his Cabinet in the course of which Lahr was berated for being much too Anglophile in the Brussels negotiations and thereby endangering Germany's much more valuable rapport with France. As the Chancellor put it: 'For us the political question is not the relationship between us and England, but the relationship between us and France.'[30] And Adenauer's attitude was most famously revealed in the course of his visit to Paris in January 1963 when, despite intense international and domestic pressure, the Chancellor refused to allow de Gaulle's recent press conference to derail the signature of the Franco-German Treaty.[31]

The policy of valuing ties with France as much as ties with Britain was never exclusively Adenauer's policy, however. Bad Kreuznach was preceded by a secret meeting between Hilgar van Scherpenberg and Maurice Couve de Murville which largely anticipated the deal to be struck between the Chancellor and President. There was little sense, moreover, in the *Auswärtige Amt* that Adenauer had 'sold out' to the French.[32] Similarly, in January 1963 the Atlanticist Gerhard Schröder was no tougher on the French than Adenauer. Face to face with de Gaulle, the Foreign Minister was obliged to admit that whereas British membership was just one problem among many, Franco-German reconciliation was 'eine Basisfrage'.[33] And even after Adenauer had left the scene, the need to balance the desire for enlargement against the necessity of good relations with Paris arose frequently. In early 1967, for instance, Kiesinger and Brandt visited Paris intent above all on mending fences with de Gaulle and securing France's blessing for the first stirrings of German *Ostpolitik*. Britain's needs were mentioned, but Germany was not prepared to use wild threats or dramatic pressure in order to force France to change its line. As Brandt told a press conference in March 1967, Germany continued to support British membership despite the restated opposition of the French. 'The Federal Government could not however force

---

[30] 'Die politische Frage ist für uns nicht das Verhältnis zwischen uns und England, sondern das Verhältnis zwischen uns und Frankreich.' BAK. BKA. B-136, vol. 2561, Beitritt Großbritannien zur EWG, Unkorrigiertes Manuskript aus der Kabinettsitzung 8.8.1962.

[31] Ludlow, *Dealing with Britain*, 219–23.

[32] Martin P. C. Schaad, *Bullying Bonn: Anglo-German Diplomacy on European Integration, 1955–61* (Basingstoke: Macmillan, 2000), 110–11.

[33] *Akten zur Auswärtigen Politik der Bundesrepublik Deutschland 1963* (Munich: R. Oldenbourg Verlag, 1994), 39.

its views on any other country. Within the EEC one country could only try to convince the other.'[34]

Second, and still more fundamentally, Germany was not prepared to pursue enlargement in a fashion which might undermine the Community itself. This was demonstrated most obviously by the consistent German emphasis—in 1961, in 1966/7, and in 1970—on the inviolability of the Treaty of Rome. In July 1961, for instance, Harkort warned Roderick Barclay of the Foreign Office that while the Treaty was very flexible and would be able to accommodate Britain's special needs, the UK should not seek to obtain any textual amendments.[35] Equally revealing was the readiness of the German government to go along with a highly defensive negotiating procedure employed in 1961–3—a procedure designed to maximize the solidarity of the Six at the expense of rapid agreement with Britain—and the positive way in which Germany responded to appeals to the solidarity of the Six throughout the 1961–3 negotiations.[36] And most important of all was the way in which the German government firmly ruled out all of the wilder schemes for retaliating against de Gaulle by co-operating with Britain instead of with France. In January 1963 it was Schröder who together with his Italian counterpart, Attlio Piccioni, poured cold water on the notion of a breakaway conference of the Five plus the British; in October 1965, at the high point of the Empty Chair Crisis, it was again Schröder who played the lead role in quashing Dutch suggestions that if the French were not willing to co-operate the British might be drafted in to replace them; and in December 1966 Brandt rebuked the Italian Socialist leader, Pietro Nenni, for suggesting just such a course of action.[37] Frank Roberts's June 1966 assessment of the German position therefore applies to all of the period under review:

The state of German feeling towards British membership is well known to you: they want us in and are prepared to do a lot to help us to surmount the obstacles in the way. They would, however, stop short of any action which in their view would be likely to cause the French to leave the Community; and they would need a great deal of persuading to agree to

[34] PRO. EW 5/8, Berlin to FO, no. 92, 9 Mar. 1967.

[35] See e.g. PRO. FO371 158277, M634/226, Barclay note on a conversation with Dr Harkort, 21 July 1961.

[36] Ludlow, *Dealing with Britain*, 55–6, and 149–50.

[37] For 1963 see Ludlow, *Dealing with Britain*, 227; for 1966, PRO, EW 5/8, Roberts to FO, no. 77, 12 Jan. 1967.

any alteration to the Treaty of Rome . . . having successfully resisted French pressure and threats on this score for seven months, they would be understandably chary of creating a precedent with us. But subject to these two reservations, we could expect the Germans to go a long way to accommodate us on specific issues.[38]

The British Response

What use, then, did Britain make of this consistently helpful German stance? The answer varies greatly according to which of the various British approaches to the EEC is looked at. In particular, it depended on whether Britain adopted what might be called its indirect strategy in order to overcome French objections or whether it employed a frontal assault on Paris. In its efforts to promote the free trade area scheme the British opted for the former. As a result, there was little direct Anglo-French diplomacy, the British relying instead on their friends among the Six, and notably therefore Germany, to pressurize the French into adopting a more reasonable approach.[39] This approach was adjudged to have failed, however, and in the course of the first application itself, British diplomatic efforts were primarily focused on France and de Gaulle.[40] Germany was not totally neglected—indeed, as illustrated by the appreciative British comments cited above, the British and German delegations struck up a good working relationship in Brussels. Schröder's November 1962 visit to Chequers, moreover, did allow some useful substantive debate. But the way in which Harold Macmillan met de Gaulle three times in the course of the application compared to his single meeting with Adenauer does accurately reflect British priorities. Likewise, at official level, the British were keen to experiment with bilateral discussions with the French. During the second application, the pendulum swung back the other way. In the aftermath of the 1963 veto, the British

---

[38] PRO, EW 5/8, Roberts to O'Neill, 27 June 1966.

[39] The most detailed study of British tactics is James Ellison, *Threatening Europe: Britain and the Creation of the European Community, 1955–8* (Basingstoke: Macmillan, 2000). See also Elizabeth Kane, 'Tilting Towards Europe? British Responses to Developments in European Integration 1955–1958' (D.Phil. thesis, University of Oxford, 1996).

[40] For details of Macmillan's personal diplomacy towards de Gaulle, see N. Piers Ludlow, ' "Ne Pleurez Pas Milord": Macmillan and France from Algiers to Rambouillet', in Sabine Lee and Richard Aldous (eds.), *Harold Macmillan: Aspects of a Political Life* (Baskingstoke: Macmillan, 1998), 95–112.

Ambassador in Paris had warned: 'I believe that the history of these negotiations proves conclusively that it is quite impossible to reason with General de Gaulle and then to achieve a compromise with him. On all important questions of high politics it is only safe to act on the assumption that one cannot do business with him.'[41] Partly as a result, British efforts in 1966–7 were directed at rallying the Five before confronting the General. Wilson's famous refusal 'to take no for an answer' and the ill-fated attempt to use the WEU to override de Gaulle's opposition all fell into the 'indirect' approach. Germany's relative importance rose as a result.[42] Indeed, Germany was considered to be particularly important in the light of its successful experience of standing up to de Gaulle in the course of the crisis of 1965–6. By 1970, however, the disappearance of the General made a new, French-centred approach possible once more. Again Germany was not ignored. On the contrary its assistance on many of the issues under discussion in Brussels was gratefully received. But central to Heath's strategy were the secret Jobert/Soames discussions in Paris and the Heath–Pompidou summit of May 1971. The road to success was seen as running more through Paris than Bonn and British diplomacy was focused on France rather than on Germany as a result.[43]

Until 1971–2, however, none of these varied approaches proved successful. It is therefore vital to assess the extent to which Anglo-German difficulties contributed to both countries' repeated failure to attain a cherished foreign policy goal. For while Britain and Germany clearly shared an interest in promoting Community enlargement, neither their bilateral relationship nor the personal rapport between their leaders was entirely easy during the period under review. Between 1958 and 1963 the uncertainties of Anglo-German relations were particularly evident when contrasted with the simultaneous and very high-profile process of Franco-German

---

[41] PRO. FO371 171449; M1092/129, Dixon to Home, 18 Feb. 1963.

[42] A great deal of research on the second application is currently under way. The best survey remains Uwe Kitzinger, *The Second Try: Labour and the EEC* (Oxford: Pergamon Press, 1968), but see also Oliver Daddow (ed.), *The Wilson Entry Bid* (Frank Cass, forthcoming).

[43] Con O'Neill, *Britain's Entry into the European Community: Report by Sir Con O'Neill on the Negotiations of 1970–1972* (Frank Cass, 2000); Uwe Kitzinger, *Diplomacy and Persuasion: How Britain Joined the Common Market* (London: Thames & Hudson, 1973); Simon Z. Young, *Terms of Entry: Britain's Negotiations with the European Community 1970–2* (London: Heinemann, 1973); Christopher Lord, *Britain's Entry into the European Community under the Heath Government of 1970–4* (London: Dartmouth, 1993).

reconciliation.[44] No British leader was accorded the welcome given to de Gaulle in the course of his triumphal tour of Germany in September 1962, nor did the British make any attempt to match the symbolism and emphasis on bilateral *rapprochement* which characterized Adenauer's July 1962 and January 1963 visits to France.[45] The gulf between Anglo-German and Franco-German relations is still more apparent if the personal rapport between leaders is considered. For while de Gaulle and Adenauer struck up an increasingly close and effective partnership, Macmillan's relations with the German Chancellor remained distant. The lack of personal chemistry, moreover, was reinforced by inept British tactics: as Martin Schaad points out, the British went on believing throughout the 1958–61 period that whereas de Gaulle needed to be bribed to allow Britain to join the EEC, Adenauer could be bullied into acquiescence.[46] Similarly, James Ellison has been critical of the whole thrust of British diplomacy during the free trade area negotiations, arguing that Britain's hopes of convincing its would-be European partners that it had genuinely rethought its whole approach to the Continent and left behind its traditional antipathy to excessive co-operation were seriously undermined by a number of simultaneous policy developments which only seemed to emphasize Britain's detachment from the Continent. Among these, the reduction of the number of troops stationed in Germany, the prominent post-Suez effort to mend fences with the USA, and the pursuit of full sterling convertibility rather than the development of the European Payments Union, all suggested that Britain had not yet made up its mind that its future lay in Europe.[47] Nor are such complaints the exclusive preserve of historians writing with the benefit of hindsight. Shortly after the abortive end of the first British application to the EEC, one British diplomat in Bonn, having warned London of the anti-British rumours being spread from France into Germany via the *Bundeskanzleramt*, continued:

But unfortunately they help to reinforce a certain basic mistrust of British motives which is endemic in our relations with the Germans . . . many Germans think that, compared to the French, the British have been

---

[44] Sabine Lee, *An Uneasy Partnership: British–German Relations between 1955 and 1961* (Bochum: Universitätsverlag Dr. N. Brockmeyer, 1996), 278–9.

[45] Jacques Bariéty, 'De Gaulle, Adenauer et la genèse du traité de l'Elysée du 22 janvier 1963', in Institut Charles de Gaulle, *De Gaulle en son siècle* (Paris: Plon, 1992), v. 358–9.

[46] Schaad, *Bullying Bonn*, 116–17, 135–6.   [47] Ellison, *Threatening Europe*, 232–7.

petty, mistrustful, critical and often directly hostile, far from stretching out the hand of friendship they have been cold, reserved and strictly practical, the British press is the most unfair in the Western world, a permanent current of hostility is apparent from questions in Parliament, and the British Government has given little lead to overcome it.

As a result the British diplomat urged the British government to make a new effort in Bonn, to build better relations, 'and generally to demonstrate that we regard the Federal Republic as a trusted ally, instead of a rather shady business partner to be tolerated but not liked'.[48]

Such Anglo-German problems should not be totally overlooked. They were not, however, primarily to blame for Britain's failure to attain the entry into the EEC that both London and Bonn so desired. Instead the failures that litter Britain's path to the Community have more to do with events in Paris and Brussels, and errors in London, than with problems in Bonn. Thus the free trade area plan failed largely because it gave the French government none of those advantages that it had managed to secure in the Treaty of Rome negotiations and because the British failed to dispel doubts, among its friends as well as in Paris, as to the sincerity of its new European policy. German suspicions, such as those voiced by Heinrich von Brentano or Hartlieb in the *Auswärtiges Amt*, were just part of a wider European phenomenon and not indicators of a specific Anglo-German malaise. Likewise, the 1961–3 membership bid did not fail because of Adenauer's misgivings or because Germany failed to deliver all the assistance its rhetoric at times implied. Instead it was unsuccessful because, through British rigidity and the defensive style of negotiation adopted by the Community member states, agreement in Brussels could not be attained before de Gaulle had built up the domestic and international strength to intervene. Macmillan tried to force his way in, not by pushing all out for agreement in Brussels—the level at which German good-will and practical help could most usefully have been employed and at which Adenauer's personal ambivalence would have been least relevant—but instead by trying to cut a deal with the General at a high-political level, where the Germans could not be (and because of Adenauer would not be) of assistance.[49] And in 1966/7 the British failed to realize that,

[48] PRO. PREM 11 4524, Rose to FO, no. 32 Saving, 2 Feb. 1963.
[49] Ludlow, *Dealing with Britain*, 244–9.

whereas Germany had been able to get the better of France in the empty chair crisis in the course of which France had sought change and Germany had protected the status quo, the Bonn government could not hope to defeat de Gaulle over enlargement, an issue on which Germany sought change and France sought to preserve the existing state of affairs.

Conclusions

The underlying nature of Germany's attitude towards the widening of the Community in general and British membership in particular thus prevented the Bonn government from assuming the central role in the enlargement process that might have been expected. Economic and political self-interest combined to ensure that Germany viewed British membership as desirable throughout the whole period under review. No great British effort to win over the Germans was therefore needed. German Anglophilia, however, was not strong enough to overcome Bonn's even greater desire to preserve good relations with France and to promote and protect the development of the European Community. As a result Bonn, while always supportive of British endeavours, would do nothing in the course of the free trade area negotiations, the two abortive British membership bids, or the successful 1971–2 approach which would jeopardize either Franco-German *rapprochement* or European integration. Such German caution thrust the responsibility for a breakthrough back on to London, Paris, or Brussels. But if Bonn could not assume leadership in the quest for Community enlargement, it did perform a vital task in ensuring that the divisive issue of British membership was not allowed to undermine or destroy the nascent EEC. It is thus to Germany's role as a Community power and not to its bilateral relationship with the United Kingdom that historians should look in their efforts to pinpoint Bonn's most valuable contribution during Britain's seventeen-year search for a satisfactory relationship with the EEC.

Part II

EUROPEAN SECURITY

6

European Security: Anglo-German Relationships 1949–1956

Gustav Schmidt

The period under review spans the time from the first public state-
ments that a West German defence contribution was necessary for
NATO to deliver on its security guarantee, to Adenauer's
Germany's first steps towards establishing the *Bundeswehr*.
However, the German defence contribution was delayed because
French governments at first insisted on tying-in West Germany
through the European Defence Community (EDC), and then
killed their own brain-child. In this period the North Atlantic
Treaty Organization (NATO) was transformed from a treaty
organization, set up to engage the United States as 'lender of last
resort', into a US-led politico-military organization; the latter,
however, devised its own strategies and force structures. NATO's
defence postures were the result of often uneasy compromises in a
three-cornered set of negotiations between (1) the USA and
Britain, (2) the USA and the so far non-nuclear continental
European members, and (3) the USA and NATO's evolving civil
and military apparatus. All of them took the German defence contribution into account, but the West Germans were not present at
the creation of the doctrines of 'defence as far east as possible'
(December 1949) and the nuclearization of NATO strategy and
force structures (December 1953),[1] even though the Germans

This essay is a shortened version of a more elaborate paper. It concentrates on comparing
the situations in 1949–50 and 1955, and on putting Anglo-German relationships into the
context of different concepts of security, especially NATO before its first 'eastern enlargement', i.e. the entry of West Germany, and European integration. Footnotes are restricted
to the bare minimum.

[1] The NATO Council at its December 1953 meeting confirmed the results of (*a*) the New
Look debate within the US government; Johannes Steinhoff and Reiner Pommerin,
Strategiewechsel: Bundesrepublik und Nuklearstrategie in der Ära Adenauer-Kennedy (Baden-Baden:
Nomos Verlagsgesellschaft, 1992), 18 f.; (*b*) the Bermuda Heads-of-Government meeting; (*c*)
US agreements with NATO-European states as to the deployment of 'tactical nuclear

believed that NATO provided the security considered essential for establishing a democratic Germany. At the New York Conference in mid-September 1950 the three Western allies had vouchsafed to come to the defence of their 'occupation zones' and Berlin;[2] they left no doubt that the rearmament of the Federal Republic, the purpose of that meeting, should be so constrained that West Germany would depend for its defence on collectively balanced forces, into which the German defence contribution would be fully integrated.

That the EDC project was stillborn did not matter too greatly from the perspective of the security guarantee because, first, strategy was beyond the EDC's realm anyway and had to be settled by NATO, and, secondly, the size and format of West Germany's defence contribution were fixed in political terms. For one, it should not exceed France's assignment to NATO's total ground forces; secondly, for Adenauer it served the double purpose of gaining access to the West's policy advisers and preventing the existing *kasernierte Volkspolizei* in East Germany from being and remaining the only German armed force; and thirdly, the French and the British claimed the right to reset the target—circumstances, for example some 'not-to-be-precluded' four-power accord, permitting. This scenario, known as Adenauer's 'Potsdam Komplex', provoked the German Chancellor into insisting on rearmament as the means of transforming Germany from 'factor (object) into actor (subject)', that is, of gaining leverage over his Western allies.

In contrast to Germany, Britain was a key player in making NATO work, and the adjuster of the EDC/West European Union (WEU)–NATO link. London and Paris, however, expected the West German state to become America's foremost ally, once it was allowed to join NATO. In its first year as a member of NATO, 1955–6, the Federal Republic of Germany (FRG) was alarmed at Britain's advocacy of a new approach to what NATO should stand for, and became critical of the USA as views from Washington increasingly came to resemble Britain's policy mix of (*a*) détente, based on 'Sicherheit durch Teilung' (cementing the status quo of

weapons'. One issue remained unresolved: should authority to use nuclear weapons be delegated to US commanders? Must the decision be reserved to ministers meeting in council?

[2] Gero von Gersdorff, *Adenauers Außenpolitik gegenüber den Siegermächten 1954: Westdeutsche Bewaffnung und internationale Politik* (Munich: Oldenbourg, 1994), 69, 180, 286.

divided Europe and divided Germany),[3] and arms control (limita-tion) regimes, run by the 'big three Us' (USA, UK, USSR); (*b*) reliance on the 'strategic deterrent' for preventing the outbreak of war; and (*c*) moving the central front in the East–West conflict from the Central Front in NATO's terminology towards focusing on meeting the Soviet challenge in the 'Third World'.

But before the story can be told, we must establish a framework. Anglo-German relationships in the period 1949 to 1956 were determined by four basic factors: (1) the consequences of the deci-sions of the three Western allies to found a West German state in response to the Soviet Union's division of Europe; (2) the funda-mental asymmetry between Britain's global power-base and the FRG's position as the better-off part of divided Germany; (3) the dominant position of the United States in shaping the course of Britain's and West Germany's foreign policies; and (4) the need to take account of France's search for a European role, and French insistence on Anglo-American commitments to vouchsafe Germany's reliability.

I

The foundation of a West German state resulted from the coinci-dence of American, British, French, and West German interests; the division of Germany was regarded as provisional. Hence the question of how to find a solution for the reunification of the occu-pation zones was the central issue in Europe's East–West relations; but even if Moscow could be lured into forgoing a socialist Germany in exchange for a say on 'free' Germany within a pan-European collective security regime,[4] the more demanding task of restoring freedom of choice to Poland, Hungary, and Czechoslovakia would put the Kremlin into a quandary. Like the other victorious allies responsible for the fate of Germany as a whole and for Berlin, Britain did conceive a series of plans for rec-onciling the conflicting objectives of reunification and settling

---

[3] Gustav Schmidt, 'Europe Divided—Divided Germany', *Contemporary European History*, 3 (1994), 145–92.
[4] Wilfried Loth, *Stalins ungeliebtes Kind: Warum Moskau die DDR nicht wollte* (Berlin: Rowohlt, 1994; dtv 1996) makes the case that such an alternative to Adenauer's policy of 'Westintegration' existed.

Europe's security. Britain's schemes competed not only with French, American, and Soviet Russian projects, but also with West German concepts. However, London, but never Bonn, could think of solving its foreign policy dilemma by directly approaching the USSR,[5] which had caused this dilemma in the first place. In this respect, British policy-makers—for example, Churchill in the spring of 1953—could even think of paying the price of a united, but neutral Germany in return for the post-Stalin Soviet leadership's consent to put an end to the Cold War, and to stop short of embarking on a nuclear arms race.[6] Britain regarded itself as a player at the same level as the two superpowers;[7] hence consideration for Germany's basic security and economic interests was just one, though at certain junctures the main, element in designing Britain's role in world affairs. The general willingness of France and of the USA[8] to advocate the process of uniting Europe, and to confront the USSR with a prospering, integrated Europe, made them, from Bonn's perspective, West Germany's favourite partners rather than Britain;[9] it was clear that in return for their backing of Germany's basic security interests, France and the USA would expect to be compensated by Germany.

---

[5] Britain, too, feared that the USSR would seek to induce Germany to throw in its lot with 'Russia', and consequently wished Germany to become more involved with the West; but the Attlee, Churchill, and Eden governments did not share Adenauer's interest in institutionalizing European co-operation, nor did they dare to foster Bonn's liking for membership in NATO for fear of provoking the French. It is well known that equality of status and influence within an integrated Europe was a big gain for West Germany, but considered by the British as a serious loss for Britain.

[6] Klaus Larres, 'Eisenhower, Dulles und Adenauer', in id. and Torsten Oppelland (eds.), *Deutschland und die USA im 20. Jahrhundert: Geschichte der politischen Beziehungen* (Darmstadt: Wissenschaftliche Buchgesellschaft, 1997), 119–50, 128.

[7] Christopher Lord, *Absent at the Creation: Britain and the Foundation of the European Community, 1950–2* (Aldershot: Dartmouth Publishing Company, 1996), 63 f.

[8] On America's motives for urging European integration and tying (West) Germany into European and NATO integration, cf. Gustav Schmidt, 'Ost-West-Konflikt und Intra-West-Spannungen: Die Position und Rolle (West)Deutschlands und Japans in der Sicht der USA', in id. and Charles F. Doran (eds.), *Amerikas Option für Deutschland und Japan: Die Position und Rolle Deutschlands und Japans in regionalen und internationalen Strukturen: Die 1950er und die 1990er Jahre im Vergleich* (Bochum: Universitätsverlag Brockmeyer, 1996), 3–97; Lord, *Absent at the Creation*, 78.

[9] 'there was little need to get Britain involved as some external counterbalance to Germany, if this role was passing on to the U.S. Not only would the U.S. play the role of guarantor more convincingly than Britain . . . U.S. publics and elites were also more enthusiastic than the British for any project of European integration. An American force motrice would be substituted for a British drag anchor' (Lord, *Absent at the Creation*, 78).

London had initially (in late 1947–8) suggested a revival of the alliance with the USA; the second-best solution was to found NATO. But whenever the USA or Supreme Allied Commander Europe (SACEUR) proposed to make NATO multilateral, Britain insisted on its older rights as a special ally of the alliance's leading power, the USA. To substantiate this claim, Britain imitated America's role,[10] rather than submerge its identity in the subordinate role of an ordinary ally.[11] Britain observed that France withdrew from 'supranationalism' once it noticed the restrictions on its global power status; the French decision to become a nuclear power was one of the reasons for dropping the EDC project in August 1954. When the FRG was allowed to join NATO directly, it met three of the powers responsible for Germany as whole and for Berlin, each of which had its own ideas for coming to terms with the fourth nuclear power, the USSR, and a NATO establishment that was thinking of promoting NATO to become the fourth nuclear power. It is obvious that Germany was torn between a French-centred European nuclear force and the American-backed NATO/fourth-power schemes.[12]

In principle, Britain shared the French, American, and German view that only European integration could prevent Germany from drifting towards neutrality, but added a warning. Even a united Europe would be too weak to balance the Soviet Union, and the pretence of an efficient European Defence System would serve as an invitation to the USA to bring its boys home. Hence such a European order would satisfy only the Soviet Union's interest in dominating the Continent without having to fight for supremacy.

[10] The USA initially objected to many of Britain's propositions—e.g. the Global Strategy concept of 1952; pre-empting the Radford concept as a cover-up for Britain's essential interest in defence cuts affecting the BAOR. In the end, however, it compromised with Britain's insistence on duplicating the American pattern, i.e. combining (1) reliance on the nuclear deterrent, (2) reducing conventional armed forces, and (3) testing chances for détente with an emphasis on arms control with respect to the European defence scenario.

[11] To tie Britain's strategic arms into a European defence organization would have prevented governments from acting independently out-of-area, especially in South-East Asia and the Middle East, which were the mainstays of Britain's position in the international economy and international finance. London acknowledged the need to commit the better part of its military outlay (e.g. airforce) to the defence of western Europe, but made sure that Britain—via the Anglo-American strategic power duopoly in NATO—retained full control over its potential.

[12] Gustav Schmidt, 'Die sicherheitspolitischen und wirtschaftlichen Dimensionen der britisch-amerikanischen Beziehungen 1955–1967', *Militärgeschichtliche Mitteilungen*, 2 (1991), 107–42.

In contrast to America and Germany, Britain claimed that Germany would be more tightly bound to the West in an Atlantic framework/expanded NATO rather than in the EDC; Franco-German co-operation could be developed by other means.[13] When the European Economic Community (EEC) got off the ground and Franco-German collaboration expanded, Prime Minister Macmillan did not hesitate to retreat from the commitments which his predecessor, Eden, had offered in order to rescue the EDC, or, more precisely, to transform the Brussels Treaty into the WEU. The Cabinet not only used the 'escape clauses' in order to achieve a reduction of British forces in Germany, but also opted for nuclear power status, confirming the American connection rather than a European option. 'U.S. support for Britain was . . . more important than a better "European" defence policy.'[14] Foreign Secretary Lloyd had warned in vain that Britain should not simultaneously reject the EEC/European Atomic Energy Community (Euratom) and some 'Europeanization' of its nuclear force.[15]

Adenauer knew that the 'West' needed Germany's willing co-operation; he was convinced that Washington, aware of the side-effects of 'Western integration',[16] but also in search of supportive actors, would press for Germany to be granted equality within the Western orbit as the inescapable consequence of integrating the FRG into European and Atlantic structures. Since the first step, restoring sovereignty to the FRG, was delayed as a consequence of France's qualms about ratifying the EDC Treaty,[17] the central issue for Adenauer was 'equality of status'; from his perspective, equality of status was the only guarantee against France and/or Britain approaching the USSR over Bonn's head. He pursued the

---

[13] Public Record Office (PRO), Cabinet Office, C/52/434, 'EDC and Alternative Plans', Eden Memorandum, 10 Dec. 1952.

[14] Anne Deighton, 'Britain and the Creation of the Western European Union, 1954', in ead. (ed.), *Western European Union 1954–1997: Defence, Security, Integration* (Oxford: European Interdependence Research Unit, St Antony's College, 1997), 22.

[15] Gustav Schmidt, 'Tying (West) Germany into the West—But to What? NATO? WEU? The European Community?', in Clemens A. Wurm (ed.), *Western Europe and Germany: The Beginnings of European Integration* (Oxford and Washington: Berg, 1995), 137–74.

[16] Adenauer knew that in April 1952 Acheson regarded 'equality' as a means of compensating the 'Westerners' among West Germany's élites for the disappointments over the issue of reunification; 'integrating' West Germany into Western systems would not automatically bring about German unification.

[17] This became a serious problem for Adenauer when the USSR granted the GDR 'sovereignty' in March 1954.

NATO track for this reason; when he shifted course to the EDC, he pressed even harder for equality rather than simply the return of 'sovereignty'. He was furious about British and French suggestions, made in public in March 1956, for determining the size and structure of the *Bundeswehr* as if the FRG were still an occupied zone.[18]

In Adenauer's view, Germany's willing co-operation—economically in the Organization for European Economic Co-operation (OEEC), the General Agreement on Tariffs and Trade (GATT), and the International Monetary Fund (IMF), and militarily through the eventual conventional force contribution—served two essential political purposes: first, to mark that the FRG was a member of the Western community and could legitimately expect to secure greater consideration for German interests, and secondly, to help ensure the maintenance of US armed forces and thus the continuation of the American security guarantee. Militarily, the Germans thought their defence contribution was needed (1) to discourage or defeat Korea-type challenges by the USSR or its proxies, (2) to reinforce the efficiency of America's power projection, (3) to counterbalance Soviet superiority in conventional armed forces, and (4) they believed that the existence of nuclear weapons would never obviate the need for substantial conventional forces. However, the division of responsibilities between the 'Anglo-Saxons', who provided and operated the nuclear deterrent, and Continental NATO-Europeans provoked talk of the introduction of a two-class system within the Atlantic Community. Until 1956, the year of crises,[19] the Adenauer government did not aim to become 'equal' to the nuclear powers; Bonn was happy to retain the American 'nuclearized security guarantee' (Article 5 of the North Atlantic Treaty) as long as the Adenauer government felt it could trust the American President to stick to, and implement, the principle of 'indivisible security'.[20]

[18] Hans-Peter Schwarz, *Adenauer: Der Staatsmann, 1952–1967* (Stuttgart: Deutsche Verlags-Anstalt, 1991), 240.

[19] Gustav Schmidt, 'Die Auswirkungen der internationalen Vorgänge 1956 auf die Strukturen des Kalten Kriegs', in Winfried Heinemann and Norbert Wiggershaus (eds.), *Das internationale Krisenjahr 1956: Polen, Ungarn, Suez* (Munich: Oldenbourg, 1999), 639–88.

[20] 'Defending Hamburg (or Hanover) as if it were New York (Chicago . . .)' is the more popular version of the principle. From Bonn's perspective, the concepts of 'areas of thinned-out forces' or 'weapons free zones' were advocating a split-up of NATO's security guarantee into areas ranging from limited defence to total warfare, with German territory belonging to 'limited'—in contrast to forward—defence and 'singularization' in the sense

II

Britain's power base included the networks of *Commonwealth* trading and the *Sterling area*; during the early 1950s, 40 per cent of world trade was still denominated on a sterling basis. Consequently, London could afford in many instances not only to resist American pressures to join Europe, but also 'to go it alone'. Instead of complying with 'Europeanization', Britain launched its projects with a view to qualifying as the Western world's second centre of command, as a complement to American leadership.[21] Britain even saw itself as a substitute for the USA, if that inexperienced superpower were to go through a recession or, in the security arena, became addicted to some sort of political extremism, either retreating into isolationism or exposing the 'free world' to nuclear warmongering.

Britain's management of the sterling area and imperial preference-system together with its nuclear-power status guaranteed independence, whereas until October 1990 the FRG depended for its defence on Anglo-American air-strike and surveillance capabilities, and for its economic prospects on the evolution of North Atlantic/West European free-market structures. 'The Germans are acutely conscious of their own exposed position in Europe and of the fact that one of the main fronts in the cold war runs through their country. They know they could not defend themselves and are sceptical of the willingness or ability of the Western allies to protect them in an emergency. They know their place is with the West.'[22] West German territory was considered essential to the defence of the West, and West Germans were thought indispensable for meeting the minimum forces requirements of NATO's strategies, but all of Germany's partners, and, consequently, Adenauer's Germany's course of alignment to the West, insisted on safeguards to establish 'Zuverlässigkeitskontrolle', that is, operational structures which were designed to prevent the

that large parts of Germany would not be defended 'to the last American (British) soldier' serving at the Central Front.

[21] The intelligent development of the Commonwealth was even viewed as a means to 'have the U.S. eating out of Britain's hands in a few years', Peter Hennessy, *Never Again: Britain 1945–51* (London: Jonathan Cape, 1992), 217; Lord, *Absent at the Creation*, 68.

[22] CP (50)80, 'Policy Towards Germany', 26 Apr. 1950, CAB 129–39.

FRG from harnessing its resources for national purposes, such as revisionism towards Poland or the CSSR, for example.

Britain's quest to have a policy of its own and its attempt to persuade the USA to adopt it resulted in the maintenance of Britain's world-power status. Beginning in 1956, this was finally backed up by an American-supported nuclear and missile defence posture, second only to that of the USA itself on the Western side. West Germany, on the other hand, though finally permitted to rearm (also in 1956), attained security through NATO's device of collectively balanced forces. Assuming that the FRG should not and could not aim to achieve self-sufficient armed forces, the *Amt Blank* decided that atomic weapons were a luxury for the *Bundeswehr*. Germany's policy stance was formulated on 6 September 1954 before Eden launched his operation to rescue the ill-fated EDC project, that is, the *entrée-billet* for Adenauer's Germany into the WEU and NATO.[23] NATO's security guarantee, however, was completely prejudiced by the divisiveness inherent in the nuclearization of NATO's strategy and defence posture. With a view to Article 5 of the Treaty, SACEUR Gruenther stated in July 1954 that he would need to have the authority to use atomic weapons so that there would be no delay whatsoever in countering a surprise attack; NATO must concentrate on retaining combat-ready forces with an integrated nuclear capacity.[24]

When the FRG finally joined NATO in May 1955, its security was embedded in a political concept which presumed that European security was, for the time being, predicated upon accepting the status quo—'Sicherheit durch Teilung', the key formula confirmed at the Geneva summit of July 1955. This implied that sooner rather than later the FRG would have to give up its role as gatekeeper for the Western allies' moves towards détente with the East; 'freezing' the German problem was a prerequisite that would allow Britain, or France, or the USA to search for a solution to the problem of how to organize a peaceful stalemate in the age of nuclear missiles.[25] It was up to them to decide how far to go in their deliberations on nuclear-weapon-free zones

[23] Hans-Heinrich Jansen, *Großbritannien, das Scheitern der EVG und der NATO-Beitritt der Bundesrepublik Deutschland* (Bochum: Universitätsverlag Brockmeyer, 1992), 240.

[24] See the final part of this essay.

[25] Dieter Senghaas coined the term 'organisierte Friedlosigkeit' to describe the post-1955 state of European security affairs.

etc., and to what extent to take account of West Germany's special situation as the 'front-line state' of the Alliance, facing the 'other Germany' at an undeclared border as the linchpin of the Soviet Union's control of its socialist empire. It was in the FRG's interest for the division of Europe, Germany, and Berlin not to become permanent, although for purposes of arms control and arms limitation etc., the status quo might have to serve as the point of reference. At about the same time (1956–7), Britain brought its status up to that of the two superpowers by attempting to consolidate the Commonwealth and sterling area networks as a base for third-power ambitions, while separating itself from the European countries' relaunch of the process to 'unite Europe', the Messina initiative.[26]

III

The 'American connection' was a voluntary option as well as 'eine Normativität des Faktischen' for the external relations of both Britain and the FRG. Neither could expect to defend themselves; both wanted NATO to become a mature institution. However, beyond that, the differences between Britain's and Germany's positions were obvious. There was no security for Germany, including protection from Soviet blackmail, except through either the USA's nuclear umbrella or German participation in a process of détente between the superpowers, an option which Adenauer envisaged as early as 1953.[27] There was also no security for Britain except by attempting to tie the USA in as a European power; Western Europe was neither willing nor able to defend itself against Soviet expansionism, or to resist Moscow's blackmailing of European states, one by one, into benevolent neutrality towards the USSR. Assuming this, Britain faced the task of coming to the rescue of continental Western Europe, in diplomatic and possibly military terms. But in order to avoid repeating the disastrous consequences of strategies adopted before the First and Second World

[26] Gustav Schmidt, ' "Master-minding" a New Western Europe: The Key Actors at Brussels in the Superpower Conflict', in George Wilkes (ed.), *Britain's Failure to Enter the European Community 1961–63: The Enlargement Negotiations and Crises in European, Atlantic and Commonwealth Relations* (London: Frank Cass & Co., 1997), 70–90.

[27] Adenauer sent Walter Hallstein to Washington in October 1953 to explain this view to President Eisenhower.

Wars, Britain had resolved in 1946 not to go to war again unless the USA were simultaneously committed to saving Europe. Conversely, beginning with National Security Council (NSC) 68 and reaffirmed by the New Look posture,[28] the USA linked its role as a European power to the fact that its NATO allies volunteered to support American hegemony. Britain was foremost. A peripheral strategy, including the defence of Britain, was the minimum objective of America's post-war global strategy. The British, but even more the French, tried to induce the USA to extend its commitment to the defence of Europe as far east as possible, that is, to reassure France and West Germany that their fate would not be 'liberation' after first being subjected to some period of occupation by an eastern invader. However, in order to accomplish this recruitment of American manpower and military-financial aid for the defence of Western Europe, Britain had to demonstrate that its aim was more than merely to enlist American support in the military defence of Europe. Hence Britain invited both its American and its Continental partners to put pressure on British policies to do more for them.[29] Britain focused attention on preserving its overseas resources and on sustaining France's dominant position *vis-à-vis* the FRG. The French were able to turn the overriding American and West German security concerns in France's favour. Both Washington and Bonn affirmed that the USA's security guarantee towards Western Europe, which had been solicited by Bevin, was tied to the evolution of the Franco-German *rapprochement*. Paris could use this self-denying ordinance of the Bonn Republic and the USA as an instrument to blackmail the USA and Germany into living with French schemes for European defence and economic integration, and also to press Britain to commit itself to a French-inspired EDC, with a view to balancing the political weight of West Germany in European organizations.

[28] The Solarium project and NSC 162-series are documented in FRUS, ser. 1952–54, vol. ii, pt. 1; on the wider connotations of the decision-making process (NATO and Far East strategy) see Robert J. Watson (ed.), *The Joint Chiefs of Staff and National Policy, 1953–54* (Washington, DC; vol. v of the *History of the Joint Chiefs of Staff*, 1986); Gersdorff, *Adenauers Außenpolitik*, 112 ff.

[29] The French and American demands on Britain were the same over the years from 1947–8 to 1956. They wanted Britain to increase its material contribution to Europe's defence and actively to participate in establishing integrational structures in Europe. In order to be balanced, a closer European union had to comprise Britain as one of its leading members. The British view is exposed in classic terms by Attlee in a memorandum of 30 Aug. 1951, CP/51/239, CAB 129–37.

IV

Research tends to neglect not only the relative absence of any serious consideration of the strategic implications of nuclear weapons for the decision to rearm Germany, but also the interactions between the processes of integrating the FRG into the Western orbit and the changes in NATO's strategy as they affected the overall relationships between the Western powers and West Germany. At the same time, when the National Security Council approved NSC 49/3 in late April 1953, it also directed its Planning Board to prepare a report of US policy towards Germany.

Alternatives were abundant; a series of options shaped the debate. For one, delays in the actual formation of German armed forces (until 1956) and the availability of a range of nuclear weapons (from 1951, and from 1953 with respect to the stationing of 'theatre weapons' on German territory) would have made it possible to think of revising views as to the indispensability and urgency of rearming Germany; the pressure on France and Britain to accommodate the American and German request to grant equality of status to Germany[30] might have been reduced. This would also induce the Alliance to think of increasing Germany's non-military contributions, that is, lend greater weight to British and French initiatives in this direction.

Secondly, this could have encouraged package deals, that is, linking the timing of West Germany's alignment to the West to the USSR's agreement to the reunification of Germany, but within a European security system in which Germany's Western allies would exercise control over the agreed and precise nature of a united Germany's rearmament.[31] Actually, in August–September 1953,[32] and again in April–May 1955, Adenauer and his military and political advisers (Heusinger and Blankenhorn), and also Dulles and the NSC were deliberating schemes which envisaged safeguards, that is, limitations on united Germany's rearmament.

[30] That is to say, within the framework of EDC during the period 1950 to 1954, and within WEU/NATO from the beginning of the search for an alternative to EDC.

[31] Marc Trachtenberg, 'America, France and the Question of German Power, 1945–1960', in Stephen A. Schuker (ed.), *Deutschland und Frankreich: Vom Konflikt zur Aussöhnung. Die Gestaltung der westeuropäischen Sicherheit 1914–1963* (Munich: Oldenbourg, 2000), 235–48.

[32] Ambassador Conant to Department of State, 16 Sept. 1953, FRUS, 1952–4, v. 806 ff.

In the summer and autumn of 1953, when the Eisenhower administration was deliberating the 'long-haul' strategy, ideas of the mutual withdrawal of American and Red Army forces from Europe were also elaborated. In August 1953 the American government prepared a policy statement[33] which proposed a broad zone of limited armament in Europe. The Red Army would have to withdraw behind USSR borders, and US forces across the Atlantic; NATO and German forces, however, would remain. If German forces were constituted as a component of an integrated Western European Union, they would be deployed on German territory, but immersed in multilateral units; the establishment of a regional arms control zone would not affect the *Schichttorten* (layer-cake) pattern, considered by the Germans as a pledge against both the neutralization and the singularization of Germany. Moreover, Germany would sit at the negotiating table as a member of 'Unit(ing)ed Europe'. All in all, the idea was that offering a package-deal would make the Russians think more constructively about securing peace in Europe and German unification.[34]

American military disengagement from West Germany involved the risk of major dislocations in present US and NATO plans; it would be extremely difficult to find places in Europe to station US troops, especially if proper allowance had to be made for deploying American atomic superiority.[35] In addition to the stalemate on the EDC issue and the resulting freeze on West Germany's military build-up, another difficulty emerged. The chief of the State Department's Policy Planning Staff, Robert Bowie, advised Dulles on this problem. The withdrawal of US troops must be linked to the control of nuclear weapons, he

[33] Cf. the debates in the National Security Council about NSC 160/1, 13 Aug. 1953, in FRUS, 1952–4, vii. 510 ff. These deliberations reflected on eventualities; Adenauer's victory in the elections of September 1953 dispelled some of the 'fears for the worst'. Klaus A. Maier, 'Die internationalen Auseinandersetzungen um die Westintegration der Bundesrepublik', in Lutz Köllner *et al.*, *Die EVG-Phase* (Munich: Oldenbourg, 1990), 155 ff.; Hermann-Josef Rupieper, *Der besetzte Verbündete: Die amerikanische Deutschlandpolitik 1949–1955* (Opladen: Westdeutscher Verlag, 1991), 352 ff.; Marc Trachtenberg, 'A Wasting Asset', *International Security*, XIII/3 (Winter 1988/89), 39 f.

[34] Klaus Gotto, 'Neue Dokumente zur Deutschland- und Ostpolitik Adenauers', in *Adenauer-Studien*, iii. 129–201, esp. 148 f.; on the Heusinger and Blankenhorn plans see Helga Haftendorn, *Abrüstungs- und Entspannungspolitik zwischen Sicherheitsbefriedigung und Friedenssicherung: Zur Außenpolitik der BRD 1955–73* (Düsseldorf: Droste, 1974); Gersdorff, *Adenauers Außenpolitik*, 212 f.

[35] It should be noted that the French government objected to the deployment of US tactical nuclear weapons on French soil, in 1952 and again in 1954.

argued, because 'we cannot withdraw our forces at the same time the Russians do without abandoning our bases. Obviously we cannot abandon our forward bases until nuclear weapons are controlled.'[36] At the same time, SACEUR Gruenther reminded the members of the Alliance that in spite of any eventual shift of emphasis towards nuclearization of NATO strategy and defence posture, which had been underway since the American project SOLARIUM,[37] the Alliance required Germany's contribution of 12 divisions to meet the minimum defence target of 30 divisions; to date, a total of 18 combat-ready divisions had been assigned to SACEUR, including 6 American and 4 British (Rhine Army) divisions.[38] 'It would be premature to consider [whether] new weapons could even with German contribution fill the gap adequately.'[39] The British government, however, asserted that in view of available new weapons there was no need to press on with conventional rearmament.

The British had always regarded German rearmament as a bargaining counter towards the USSR: 'if it were true that the Soviet Gvt. were genuinely apprehensive about the rearmament of West Germany, we might be in a position to extract some real concession from them.'[40] Fearing that American 'nuclear trigger-happiness'[41] could expose Britain, as America's foremost and global ally, to uncertain risks, the British had another reason for advocating a dual strategy at the political level of managing the East–West contest: to combine the maintenance of the West's position of strength with détente.[42] Bonn became suspicious that London's willingness to accommodate the Kremlin might imply

---

[36] Robert Bowie to J. F. Dulles, 19 Oct. 1953, FRUS, ii. 1228.

[37] Oliver Gnad, *Konfrontation und Kooperation im Kalten Krieg: Amerikanische Sicherheitspolitik 1950 bis 1956* (Wiesbaden: Deutscher Universitätsverlag, 1997), 59–107.

[38] According to Gersdorff, *Adenauers Außenpolitik*, 26, 65 ff., 110 ff.—NATO had a force at its disposal which could make the attack extremely costly for an aggressor.

[39] FRUS, 1952–4, V/1, 470; cf. Steinhoff and Pommerin, *Strategiewechsel*, 20, 18 f.

[40] Attlee, Feb. 1951, Cab.Concl. 51/12, CAB 128–19.

[41] The British government intervened in Washington when rumour had it that the American government was about to authorize nuclear strikes against China, in the context of the Korean war (late November–early December 1950), and in various stages of the Taiwan-Peoples' Republic of China warmongering.

[42] On Churchill's May 1953 initiative cf. Rolf Steininger, 'Ein vereintes, unabhängiges Deutschland? Winston Churchill, der Kalte Krieg und die deutsche Frage im Jahre 1953', *Militärgeschichtliche Mitteilungen*, 34 (1984), 105–44; Saki Dockrill, 'The Eden Plan and European Security', in Günter Bischof and Saki Dockrill (eds.), *Cold War Respite: The Geneva Summit 1955* (New Orleans: Louisiana University Press, 2000), 161–89.

disregard for Germany's precarious position and lead to the deterioration of the FRG's political stability.

The German schemes were intended to sell the USSR the message that a united Germany firmly entrenched in EDC, or WEU and NATO, was the best security guarantee that the Kremlin could buy.[43] The thoughts on security arrangements were intended to provide security for as well as against Germany. They were also designed to satisfy legitimate Soviet Russian security demands.[44] The package-deal comprised the following items:

- Germany would not become an atomic power;
- German integration into EDC/WEU-NATO would prevent Germany from forcibly challenging the integrity of its neighbours in Eastern Europe;
- Germany had renounced 'resort to force' (*Gewaltverzicht*) in order to qualify for EDC/WEU-NATO membership.

On the other hand, the three Western allies also aimed to prevent Germany from seeking accommodation with the USSR on its own terms.[45] But as the Western allies were united in their resolve to forestall a neutralized united Germany, they thereby created a conflicting objective (*Zielkonflikt*). What was to be visualized first, integration of the FRG into the West, or reunification? Priority was accorded to the reaffirmation of the ties that bound West Germany to the Western system. No serious discussion with the USSR, Dulles ruled on 8 September 1953,[46] should take place on mutual troop withdrawals until progress had been made in establishing the EDC, that is, realizing the German defence contribution to the safety of the West; he thought there might be a fair chance of some settlement with the Russians if the 'West' had a firm foundation in

---

[43] Comments of the *Auswärtige Amt*, Abteilung III, Ref. L I a, 17 Dec. 1953, on the Van Zeeland Plan, Politisches Archiv des Auswärtigen Amtes, 232–00 III 27111/53; MemCon. of Adenauer meeting with Prime Minister Scelba (Italy), 26 Mar. 1954, AA-PA, III, 232–00. On Blankenhorn's visit to Washington in June/July 1953 see Gotto, 'Neue Dokumente zur Deutschland- und Ostpolitik Adenauers', 141 ff.

[44] Blankenhorn emphasized this aspect when presenting the first Heusinger–Blankenhorn plan in Washington—cf. Gotto, 'Neue Dokumente zur Deutschland- und Ostpolitik Adenauers', 141 ff.

[45] Gersdorff, *Adenauers Außenpolitik*, 315 f.

[46] J. F. Dulles, 8 Sept. 1953; cf. John Lewis Gaddis, 'The Unexpected John Foster Dulles: Nuclear Weapons, Communism, and the Russians', in Richard H. Immermann (ed.), *John Foster Dulles and the Diplomacy of the Cold War* (Princeton: Princeton University Press, 1990), 69.

Western Europe, 'but not before'.[47] Once a position of strength became a reality, the USA could afford to search for some *modus vivendi* with the USSR, encompassing mutual withdrawals of the superpowers' forces and control over atomic and H-bombs; the satellites would be politically liberated, but orientated towards the USSR. Anticipating defence cuts in all the major Western countries and the relative decline of America's nuclear superiority compared to the USSR's progress, Dulles and Eisenhower were thinking of taking the initiative to relax world tensions.[48]

Facing his electorate at about the same time (September 1953), Adenauer and his military experts (Heusinger and Kielmannsegg) wished to influence these discussions. Their concept envisaged an attempt to square the circle by reconciling reunification and the continuance of NATO on the one hand, and the legitimate security interests of the USSR on the other. For Adenauer, the concept was a tactical device, primarily designed to forestall British and American ideas tending towards disengagement and perhaps even neutralization. Adenauer was concerned that disengagement schemes would lead to the erosion of NATO because US troops would have to be removed from German territory. The creation of a military vacuum in the neighbourhood of the USSR would entice different types of 'German nationalists' to draw nearer to the USSR. Adenauer also feared that a minimum 'equidistance' (towards both superpowers) would replace the mutually fruitful alignment of West Germany with the West. Above all, the status gains of the FRG *vis-à-vis* France and Britain would be irrevocably lost because all of their proposals limited the demilitarized or de-nuclearized areas in the West to the territory of the FRG, exempting British and French territory.[49] The West had first to

[47] J. F. Dulles to President Eisenhower, 23 Oct. 1953, in FRUS, 1952–4, ii. 1234. Anne-Marie Burley, 'Restoration and Reunification: Eisenhower's German Policy', in R. A. Melanson and D. Mayers (eds.), *Reevaluating Eisenhower: American Foreign Policy in the 1950s* (Urbana: University of Illinois Press, 1987): 'From March 1952 through April 1955, it was plain that the West intended to let nothing deter them from the primary objective of bringing West Germany into their system of alliances; the Soviet Union could fairly consistently give emphasis to plans for the solution of German unification—this was in large part a bluff.'

[48] Maier, 'Die internationalen Auseinandersetzungen um die Westintegration der Bundesrepublik', 159 ff.; FRUS, 1952–4, ii. 1228 ff.

[49] Hans-Jürgen Grabbe, 'Konrad Adenauer, John Foster Dulles, and West German–American Relations', in Immerman (ed.), *John Foster Dulles and the Diplomacy of the Cold War*, 114 ff.

obtain ratification of the EDC;[50] German plans envisaged EDC forces being stationed on the western side of the zone of restricted armament, and NATO forces west of the West I zone.

From Adenauer's perspective it was a different matter if the USA and the USSR engaged in negotiations on the reduction and control of nuclear weapons. If the two superpowers were able to agree on an arms control process, the resulting détente would provide hope of reducing tensions elsewhere. Given the difficult domestic situation in the USSR, the Kremlin might see an advantage in negotiating East–West agreements, and eventually release the GDR from its bloc.[51] The deliberations between Washington and Bonn in the autumn of 1953 and again in spring 1955 about using a firm regime of Western control over a Western integrated Germany as a means of inducing the USSR to release the GDR and allow for German unification did not attain a dynamic of their own. One reason was that the consolidation of the Western bloc, and especially interest in incorporating German defence forces into Western systems, either through ratification of the EDC or the WEU/NATO link, became the overriding political concern of both the USA and the FRG.[52] Secondly, it was not enough to address the matter of finding a mutually acceptable status for Germany if the issue of the Soviet 'satellites' was ignored. The Kremlin, as Dulles and Adenauer pointed out correctly, considered the fact that the GDR belonged to the Soviet bloc as a tool for exercising perennial control over Poland; the other instrument for assuring the USSR's predominance in its enlarged *glacis*, namely Poland's (and the CSSR's) fear of Germany, was bound to lose its effectiveness if Bonn, under the impact of domestic pressures and the advice of its Western allies, ever started a meaningful 'peace offensive' towards its eastern neighbours, replicating reconciliation (integration) with the 'West'.

Dulles conceded that 'Soviet atomic plenty' was at the heart of the problem. Even if Soviet control over Eastern Europe should somehow break down, or a split occur between Moscow and Beijing, the problem of how to decrease the USSR's nuclear capabilities would

---

[50] *Staatssekretär* Hallstein in a meeting with President Eisenhower, Oct. 1953.

[51] Adenauer, 18 Jan. 1954, meeting of the *CDU-Bundesvorstand*; Gotto, 'Neue Dokumente zur Deutschland- und Ostpolitik Adenauers', 145 f.

[52] Blank report of 30 July 1953 on his talks with US officials, 30 June–15 July 1953, Bundesarchiv/Militärarchiv Freiburg, BW 2/2734 NfD.

remain.[53] Negotiations on atomic arms control might offer a way out of the problems which confronted the USA; this, in turn, would create an opportunity to get negotiations on related issues off the ground. If Dulles and the State Department could perceive any solution to the interrelated issues of the German question and European security at all favourable to the West, their debate converged at the sticking point: solutions would depend upon a global *rapprochement* with the Soviets on controlling nuclear weapons, which in itself was the prerequisite for some sort of disengagement in Europe.[54] Counting, as Adenauer also did, on a Sino-Soviet rift and on the inherent instability of Communist regimes, Dulles saw some chance of a settlement with the USSR, especially if the USA–WEU(EEC) line held firm. In general, however, he realized that the Soviet leadership would not contemplate changes in East Germany and in Eastern Europe, especially when the USA was ahead of the Eastern superpower; conversely, none of the Western powers was willing to accept the terms for a settlement which the Kremlin presented in the period from 1950 to 1955.[55] To enter into negotiations on ending the Cold War on the basis of anything less than two prerequisites—a fundamental shift within the Soviet Union and Eastern Europe towards pluralism, and restoring at least some freedom of choice in the economy—would be a signal that the West accepted defeat in the contest with the Soviet superpower, and Eisenhower/Dulles and Adenauer insisted that this should not happen. They perceived the need for more activities on the diplomatic front to cope with problems resulting from the shift of emphasis in NATO's strategy and

[53] Notes on NSC meeting, 21 Dec. 1954, FRUS, 1952–4, ii. 833 ff.; meeting of Dulles with State Department advisers, 29 Dec. 1954, FRUS, 1952–4, ii. 1585 f.

[54] This has to do with Dulles's perception that the USA and its allies could never match Soviet and 'Red' Chinese superior military manpower; the security which the USA could 'export' to their allies in the 'free world' rested upon the superiority of America's deterrent; the series of earlier-than-expected Soviet successes forced the powers-that-be in Washington to get the balance right between American efforts to maintain their own 'reliability' and American pressures on their allies, especially Britain, Germany, and Japan, to do more to strengthen the stability of their 'region'.

[55] The Soviet leadership demanded not only the withdrawal of US forces from West Germany (and Europe), but also the dissolution and abrogation of bases; another demand, which Western governments likewise considered as spelling the end of NATO, was a ban on introducing atomic weaponry. The American top military echelon and SACEUR asserted that the USSR gained additional advantages through the motorization of its units, the build-up of forward stockpiles, etc., and argued that the introduction of tactical atomic weapons into NATO's forces structure was required to reduce the imbalance between Soviet and NATO military power.

defence forces posture. The first charge, however, was on solving intra-Western tensions over the question of anchoring (West) Germany firmly in European and Atlantic integration and accommodating Bonn's claim for equality of 'Mitwirkung'.[56]

With a view to Moscow's need for respite, or the unresolved disputes among Stalin's successors, Britain took the position that a further military build-up by European countries was neither possible (for economic reasons) nor necessary.[57] Assuming that any pan-European security arrangement must have regard to what the Western European members accepted voluntarily as the force level they could afford, the British view implicitly contradicted American and German thinking in terms of accomplishing a position of strength through efforts to attain NATO's collectively balanced forces requirements. The British Chiefs of Staff had their doubts as to whether the strategic guidance of SACEUR's planning, namely 'the holding of as much of NATO territory as possible', was wise;[58] they realized, however, that for political reasons no departure from the device of engaging in 'defence as far to the East as possible'—on which France as well as the FRG insisted—was possible. In July 1953 Supreme Headquarters, Allied Powers, Europe (SHAPE) and SACEUR estimated that to carry out such strategy needed forces requirements in all categories higher than Britain was willing to support. The difference originated not only on military grounds, but also in London's new perception of the 'Soviet threat'. According to Britain's assessment, the West's best hope of gaining a position of strength would be as the result of domestic and internal pressures in the Communist bloc (China) working on the minds of the Soviet leadership; if these pressures began to work, a situation might evolve in which the Kremlin would think of abandoning East Germany. However, the West should consider the price it would be willing to pay in return for

[56] See my articles in Wurm (ed.), *Western Europe and Germany*; Wilkes (ed.), *Britain's Failure to Enter the European Community 1961–63*; CEH, III (1994), 145–92. Four-Western-power consultations were formally established in spring 1955; the formal equivalent with respect to 'nukleare Mitwirkung' had to wait until 1966.

[57] John S. Duffield, 'The Evolution of NATO's Conventional Force Posture' (Ph.D. thesis, University of Princeton, 1989), 161 ff.; Hermann-Josef Rupieper, 'Deutsche Frage und europäische Sicherheit: Politisch-strategische Überlegungen 1953/55', in Bruno Thoß and Hans-Erich Volkmann (eds.), *Zwischen Kaltem Krieg und Entspannung* (Boppard: Harald Boldt Verlag, 1988), 193 ff.

[58] PRO, DEFE 5–50, COS (53) 609, 'SACEUR's estimate of the situation and force requirements for 1956', 23 Dec. 1953; COS (53) 490, 2 Oct. 1953.

Moscow removing the Berlin danger and extending Western influence to the Polish border. The Kremlin might consent to the idea of a neutralized zone extending from East Germany through Austria and making use of Yugoslavia's middle position, if the eastern portion of united Germany were to be demilitarized; such acts could help the Soviet leadership save face over including united Germany in NATO, but the USSR would have to be embedded in a security regime which would assure the USSR of a 'weighty' voice.

Confronted with the need to close the gap between NATO's armed forces requirements and the resources which members were willing to designate to defence,[59] the USA rediscovered the importance of Germany's conventional contribution. Troop withdrawals could not effect major savings in the defence budget for some time. Consequently, the discussion focused on revising America's and NATO's policy on the use of atomic weapons, which alone now promised the possibility of budget cuts. The USSR's possession of the H-bomb seemed to cancel out the importance of strategic nuclear weapons as a deterrent to 'limited wars' resulting from the Soviet Union's exploitation of the superiority of 'intervention' forces,[60] and made the size of conventional forces critical. This assumption called for European political unity[61] as the appropriate response, because only a 'united Europe' could assemble and finance the large conventional forces necessary to deter the USSR. This view of Eisenhower, Dulles, US representatives in Europe, and SACEUR was shared by Adenauer's top military advisers.

[59] Reliance on nuclear weapons had become the solution of countries 'unwilling or unable to make the sacrifice of economic resources necessary to sustain large conventional forces and sacrificing political sovereignty', Thomas H. Schwartz, 'The "Skeleton Key"— American Foreign Policy, European Unity, and German Rearmament, 1949–54', *Central European History*, 19 (1986), 384. Britain also stated in 1954–5 that the USSR was less prone to launch a war in Europe in order to expand its influence. Remembering American officials advocating nuclear blackmail towards China without due consideration to the security interests of America's allies, Britain urged entering negotiations with the USSR on arms agreements as a first step to ensure peace; these negotiations should not be loaded, as Bonn and Washington emphasized, with requests to tackle the political origins and causes of the Cold War.

[60] The perception of threat rested on the 'fact' that the tanks which were used to suppress revolts against Communist Party rulers could also serve as a spearhead in 'limited (local)' conflicts, e.g. should revolts spill over from Poland or the CSSR into the GDR, and West Germans attempt to come to the rescue of compatriots in Eastern Germany.

[61] 'Political unity' had various meanings, ranging from unity of purpose (speaking with one voice) to organizing 'common action'.

However, neither the French nor the British took 'conventional deterrence' as an answer to the 'Soviet threat', and moved towards provisioning their own national strategic deterrent force (Britain from 1953, and France from 1954 onwards), whilst the USA and the FRG still considered the build-up of a conventional defence posture[62] as an indispensable pillar of NATO's security.

Since mid-1952, the British had attempted to revise NATO strategy to take account of the growing stockpile of nuclear weaponry. The British Chiefs of Staff's review of British strategy in the light of the immense burden of rearmament and the growing power of the US atomic stockpile had concluded in mid-1952 that by 1954 NATO's ready forces, coupled with the use of tactical nuclear weapons, would be sufficient to win the decisive but brief initial phase of any future war. Hence there would be no need to continue the conventional build-up after that date. Although the US military had challenged Slessor's case in July 1952,[63] British officials explored the problem of how best to relate NATO force requirements to the deterrent theory.[64] For them the problem was how to persuade NATO that in calculating its forces requirements it should consider what was required to deter the Russians from making an attack, and not what might be required to defeat a Russian attack. The British took the view that NATO's present level of forces constituted an effective deterrent. The British urged SHAPE and SACEUR Ridgway to study the effects of nuclear weapons on NATO's force requirements for 1956. This study, known as the New Approach, examined not future requirements, but how NATO could fight most effectively given the forces likely to be available three years hence, including tactical nuclear weapons.

The US New Look exercise was completed and approved (NSC 162/2) just as NATO's New Approach got underway. In the

---

[62] For Eisenhower and for Adenauer, 'atomic weapons' were another sort of 'artillery'; Adenauer was accused of ignorance when he made such a statement, but because neither the USA nor the allies—i.e. NATO's collectively balanced forces—thought they could afford separate 'conventional' and tactical atomic weapons force-units, 'non-strategic' nuclear weapons had to be immersed in the equipment of 'conventional' armed forces.

[63] Slessor, the moving spirit behind the Global Strategy paper, presented the recommendations of the Chiefs of Staff to his counterparts in Washington; neither the Royal Navy nor the Army were inclined to implement the new strategic doctrine. The Sandys White Paper of April 1957, with Macmillan's backing, revived the concept behind the 1952 Global Strategy paper.

[64] N. Brook to Prime Minister Churchill, 25 Mar. 1953, PREM 11–369.

following months US officials pursued two primary objectives: (1) to obtain an alliance agreement allowing NATO military authorities to base their plans on the use of nuclear weapons just as the US military had been effectively authorized to do under NSC 162/2; without such authority, the military stated, they would have to prepare for two types of conflict, one conventional and one nuclear, at considerably greater expense. The military should be authorized to assume, for planning purposes, that if it might be of military advantage to use nuclear weapons, the USA and the alliance would do so. Nuclear weapons should be considered available for use, like other munitions, in the event of hostilities.[65] Although certain allies drew a sharp distinction between the use of conventional weapons and atomic weapons, from late 1953 through to the North Atlantic Council meeting in April 1954, US officials insisted that it no longer made any sense to refuse to prepare to use tactical nuclear weapons, given recent Soviet advances in this field, or to maintain two separate military establishments, which would result in unnecessarily high defence expenditures. A new concept had to be considered by which atomic and new weapons would be meshed in with conventional armaments, Dulles told Eden and Bidault at the Bermuda Conference in December 1953.[66] (2) In order to obtain prior approval by the European allies for the use of nuclear weapons from their territory by US and NATO forces in the event of hostilities and, concomitantly, to assist the European partners in the use of atomic energy for civil and, possibly (depending on progress towards European Union), for military purposes, the Eisenhower administration asked Congress to amend the McMahon/Atomic Energy Act to allow for sharing-arrangements and stockpile agreements.

[65] On the Review of US Basic National Security Policy, see Duffield, 'The Evolution of NATO's Conventional Force Posture', 165 ff.; FRUS, 1952–4, ii. 435 ff., 532 ff.

[66] Eisenhower/Dulles–Eden–Bidault meetings (Bermuda Conference), 4–8 Dec. 1953, FRUS, 1952–4, v. 1710 ff. At the NAC meeting in Paris on 24 April 1954 Dulles asserted that it should be agreed policy, in case of either general or local war, to use atomic weapons as conventional weapons 'whenever and wherever it would be of advantage to do so'; on Dulles's thinking about nuclear policies see, however, Christian Greiner, 'Das militärstrategische Konzept der NATO von 1952–57', in Thoß and Volkmann (eds.), *Zwischen Kaltem Krieg und Entspannung*, 211 ff.; Gersdorff, *Adenauers Außenpolitik*, 25 ff.; Robert Wampler, *NATO Strategic Planning and Nuclear Weapons 1950–1957* (NHP, University of Maryland, 1990); Saki Dockrill, *Eisenhower's New Look National Security Policy, 1953–61* (London: Macmillan, 1996), 98 ff.

The debate on the 'nuclearization' of NATO's strategy, especially the 'conventionalization' of tactical atomic weapons, held serious implications for Germany. The British and American-induced decisions to introduce tactical atomic weapons to compensate for the deficiencies in the deterrent role of conventional armed forces resulted in the meshing in of conventional and nuclear weapons in the structure of NATO forces; there were no separate forces to react to different types of threat and limited wars. The shift towards heavy reliance upon tactical and, later, on 'Euro-strategic' nuclear weapons (medium-range ballistic missiles: THOR and JUPITER 1958/9–63) ensured that 'any war in Europe would be a total war for the Germans'.[67] Once again, the prospect of (West) Germany's 'singularization' turned up in the debates about authorization of the military, that is, the Joint Chiefs of Staff and SACEUR with their respective command chains, to plan for the use, and perhaps eventually even to use the range of nuclear weapons in the defence of Western Europe. In December 1953, SACEUR Gruenther suggested that the presence of the long-awaited German divisions was no less important than the ability to use nuclear weapons if NATO was to have a reasonably good chance of defending Europe successfully against all-out aggression. One month later, in January 1954, studies undertaken by NATO's top military echelon indicated that an atomic defence of Western Europe would still require a shield of ground forces strong enough to force the enemy to concentrate its own troops in an attempt to break through NATO lines, thereby providing targets against which it would be worth using nuclear weapons.[68] To deploy Germany's overdue contribution of twelve divisions would concentrate NATO forces; this would force the 'enemy' (USSR) to a considerable build-up before it could attack, thus providing NATO with both an extended warning time and the potential to deter an 'invader' from testing NATO's security guarantee.

Although Dulles had been instrumental in the development of the 'new look' concept of US national defence and global strategy, and in revising NATO's strategy accordingly, he stated in

---

[67] Emil J. Kirchner and James Sperling, 'From Instability and Stability', in eid. (eds.), *The Federal Republic of Germany and NATO: 40 Years After* (London: Macmillan, 1992), 11; Wolfram F. Hanrieder, 'The FRG and NATO: Between Security Dependence and Security Partnership', ibid. 209.

[68] Gruenther, 12 Jan. 1954; Gersdorff, *Adenauers Außenpolitik*, 25 ff.; Watson, *History of the Joint Chiefs of Staff*, v. 309 f., 288 ff., 43 f.

December 1953 that 'Western Europe was the one region in the world where the doctrine of massive retaliation was expressly not intended to apply'. 'That is one situation where we are *not* relying exclusively by any means upon the deterrent of striking power.'[69] Against the views of the Pentagon (Secretary of Defence Wilson) and the Joint Chiefs of Staff, President Eisenhower insisted that the JCS should not plan to employ nuclear weapons in minor affairs, pointing out that there were certain places where the USA would not be able to use these weapons because if it did, it would look as though the USA were initiating a global war.[70] The Eisenhower administration regarded it as necessary to maintain an adequate defence-in-being in Western Europe. Dulles declared the ability to provide a forward defence as the strongest deterrent against military aggression in the (European) region. In this respect, the German defence contribution mattered; hence the German government must be given a say in defining, implementing, and revising the Alliance's foreign policy and defence affairs.

V

The 'nuclearization' of NATO's strategies and force structures had serious implications. On the one hand, the European allies welcomed the US commitment to deploy the new atomic theatre weapons with their own forces and the air and ground forces of the allies assigned to SACEUR because the nuclearization of NATO forces meant that the Americans would have to stay in Europe for a considerable period of time.[71] On the other hand, by accepting

[69] For Dulles's statements (21 Dec. 1953) see Duffield, 'The Evolution of NATO's Conventional Force Posture', 180 ff.; on the critics of massive retaliation and 'self-deterrence' see Peter J. Roman, *Eisenhower and the Missile Gap* (Ithaca: Cornell University Press, 1995), 63 ff. Among the reasons for Europe's exemption from America's unilateral threat of nuclear retaliation in all instances, two stand out: (1) an all-or-nothing scenario had to be prevented because the 'region' (western Europe) was so vital to the security of the USA; the Europeans had to be convinced that they had the means to put a special guard around this core-area—they 'only' had to allow German integration into Western systems; (2) talk of atomic attacks would be dangerously counterproductive, i.e., create a movement for 'peace-at-any-price' in allied countries; on the latter aspect, with respect to Germany and Japan, see Schmidt, *Amerikas Option*.

[70] NSC, 265th meeting, 7 Oct. 1953, discussing NSC 162; cf. Dockrill, *Eisenhower's New Look National Security Policy*, 86–105; see esp. the contributions by R. Wampler and M. Trachtenberg in Francis H. Heller and John R. Gillingham (eds.), *NATO: The Founding of the Atlantic Alliance and the Integration of Europe* (London: Macmillan, 1992), 353 ff., 413 ff.

[71] Trachtenberg, in Heller and Gillingham (eds.), *NATO*, 420 f.

the nuclear strategy, the Europeans were transferring the authority to start a war to the American President, which meant, in certain cases, to American military commanders.[72] Furthermore, the apparent reduction of the role of conventional warfare in American and British strategy, of which the French became fully aware at the Bermuda summit and the North Atlantic Council meetings in December 1953, from the French point of view occurred at the wrong time. Given the perception that Europe need not expect a deliberate military attack from the East, which also helped to justify New Look, at least on Britain's side, the French insisted on a more or less permanent Anglo-American security guarantee against some future German menace.[73] How, then, could a nuclearized security guarantee, which the FRG was bound to ask for in return for its crucial defence contribution to NATO strategy, ever meet the French desire to control Germany's resurgence as a European power? Above all, SACEUR and SHAPE postulated that the introduction of nuclear weapons and the expected German defence contribution were intertwined. One could not be had without the other. Could Germany's Western European partners ever be happy with the prospect of depending, in a worst-case scenario, on the US decision to release the atomic chain of command on the one hand, and on the military effectiveness of the *Bundeswehr* on the other?

The second aspect of 'nuclearization', which the British stood for as much as the American government, was that it changed the prospects of negotiations with the USSR. Whilst Adenauer and his political and military advisers could (and did) argue that EDC assured control—albeit Western—of Germany's power and would therefore also solve Russia's legitimate security concerns, this option dissipated before the French declared EDC a lost case. In the meantime, the meshing of allied nuclear weapons and conventional forces, while desperately awaiting Germany's actual contribution, in NATO's defence posture, raised in the USSR the spectre of a military threat being launched from German soil. The British government was disturbed about this consequence of its own

---

[72] Ibid. 421; Klaus A. Maier, 'Amerikanische Nuklearstrategie unter Truman und Eisenhower', in id. and Norbert Wiggershaus (eds.), *Das Nordatlantische Bündnis 1949–1956* (Munich: Oldenbourg, 1993), 265 ff.

[73] Saki Dockrill, *Britain's Policy for West German Rearmament, 1950–1955* (Cambridge: Cambridge University Press, 1991), 135, 139, 148.

doings, but further enhanced NATO's dilemma on the one hand by preaching the virtues of tactical and strategic nuclear forces as substitutes for conventional forces, and on the other by admonishing Washington and Bonn to compensate for the offset costs of Britain's military outlay. Otherwise, it suggested, London would be forced to reduce the Rhine Army and cut by nearly a half the air-force assigned to NATO's Tactical Air Force.

7

Britain and the Federal Republic of Germany in NATO, 1955–1990

Beatrice Heuser

[West] Germany was finally admitted to NATO on May 5th,
1955 . . . And West Germany has remained a loyal ally ever
since.

Denis Healey, *The Time of My Life*, 165 f.

Unser Verhältnis zur NATO ist, wie ich im letzten Gespräch
mit [Defence Secretary Denis] Healey feststellen konnte,
genauso eng wie das britische. Wir halten beide die NATO für
unerläßlich und sind entschlossen, an den Grundprinzipien
des Bündnisses, nämlich dem der Integration und vor allem
des gemeinsamen, unter amerikanischer Führung schon in
Friedenszeiten bestehenden Oberkommandos festzuhalten.

Herbert Blankenhorn, *Verständnis und Verständigung*, 483 f.

Britain Proposes the FRG's entry into NATO

Initially, the positions of Britain and the FRG in NATO could not
have been more different. Yet with Britain the victor and Germany
the vanquished of the Second World War, the British Foreign
Secretary, Ernest Bevin, was among the earliest to advocate, in the
winter of 1948–9, the admission of the FRG into the Western system of defence of which he was an architect.[1] Britain backed the
Pleven Plan of 1950, which aimed to create a European Defence
Community (EDC) and, with it, a West German military component in a European army. When this project foundered, it remained

---

[1] N. Wiggershaus, 'The Decision for a West German Defence Contribution', in O. Riste
(ed.), *NATO: The Formative Years* (Oslo: Universitetsforlaget, 1985), 198–214; S. Dockrill,
Britain's Policy for West German Rearmament, 1950–1955 (Cambridge: Cambridge University
Press, 1991).

the British government's priority to secure a German contribution to Western defence and to tie the FRG into the Western treaty systems in some way, even at the cost of gravely antagonizing the French—indeed, if necessary, at the risk of losing French membership of NATO.[2] In order to facilitate this in the absence of a supranational framework (such as the EDC Treaty), Britain went further than any other country bar the USA by unilaterally committing forces to Germany. The stationing of the British Army on the Rhine (BAOR) was part of the Lancaster House package that also contained the agreement to incorporate West Germany into the Western Union (recast to become the West European Union) and into NATO. With its commitment to deploy forces in West Germany indefinitely, Britain had the second-largest force in the FRG after the USA, particularly after France withdrew from the integrated military structure and deployed only token forces on German soil, near the Franco-German border.

Yet no sooner had Britain made this exceptional commitment than ministries began to wonder whether it had been a wise decision. British interest in proposals for a mutual disengagement from Germany (and the rest of central Europe), the most famous of

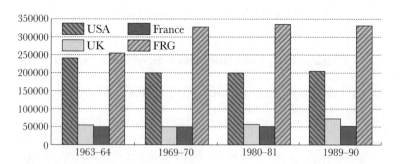

Figure 7.1. Forces deployed in the FRG
Source: IISS: Military Balance.

[2] O. Mager, *Die Stationierung der britischen Rheinarmee: Großbritanniens EVG-Alternative* (Baden-Baden: Nomos, 1990), 85–100, esp. 89; see also B. Thoß, 'Der Beitritt der Bundesrepublik Deutschland zur WEU und NATO im Spannungsfeld von Blockbildung und Entspannung (1954–1956)', in H. Ehlert, C. Greiner, G. Meyer, and B. Thoß, *Die NATO Option*, vol. iii of *Anfänge westdeutscher Sicherheitspolitik* (Munich: Oldenbourg, 1993), 155–64.

which is associated with the Polish foreign minister Adam Rapacki, was widespread. Sir Anthony Eden, Air Chief Marshall Sir John Slessor, Hugh Gaitskell, Harold Wilson, and his defence secretary were among those favouring the withdrawal of nuclear weapons and conventional forces from a wide strip of land on both sides of the Iron Curtain which would have left the two Germanies neutralized.[3] The fear of abandonment by their allies was a factor which troubled German–British relations in this period, particularly because London gave this option such serious consideration.[4] Bonn governments consistently opposed such proposals, and, in the end, it was Bonn's views, not the drift towards disengagement, which prevailed.

Britain, Germany, and the NATO Crisis 1957–1967

The lure of disengagement proved relatively short-lived, but underlying economic considerations accompanied British–German defence relations throughout the Cold War. From 1957, if not earlier, British governments saw the maintenance of the BAOR as a burden for the British economy, which had not recovered from the Second World War as swiftly and completely as the British had hoped. Consequently, commitments had to be cut back. Henceforth a main theme was that of British requests for increased German payments for the British force stationed in Germany. In 1957 the British defence minister under Macmillan, Duncan Sandys, produced the first of his White Papers which proposed the end of conscription and a drastic reduction in British conventional forces coupled with greater emphasis on nuclear (including short-range, tactical) forces. 'The Germans seemed shaken', Macmillan recalled after trying in vain to explain the reasoning to Chancellor Konrad Adenauer, foreign minister Hallstein, defence minister Franz-Josef Strauss, and Inspector General of the *Bundeswehr*

---

[3] Cf. C. Gasteiger, 'Der Atlantikpakt und das Problem der europäischen Sicherheit', *Europa Archiv*, vol. 13, no. 7 (5 Apr. 1958), esp. 10647–59; on British disengagement plans under Wilson and Healey, see A. Frisch, 'Truppenverringerung in Europa?', *Süddeutsche Zeitung*, 15 Mar. 1965; 'Bonn über die britischen Pläne zum Abzug von Raketenwaffen besorgt', *Der Kurier* (Berlin), 27 Aug. 1965; 'Ziehen die Amerikaner ab?', *Christ und Welt*, 27 May 1966.

[4] H. Macmillan, *Diaries*, vol. iv: *Riding the Storm, 1946–1959* (New York: Harper & Row, 1971), 639.

General Heusinger on his visit to Bonn in May 1957.[5] The issue of the financing of the BAOR became a recurrent and long-term problem in Anglo-German relations. Herbert Blankenhorn, German ambassador to the court of St James's, sighed under the burden of never-ending discussions about export deficits and British requests to link these with the British contribution to European defence.[6] The issue put in regular appearances in the 1960s and 1970s.

Adenauer, like his successors, did his best to persuade the United Kingdom of the need to leave forces in Germany. He convinced all the Western leaders, including those of Britain, of his own impeccable anti-Communist and anti-nationalist standing, but in doing so, and for his own purposes, he consciously fuelled fears that without foreign forces (but also without himself in government), Germany might revert both to nationalism and to the old temptation of flirting with the East.[7] The consequences were double-edged. On the one hand, it arguably increased Adenauer's own standing with the Western powers. On the other, it fed fears that latent revanchist or racist tendencies in Germany might break out again. This had repercussions also on co-operation within the Atlantic Alliance. Macmillan and de Gaulle shared suspicions of the FRG and agreed that it 'would be very serious' if the FRG developed its own nuclear weapons, which it might do if the USA pulled its forces out of Germany.[8] Clearly, London's and Bonn's preferences diverged considerably. What was the West German perspective on this?

From the mid-1950s, Chancellor Konrad Adenauer and his first minister for atomic energy and subsequently second defence minister, Franz-Josef Strauss, were as keen on nuclear weapons as anybody else in NATO. Most European members of NATO, and also some non-members, were at the time exploring nuclear options, either on a national basis, or in collaboration with other powers. This was true even of a neutral country like Sweden,[9]

[5] H. Macmillan, *Diaries*, vol. iv: *Riding the Storm, 1946–1959* (New York: Harper & Row, 1971), 292.

[6] H. Blankenhorn, *Verständnis und Verständigung: Blätter eines politischen Tagebuchs, 1949–1979* (Frankfurt am Main: Propyläen, 1980), 480, and 484–562, *passim*.

[7] Macmillan, *Riding the Storm*, 335.

[8] UK, Public Records Office [henceforth PRO], FO371/161097, WF 1051/22/G 28 Jan. 1961, transcript of CdG's and Macmillan's conversations in Rambouillet.

[9] T. Larsson, 'Swedish Nuclear and Non-Nuclear Postures', in Leopoldo Nuti and Cyril Buffet (eds.), *Dividing the Atom*, special issue of *Storia delle Relazioni Internazionali* (Summer 1998).

and it was certainly true of France, Italy, and the FRG. During the years 1956 to 1958, when the Treaties of Rome were negotiated, signed, and implemented, the three of them pursued the development of a European nuclear force. As a maximum aim, this would have driven European integration in the area of defence and security policy to its logical, supranational conclusion. As a minimum aim, it was designed to make the Americans more generous in sharing their own nuclear forces with their allies.[10]

Cutting across this project were various American proposals. One was the Norstad proposal; another was that for a Multilateral Nuclear Force. Neither was welcome in London. The former was a proposal put forward by the Supreme Allied Commander Europe (SACEUR), General Lauris Norstad, for a European Medium-Range Ballistic Missile (MRBM) force independent of a US veto to be created, but not one which would allow individual European powers to launch nuclear weapons on their own—with the exception of Britain, which already controlled its own nuclear weapons. British and French hostility to the Norstad project was barely concealed. As Christoph Bluth noted, it is striking 'in the light of later British arguments about the benefits of multiple centres of decision-making' that one objection they raised against the Norstad proposal was that 'two nuclear centres of decision would split the Alliance'.[11] From a British point of view, the Norstad proposal supported German, but not British, interests. As one German-American observer noted:

The attitude in London was generally hostile toward SHAPE[12] increasing its role and concomitant influence in nuclear defence through acquiring weapons capable of striking the Soviet Union. To the extent that SHAPE acquired a 'Continental attitude', Her Majesty's Government appeared concerned that SHAPE was susceptible to excessive influence from countries having Soviet forces at their frontiers.[13]

---

[10] On this, see B. Heuser, *NATO, Britain, France and the FRG: Nuclear Strategies and Forces for Europe, 1949–2000* (London: Macmillan, 1997), ch. 6: 'Projects for a European Nuclear Force'.

[11] C. Bluth, *Britain, Germany and Western Nuclear Strategy* (Oxford: Clarendon Press, 1995), 72.

[12] SHAPE = the Supreme Headquarters of the Allied Powers in Europe.

[13] Robert von Pagenhardt, quoted in Bluth, *Britain, Germany*, 70 f.

Worse still, wilfully misrepresenting Norstad's proposal, some Britons argued that the proposal 'could mean German commanders having power to use nuclear weapons'.[14]

The second American proposal cutting across European moves towards nuclear independence came in 1960, when the outgoing second Eisenhower administration advocated the formation of a 'Multilateral Force' (MLF). The subsequent Kennedy administration interpreted this as something that might bring the British and nascent French nuclear forces under US control. While the British were prepared to link their nuclear forces to NATO in some way, they were determined to keep the final say over their use, and succeeded in negotiating a special deal to this effect with the USA in Nassau in December 1962. But the threat of the American veto being imposed remained as long as there was talk of the MLF, and it grew with Britain's procurement dependence on the USA, when in the early 1960s Britain abandoned all indigenous missile production. Britain was thus fundamentally hostile to the proposed MLF, while the FRG's leaders saw it as the only way for their forces to gain security equal to that of their nuclear-armed allies along the Central Front.

There was such yearning for European nuclear forces in the early 1960s because, with the Soviet development of intercontinental nuclear missiles, the USA had become vulnerable to Soviet nuclear retaliation, and all sides knew that the USA would henceforth hesitate to use nuclear weapons in defence of the Europeans. Or, in the words of a British official summary of the different positions in 1963:

The US view
The Dulles doctrine of 'massive retaliation' with nuclear weapons 'at a time and place of our choosing', against any major conventional encroachment by the Soviet Union, though never formally abandoned by the Kennedy Administration, has been retained only in the form of a refusal to undertake *not* to initiate the use of nuclear weapons in any circumstances. Recent US strategic thought has concentrated on the problems of raising the nuclear threshold so as to defer the moment at which nuclear weapons are used, and of minimising damage to non-military targets if they are used. . . .

---

[14] PRO, FO371/161240, Steering Committee NATO Strategy, report of 28 Aug. 1961; see also conversation between the French and British defence ministers, Pierre Messmer and Peter Thorneycroft, in Paris, 17 Oct. 1962, PRO FO371/166328.

The French view
The French show no interest in raising the nuclear threshold, feeling
rather that deterrence would be made less credible by measures (such as
a considerable increase in conventional forces) which suggested unwillingness to make early use of nuclear weapons. Nor do they at present
seem interested in a collective NATO deterrent.

The West German view
The West German attitude to the nuclear threshold resembles that of the
French. Since the most likely battleground for a 'tactical' nuclear war is
West Germany, West German interest [*sic*] are held to lie in making such
a war unlikely by threatening the use of battlefield or interdiction nuclear
weapons as soon as possible after the outbreak of hostilities. The West
Germans have resisted suggestions for an increase in manpower beyond
500,000 which might be interpreted by the Soviets as indicating reluctance to resort to nuclear weapons. Unlike the French, the West
Germans are keenly interested in the creation of a NATO nuclear force,
although they hope for the ultimate removal of the US veto on its use. To
the West Germans the force represents an essential means of maintaining the credibility of the Western deterrent as a whole and of gaining a
say in its use.[15]

British views were moving in a different direction at the time.
British planners favoured the concept of attempting to restore
deterrence, if it had failed, by using nuclear weapons selectively,
ideally 'against the invading Warsaw Treaty Organization troops
within the territory of the NATO countries attacked'. Alternatives,
such as using nuclear weapons against the attacking forces' rear
support, were thought more dangerous as this might 'spread the
area of conflict' unnecessarily. While the attacked NATO ally 'may
regard it with distaste' that NATO nuclear weapons would be used
on its territory, 'since the area to be bombed will be in enemy
hands, such objections could be overcome'. British government
strategists at the time still estimated the fall-out effects of ground-
bursts (they were thinking in terms of 1 megaton bursts with blast
and thermal effects throughout a 5–10 mile radius) as 'trouble-
some', but not much more.[16]

This was the point at which British and West German views
diverged most dramatically. During the first decade of NATO

[15] PRO, DEFE 7/2236, D13.112 SRS.64/63, Annex 'Attitudes to Deterrence', JIB, 25
June 1963.
[16] PRO, Air Council Files: Report by the Air Ministry Strategic Scientific Policy
Committee on 'N.A.T.O. Shield Forces', AC(62)14 of Mar. 1962.

membership, West German governments were only selectively informed about the military strategy which their nuclear allies intended to follow in case of war. Not until the mid-1960s were they fully aware of how much nuclear ordnance the Americans intended to detonate on West German territory in the case of a WTO invasion. Likewise, they only fully grasped the extent of nuclear destruction which their country was likely to suffer at the hands of the British when this was demonstrated in joint military exercises. In 1960, for example, British tactical nuclear employment plans became known to the West German military leadership, and these provided for the use of short-range nuclear weapons primarily on either side of the inner-German border.[17]

In full realization of these British (and similar US) plans, the FRG's government and military chiefs urged the adoption of a new strategic concept which aimed to defend West Germany along the inner German border, rather than in the depth of the FRG's territory. Given persistent German pressure, London gradually gave in, and finally agreed to defend further to the east, if possible, even though this meant 'the abandonment of a natural river obstacle and a greater reliance on nuclear weapons', as Lord Mountbatten told General Lyman Lemnitzer, Chairman of the US Joint Chiefs of Staff, in May 1962.[18]

Britain had political as well as military reasons for seeking to fulfil German requests. Obviously, on balance, it was important for Britain to retain the FRG as a military ally and to adapt its defence strategy, rather than to run the risk of German neutralism. But the political reasons lay elsewhere. Britain was hoping for German support in its belated quest for EEC membership. While Britain was wooing the six EEC members in 1960–3, the UK government took very seriously the possibility that a condition for joining might be for Britain to turn its nuclear force into a 'jointly owned and operated nuclear force in Europe'. Large sections of the government—particularly on the defence side—were reluctant to take this step and hoped that Britain could, 'as long as this was possible', stay with an 'Interim Arrangement' 'designed to preserve the substance of the existing situation while accepting the form of

---

[17] Letter to Major-General Trettner (16 Sept. 1960), Nuclear History Project, Bonn Document collection, Doc. 52 p. 2.

[18] PRO, DEFE 4/144, COS(62)31st Mtg., 1 May 1962, Item 1.

greater multilateralism', at the same time 'retaining the options open to us including the possibility of continuing the British independent deterrent'.[19]

Britain eventually assigned all its nuclear forces to NATO as part of this interim arrangement. Britain's aims were above all, and quite pragmatically, to retain an effective deterrent, to retain US military support for Europe (that is, not to do anything that would push the USA out of Europe), to prevent the creation of a German independent nuclear force, to maintain British influence in European defence, to satisfy the other European countries' wish for less dependence on the USA, and to avoid the duplication and waste of scarce resources.[20] The problem of US detachment from Europe, however, and of the perceived hollowness of the US nuclear guarantee, continued to bedevil NATO as a whole. And it was really this pressure which brought Britain and the FRG together in the second half of the 1960s. In mid-1965, FRG ambassador Blankenhorn noted that the German and the British attitudes towards NATO were similar in the prevailing NATO crisis.[21]

But British–German co-operation was still complicated by divergent policies towards nuclear weapons. Britain actively scuppered the Multilateral Force and tried to drive the FRG, Italy, and all the other non-nuclear powers into a two-tier system confirmed by the Non-Proliferation Treaty (NPT). Meanwhile, as the MLF rapidly sank, Bonn still desperately clung to the buoy of hope for a European nuclear force or a collective NATO nuclear force of sorts (which the NPT's formulation ruled out). All sides were aware that the alternative Britain put forward to the MLF, an 'Atlantic Nuclear Force', was designed to sink the MLF by confusing the argument even further. 'As Franz-Josef Strauss put it, the ANF was the only fleet in history which had not been created, yet torpedoed another fleet which had never sailed.'[22] The death-blow thus dealt to the MLF by the Wilson government was seen by German observers as a serious problem for British–German relations. One of the FRG's leading security specialists, ambassador Wilhelm

[19]   PRO, DEFE 7/2236, Lord Mountbatten of Burma to Minister (12 Dec. 1962).

[20]   PRO, AIR 19/999, British Nuclear Deterrent Study Group, Annex to COS(62)473, 11 Dec. 1962.

[21]   Blankenhorn, *Verständnis und Verständigung*, 483.

[22]   D. Healey, *The Time of My Life* (1989; quotation from Harmondsworth: Penguin, 1989), 305; Blankenhorn, *Verständnis und Verständigung*, 495.

Grewe, characterized Harold Wilson in this context as a 'sly opportunist, full of tricks', whom even members of his own party regarded as insincere. Grewe accused Britain of selling the same horse several times over in offering to assign British nuclear forces to NATO at the Ottawa NATO summit in May 1963, and then supporting the NPT which would make any collective control of nuclear weapons impossible.[23]

The NPG from Healey–Schröder to the Euromissile Crisis

Both Britain and the FRG have a share in the origins of the Nuclear Planning Group. This is usually credited to McNamara, but it was first proposed no later than early 1962 by the UK in reaction to the Kennedy administration's insistence on a more conventional defence strategy.[24] In September 1963, the British and German defence ministers, Peter Thorneycroft and Kai-Uwe von Hassel, jointly held a seminar on NATO strategy. It was on this occasion that they found their views converging, as eye-witnesses recorded, 'somewhere in the middle between two extremes'.[25] These two extremes were the French and the US views. The former advocated the retention of the declaratory strategy of Massive Retaliation and emphasis on nuclear deterrence above all else. Paris wanted to keep conventional forces small to demonstrate NATO's determination not to fight a conventional war but to resort early and decisively to nuclear use if attacked. The contrasting US position was most clearly articulated from 1961 in Dean Acheson's campaign for a conventional defence posture, with nuclear weapons to be held well in the background. The nuclear threshold would thus be raised much higher than any of the Europeans liked to contemplate. The British and German views on the matter were not identical. The British were somewhat closer to the French, while the Germans favoured nuclear use against the enemy's conventional forces to stop aggression on the battlefield. Still, they were closer to each other than to the views of any third country.[26]

---

[23] W. G. Grewe, *Rückblenden, 1976–51: Aufzeichnungen eines Augenzeugen deutscher Außenpolitik von Adenauer bis Schmidt* (Frankfurt am Main: Propyläen, 1979), 621 f.

[24] PRO, DEFE5/126, COS(62)163, 'Briefs for the Anglo-French Staff Talks', 17 Apr. 1962.

[25] Bluth, *Britain, Germany*, 138.   [26] Loc. cit.

A real turning point in British–German defence relations came when Denis Healey was appointed Defence Secretary in 1964. However, the closeness between him and members of the German government only began to have a real impact once NATO pulled out of its crisis and the Nuclear Planning Group truly started working in 1967. But even in 1965, ambassador Blankenhorn reported on the commonality of interests between Healey and his own government where NATO was concerned.[27] Denis Healey was genuinely unbiased with regard to the Germans, and himself recalled that 'I never shared the strong anti-German feeling so widespread in Britain after the war'. He attributed this to a holiday spent in Germany in 1936, and the annual Anglo-German Conferences held at Königswinter, where he met and became friendly with a number of German intellectuals.[28] Although (like many other respectable British thinkers) Healey had been in favour of disengagement from Germany in the late 1950s, he subsequently ceased to see this as a promising policy for NATO to pursue.[29]

Healey himself thought later that West German leaders ceased to pursue the option of a shared NATO or even independent German nuclear force after the late 1960s because of the existence of the Nuclear Planning Group, which satisfied many of their needs.[30] The first great joint British–German venture within NATO was the co-operation between Denis Healey and Gerhard Schröder on a report on nuclear targeting which formed the basis of the Provisional Political Guidelines (PPGs), adopted in 1969. According to his own accounts, Healey got on particularly well with the Inspector General of the Bundeswehr, General Ulrich de Maizière, and with Helmut Schmidt, who followed Gerhard Schröder as defence minister in 1969.[31] As Christoph Bluth has shown, NATO charged Britain and the FRG with the task of jointly drafting guidelines for criteria to govern NATO's first use of nuclear weapons, and this assignment was made despite initial American resistance.[32] Denis Healey also created the Eurogroup ministerial meetings in NATO, which have variously been praised as fruitful and engaging in serious negotiations,[33] or else dismissed as an elegant form of dining club.

[27] Blankenhorn, *Verständnis und Verständigung*, 483.
[28] Healey, *The Time of My Life*, 163 f., 315.   [29] Ibid. 178 f.   [30] Ibid. 314.
[31] Ibid. 315.   [32] Bluth, *Britain, Germany*, 185.   [33] Grewe, *Rückblenden*, 603 f.

Following this period of heightened NATO activity and
British–German co-operation, the early and mid-1970s were a
relatively uneventful period for NATO. Attention lay elsewhere—
in *Ostpolitik*, hopes for a relaunch of EEC integration, and arms
control. Anglo-German relations became particularly close and
productive once again in the period 1977 to 1985. This period
opened with Helmut Schmidt's Alastair Buchan Memorial
Lecture at the International Institute of Strategic Studies in
London in 1977. Chancellor Schmidt drew attention to the danger
of US–Soviet bilateral arms control. With the Strategic Arms
Limitation Talks (SALT) this addressed only strategic nuclear systems, leaving the way open for the unlimited growth of Soviet
'theatre' nuclear arsenals and conventional forces in Europe which
threatened European NATO countries, but not the USA. Schmidt
argued that this created a dangerous imbalance, and that 'theatre'
systems should be taken into account in arms control talks.[34] This
evoked a letter from the British Ministry of Defence to the
Pentagon, proposing a consideration of this matter, which eventually led to the creation of the High Level Group in NATO to study
NATO's nuclear force structure in connection with arms control
issues.[35] In this High Level Group, co-operation between the
British and German representatives was particularly close, to the
point where the two often concerted their views in advance of
meetings and pushed what was essentially a common European
agenda. As Ivo Daalder has shown, the two delegations saw the
need for the deployment of missiles accurate enough and reliable
enough credibly to threaten nuclear first use against non-urban
targets in the WTO area, with the purpose of creating conditions
in which the Soviet leadership would be forced to consider war
termination. The two delegations worked jointly in NATO 'to shift
emphasis away from the large-scale use' of nuclear weapons on the
battlefield 'to interdiction strikes deep inside the WTO territory',
as Christoph Bluth has documented.[36] The second 'track' of the
argument was that in deploying long-range missiles within the
European theatre, which had not existed in NATO's arsenal since
the withdrawal of the Jupiter and Thor missiles, NATO would

---

[34] H. Schmidt, 'The 1977 Alastair Buchan Memorial Lecture', *Survival*, vol. 20, no. 1
(Jan./Feb. 1978), 4–5.
[35] Bluth, *Britain, Germany*, 236.   [36] Ibid. 238 f.

create for itself a position that would allow it to bargain for an elimination of Soviet intermediate-range missiles not covered in the SALT negotiations.[37]

The policy eventually adopted by the HLG in December 1979, as the Soviet Union invaded Afghanistan, was to deploy 'long-range theatre nuclear forces'—Cruise and Pershing II missiles—on the soil of European member states. FRG Foreign Minister Hans-Dietrich Genscher supported the work and findings of the High Level Group.[38] Chancellor Helmut Schmidt and his Defence Minister Hans Apel, however, had last-minute misgivings. Even at a late stage Schmidt returned to the option of exclusively sea-based nuclear forces in order to avoid turning European territory into the targets for pre-emptive Soviet nuclear strikes. Nevertheless, once this decision had been taken by the Alliance, Helmut Schmidt pledged himself to its implementation, to the point of splitting his party and losing government over it. Under the coalition government of Schmidt and Genscher and the subsequent coalition government of Helmut Kohl and Genscher, Bonn and London were united in their efforts to implement the dual track decision and to cope with criticism at home and in the Eastern bloc. Both capitals were shaken by anti-nuclear protest marches and a ground swell of popular resistance to the deployment of 'Euromissiles', and stood together in their determination to see the deployment through until the USSR was willing to begin a new round of arms control talks. But in the process of developing this rationale for arms control, the strategy experts of both countries became so keen on the particular weapons they were deploying (which allowed *selective* use beyond NATO territory) that they found it difficult to follow the Americans and Soviets in 1986–7 when these agreed on the elimination of what were now called 'Intermediate Range Nuclear Forces' or INF. For the negotiations of the General Political Guidelines by NATO in 1986 were, in respect of British and German targeting preferences, a high-water mark of British–German agreement and co-operation against distinctly different interests defended by the USA.[39] And to implement these targeting preferences, NATO needed the 'Euromissiles'.

[37] I. H. Daalder, *The Nature and Practice of Flexible Response: NATO Strategy and Theater Nuclear Forces since 1967* (New York: Columbia University Press, 1991); H. Haftendorn, 'Das doppelte Mißverständnis', *Vierteljahreshefte für Zeitgeschichte*, vol. 33, no. 2 (1985).
[38] Bluth, *Britain, Germany*, 233.   [39] Ibid. 304.

The British and FRG governments also reacted similarly in 1983 to the American Strategic Defence Initiative. They reluctantly climbed on to the bandwagon when they were persuaded that this might be of economic benefit to their industry. Both feared a decoupling of America from the European part of the Alliance as a result of the protective shield, which might leave the European 'theatre' to its fate while giving the Americans a (false?) sense of security. Thus, on a variety of issues, the British and West German governments in NATO were as close as could be.

The End of the Cold War, German Unification, and the Demise of the Silent Alliance

During the final years of the Cold War and the watershed of 1989–90, however, the close British–German relationship in NATO began to disintegrate. The second half of the 1980s saw the Alliance nearly torn apart over the question of whether developments in the Soviet Union were likely to last and Soviet disarmament proposals—most importantly, the INF Treaty—were sincere, or whether the Alliance was being led to drop its guard only to find itself more vulnerable after abandoning its complex nuclear deterrence posture. The UK government was most adamant that short-range nuclear forces should be modernized, while the Federal Government was painfully aware that it would not be able to impose such a decision on its domestic opinion. While still agreeing with the views of the British strategists, German government planners saw it as increasingly unfeasible to pursue this aspect of their government's own preferred strategy. Agreement ceased when Prime Minister Thatcher spoke out in favour of creating a 'fire break' between short-range and strategic nuclear forces, which would destroy the 'seamless gown of NATO deterrence' (nuclear weapons of all ranges) of which previous NATO planners had been so proud, and which would have cloaked all NATO countries in equal security. Short-range nuclear forces, by contrast, could only target German territory, while the 'fire-break', leaving Germany exposed, would have excluded its neighbours from a nuclear exchange. It is not difficult to understand why this posture was anathema to Bonn.

Symptomatic of this divergence of perspectives and interests was WINTEX 89. NATO exercises, particularly at the highest (command post) level, have always been more than mere exercises and in themselves something of a political statement. This was true of the 'LION NOIR' exercise of 1955 as much as of the series of autumn exercises 'FALLEX' in the 1960s and 1970s, which marked the evolution of NATO's nuclear strategy. In the 1980s, the most important exercises were the winter exercises 'WINTEX', the last of which took place in 1989. (Ever since, there have merely been Crisis Management Exercises at the command post and political level, called CMX.) In WINTEX 89, Britain was prepared to support the FRG against attack by 'using' nuclear weapons against Soviet territory, only to find that the Bonn government terminated the exercise in protest against the fact that some nuclear weapons were also 'used' against West German territory, and the circumstances of the entire exercise were leaked to the press in Bonn. The major British players saw this as something of a German betrayal, and feelings on all sides were strong.

In the following year, German reunification had a thoroughly upsetting effect on the British–German partnership that had emerged. That Prime Minister Margaret Thatcher was 'against it, ho-ho', as Alan Clark was told by her close collaborator Archibald Hamilton,[40] did not remain a secret, and it was certainly no secret to the Bonn government. Horst Teltschik, adviser to Helmut Kohl during the negotiations leading up to reunification, was aware less than a month after the Berlin Wall had come down that the British Prime Minister had been trying to delay this development. In January 1990 she even said so clearly in an interview with the *Wall Street Journal*.[41]

By 1993, RAF pilots were no longer aware that Britain had a nuclear commitment to the defence of the FRG and of other NATO (or at least WEU) members; the absence of nuclear exercises had led to swift oblivion of what the close co-operation of the Cold War had been about.[42]

---

[40] A. Clark, *Diaries* (orig. 1993; quotation from London: Phoenix pb., 1994), 275.

[41] H. Teltschik, *329 Tage: Innenansichten der Einigung* (Berlin: Siedler, 1991), 66 f.; 72, 115 f.; interview M. Thatcher in *The Wall Street Journal Europe*, 26 Jan. 1990.

[42] The author's experience of teaching at the RAF Staff College in Bracknell, 1992–6, demonstrated that little or no knowledge of the 'Silent Alliance' survived the end of the Cold War.

British Attitudes towards Germany . . .

Why did this 'special relationship' within NATO disintegrate quite
as quickly as it did? The answer lies both in the waning of the Cold
War constellation (the common threat, and the common European
strategic preferences had pushed Britain and the FRG together) and
in a metaphysical dimension, that of collective beliefs and *mentalité*.[43]
Ever since the end of the Second World War, British attitudes to the
FRG in NATO have been ambiguous. British commentators peri-
odically linked the British possession of nuclear weapons with the
need to keep the FRG away from nuclear ownership, and British
willingness to co-operate closely with the FRG in NATO was driven
in good part by the desire to keep track of what the FRG was doing
and to prevent it from drifting into a unilateral pursuit of security
and nuclear weapons ownership.[44] Just as doubts about the
American guarantee were occasionally packaged in an indirect
attribution of these doubts to Moscow, rather than to London,
British politicians liked to point to an adverse Soviet reaction as an
argument against any German access to nuclear forces. Thus
Harold Wilson as leader of the Labour Party criticized Douglas-
Home's government for its 'nuclear pretence' which would make it
'inevitable that Germany will develop nuclear ambitions. And a
German finger on the nuclear trigger will render it more difficult to
reach any understanding between Russia and the West.'[45]

While suspicions with regard to Germany thus lived on, the Cold
War brought out many instances of British gallantry *vis-à-vis* the
FRG. These were encapsulated in Britain's acknowledged obliga-
tions under the revised Brussels (WEU) Treaty of 1954, repeated by
Sir Geoffrey Howe as Foreign Secretary in 1987: 'We regard the forward defence of the FRG as the forward defence of the UK itself.'[46]
This ambiguous mix of suspicion and gallantry was noted by one
commentator, drawing attention to the Labour Party's instrumen-
talization of the German factor in the mid-1960s. On the one hand,
he argued, the Germans were thought by the Labour Party

---

[43] For more on this subject, see B. Heuser, *Nuclear Mentalities? Strategies and Belief Systems in Britain, France and the FRG* (London: Macmillan, 1998).
[44] 'World War III', *Observer*, 17 June 1962.
[45] 'Wilson attacks "atom pretence" ', *Observer*, 1 Dec. 1963.
[46] Sir G. Howe, 'European Security', *Studia Diplomatica*, no. 1 (1987), 48.

to be so potentially *dangerous* as not to be trusted even with tactical atomic weapons. On the other, they are deemed so *sentimental* that a British nuclear self-denying ordinance will lead them to join in. But those people in Germany who want their country to have these weapons . . . are not primarily interested in becoming equal to Great Britain . . . [but] think that their possession will increase Germany's security *vis-à-vis* the USSR and give them more control over their national future. . . . their opinion is . . . not likely to be changed by a British renunciation.[47]

Even during the Cold War, waves of anti-German sentiment swept across the UK at regular intervals. The journalist John Mander, himself not a sentimental Germanophile by any means, commented on the generally xenophobic, but particularly anti-German mood which seized Britain, the one European country that had not suffered German or other fascist rule, from the 1950s, particularly on its political far Left and far Right. Mander saw this as a function less of fear of neo-Nazism than 'of Britain's own malaise'.[48] It was perhaps not surprising to find this xenophobic backlash in the context of the perception of Britain's own decline, and, indeed, Mander's observations could well be applied to British feelings towards Germany during other spells of malaise.

Admittedly, however, there were aspects even of the Federal Republic which reminded British observers all too much of Germany's past. One commentator, fearful of the spread of nuclear weapons, was particularly concerned about the chance that 'the infection could be spread to West Germany in time':

For a decade the government of West Germany had put up maps in every army barracks and in every train and station showing not only East Germany but also the western territories of Poland and even East Prussia itself as 'temporarily under foreign administration'.[49] Every year a cabinet minister called Seebohm claimed the Sudetenland for Germany without losing his post. . . . If such a country were to make and absolutely control a nuclear strike force, it would be more than even the most long-suffering

---

[47] A. Hartley, 'The British Bomb', *Encounter*, May 1964, reprinted in *Survival*, vol. 6, no. 4 (July–Aug. 1964), 177.

[48] J. Mander, *Great Britain or Little England* (Harmondsworth: Penguin, 1963), 121 ff.

[49] This is quite true. See also, for example, the contemporary road atlases sold in Germany. Even the *Shell Atlas Deutschland* of 1965 had precisely these words printed over Western Poland, where the place names were given exclusively in German. As the signposts in Western Poland in turn only bore the Polish names, this was a rather self-defeating exercise, as the one thing these German maps certainly did not do was to help West German tourists—if ever there were any—to find their way.

of its former victims could be expected to bear, and the Soviet Union is not especially long-suffering.[50]

'The plain fact', according to Nigel Lawson, a journalist before becoming a leading Conservative politician and Cabinet minister, 'is that with a history of instability for the greater part of the present century, Western Germany remains today the only nation in Europe with open and unsatisfied territorial ambitions.' The result: 'half of Europe is still scared stiff' of Germany. Therefore there could be 'no question of Britain accepting military nuclear equality with Germany'.[51] There was a large degree of consensus in Britain on this point. Even an increase of German influence in NATO was seen as dangerous: it 'would not help East–West relations and would cause some uneasiness even within NATO'.[52]

The proposal that Continental European members of NATO should fill the gaps left by US force reductions during the Vietnam War invariably aroused in Britain the bogey of an excessively strong Germany.[53] The idea of Franco-German nuclear co-operation (which, as we shall see, was far from a real possibility under the Fifth Republic) only made this bogey more scary in British eyes.[54] West Germany's geostrategic importance meant that it would be 'the dominant European partner if the UK were not a nuclear power', and this was reason enough for Britain to keep the deterrent, it was argued in late 1979.[55] This was the height of British–German nuclear co-operation within NATO—when Helmut Schmidt was imploring Britain to modernize its strategic nuclear weapons so that France would not be the only nuclear power in Europe![56]

One journalist, writing in the *Guardian*, represents those with a completely different frame of mind who saw Germany as an ally there was little reason to vex. He felt that Prime Minister Wilson,

---

[50] W. Young, 'MLF—A West European View', *Bulletin of the Atomic Scientists*, vol. 20, no. 9 (Nov. 1964), 19.

[51] N. Lawson, 'Britain & Germany—and a Child's Guide to the Home Front', *Financial Times*, 24 Nov. 1965.

[52] J. Garnett, 'BAOR and NATO', *International Affairs*, vol. 46, no. 4 (Oct. 1970), 672; see also Lord Wigg, 'The perils of defence on the cheap', *The Times*, 19 Feb. 1970.

[53] 'US double vision over Europe', *The Times*, 15 Dec. 1972.

[54] Bluth, *Britain, Germany*, ch. on 'The MLF—the British response'.

[55] R. Dale, 'The balance of arguments for a UK deterrent', *Financial Times*, 13 Nov. 1979; J. Critchley, MP, 'Why Britain must now have a Trident', *Guardian*, 17 Dec. 1979.

[56] As Callaghan recollected: 'Callaghan's case for Trident', *Sunday Times*, 29 Mar. 1987.

by reiterating the British Government's opposition to a German finger on the trigger of any multilateral nuclear force, had slid 'yards back'. 'Such phrases make people in Germany feel that we think them vicious, untrustworthy, and uncouth. They play on latent German inferiority complexes. . . . This is what has driven some dispirited Atlanticists back into the arms of de Gaulle.' This, he felt, was not the way to create a greater feeling of unity in the Atlantic Alliance.[57] Philip Windsor, expert on German affairs at the London School of Economics, was also more optimistic about the Anglo-German ability to co-operate. In 1970, he discerned a 'growing alliance between Britain and Germany in the past few years'. He saw this as a function of Britain's determined efforts to sidestep French blocking by working bilaterally with Continental allies, and mainly through NATO, where the French could not block them in view of their own absence.[58] A decade later Hedley Bull emphasized how much Europe would benefit from West Germany playing a more positive role in European defence. 'It is only on the basis of West German power that a West European counterpoise to the Soviet Union can be constructed.' And he sanguinely added: 'This means that West Germany will need to play some role, even if at first a small one, in the control of European nuclear forces.' Arguing that over forty years West Germany had shown itself 'an exemplary social democracy', and that its territory was the most likely battlefield in a war involving Western Europe, he thought it was time the Germans returned to 'a "normal" status in world affairs'.[59]

The relative rise of Germany as a force to be reckoned with, without any value judgement attached to this fact, is reflected in a throwaway line in the writing of the Conservative academic Christopher Coker. Arguing against British nuclear divestment, as proposed again by the Labour Party in the 1980s, he wondered whether a Labour government would really 'retain any influence in Washington or Bonn'.[60] The underlying assumptions of this are worth spelling out (which Coker does not do in that essay). With

---

[57] A. Hetherington, 'Questions on the Bonn agenda', *Guardian*, 18 Jan. 1965.

[58] P. Windsor, 'Current Tensions in NATO', *The World Today*, vol. 26, no. 7 (July 1970), 289.

[59] H. Bull, 'European Self-Reliance and the Reform of NATO', *Foreign Affairs*, vol. 61, no. 4 (Spring 1983), 887.

[60] C. Coker, 'Naked Emperors: The British Labour Party and Defense', *Strategic Review*, vol. 12, no. 4 (Autumn 1984), 44.

regard to Germany they are that (*a*) West Germany was now a force important enough to be named in one breath with the USA, and (*b*) that this Germany would be impressed in its dealing with an ally by that power's possession of nuclear weapons. That Germany was still feared more than trusted towards the end of the Cold War is shown in an article by a British diplomat, who at the beginning of the 1980s was still arguing that any potential future form of nuclear co-operation in Europe must above all avoid a German finger on the trigger: a European finger seemed more acceptable.[61]

. . . and West German Attitudes towards Britain

Western Germany paid no comparable attention to the UK during the Cold War. Occasionally there was grumbling that NATO was an 'American–British Club', as Georg Leber once said, in which most crucial posts were held by Americans or Britons.[62] But other than that, Germans dwelt less on Britain and British attitudes to defence, inside or outside NATO, than on US or French attitudes, which were more important to their thinking.

Britain and its nuclear force were thus marginal to German thinking.[63] Young German scholars, unless their studies focus specifically on British politics or British policies towards Germany, barely register that the United Kingdom played any role at all in NATO, let alone in the formulation of nuclear strategy, which is perceived as an almost exclusively US–German product.[64] Obviously, the select members of Bonn governments involved in defence co-operation in NATO were aware of the contribution Britain was making to NATO's nuclear posture in conceptual but also in physical terms, and they were aware of the closeness of

[61] P. Unwin, 'Britain's Foreign Policy Opportunities: Part I: The Global Context', *International Affairs*, vol. 57, no. 2 (Spring 1981), 231.

[62] A. Weinstein, 'Die Nato ist immer noch ein "amerikanisch-britischer Club" ', *Frankfurter Allgemeine Zeitung*, 20 May 1977.

[63] J. Digot, 'Défense et sécurité: points de vue allemands: 1. Les doctrines officielles', *Revue Défense Nationale*, vol. 36, no. 1 (Jan. 1980), 439 f.

[64] See e.g. S. Peters, *The Germans and the INF Missiles: Getting their Way in NATO's Strategy of Flexible Response* (Baden-Baden: Nomos, 1990), and H. Mey, *NATO Strategie vor der Wende: die Entwicklung des Verständnisses nuklearer Macht im Bündnis zwischen 1967 und 1990* (Baden-Baden: Nomos, 1992).

British–German understanding on these matters. An anonymous German official, writing in 1984, acknowledged that

Today, and in contrast to the 1960s, the American strategic potential benefits from being supplemented by another nation's and the consequent uncertainty about the moment and degree of nuclear escalation. In this respect, the British strategic nuclear contribution becomes a decisive weight in the balance of power.[65]

It is significant that this anonymous article appeared not in a German, but in an English-language journal. Neither the German nor the British public ever found out about the close nuclear co-operation and the high degree of agreement between their governments.

Conclusions

British–German relations in NATO went through several phases. In the first phase, roughly spanning the 1950s, Britain played a crucial role in pushing for and later facilitating the FRG's integration into the Western alliance. By unilaterally committing British forces to be deployed in Germany on a permanent basis in the British Army of the Rhine, Britain helped overcome the reluctance on the part of other European powers to see the FRG in NATO and Germans once again in uniforms and barracks.

The second phase was marked more by dissonance than by harmony: it was the period roughly from 1957 until 1967, when the FRG's leadership fought for a European nuclear force independent of a US veto, and Britain fought for the independence of its national force from any joint European (or US) control. But out of this period of rivalry grew the increased awareness that European strategic interests coincided more than did strategic interests on either side of the Atlantic. This led to the joint pursuit of influence on the USA, finally expressed through the input made by the Nuclear Planning Group and the work of the committees that was later enshrined in the PPGs.

Founded on the Healey–Schröder period's co-operation and kept alive through the regular meetings of the NPG, the British–German

---

[65] Anon., 'NATO and the British Nuclear Deterrent—Necessity or Burden?', *The Hawk*, Mar. 1984, 66.

relationship in NATO became increasingly harmonious in the 1970s, until, in the period of the Euromissiles, from 1978 until 1989 it blossomed into a 'silent alliance', silent but close, in the bosom of NATO.

But this alliance was an all too closely guarded secret. It was never backed by popular feeling, and never took root. Thus it did not withstand the turbulence brought on by the end of the Cold War and by German reunification. Instead it gave rise to a relatively harmless, but none the less palpable sense of rivalry, which was expressed not only in relations between London and Bonn, but also in international organizations such as NATO. Football encounters and press polemics are only part of the picture; a sporting rivalry can also be found among diplomats and other government representatives.

British–German relations in NATO thus had their ups and downs, with a tendency towards close co-operation when America's behaviour seemed particularly erratic. Without the Soviet threat forcing them together, the imperative for close co-operation is lacking, and a degree of re-nationalization can be observed in the policies of both countries, and with it, of old-fashioned national rivalry.

8

Britain as One of the Four Powers in Berlin

Lothar Kettenacker

The history of Berlin is full of contradictions and as such is a mirror-image of German and European history in the twentieth century. During the First Empire and throughout the first half of the nineteenth century most Germans looked on Vienna as their capital. It was only with the unification of Germany under Prussia that Berlin rose to prominence as the seat of an all-German government, and not until 1900 that Berlin came to overshadow Munich as Germany's cultural metropolis.[1] The city symbolized the inherent German antagonism between 'Geist' and 'Kultur' in that it reached its zenith as a centre of dynamic culture in the 1920s when Germany, with its armies vanquished, was in political turmoil: the Twenties were not as 'golden' as that.[2] Again after unconditional surrender in 1945 cultural life amidst the rubble of the bombed-out city was much more vibrant than during the previous twelve years of Nazi power-politics.[3] This was due in no small part to the efforts of the occupying powers, not least Great Britain, who saw German culture as a redeeming feature.

Berlin's real career began at the very moment when it had lost its function as the Reich's capital and was occupied and divided among the four victorious powers. It took on a symbolic quality both as the defiant citadel of the West in the ensuing Cold War, and as the only remaining platform for Germany's claim to reunification. When a

---

[1] For the change from Prussian to Imperial capital: Ruth Glatzer, *Berlin wird Kaiserstadt: Panorama einer Metropole 1821–1890* (Berlin: Siedler, 1993). The most authoritative history of Berlin is that edited by Wolfgang Ribbe, *Geschichte Berlins*, 2 vols. (Munich: Beck, 1987). In English, still useful: Gerhard Masur, *Imperial Berlin* (London: Routledge & Kegan Paul, 1971).

[2] See Peter Alter (ed.), *Im Banne der Metropolen: Berlin und London in den zwanziger Jahren* (Göttingen: Vandenhoeck & Ruprecht, 1993).

[3] See Brewster S. Chamberlain, *Kultur auf Trümmern: Berliner Berichte der amerikanischen Information Control Section, Juli–Dezember 1945* (Stuttgart: Deutsche Verlags Anstalt, 1979).

small majority of *Bundestag* Deputies voted for the reinstatement of Berlin as the German capital in 1991 it was chiefly to honour the promise made during forty frustrating years of division.[4] For the world at large Berlin redeemed its past as the nucleus of German militarism when its population withstood—against all odds and predictions—the blockade imposed by the Soviet Military Administration in 1948. The various crises, and the brinkmanship that defined them, kept Berlin in the news for the next twenty-five years. After all, the besieged city, where the antagonistic super-powers confronted one another every day, was one of the most volatile power-kegs with potential to unleash a Third World War.

Britain's relationship with Berlin is much closer than is generally realized, one reason being that Britain fought Prussian militarism in both the First and the Second World Wars.[5] The demise of the hated Nazi regime was a foregone conclusion, that of the Prussian spirit was not, and Berlin was identified more with Prussianism than with Nazism. Decision-makers in Whitehall were unaware of the extent to which the idea of Prussia and the Prussian officer corps had been corroded and corrupted by the Nazi regime. Nor was the nature of the Führer's rule properly understood, the polycratic structure with competing power centres.[6] Berlin, that is, its administrative machinery, was perceived as the undisputed centre of power for the implementation of Hitler's decisions throughout the Reich. Not surprisingly then, a separate zone for Berlin was the brainchild of British political ingenuity. The first plans, submitted to the other two Allies as early as mid-January 1944, were finally approved by the three governments in July. A separate zone around Berlin recommended itself for two reasons: first, the application of indirect rule by means of an Allied Control Commission which would supervise a German central government or, more likely, central administrative authorities ('oberste Reichbehörden'); second, to 'stress further the

---

[4] Deutscher Bundestag (ed.), *Berlin–Bonn: Die Debatte. Alle Bundestagsreden vom 20. Juni 1991* (Cologne: Kiepenheuer & Witsch, 1991). See also Ekkehard Kohrs, *Kontroverse ohne Ende: Der Hauptstadt-Streit. Argumente, Emotionen, Perspektiven* (Weinheim: Beltz, 1991).

[5] See Lothar Kettenacker, 'Preußen-Deutschland als britisches Feindbild im Zweiten Weltkrieg', in Bernd-Jürgen Wendt (ed.), *Das britische Deutschlandbild im Wandel des 19. und 20. Jahrhunderts* (Bochum: Brockmeyer, 1983), 145–70.

[6] This is now emphasized in Ian Kershaw's new biography, *Hitler 1889–1936: Hubris* (London: Allen Lane, 1998). See also Gerhard Hirschfeld and Lothar Kettenacker (eds.), *The 'Führer State': Myth and Reality: Studies in the Structure and Politics of the Third Reich* (Stuttgart: Klett-Cotta, 1981).

combined occupation of Germany'.[7] If Prussia were to disappear from the map it would not be necessary to dismember Germany. On the contrary, a Germany intact and controlled from above would also hold the alliance together and prevent the zones of occupation from drifting into separate spheres of interest. In other words, Berlin was supposed to be the counterweight to the principle of occupation by zones.[8] There was also the unspoken assumption that any one power in control of Berlin would exercise supreme authority over the whole of Germany. Churchill therefore urged Eisenhower— Supreme Commander Allied Expeditionary Force (his official title in March 1945)—to push on to Berlin. Eisenhower, however, was not amenable because he knew that Berlin itself was 'no longer a particularly important objective',[9] and that the western zones would be limited in the east by a line 200 miles west of the city. In his view Churchill's insistence on taking Berlin ahead of the Russians must have been based on the conviction that this would later give the Western Allies greater prestige and influence.

British hopes and fears for Berlin were greatly exaggerated. Between January 1944 and July 1945, when the Anglo-American forces took up their positions in the capital, the original concept for Berlin was watered down to the extent that the separate central zone was but an empty shell. The British Chiefs of Staff would not agree to serve under a Russian Commander-in-Chief in Germany. At the end of June the Russians submitted their plan for carving up Berlin into occupation sectors similar to the division of Germany into separate zones. In November a judicious compromise was reached on the question of supreme authority in Germany. It was to be exercised by the Commanders-in-Chief 'each in his own zone of occupation, and also jointly, in matters affecting Germany as a whole', in their capacity as members of the Control Council.[10]

---

[7] Areas of Occupation of Germany by the Allies after Cessation of Hostilities (MSC 22/2), 8.6.1943, FO 3371/35319/U2681. For the general context of British planning see Lothar Kettenacker, *Krieg zur Friedenssicherung: Die Deutschlandplanung der britischen Regierung während des Zweiten Weltkriegs* (Göttingen: Vandenhoeck & Ruprecht, 1989).

[8] Cf. Tony Sharp, *The Wartime Alliance and the Zonal Division of Germany* (Oxford: Clarendon Press, 1975).

[9] Eisenhower to Marshall, 30 Mar. 1945, quoted by Dwight D. Eisenhower, *Crusade in Europe* (London: William Heinemann, repr. 1949; 1948), 438. See also Sharp, *Wartime Alliance*, 125–9.

[10] F. S. V. Donnison, *Civil Affairs and Military Government: Central Organization and Planning* (London: Her Majesty's Stationery Office, 1966), 105; also William (Lord) Strang, *Home and Abroad* (London: André Deutsch, 1956), 218.

Thus the division of Germany was virtually preordained if the Four Allies and Berlin could not agree on a common policy for the whole of the country.

There is another scenario eclipsing Berlin as the seat of the Control Council which at one stage looked like being transformed into reality. By the end of the war Anglo-American forces had penetrated deep into Mecklenburg and Thuringia, into that part of Germany which, on the initiative of the British government, had been allocated to the Soviets as their zone of occupation. Now Churchill implored the new American President, Harry Truman, to stay put until the Russians could be persuaded to make certain concessions, above all not to detach the agrarian east from the west of Germany, at least for the time being. However, Truman was not willing to compromise his relationship with the Russians by introducing *Realpolitik* through the back door. When the Allies met in Berlin on 5 June 1945 to take over control of Germany General Shukov told Montgomery quite unequivocally that retirement to the zones and the establishment of the Control Commission in Berlin were 'inextricably linked'.[11] The withdrawal of Anglo-Saxon forces from Mecklenburg and Thuringia was the price the West had to pay for its part of a devastated metropolitan landscape and the shaky premiss of joint Allied responsibility for Germany as a whole. Anxious to avoid a scramble for Germany, and to come to an early settlement on the zones of occupation, the British had, in fact, tied their own hands. This was due to their reluctance to cross the Channel and the concomitant fear that the Russians might be the ones to reach the Rhine first, and would then have to withdraw to their allocated zone.[12] The British military planners could not be accused of being over-optimistic; on the contrary, the worst-case scenario more often than not seemed to them to be the most realistic assumption.

The idea of joint occupation was a farce right from the start, except that it lasted for nearly fifty years. More important, however, was the principle, closely linked to Berlin's status, of supreme Allied authority, jointly administered, for Germany as such. It was never abrogated by any of the four powers. Berlin became a *pars pro*

---

[11] Verbatim protocol, 5 June 1945, FO 371/50767/U4470. See also Winston S. Churchill, *The Second World War*, vi (London: Cassell, 1954), 520–31 ('A Fateful Decision').

[12] See the memoirs of the British negotiator in the inter-Allied European Advisory Commission, William (later Lord) Strang, *Home and Abroad*, 213.

toto and as such gained a symbolic significance which nobody could have anticipated or foreseen in 1945. According to the final proto-col of 26 July 1945, the British or north-western part of Greater Berlin comprised the districts of Rheinikendorf, Wedding, Tiergarten, Charlottenburg, Spandau, and Wilmersdorf. Four days later, at the first meeting of the Allied Control Council, the districts of Reinikendorf and Wedding were ceded to the French.[13] Thus the British sector was sandwiched between the French and American zones, and occupied the main commercial centre, including the Kurfürstendamm and a residential area.

The change of perception in the British official mind as to the role Berlin was to play reflected the general assumptions about Soviet intentions. The conference at Potsdam was still based on the concept of a unitary, though decentralized, German state with Berlin as its capital. For the time being no central German gov-ernment was to be formed. 'However, certain essential central German administrative departments, headed by State Secretaries, shall be established, particularly in the fields of finance, transport, communications, foreign trade and industry. Such departments will act under the direction of the Control Council.'[14] This was the last chance for Berlin to reassert itself as Germany's capital and to hold the country together. France was not prepared to go along with these resolutions since it had not been invited to Potsdam, and rejected the concept of a unitary German state. Elisabeth Kraus and Ann Deighton have demonstrated that Britain, too, had reser-vations about American plans to press ahead with these central departments. In fact, the British were only too happy to hide behind the French in the Control Council on this issue.[15]

Contrary to previous intentions, the British government used its presence in Berlin to gain intelligence about Soviet intentions rather than to commit itself to any firm policy. Having designed the Control Council mechanism, the British were becoming increasingly aware that the Russsians were not playing the game by these new Club rules. Instead of co-ordinating their approach

[13] Cf. Sharp, *Wartime Alliance*, 202–8.

[14] See the Potsdam Declaration, 2 August 1945, Appendix II; Charles L. Mee, *Meeting at Potsdam* (London: André Deutsch, 1975), 322–3.

[15] Elisabeth Kraus, *Ministerien für ganz Deutschland? Der Alliierte Kontrollrat und die Frage gesamtdeutscher Zentralverwaltungen* (Munich: Oldenbourg, 1990), 86–9. See also Anne Deighton, *The Impossible Peace: Britain, the Division of Germany, and the Origins of the Cold War* (Oxford: Clarendon Press, 1993), 67–76.

with the Control Council the Soviets were eager to create *faits accomplis* in their own zone, not only by forcing the newly-founded parties into the straitjacket of a grand coalition, but also by setting up central administrations in their own zone. British officials referred to these eleven departments as a 'shadow government'.[16] It was not clear whether these authorities were only meant to operate in the Soviet zone or in the whole of Germany. It turned out that Order No. 12 of the Soviet Military Administration had been issued three days before Molotov proposed central departments for Germany at the Potsdam Conference on 30 July 1945. In London both interpretations vied for recognition. No wonder the German capital underwent a metamorphosis in British eyes: from the shining example of Allied co-operation to the Trojan Horse of Soviet influence over the whole of Germany. Heinrich Maetzke observed that Whitehall could not get away from thinking in terms of stark alternatives, not realizing that Soviet policy was also in a state of flux and that minimum goals and maximum ambitions were being pursued simultaneously.

In the course of the years 1947–8 the Western Allies abandoned all hope of a consensual policy to be implemented via the Control Council. It was now a matter of safeguarding access to Berlin and of preserving the special status of the city once it had ceased to have any practical significance as the seat of a German government under joint Allied supervision.

Access to the British parts of Berlin, as well as to the other Western sectors, proved to be the test-case for the West's determination during the Cold War, at least until the signing of the Quadripartite Protocol on Berlin in June 1972. The crucial mistake concerning transit to Berlin was made in the summer of 1944 when Whitehall decided that this question 'need not be covered by the protocol'.[17] However, the Americans perpetuated this policy of taking access for granted. When, a year later, General Shukov suggested the allocation of one road, one train-track, and a 32-kilometre-wide air corridor, Lucius D. Clay, the US Deputy Governor, rejected the offer as incompatible with Allied rights of free movement in Germany.[18]

---

[16] Heinrich Maetzke, *Der Union Jack in Berlin: Das britische Foreign Office, die SBZ und die Formulierung britischer Deutschlandpolitik 1945/47* (Constance: Universitäts-Verlag, 1996), 40–4.

[17] Minutes of a FO meeting, 4 July 1944, FO 371/40648/U6259, quoted in Kettenacker, *Krieg zur Friedenssicherung*, 333.

[18] John H. Backer, *Winds of History: The German Years of Lucius D. Clay* (New York: Van Nostrand Reinhold, 1983), 24.

Even though the British had devised four-power control, they were the first to abandon it when it turned out to have been based on false assumptions. When Bevin first contemplated the pros and cons of a West German state he was ready to abandon Berlin as the capital. This meant: in strategic terms the city was indefensible, from a political point of view it could all too easily become the platform for a Communist takeover. In February 1948 a Foreign Office committee did not rule out an eventual orderly evacuation 'if and when it becomes clear the Russians intend to take drastic steps to force us out'.[19]

However, the Communist coup in Czechoslovakia on 27 February hardened attitudes in the capitals of the West. Now the Western powers could not abandon Berlin without losing face and risking disillusionment in their zones of occupation. On 20 March the Russians withdrew from the Control Council. At the same time they tightened their grip on Berlin. While Lucius D. Clay, by then American Military Governor, was making plans to force an armed convoy through the Russian checkpoint, General Robertson was still thinking of an undramatic solution that 'would get our trains running without too much loss of face'.[20] He was not pleading, though, for appeasement at all costs. In the event of Soviet intimidation prompt action could be expected. When a Soviet fighter strafed a BEA passenger aeroplane, Robertson and Clay at once ordered fighter protection for all British and American planes. At the time it was generally believed that this show of force kept the air corridor open at the height of the blockade. According to David Williamson's biography, the idea of supplying by air the whole population of the Western sectors was first suggested to Brian Robertson by Air Commodore Waite, who led the inquiry into the air incident.[21] They both went to see Clay, who agreed to the airlift as a temporary measure which would be acceptable to the doves in Washington. What is interesting about the airlift is not so

[19] Resumé of Discussions in the German Section of the FO, 17 Feb. 1948, FO 371/70489. Quoted by David Williamson, *A Most Diplomatic General: The Life of General Lord Robertson of Oakridge* (London: Brassey's, 1996), 118.

[20] Quoted ibid. 120.

[21] Cf. ibid. 127. For the British stance on the Berlin blockade see also: Michael Bell, 'Die Blockade Berlins—Konfrontation der Alliierten in Deutschland', in Josef Foschepoth (ed.), *Kalter Krieg und Deutsche Frage: Deutschland im Widerstreit der Mächte 1945–1952* (Göttingen: Vandenhoeck & Ruprecht, 1985), 217–39. For the technical achievement see now John Provan, *Big Lift: Die Berliner Luftbrücke* (Bremen: Edition Temmen, 1998).

much the technical achievement but the observation that the top-ranking military, both in London and Washington, were inclined to think that it would not work, while the politicians saw no alternative but to attempt the impossible. Montgomery, for instance, pointed out that the bulk of the electricity supply was in the Russian sector. Cutting supply lines would stop factories and lead to mass unemployment. 'The Germans might well begin to ask us to go.'[22] The Pentagon was equally defeatist. However, Bevin, the British Foreign Secretary, minuted on a departmental paper on the situation in Berlin of 19 March: 'We must stay.' Now under pressure, a withdrawal was just not on. The mild-mannered Lord Pakenham, in charge of German matters in London, stressed the moral obligation: 'the special responsibility for defending them [that is, the citizens of Berlin] from external aggression and persecution'. His appeal reinforced Bevin's attitude. On 4 May he announced in the House of Commons: 'We are in Berlin as of right and it is our intention to stay there.' General Robertson on the spot was less outspoken. His advice was most diplomatic: 'Simply say nothing and stay put', in other words, to hold out as long as possible, but without any further pledge.

For some time the West had been embarking on a policy of state-building in the Western zones. The Russians interpreted this as a clear violation of the Potsdam Agreement. The blockade of Berlin was meant to prevent this, as was pointed out to the Western Allies on many occasions. However, there was a certain degree of uncertainty as to whether Stalin wished to force the West back to the negotiating table or to drive the Allies out of Berlin altogether in order to consolidate his own zone in a similar fashion. The dilemma was that both alternatives appeared to be unacceptable to the two Anglo-Saxon powers, since they risked endangering their whole political strategy in western Europe.

As an act of defiance the Berlin Airlift turned out to be the most spectacular propaganda coup the Allies could conceive of. It gave a boost to German morale at the height of the Cold War, and within a few weeks the occupying powers were perceived as Germany's 'Schutzmächte'. It was now less likely that the Germans in the Western zones would ever fall for the lures of the Socialist Unity

---

[22] For this and further quotations see Williamson, *General Lord Robertson*, 122–6.

Party. In this situation General Sir Brian Robertson, who had been Commander-in-Chief of the British zone since 1 November 1947, came forward with his own plan for solving the German question. He felt that the Allied position in Berlin was not tenable in the long run. It might also have hurt his pride that the RAF was clearly the junior partner to the American Air Force in the whole operation to keep the Western sectors supplied by air.[23] The British managed to contribute one quarter of the daily deliveries deemed necessary to sustain the city. Robertson believed that a political settlement was unavoidable unless the West was prepared to go to war over Berlin. He suggested a new approach, by which 'faces all round are saved'. His central idea was the withdrawal of all Allied troops into given frontier areas, leaving Berlin and the main part of Germany to a single central government.[24] He thought that a German government had a fair chance of securing its political independence. He was aware that the Germans in the Western zones, left to themselves, would never opt for Communism, not even in order to regain their Eastern territories. However, he could not persuade officials at the Foreign Office who dissected his ideas. Rapallo had not been forgotten: Germany, though itself not a threat to world peace any longer, would, in combination with Russia, unsettle the balance of power and 'could be a mortal danger'.[25] Precisely because the British had set great store by ruling Germany via Berlin, they were now certain that the Russians would try the same approach. 'A government in Berlin such as General Robertson plans, would come, in fact, if established in anything like present circumstances, inevitably under Soviet control.'[26]

It is interesting to note that several months later George Kennan was to develop a similar plan which met with the same negative

---

[23] As to the still substantial British contribution ('Operation Plainfare'), see Provan, *Big Lift*, 106–29.

[24] Cf. Rolf Steininger, 'Wie die Teilung Deutschlands verhindert werden sollte: Der Robertson-Plan aus dem Jahre 1948', *Militärgeschichtliche Mitteilungen*, 33 (1983), 49–90. See also Lothar Kettenacker, 'Ein Axiom europäischer Politik: Kein neutrales Deutschland', in Frank Otto and Thilo Schulz (eds.), *Großbritannien und Deutschland: Gesellschaftliche, kulturelle und politische Beziehungen im 19. und 20. Jahrhundert. Festschrift für Bernd-Jürgen Wendt zu seinem 65. Geburtstag*, Historische Forschungen 44 (Rheinfelden: Schäuble, 1999), 161–76.

[25] Ivone Kirkpatrick (later High Commissioner for the Federal Republic), 25 Nov. 1948, FO 371/70603/C10710, quoted by Steininger, 'Wie die Teilung Deutschlands verhindert werden sollte', 83 f.

[26] Patrick Dean, 19 June 1948, FO 371/70501/C5540, quoted ibid.

response in Washington. In Kennan's plan Berlin figured as the seat of a provisional German government emanating from free elections. The occupation forces would withdraw to garrison quarters at the periphery of Germany.[27] George Kennan was head of the State Department Planning Staff and it is more than likely that he had knowledge of General Robertson's July memorandum. However, the points for a separate West German state were set, a course had been mapped out, and nobody was to stop this development, neither Stalin nor any clever general or diplomat in the West. And Berlin was not to be the train's destination.

The future of Berlin could never be fully separated from the question of German unification: any lasting settlement of both these issues was a matter for the Four Allies. Ever since Stalin tempted the West with the prospect of free elections in his diplomatic offensive of 1952, it has generally been assumed that neutrality was the condition *sine qua non* for Moscow's consent to German unification. For a last time the Soviet government tried to regain the political initiative and, as it were, the territory lost since Potsdam, by offering free elections and the prospect of a reunified country on the basis of armed neutrality. Was Stalin's chalice poisoned or not? His offer triggered off a heated debate as to whether Adenauer deliberately ignored the last chance to liberate East Germany.[28] Again the British feared that an all-German government run from Berlin would be tempted to return to the bad old ways of power-politics. They were much relieved that Adenauer would not deviate from his course of integrating the Federal Republic into the Western alliance.

In the 1950s it became all too obvious that the division of Germany and that of Europe into opposing camps were inextricably linked. But nobody in the West was prepared to allow for an unfettered and united Germany in the middle of Europe, except for one person: Winston S. Churchill. After Stalin's death he saw a chance to end the Cold War and he was eager to grasp it in order to supplement his reputation as a warlord with that of a peacemaker. His grand design, outlined in his House of Commons

---

[27] Cf. George F. Kennan, *Memoirs 1925–1950* (London: Hutchinson, 1968), 418–19, as well as FRUS 1948/II, pp. 1324–38; also most recently, Alexander Gallus, *Die Neutralisten: Verfechter eines vereinten Deutschland zwischen Ost und West 1945–1990* (Düsseldorf: Droste, 2001).

[28] See Rolf Steininger, *The German Question: The Stalin Note of 1952 and the Problem of Reunification* (New York: Columbia University Press, 1990), 1–20.

speech of 11 May 1953, addressed the Soviet Union's security concerns and accepted the possibility of German neutrality.[29] The British Prime Minister overestimated his own and Britain's standing in the world. The old man had to be talked out of his plan by both his own Foreign Office and the Eisenhower administration.[30] He was told that a neutral Germany was bound to be at the mercy of the Soviet Union, which had strengthened its bargaining position by holding out hopes for a renegotiation of the Eastern border. While Churchill had referred to the Locarno Treaty when Britain was still one of the leading peacemakers, his officials conjured up the ghost of Rapallo. The idea of a German–Russian *rapprochement* without the West's blessing came to haunt Whitehall again in 1989. Diplomatic initiatives leading to German neutrality would have meant having 'created by our own action the most deadly danger to our security and to that of the world'.[31] For once Adenauer could not have agreed more with the political assessment of British diplomats.

The uprising in East Berlin on 16–17 June 1953 put a definitive stop to Churchill's aspirations. It proved beyond doubt that Moscow was not prepared to accept political self-determination or to abandon the Stalinist regime in East Berlin, the cornerstone of its satellite empire. Churchill tried to play down the significance of the revolt and gave full support, though not in public, to the Soviet authorities' brutal intervention: they were quite within their legal rights as the occupying power to restore law and order. The Prime Minister objected explicitly to the wording of the protest note sent by the three Western Commanders in Berlin, which referred to 'irresponsible recourse to military force'.[32] There was agreement amongst British observers that the Red Army had 'acted with marked restraint and moderation'.[33] They nevertheless backed the

---

[29] Parl. Debates, House of Commons, vol. 515, cols. 883–98.

[30] See Klaus Larres, *Politik der Illusionen* (Göttingen: Vandenhoeck & Ruprecht, 1995), 133–54.

[31] Memo by Frank Roberts to William Strang ('A united, neutralised Germany'), 19 May 1953, FO 371/103660/C1016.

[32] Published in Royal Institute of International Affairs (ed.), *Documents on International Affairs*, vol. 1953, p. 159.

[33] Ward to FO, 20 June 1953, PRO: PREM 11/673. For the vast literature on the rising, see Larres, *Politik der Illusionen*, 172–3, n. 192. See, in particular, Gerhard Beier, *Wir wollen freie Menschen sein* (Frankfurt am Main: Büchergilde Gutenberg, 1993), and Armin Mitter and Stefan Wolle, *Untergang auf Raten: Unbekannte Kapitel der DDR-Geschichte* (Munich: Bertelsmann, 1993).

decision by the three Western Commanders to express their concern, in view of German and American opinion. Ian Kirkpatrick, the British High Commissioner, actually felt the need to enlighten his American colleagues about the wisdom of keeping their own counsel. 'The Germans were a hysterical people, rioting was contagious and if we deliberately inflamed passion for propaganda purposes we might one day find the Germans using violence to express disapproval of our own policy.'[34] Some such comments may well have been made behind closed doors in 1989. They were significant for the over-cautious British approach to the Berlin question: sticking to the legality of four-power occupation and not causing the Soviet government any trouble.

The second Berlin crisis, ten years later, was less dramatic but more significant in the context of Anglo-German relations. As a member of NATO and the European Economic Community, the Federal Republic had been fully integrated into the West. Since 1954 the Western Allies had been pledged to support German unification by peaceful means. Nikita Khrushchev's ultimatum of November 1958 was judged to be the first serious test of British resolution and Macmillan's Britain was found wanting. It was during the second Berlin crisis that Britain gained a reputation for being an 'appeaser', an 'unsicherer Kantonist', as the Germans say. On 20 November 1958 the Soviet ambassador to Bonn informed the Chancellor that the Soviet government was about to 'liquidate the Occupation Statute concerning Berlin'.[35] At the request of Adenauer, Macmillan sent a telegram to Khrushchev saying: 'The British government has every intention of upholding their rights in Berlin which are soundly based.'[36] Moscow responded with a note of 27 November to the three Allied powers and the Federal government, confirming its plans in more threatening language and giving a time-limit of six months. West Berlin was offered the status of a demilitarized free city. Later the Western Allies were told that the Soviet government was determined to conclude a separate peace treaty with the GDR. These are the bare facts which triggered off the second Berlin crisis.

---

[34] Kirkpatrick to Roberts, 25 June 1953, FO 371/10985/CW 10715/5, quoted by Larres, *Politik der Illusionen*, 177, n. 205.

[35] Harold Macmillan, *Riding the Storm: 1956–1959* (London: Macmillan, 1971), 571–2.

[36] Macmillan to Khrushchev, 22 Nov. 1958, PRO: T 584/58, PREM 11/2503.

For the following three years the British government considered all sorts of concessions, generally at the expense of German national interests, to satisfy the Soviet Union, short of walking out of Berlin. This is more or less the conclusion reached by John Gearson in his study entitled *Harold Macmillan and the Berlin Wall Crisis 1958–1962*. It was the old story of Britain's inclination towards appeasement in a crisis situation, coupled with high-level diplomacy at the expense of others. Summing up, Gearson writes:

The British, predisposed towards compromise, quickly settled on the possibility of recognising the East German regime as a price worth paying for a Berlin settlement, to the dismay of their main allies. The debate over how to respond to Khrushchev saw little agreement, either militarily or politically, among the three allied occupying powers and the FRG, but Britain was singled out as the weakest link and accused of defeatism. This resulted from an ill-conceived decision by the Foreign Office to present the problem as a stark choice between compromising on dealing with the East German regime, or preparing for war.[37]

The British Prime Minister was desperately trying to find the transition from power to influence, only to end up exposing Britain's subordinate position *vis-à-vis* the United States. First of all, he unnerved his allies by his unwarranted visit to Moscow in the midst of the crisis. Though he returned empty-handed, he had still not given up his belief in the merits of summit diplomacy. Throughout the crisis the US government, whether under Eisenhower or Kennedy, felt the need 'to press strongly upon the British our determination to stand firm' on Berlin. The Americans knew that in the last resort there was no solution to the Berlin problem short of reunification. The British Prime Minister was not so sure and was always seen to be wavering. During the ill-fated summit in Paris in May 1960 the three Western leaders discussed the Soviet proposal to give Berlin special status. Macmillan, haunted by the spectre of a hasty retreat from the city, suggested: 'A free city under the United Nations might not be such a terrible thing. It was not like agreeing to annihilate West Berlin.' He failed to see that the withdrawal of the Western forces would seriously impair the security of West Berlin. On this occasion Eisenhower reminded the British that he had pressed for a new German capital at the end of

---

[37] John P. S. Gearson, *Harold Macmillan and the Berlin Wall Crisis, 1958–62: The Limits of Interests and Force* (London: Macmillan, 1998), 33.

the war but had been overruled.[38] It was the British in the first
instance who had conceived of the idea of a special Berlin zone,
without now being prepared to shoulder the consequences once
the original plans for amicable four-power control from the centre
had gone awry. During the last leg of the crisis Macmillan was
opposed to Kennedy's military build-up and was therefore not
prepared to enter into contingency planning. Among the Western
Allies the impression prevailed that Britain was certainly not
willing to go to war over Berlin. No doubt the failure to secure
Adenauer's support for Britain's plans for Europe, that is, a free
trade area in preference to a more regulated common market, did
not help to inspire friendly feelings towards the West Germans'
refusal to recognize the 'bastard state' in the East.[39]

The second Berlin crisis came to a conclusion with the erection
of the Wall in August 1961 or the closing of the sector boundary, as
British officials preferred to call it, thereby, of course, playing down
the importance of this move by a government which they did not
recognize. Though not anticipated at the time, this closing of the
last gap was regarded by the British as an inevitable measure to
stop the flood of refugees which threatened the East German economy. Christopher Steel was surprised that it had taken the GDR so
long to take action.[40] The protest by the Western Allies, who were
only concerned with the security of West Berlin, was a mere for-
mality. Had they known at the time that the crisis was over to all
intents and purposes they would have been even more relieved
than they actually were. Nikita Khrushchev had deferred his ultimatum so many times that it was by no means clear whether the
last deadline was still to be taken seriously. As we know today, high-
level negotiations petered out in fruitless exchanges and the Berlin
question was pursued at a lower level, that is, between the West
Berlin senate and the GDR, only to evolve, *peu à peu*, or rather by
a 'Politik der kleinen Schritte', into *Ostpolitik*. That the focus of
the Cold War had to some extent shifted away from Berlin to
other areas was not yet clear. For the West, Berlin remained a
potentially explosive spot, either because the Soviets might decide

---

[38] Statements by the Prime Minister and Eisenhower at the Elysée, 15 May 1960, PREM
11/2992.

[39] See the essay by Martin Schaad in this volume.

[40] Steel to Foreign Office, 14 Aug. 1961, FO 371/160509. Cf. also Gearson, *Harold
Macmillan*, 184.

to turn the screw, or because some unforeseen incident could get out of control.

By the early 1960s a certain pattern of the Allied presence had evolved. The duties of each of the Allied forces were similar. They all carried out border patrols and mounted guard at the head-quarters of the Allied Kommandantura. British and American planes also made routine flights along the length of the Wall. The Western Allies and Soviet soldiers shared the task of guarding the sole inmate of West Berlin's Spandau Prison, Hitler's deputy Rudolf Hess. Altogether the Western Allies maintained about 12,000 troops in West Berlin, half of them American. The central British garrison was located in the buildings of the former German 'Sportforum' near the Olympic Stadium.[41] As a rule three infantry batallions, each with four armoured vehicles, were on duty for a 'tour' of two years. They had the support of 14 chieftain tanks. After 1953 the Allies had no fighter planes stationed in Berlin.

Not surprisingly, it was another minor Berlin crisis which, in the end, led to a final settlement. Walter Ulbricht strongly objected to the election of the Federal President taking place in West Berlin in the spring of 1969. Bonn was only prepared to opt for another venue if the Soviet government would enter into negotiations to reach a definite agreement on access to Berlin. William E. Griffith, the foremost American expert on *Ostpolitik*, points to the Ussuri incident on 2 March 1969, along the Chinese–Soviet border, which predisposed Moscow to seek an accord with the West over Berlin.[42] Even before the new government of Willy Brandt and Walter Scheel was sworn in, Moscow responded positively to ini-tiatives by the Western powers on 7–8 August regarding talks designed to remove points of friction with the GDR and to prevent further crises over Berlin. What worried the West was that the GDR was increasingly left in control of access to West Berlin, thus eroding four-power responsibility. The election results of 28 September 1969 were a great boost to détente. On 16 December the three Western ambassadors made the next move. A week earl-ier negotiations between the Federal and the Soviet governments on a declaration renouncing the use of force had begun in earnest.

---

[41] Cf. Udo Wetzlaugk, *Die Alliierten in Berlin* (Berlin: Berlin-Verlag, 1988), 132–3.
[42] William E. Griffith, *The Ostpolitik of the Federal Republic of Germany* (Cambridge, Mass.: MIT Press, 1978), 166.

Henceforth the following lines of high-level communication were pursued in parallel, requiring close co-ordination: the West was mainly interested in a binding agreement on West Berlin, the Soviet government was striving for recognition of the post-war order, including the GDR and the Oder–Neiße line. Because of the many technical matters which had to be sorted out between the two German governments, timing was all-important. This was not lost on Allied, especially British diplomats, who tried to synchronize their moves with Bonn as best they could. The British ambassador in Moscow assumed that all these agreements, once reached by a European Security Conference, served as 'a sort of substitute Peace Treaty'. Brandt, he felt, was 'the best West German chancellor that the Soviet Union can expect for a long time to come'.[43] The GDR, though desirous of diplomatic recognition, disliked any settlement of the Berlin issue which would guarantee the city's survival as a citadel of the West. But that was the price of international recognition and it was imposed by Big Brother in Moscow.

During the four-power discussions on Berlin Britain's loyalty and constructive co-operation with the other two Western powers in the interests of the Federal Republic were never in doubt, with none of the posturing as mediator between the two superpowers that had characterized Macmillan's unfortunate diplomacy during the second Berlin crisis. Now, of course, Bonn was ready to make the very same concessions of its own accord as the British had suggested a decade earlier, such as recognition of the GDR and Poland's western border in exchange for guarantees of Western rights in, and Bonn's links to, West Berlin. Moreover, the British were not faced with unilateral threats of a nuclear holocaust, which would expose them to the other Allies as natural-born appeasers. On the contrary, now they seemed to be less enthusiastic about détente in general than the Federal government. On 27 October 1970 Sir Alec Douglas-Home and Mr Gromyko discussed the linkage between Bonn's *Ostpolitik* and the future of Berlin. 'The British Government', Sir Alec explained, 'were interested in a more tolerable life for the West Berliners, and especially in access questions.'[44] The British Foreign Secretary stressed that 'the three

---

[43] Letter from Sir Duncan Wilson, 3 July 1970, published in *Documents on British Policy Overseas*, series III, vol. i: *Britain and the Soviet Union, 1968–1972* (London: The Stationery Office, 1997), 244.

[44] Record of conversation, 27 Oct. 1970, published ibid. 269.

Western Allies governed the city, and not the Federal government'. This was the agreed Western position and it was only in this way that the GDR could be kept at bay. Yet one can also detect a certain pride at being on a par with the superpowers as one of the four in control of the former Reich's capital. The prestige accruing from this position was not unlike British membership of the United Nations Security Council. Be that as it may, the British did not deviate from the joint Western approach. However, whatever the legal situation, the Foreign Office was not fooled as to who really ruled West Berlin. Diplomats knew that the Federal presence in the city, including representation abroad, was crucial for West Berlin's survival, provided that, as Sir Duncan Wilson put it, 'the façade of West Berlin's "independent status" is preserved'.[45] The latter was a necessary optical illusion for the Russians to sell the Berlin Agreement to the East Germans who had to live with it.

Brandt left no doubt that a satisfactory outcome to the Berlin talks was a necessary precondition for Germany's détente with Moscow. NATO fell in with this demand (4 December 1970) inasmuch as it would not otherwise proceed with planning the Conference on Co-operation and Security in Europe (CSCE) which, in Russian eyes, was to sanction the Pax Sovietica in Eastern Europe. This pressure by the West included a *rapprochement* between the USA and China through ping-pong diplomacy. The first stage of the Quadripartite Agreement on Berlin was signed on 3 September 1971,[46] only to come into force after completion of the negotiations between the two German states (3 June 1972). The sticking point had been the notion of what constituted Berlin, which was then described as 'the relevant area'. In exchange for unimpeded access to West Berlin and recognition of non-political ties between the Federal Republic and West Berlin, the Russians received guarantees as to the political independence of the Western sectors, as well as diplomatic recognition of the GDR. Tacit acceptance of the Berlin Wall implied that the interests of the

---

[45] Letter from Sir Duncan Wilson, 9 Nov. 1970, ibid. 282.

[46] For the text of the agreement which secured access to West Berlin see *Documentation Relating to the Federal Government's Policy of Détente*, published by the Press and Information Office of the FRG (Bonn, 1978), 87–108. The final protocol was signed on 3 June 1972 bringing the previous agreement 'into force' (ibid. 109–10). In the meantime, various technical agreements between Bonn and East Berlin, as well as the West German senate and the GDR government, had been signed.

Western Allies would in fact, if not in theory, be confined to their half of the city, and not extend to Berlin as a whole.

In August 1975 the head of the British military garrison, which still styled itself 'British Military Government Berlin', described the situation in the city following the Helsinki Accord. West Berlin had not been harassed for three years and 'no dramatic change in Soviet policy was to be expected'. British officers noted that in their day-to-day contact with Soviet diplomats the latter under-lined the 'importance of avoiding tension over Berlin'.[47] Neverthe-less, the British were very alert to the 'opportunity for an ugly incident which can quickly inflame West Berlin public opinion and lead to a slanging match'. Incidents of this kind were hence-forth more likely to emanate from the Germans than from any Soviet move. Berlin's traditional role of standing ready as the capital of a reunited Germany had lost, so it seemed, much of its meaning. Was the city in danger of withering 'into provincial obscurity'? After all, Berlin seemed to have lost its claim to be the Federal Republic's capital-in-waiting. The British on the spot were somewhat sceptical about attempts by the Senate to find a new role for Berlin as 'Mittelpunkt' between East and West. As it turned out West Berlin did rather well as a meeting place, even though it was no longer the touchstone for the state of relations in Europe. Nor did the final act of the CSCE confirm 'the unsavoury truth implied in the Eastern Treaties that the division of Germany is here to stay for a very long time'. Indeed, this was the impres-sion conveyed: 'Non-Germans will claim that this is obvious to all but the most obtuse.'

No doubt Bonn's *Ostpolitik* could be, and was, interpreted as the final seal on the division of Germany. However, Berlin's legal sta-tus, its geographical location, and the miserable Wall dividing the city, were constant reminders that there was something manifestly absurd in the central European *status quo*. The cunning of history is very rarely anticipated by men. It was by recognizing the post-war realities that it was possible to overcome them in the end.

With the fall of the Wall on 9 November 1989, and Chancellor Kohl's Ten-Point Plan less than three weeks later (28 November),

---

[47] Major-General D. W. Scott-Barrett to Mr Julian Bullard (Bonn), 15 Aug. 1975, pub-lished in *Documents on British Policy Overseas*, series III, vol. ii: *The Conference on Security and Cooperation in Europe, 1972–1975* (London: The Stationery Office, 1997), 470–4.

German unity was back on the international agenda.[48] It was a matter of crisis management, unrelated to previous Berlin crises, which had been deliberately provoked. Now it was a groundswell caused by a flood of refugees from the GDR which could at best be controlled, but not stopped, by diplomatic means. In the end even attempts by the British Prime Minister to slow down this process proved futile. Margaret Thatcher knew how to control her Cabinet, but was totally powerless in the face of mass demonstrations in the streets of East Germany. When she failed to put a brake on the German 'juggernaut'[49] by seeking to involve first the thirty-five nations of the Helsinki Forum, then the French President, she put her faith in the Four Powers who governed Berlin and as such were responsible for Germany as a whole. She therefore welcomed the Soviet initiative to convene a meeting of the ambassadors of the Four Powers, the first for eighteen years, in the building of the Allied Control Council. While the Soviet ambassador, Kotschemassov, hoped to enlarge the agenda and discuss the further development of the two German states, the three representatives of the Western Allies insisted on confining the talks to Berlin, on the basis of the Quadripartite Agreement.[50] Clearly the Soviet government had hoped to install a 'four plus zero' (that is, the four Allies and no German government) process to deal with the German question in more or less the same way as during the post-war conferences. It is probably not unfair to suggest that Margaret Thatcher would have been happy to go along with this approach, if only the Americans had let her. The US ambassador Vernon Walters had been in the chair and knew how to direct the discussion, the details of which were communicated to Bonn by the French ambassador, Serge Boidevaix. Sir Christopher Mallaby had no choice but to toe the line. In any case he was probably briefed not by Downing Street but by the Foreign Office, which was more sympathetic to German sensitivities. The subsequent photo-call of the four ambassadors created a bad impression in the German media. Hans-Dietrich Genscher was particularly upset about this meeting and made sure that there would be no repeat performance. At a NATO meeting a

---

[48] Helmut Kohl, *Ich wollte die Einheit*, based on interviews conducted by Kai Diekmann and Ralph Georg Reuth (Berlin: Propyläen, 1996), 157–211.

[49] Margaret Thatcher, *The Downing Street Years* (London: HarperCollins, 1993), 797.

[50] Wjatscheslaw Kotschemassov, *Meine letzte Mission: Fakten, Erinnerungen, Überlegungen* (Berlin: Dietz, 1994), 196–8.

couple of days later in Brussels he told his colleagues in no uncertain terms that this kind of discrimination was incompatible with German membership of the alliance and of the European Community. According to Genscher's memoirs, James Baker took his hands and said: 'Hans-Dietrich, we have got your message.'[51] Henceforth the official line of the *Auswärtige Amt* was 'no special status for Germany, nor singularization or discrimination'.

In spite of the unease it caused, the Berlin meeting of the Four Powers proved to be a blessing in disguise. It had now become obvious that some mechanism had to be designed in order to address the legitimate concerns of the Four Powers, which were indeed responsible for Germany as a whole. According to Philip Zelikow and Condoleezza Rice, authors of the most comprehensive study of the diplomatic process, the crucial formula 'two plus four' had first been proposed by two of James Baker's advisers. The President's advisers in the National Security Council were more in favour of *de facto* unification brought about by the two German states. However, Robert Zoellick argued persuasively that without a multilateral forum the Federal Republic would probably be obliged to work out a private deal with Moscow. If that were the case, he said, 'NATO will be dumped and will become the obstacle'.[52] For the United States Germany's continued membership of NATO had top priority and only by backing Bonn's bid for unification could the USA hope to retain Germany's loyalty and achieve this goal.

With the 'two plus four' mechanism formally agreed upon at the NATO conference in Ottawa (13 February 1990) Britain was happily back on board. While Margaret Thatcher claimed to share Washington's concern about NATO, she saw no need to speed up the diplomatic process in order to synchronize the internal and external development of unification. She would have preferred to prolong four-power control in Berlin beyond the actual fusion of the two German states. At one point she even egged on President Bush to suggest that Soviet troops be allowed to stay on indefinitely in a united Germany.[53] In her memoirs she poses as Gorbachev's

---

[51] Hans-Dietrich Genscher, *Erinnerungen* (Berin, 1995), 695–6. See also Frank Elbe and Richard Kiessler, *A Round Table with Sharp Corners: The Diplomatic Path to German Unification* (Baden-Baden: Nomos Verlagsgesellschaft, 1996).

[52] Philip Zelikow and Condoleezza Rice, *Germany Unified and Europe Transformed: A Study in Statecraft* (Cambridge, Mass.: Harvard University Press, 1995), 168.

[53] Cf. ibid. 207.

champion in Western councils: 'If all Soviet forces had to leave East Germany that would cause difficulties for Mr Gorbachev and I thought it best to allow some to stay for a transitional period without any specific terminal date.'[54] The Prime Minister pursued a policy of procrastination up to the eleventh hour. She was clearly most reluctant for Britain to give up its role as one of the four occupying powers, the last vestiges, as it were, of victory in the Second World War and great-power status. Following the Ottawa Accord, Douglas Hurd made a statement in the House of Commons which was meant to dispel the bad feelings aroused in Germany by Mrs Thatcher's stance. During the subsequent debate it was the former Labour Chancellor Denis Healey who really hit the nail on the head when he said: 'Germany of today is by far the least nationalistic of all the European powers. The one thing that could revive nationalism in Germany today would be an attempt by former occupying powers to continue acting as occupying powers.'[55]

[54] Thatcher, *Downing Street Years*, 798–9.
[55] Parl. Debates (Hansard), House of Commons, vol. 166, col. 1110 (22 Feb. 1990).

Part III

THE GERMAN QUESTION

9

Britain and the GDR in the 1960s
The Politics of Trade and Recognition by Stealth

Klaus Larres

Ever since the founding of the German Democratic Republic (GDR) in October 1949, British governments of all political persuasions refused to recognize the East German state.[1] During the first two decades of the Cold War the British Foreign Office (FO) argued that 'in the absence of a peace treaty with a unified Germany' and in view of the fact that the GDR was 'not regarded as a state, no question of recognising the German authorities there as a "government" ' arose. London was convinced that 'the German authorities in East Germany, being entirely dependent on the presence of Soviet troops . . . fail the test for recognition as a government, since they are not independent'.[2] Throughout the 1950s and 1960s Britain claimed to be adhering to the Western world's non-recognition doctrine as officially adopted by the Western foreign ministers and the Permanent Commission of the Brussels Treaty Organization in December 1949.[3] It was always emphasized that 'Her Majesty's Government consider that the Federal German Government is the only truly constitutional and legitimate government in Germany and is the only government entitled to speak for Germany in internal affairs'.[4] This would

---

[1] In December 1949 London and all other NATO states agreed to ignore the very existence of the 'artificial' East Berlin government. See *Foreign Relations of the United States* (hereafter FRUS), 1949, iii. 532; see also n. 3.

[2] Public Record Office, Kew (hereafter: PRO): FO 371/189 154/RG 1011/4, 17/2/1966. On occasion the FO even argued that recognition was not so much a policy issue 'but a question of whether certain criteria' were met. PRO: FO 371/169 212/CD 1075/3, 6/8/1963.

[3] See PRO: FO 371/76619/C 9776, 15/12/1949 (Document no. A/561, Final Version).

[4] PRO: FO 371/172 131/RG 1062/1, 13/9/1963. In April 1954 Britain, France, and the United States had already set out the Western world's strategy in public. They announced

remain Britain's official position until 1972–3 when, following the German–German Basic Treaty, paraphrased and signed in November/December 1972, the GDR became an internationally recognized state. Britain entered into diplomatic relations with the East German regime in early 1973.[5]

During the 1950s and 1960s, British policy-makers were convinced that any official or unofficial dealings with East Berlin would boost the prestige of the undemocratic and illegal regime in the Soviet zone of occupation. It was also obvious that any contacts with East Germany would be deeply resented by the West German government in Bonn which viewed itself as the only legal representative of the whole of the German people.[6] It could be assumed that once one of the allied powers recognized the GDR, many other governments all over the world would also do so, thereby strengthening the Soviet Union's dictatorial client state in eastern Germany and enabling Moscow to lay claim to an important victory in the Cold War. Thus political recognition was out of the question for decision-makers in Britain. London could not afford to endanger its friendly relations with Bonn and Washington. Moreover, particularly in the early part of the 1960s, East Germany's image remained badly tarnished by the Berlin Wall, erected in August 1961.

Still, in the late 1950s and, above all, during the 1960s, the Western world's non-recognition doctrine was gradually undermined. Largely as a result of the prolonged Berlin Crisis of 1958–63

that 'the three Governments represented in the Allied High Commission will continue to regard the Soviet Union as the responsible Power for the Soviet Zone of Germany. These Governments do not recognise the sovereignty of the East German regime which is not based on free elections, and do not intend to deal with it as a Government. They believe that this attitude will be shared by other states who, like themselves, will continue to recognise the Government of the Federal Republic as the only freely elected and legally constituted government in Germany.' Joint Declaration by the three Western Allied High Commissioners on 8 April 1954. Quoted in PRO: FO 371/189 154/RG 1011/4, 17/2/1966.

  [5] Simultaneously France entered into relations with the GDR. The United States followed suit a year later although both German states had been admitted to full membership of the United Nations on 18 September 1973.

  [6] In the course of the allied nine-power conference in London in Sept./Oct. 1954, during which a solution for the FRG's rearmament and integration with the West was found, the Western Allies also made it clear that they considered 'the Government of the Federal Republic as the only German Government freely and legitimately constituted and therefore entitled to speak for Germany as the representative of the German people in international affairs'. Quoted in PRO: FO 371/189 154/RG 1011/4, 17/2/1966. See also Michael Bothe, 'Deutschland als Rechtsproblem', in Hans-Jürgen Schröder (ed.), *Die deutsche Frage als internationales Problem* (Stuttgart: F. Steiner, 1990), 39–49.

and the fallout from the 1962 Cuban Missile Crisis, the Soviet Union succeeded in dividing the united anti-Communist and non-recognition front of the Western alliance to a considerable extent. Indeed, throughout the 1960s a certain 'creeping recognition' of the GDR in the Western hemisphere and notably in the developing and non-aligned world could be observed.[7] Not only in the political sphere but, above all, in the field of economic relations the Ulbricht regime was able to make progress towards *de facto* recognition. This was also the case as far as Britain was concerned. Thus it was in the sphere of trade relations that the GDR appears to have become increasingly accepted in Britain as a state in its own right during the 1960s.

This essay looks at the political and the complex economic relationship between Britain and the GDR from the late 1950s to the late 1960s. It asks whether Britain had in practice already recognized the GDR as a sovereign country on the world stage as a result of its increasingly intensive trade relations with East Germany during the 1960s, before it officially did so in 1973. Did British decision-makers officially subscribe to the West's non-recognition policy while in practice contributing to undermining West Germany's and the Western alliance's rigid anti-Communist policy? This essay will also briefly examine how, if at all, Britain came to the aid of the West German government in obstructing East German attempts to obtain international recognition in the 1960s. A brief survey of British–German relations in the 1950s lays the groundwork for the subsequent analysis.

The German Question and the Politics of Trade in the 1950s

As far as Britain and the Western alliance were concerned, at issue in the first half of the 1950s was not so much the recognition of a separate East German state, but the likelihood of imminent West German rearmament within the framework of the controversial European Defence Community and the possibility of German reunification on a neutral basis. The great opposition to West German rearmament in Britain, France, the FRG itself, and other

---

[7] For the expression see e.g. with reference to countries such as Ceylon, PRO: FO 371/177 933/RG 1062/10, 11, 20 and 19/2/1964; also FO 371/177 904/RG 1023/3, 19/3/1964.

Western states, meant that the West's dismissal of the Stalin note of March 1952 caused much public controversy. After all, the rejection of Moscow's proposal to conclude a peace treaty with a reunited neutral Germany equipped with only a small army seemed to offer a way of avoiding German rearmament and bringing the Cold War to an early end. Western politicians however insisted on their belief that the Stalin note was merely a Soviet ploy to prevent the Bonn Republic from rearming and integrating with the Western world.[8] With respect to Britain's German policy, Prime Minister Churchill's controversial détente initiatives between 1953 and early 1955 were even more important. They initially included a proposal for a reunified neutral Germany and a German–Soviet friendship treaty guaranteed by Great Britain. Not only Bonn and Washington but also the Foreign Office in London were strongly opposed to the Prime Minister's proposal to start negotiating with the post-Stalin leadership in the Soviet Union. This threatened to reopen the complex and controversial question within the Western world of how to deal with the German problem.[9]

Neither German reunification on a neutral basis nor recognition of a separate East German state were considered to be serious alternatives to the existing policy of supporting the development of a democratic, stable, and prosperous West Germany fully integrated with the West. Britain's political élite were fully committed to this strategy, which was eventually achieved in May 1955 when the FRG became a member of both the Western European Union (WEU) and NATO, and was given semi-sovereignty in return.[10] In

[8] See David C. Large, *Germans to the Front: West German Rearmament in the Adenauer Era* (Chapel Hill: University of North Carolina Press, 1966); Saki Dockrill, *Britain's Policy for West German Rearmament, 1950–1955* (Cambridge: Cambridge University Press, 1991); Rolf Steininger, *The German Question: The Stalin Note of 1952 and the Problem of Reunification* (New York: Columbia University Press, 1990); Gerhard Wettig, 'Stalin and German Reunification: Archival Evidence on Soviet Foreign Policy in Spring 1952', *Historical Journal*, 37 (1994), 411–19; id., *Bereitschaft zu Einheit in Freiheit? Die sowjetische Deutschland-Politik 1945–1955* (Munich: Olzog, 1999), 205 ff. For the view of the British government on the Stalin note, see PRO: PREM 11/168; FO 800/793; FO 800/777.

[9] See my book *Politik der Illusionen: Churchill, Eisenhower und die deutsche Frage 1945–1955* (Göttingen: Vandenhoeck & Ruprecht, 1995), ch. 4; and my article 'Integrating Europe or Ending the Cold War? Churchill's Post-War Foreign Policy,' *Journal of European Integration History*, 2 (1996), 15–49.

[10] See Anthony Eden, *Full Circle* (London: Cassell, 1960), 146–74; Konrad Adenauer, *Erinnerungen, 1953–55* (Stuttgart: DVA, 1966), 305 ff., 360 ff.; see also Anne Deighton, 'British–West German Relations, 1945–1972', in Klaus Larres with Elizabeth Meehan (eds.), *Uneasy Allies: British–German Relations and European Integration since 1945* (Oxford: Oxford University Press, 2000), 27–44; Spencer Mawby, *Containing Germany: Britain and the Arming of*

the same month, the Soviet Union invited the GDR to join the Warsaw Pact; two months later Soviet leader Nikita Khrushchev proclaimed his 'two-state theory' regarding the existence of two German states.[11] Moscow granted 'full sovereignty' to the GDR later in 1955 after the Kremlin had entered into diplomatic relations with the Federal Republic during Chancellor Konrad Adenauer's visit to Moscow in September 1955.[12] Still, even after these developments, which had undoubtedly deepened the division of Germany (though hardly anyone in Bonn wished to recognize this), British politicians continued to subscribe wholeheartedly to NATO's strategy of ignoring the very existence of the second German state. After all, this seemed to be important in order to show support for Adenauer's 'magnet theory' as well as for Bonn's and Washington's belief that the Hallstein Doctrine, formulated after the Chancellor's Moscow visit, and a continued 'policy of strength' would eventually bring about German unification and the integration of the whole of Germany with the West at some unspecified time in the not too distant future.[13]

Yet by the mid to late 1950s, the beginning of an indirect and informal relationship with the GDR as well as a certain mental weakening of the non-recognition doctrine could be observed in Britain and in some other countries. As far as the political sphere was concerned, Prime Minister Anthony Eden and, during the Berlin Crisis, even more clearly his successor, Harold Macmillan,

---

the Federal Republic (Basingstoke: Macmillan, 1999); Kevin Ruane, *The Rise and Fall of the European Defence Community: Anglo-American Relations and the Crisis of European Defence, 1950–55* (Basingstoke: Macmillan, 2000).

[11] In the 1960s the GDR's National People's Army (NVA) became a fully developed military force and was integrated into the Warsaw Pact's First Strategic Echelon in 1965. As early as 1964 the GDR's armed forces were equipped with nuclear-capable short-range missiles. See Hans-Joachim Spanger, *The GDR in East–West Relations*, Adelphi Papers, 240 (London: Brassey's, 1989), 14.

[12] For Adenauer's Moscow visit and further literature, see my article 'Germany and the West: The "Rapallo Factor" in German Foreign Policy from the 1950s to the 1990s', in K. Larres and P. Panayi (eds.), *The Federal Republic of Germany since 1949: Politics, Society and Economy before and after Unification* (London: Longman, 1996), 285–301.

[13] On the origins of the Hallstein Doctrine, see Wilhelm Grewe, *Rückblenden 1951–1976* (Frankfurt am Main: Propyläen, 1979), 251–62. On the policy of strength see the still useful book by Coral Bell, *Negotiation from Strength: A Study in the Politics of Power* (London: Chatto & Windus, 1962). For Adenauer's Western policy, see Anthony J. Nicholls, *The Bonn Republic: West German Democracy, 1945–1990* (London: Longman, 1997), ch. 6; Henning Köhler, *Adenauer: Eine Politische Biographie* (Frankfurt am Main: Propyläen, 1994), 553 ff.; also my article 'Konrad Adenauer (1876–1967)', in Torsten Oppelland (ed.), *Deutsche Politiker, 1949–1969: Biographische Skizzen aus Ost und West*, i (Darmstadt: WBG, 1999), 13–24.

were interested in overcoming the dangerous instability of the Cold War in Europe by achieving a *rapprochement* between East and West. The setting up of neutral zones in the middle of Europe to disengage East from West was seen as a way of reducing Cold War tension; it was also a solution viewed favourably by the Soviet Union. Such schemes, which indirectly acknowledged the reality of a divided Germany, were, however, strongly opposed by both Bonn and Washington.[14] Macmillan's ten-day visit to Moscow between 21 February and 3 March 1959, including Foreign Secretary Selwyn Lloyd's tentative declaration that Britain might be prepared to recognize the GDR, resulted in only moderate relaxation of tension in the Berlin Crisis, but it caused a severe crisis in British–West German and to some degree also in Anglo-American relations.[15] Thus for the time being this kind of thinking was buried in London and the policy of non-recognition upheld.

However, in the second half of the 1950s, unofficial British–East German trade relations were gradually entered into, and London's policy of strict non-recognition effectively deteriorated in practice. After all, the official strategy of non-recognition as agreed upon by the major Western European countries (and an American observer) in December 1949 included governmental trade relations. Entering into trade relations could easily be misunderstood and the West was adamant that neither *de jure* nor *de facto* recognition of the GDR should be extended. For the same reasons it was agreed that the GDR ought not to be allowed to join any international bodies.[16] Yet the first British–East German business deal, albeit a private one, was concluded less than four years later during the Leipzig trade fair in the autumn of 1953. Conservative MP Barnaby Drayson was responsible for negotiating such an agreement between an independent British and an East German company on behalf of the firm Dominions Export Ltd., in which

---

[14] See e.g. John van Oudenaren, *Détente in Europe: The Soviet Union and the West since 1953* (Durham, NC: Duke University Press, 1991), 24 ff., esp. 29, 46, 206, 226; John P. S. Gearson, *Harold Macmillan and the Berlin Wall Crisis, 1958–62: The Limits of Interest and Force* (Basingstoke: Macmillan, 1998), 26–30; also Michael Howard's classic *Disengagement in Europe* (Harmondsworth: Penguin Books, 1958).

[15] For the discussions during the Moscow visit, see in detail PRO: CAB 133/293, including Top Secret annex; also PREM 11/2690, 11/2716; FO 371/143433–440 and 143686–688; CAB 21/3233; PRO: FO 371/143 439/NS 1053/179, 9/3/1959; FRUS 1958–1960, vol. 7, part 2, 837–41. See also Harold Macmillan, *Riding the Storm: 1956–1959* (London: Macmillan, 1971), 592–634; Gearson, *Harold Macmillan*, 70–5.

[16] See PRO: FO 371/76619/C 9776, 15/12/1949 (Document no. A/561, Final Version).

he had a substantial private interest.[17] The Foreign Office's later conviction that the 'East Germans derive particular value from their contacts with individual Members of Parliament' proved to be fully justified.[18]

This first British–East German business deal was concluded only a few months after the East German uprising on 16 and 17 June 1953 had displayed the widespread unpopularity and fragility of the GDR system.[19] Once Walter Ulbricht had managed to overcome this crisis and, with firm Soviet support, had eliminated the opposition to his leadership from within the SED by 1957–8,[20] the East German regime made increasingly strenuous efforts to enter into trade relations with Western countries. Not only did East Berlin want to use the device of trade agreements to further the international recognition of the GDR, but more intensive trade relations with the Western world were also urgently required in view of the continued existence of economic hardship in East

[17] See PRO: FO 371/103 857/CS 1111/11, 13, Sept.–Nov. 1953; Marion Bell, 'Britain and East Germany: The Politics of Non-Recognition' (unpubl. M.Phil. thesis, University of Nottingham, 1977), 136; Bert Becker, *Die DDR und Großbritannien 1945/49 bis 1973: Politische, wirtschaftliche und kulturelle Kontakte im Zeichen der Nichtanerkennungspolitik* (Bochum: Brockmeyer, 1991), 193–4. France and, in particular, the Scandinavian nations were also busily intensifying their trade links with East Germany.

[18] See e.g. PRO: FO 371/163 695/WG 1052/17, 17/11/1960. In this memorandum by its Western Dept. the FO was, however, thinking less in terms of trade contacts than in terms of MPs helping the GDR to sponsor visits to the UK and paying too much attention to East German propaganda and making pro-GDR statements in the House of Commons. See also Henning Hoff, ' ". . . Largely the Prisoners of Dr Adenauer's Policy": Großbritannien und die DDR (1949–1973)', in Ulrich Pfeil (ed.), *Die DDR und der Westen: Transnationale Beziehungen 1949–1989* (Berlin: Ch. Links Verlag, 2001), 185–206.

[19] Moreover, in the course of the succession struggle in the Soviet Union after Stalin's death in March 1953, the sacrifice of the GDR in favour of a deal on unification and West German economic aid had been considered for a few weeks in Moscow (above all by Interior and Security Minister L. Beria). Paradoxically, the subsequent uprising put an end to this and ensured that GDR leader Walter Ulbricht would be able to remain in power. Once the widespread demonstrations in the GDR had been put down with the help of Soviet tanks and Beria had been arrested (he was executed in December 1953), the USSR convinced itself that Ulbricht's hard-line policies were needed to keep the GDR and, by implication, the other East European satellite states under control. See Elke Scherstjanoi, ' "In 14 Tagen werden Sie vielleicht keinen Staat mehr haben": Vladimir Semenov und der 17. Juni 1953', *Deutschland-Archiv*, 31 (1998), 907–37; see also my article 'Preserving Law and Order: Britain, the United States and the East German Uprising of 1953', *Twentieth Century British History*, 5 (1994), 320–50.

[20] See Martin Jänicke, *Der dritte Weg: Die antistalinistische Opposition gegen Ulbricht seit 1953* (Cologne: Neuer Deutscher Verlag, 1964); Karl Schirdewan, *Aufstand gegen Ulbricht: Im Kampf um politische Kurskorrektur, gegen stalinistische, dogmatische Politik* (Berlin: Aufbau, 1994). For a recent biography of Ulbricht, see Norbert Podewin, *Walter Ulbricht: Eine neue Biographie* (Berlin: Dietz, 1995).

Germany which had ultimately been the reason for the 1953 uprising. Between 1957 and 1959 a certain consolidation of the GDR economy was noticeable. The number of people leaving the GDR declined considerably and the general standard of living improved, with the result that food ration cards could eventually be abolished.[21] However, the GDR still needed to import many important products from West Germany and other Western countries. In fact, throughout its existence the GDR remained economically dependent on Western imports.

East Germany's improving economic situation in the late 1950s and its success in entering into informal trade contacts with a considerable number of Western countries tempted Ulbricht to exaggerate the economic potential of his state. He embarked on a course of 'catching up' with West Germany in particular, as far as industrial productivity and efficiency, and general consumption levels were concerned. The GDR leadership also misinterpreted the tendency of a large part of the East German population grudgingly to come to terms with the GDR state. In line with Ulbricht's forceful ideological crusade from 1957 to 1958, the SED believed that the time was ripe to eliminate any surviving capitalist elements by collectivizing the GDR's remaining private firms and farms. Socialism was to be firmly established within the hearts and minds of the East German people.[22] Yet this attempt backfired, as did the attempt to emulate the West German economy. Difficulties with respect to a lack of resources, insufficient workers' discipline and productivity, and the inflexibility of the GDR's bureaucracy prevented longer-term strategic economic planning. Between 1959 and 1961 industrial expansion fell from 12 to 6 per cent.[23] A severe scarcity of food and many consumer products developed, which led to renewed popular discontent and emigration to the West. Young and skilled workers in particular were attracted by the FRG's economic miracle, and these were people the East German economy could ill afford to lose. By late 1959, ten years after the founding of the GDR, almost 2.5 million people had gone to the

---

[21] See e.g. Ulrich Mählert, *Kleine Geschichte der DDR* (Munich: Beck, 1998), 86–7, 91–2.

[22] Ibid. 91–5; Hermann Weber, *Die DDR 1945–1986* (Munich: Oldenbourg, 1988), 46–8; Hermann Weber, *Geschichte der DDR*, 2nd edn. (Munich: dtv, 1986), 297–301.

[23] Weber, *Die DDR*, 60. Between 1956 and 1965 the GDR was able to run its economy only on the basis of *ad hoc* one-year plans.

West.[24] Although Ulbricht's ultimate political goal remained the reunification of a socialist Germany, the building of the Wall on 13 August 1961 seemed to be the only way to guarantee the further economic survival of the GDR.[25]

Both before and after the erection of the Wall, the British government rejected any *official* trade links with the GDR; it also remained very cautious about political and cultural contacts with East Germany.[26] In the 1950s and 1960s Britain's policy continued to be 'based on the general principle that contacts with East Germany should not be encouraged (except in certain circumstances, for trade contacts) and that all East Germans whose visits have a predominantly political character should be excluded [from visiting the UK]'.[27] Thus there were only muted objections in London to the exploitation of *private* business contacts between the independent Federation of British Industry (FBI) and its successor organization the Confederation of British Industry (CBI), and their East German counterparts. In view of increasing pressure by British industry and a number of MPs with close business links, the Macmillan government felt that it was imprudent to take too much account of West German protestations. Then, as later, Bonn claimed that its own trade with the East Germans facilitated the purchase of 'major political concessions' and substantially helped 'to humanise conditions in the Soviet zone by offers of economic benefits in exchange'. In contrast, it was argued that British and other Western trade contacts with East Berlin would 'stabilise the regime'; it was therefore 'anathema' to the Federal Republic.[28]

The Macmillan government and subsequent British governments had little sympathy for this not entirely convincing West German point of view. Not least because of Britain's increasingly

---

[24] Quoted in Weber, *Geschichte der DDR*, 325; see also Thomas Ammer, 'Stichwort: Flucht aus der DDR', *Deutschland-Archiv*, 22 (1989), 1207.

[25] See e.g. Martin McCauley, *The German Democratic Republic since 1945* (Basingstoke: Macmillan, 1983), 96–102; A. James McAdams, *Germany Divided: From the Wall to Reunification* (Princeton: Princeton University Press, 1993), 49–55; Norman Gelb, *The Berlin Wall* (London: Michael Joseph, 1986), 90 ff.; also Jochen Staadt, *Die geheime Westpolitik der SED 1960–70: Von der gesamtdeutschen Orientierung zur sozialistischen Nation* (Berlin: Akademie Verlag, 1993).

[26] For an overview regarding the cultural links between Britain and the GDR, see PRO: FO 371/163 695/WG 1052/17, 17/11/1960; and Becker, *DDR und Großbritannien*, 236 ff.

[27] PRO: ibid.

[28] PRO: FO 371/177 920, 16/10/1964. See also FO 371/ 189 250/RG 1154/10, 9/2/1966; FO 371/177 963/RG 1154/42, 29/12/1964.

difficult economic situation and its rising trade deficit with the out-side world, West Germany's flourishing inter-zonal trade with the GDR was regarded with envy in Whitehall. As early as April 1955, an East German Leipzig Fair Agency had been set up in London. In 1959 permission was given for the opening of the office of an 'independent' agency of the East German Department of Foreign Trade, KfA Ltd. (Kammer für Außenhandel), in the British capital.[29] The FBI, however, was discouraged from establishing a trade representation in either East or West Berlin.[30] The Board of Trade and the Treasury were kept well-informed about the inten-sifying contacts between the GDR and the FBI, and more often than not guided Britain's industrial umbrella organization in its dealings with the representatives of East Berlin. A member of the Board of Trade tended to be on the FBI's negotiating team with the KfA to discuss annual export and import volumes, including the lists of goods to be traded between the two countries. In addi-tion, the trade exhibitions organized by the FBI during the Leipzig spring and autumn trade fairs were subsidized by the British Government.[31] Despite the successful beginning of intensified pri-vate or semi-official trade contacts between Britain and the GDR in 1959, initially the Board of Trade proved to be inflexible as far as exports to the GDR were concerned. A major steel export deal to the value of 40 million pounds was lost when the Board refused to give a credit guarantee which would have gone beyond the KfA–FBI agreement of 1959, and of which West Germany might have disapproved.[32] There was much public criticism of this inflex-ibility and Britain's exaggerated willingness to take West Germany's wishes into consideration. By the mid-1960s this and similar cases had made some sections of British business and indus-try develop the view that the British government was in Bonn's pockets.[33]

---

[29] See on the KfA Ltd., Friedrich Eymelt, *Die Tätigkeit der DDR in den nichtkommunistischen Ländern*, v: *Großbritannien* (Bonn: DGfAP, 1970), 15–19; Bell, *Britain and East Germany*, 147 ff.

[30] PRO: FO 371/177 944/RG 1082/64, 6/7/1964.

[31] It was realized that the leakage of this information regarding the 20 per cent subsidy would make it 'extremely difficult to insist on the non-official nature of the F.B.I.'. See PRO: FO 371/163 702/CG 1861/18, 22/2/1962; also FO 371/189 308/RG 1861/9, 18/8/1966. The subsidy was discontinued in 1963.

[32] See Becker, *DDR und Großbritannien*, 222.

[33] See PRO: FO 371/183 049/RG 1054/21, 17/5/1965.

The Recognition Question and the Politics of Trade in the 1960s

During the 1960s the GDR's foreign policy consisted largely of the struggle for international recognition as an independent state. Together with the attempt to undermine the Federal Republic's contention that it possessed the sole right to represent the German nation, this became the leitmotiv of the GDR's foreign policy.[34] Both before and after the downfall of Khrushchev in 1964, the USSR strongly supported this strategy. East Berlin was, however, not merely a Soviet proxy; it also pursued its own foreign political interests, both in Europe and, perhaps especially, in the non-aligned world.[35] East Germany's activities in this context were characterized by a three-pronged approach, driven by both political and economic motives: while attempting to obtain indications of political recognition, East Berlin was above all interested in intensifying trade links with Western Europe in order to obtain a degree of recognition by the back door. After all, it was unlikely that Western countries would extend direct political recognition to the GDR in the foreseeable future; moreover, intensified trade would help to improve the GDR's economic performance and satisfy the consumer demands of the East German population. For the same reasons the GDR also pursued a deliberate strategy of entering into closer contacts with many of the non-aligned and developing states, and attempting to join international organizations. However, for reasons of space, this essay will largely focus on the East German attempts to enter into and then intensify trade links with Great Britain and to obtain political recognition.

---

[34] See Spanger, *The GDR in East–West Relations*, 11. See also e.g. Ingrid Muth, *Die DDR-Außenpolitik 1949–1972: Inhalte, Strukturen, Mechanismen* (Berlin: Ch. Links Verlag, 2000); Heiner Timmermann (ed.), *Die DDR: Politik und Ideologie als Instrument* (Berlin: Duncker & Humblot, 1999); Renate Stegmüller, *Die Westpolitik der Deutschen Demokratischen Republik von 1949–1961: Grundlagen, Strategie und Taktik in bezug auf England, Frankreich, Italien und Skandinavien* (Ph.D. thesis, University of Munich, 1976). For the years after recognition, see Benno-Eide Seibs, *Die Außenpolitik der DDR 1976–1989: Strategien und Grenzen* (Paderborn: Schöningh, 1999).

[35] Regarding the impact of Khrushchev's fall on Ulbricht's policy, which cannot be analysed here, see the analysis in PRO: FO 371/ 183 007/RG 1023/2, 15/2/1965. See also Michael J. Sodaro, *Moscow, Germany, and the West from Khrushchev to Gorbachev* (London: I. B. Tauris, 1991), 52–71. For a discussion on whether or not the GDR was merely Moscow's proxy, see Gareth Winrow, *The Foreign Policy of the GDR in Africa* (Cambridge: Cambridge University Press, 1990), 6–10.

Unlike the situation in the FRG, in the GDR a Ministry of Foreign Affairs had been set up to co-ordinate the GDR's recognition strategy immediately after the founding of the East German state in 1949. However, confronted with Bonn's Hallstein Doctrine, by the late 1950s East Berlin had been able to establish full diplomatic relations only with Communist states such as the Soviet Union, its Eastern European satellite states, Mao's China, North Korea, the Mongolian Republic, and North Vietnam. In 1957 diplomatic representatives were also exchanged with Yugoslavia (which led to West Germany's first use of the Hallstein Doctrine), although the GDR mission was not elevated to ambassadorial status until 1966, after Tito's visit to East Berlin the year before.[36]

The first real breakthrough as far as some degree of recognition of the GDR by the Western world was concerned occurred in the course of the Berlin Crisis of 1958–63 and under the impact of the 1962 Cuban Missile Crisis. It became clear that under American leadership the West was slowly moving away from wholeheartedly supporting West Germany's rigid non-recognition policy in favour of a new spirit of *rapprochement* with the Eastern bloc. In particular, it soon became clear that President John F. Kennedy's interest in embarking on a policy of détente with the USSR without further insistence on simultaneous progress in the German question would slowly weaken the West's non-recognition doctrine.[37] However, as early as Dwight D. Eisenhower's presidency, delegations from both German states were given permission for the first time ever to attend the Four Power Foreign Ministers' Conference in Geneva in May/June 1959 as advisers. This was interpreted by East Berlin and Moscow as *de facto* international recognition of Ulbricht's state.[38] Paradoxically, despite all the short-term anger expressed all

---

[36] See Rüdiger Thomas, *Modell DDR: Die kalkulierte Emanzipation*, 7th edn. (Munich: Hanser, 1981), 124–5. For an analysis of the development and importance of the Hallstein Doctrine, see Winrow, *The Foreign Policy of the GDR*, 37–42. For a table which lists the various East German commercial and diplomatic representations abroad as of June 1969, see Walter Osten, *Die Außenpolitik der DDR: Im Spannungsfeld zwischen Moskau und Bonn* (Opladen: Leske Verlag, 1969), 115–18.

[37] See e.g. John C. Ausland, *Kennedy, Khrushchev, and the Berlin–Cuba Crisis, 1961–64* (Oslo: Scandinavian University Press, 1996). This would lead to Adenauer's great disenchantment with the new American government and make him move closer to French President Charles de Gaulle. See PRO: PREM 3804, Washington telegram, no. 543, 19/2/1962. For the importance of the Cuban Crisis on the West's readiness to negotiate about an end to nuclear testing in the atmosphere, see PRO: PREM 11/3806, Minute Zulueta, 1/11/1962.

[38] See Becker, *DDR und Großbritannien*, 133–4.

over the world, the building of the Berlin Wall on 13 August 1961 also gradually led to a certain worldwide acknowledgement that the GDR was indeed a separate state with its own distinct territory and political and cultural identity.[39] As early as December 1961 the *Volkskammer*'s interparliamentary group invited an international conference of parliamentarians to Weimar in order to outline to them the necessity of the 'security measures' of August 1961. In March 1962 the GDR made known its desire to explain East Berlin's own distinctive disarmament concept to the UN disarmament conference in Geneva.[40]

With the Berlin Crisis lingering on after the building of the Wall and the Soviets 'engaging in a sort of noisy inactivity vis-à-vis the West', Britain considered taking the initiative in early 1962. Once again, the Macmillan government began toying with disengagement schemes and other 'fall-back positions' including the recognition of the GDR as a sovereign state in order to de-escalate East–West tension.[41] In a conversation with Soviet Foreign Minister Andrei Gromyko in Geneva on 21 March 1962, Foreign Secretary Lord Home referred to the GDR regime as a sovereign government and the possibility of *de facto* recognition. He told Gromyko: 'The Russians must not expect us to give *de jure* recognition to East Germany, but he could say that we did not want to upset the Government of East Germany or infringe upon their sovereignty.'[42] Most politicians and officials in London were, however, aware that the prospects for the conversion of such views into practical politics were severely limited. Apart from firm West German resistance, it was also highly questionable whether the Americans were 'prepared to go as far as we should consider acceptable in the direction of recognising the sovereignty of the D.D.R.; accepting its frontiers; restricting nuclear weapons for German forces; and so on'.[43] Still, this kind of thinking did not

---

[39] See e.g. A. James McAdams, *East Germany and Détente—Building Authority after the Wall* (Cambridge: Cambridge University Press, 1985), 10.

[40] See Becker, *DDR und Großbritannien*, 139–40; also Anita Dasbach-Malinckrodt, *Propaganda hinter der Mauer: Die Propaganda der Sowjetunion und der DDR als Werkzeug der Außenpolitik im Jahre 1961* (Stuttgart: F. Steiner, 1971).

[41] PRO: PREM 11/3805, Brief no. 1 by E. Shuckburgh, 20/6/1962. This inclination may well have been reinforced by dismay about Adenauer's failure to support strongly Britain's first application to join the European Economic Community (EEC). See Gearson, *Harold Macmillan*, 203.

[42] PRO: PREM 11/3805/IAD 410/614, 29/3/1962.

[43] PRO: PREM 11/3804, FO telegram no. 1692, 24/2/1962.

help to reverse the rapid deterioration in British–West German relations which had begun with Macmillan's Moscow trip in 1959. It continued unabated; in late September 1962 the German ambassador was told about the undesirability of a visit by the Chancellor to London with the thinly disguised excuse that 'there was always the problem of our climate at this time of the year'.[44]

Although Lord Home's sentiments regarding the GDR's sovereignty were not subsequently repeated,[45] Macmillan's trusted Private Secretary Philip de Zulueta was still arguing in November 1962 that 'much the best solution would be a tacit acceptance by both sides of the *status quo*, i.e. Soviet acceptance of the allied presence and rights in Berlin and allied acceptance of the existence of the D.D.R.'. He was hopeful that 'President Kennedy might be ready to speak frankly to Dr. Adenauer when the latter visits Washington and to tell him that he must now swallow some form of recognition of the D.D.R.'.[46] However, continued West German and American opposition to the Macmillan government's readiness to give in over Berlin and to recognize the GDR as Khrushchev requested, and also accusations that Britain was attempting to appease the Soviet Union which surfaced in the German press, prevented any serious consideration of the British proposals.[47] The gradual development of East–West détente in the aftermath of the Cuban Missile Crisis and the simultaneous disappearance of the Berlin question in Soviet policy ensured instead that the status quo of the West's official non-recognition of the GDR was maintained.

---

[44] PRO: FO 371/163 559/CG 1051/17, 20/9/1962.

[45] See e.g. PRO: PREM 3806/CG1071/233, 21/7/1962; CG 1071/240, 23/7/1962; WP 7/54, 28/9/1962; WP 7/55, 1/10/1962; also FO telegram no. 4155, 9/10/1962. However, in late 1964, Patrick Gordon Walker, the new Labour Foreign Secretary, considered raising the issue of British 'support for the Oder–Neisse line as the eventual frontier of Germany' with Schröder. It was believed that this was 'what many Germans already accept in their heart of hearts'. PRO: FO 371/177 843/RG 1081/15, 5/12/1964, 13/11/1964.

[46] PRO: PREM 11/3806, Top Secret Minute Zulueta to Macmillan, 1/11/1962. Other officials shared his reasoning. For example, Sir Christopher Steel at the Bonn Embassy wrote to the FO: 'I consider, as you know, that there is fundamentally only one direction in which a long-term *modus vivendi* over Berlin can be obtained. That is the exchange of some degree of recognition for the East German regime against new hard and fast arrangements for access, our troops of course remaining.' PRO: PREM 11/3806, Bonn telegram no. 898, 30/10/1962.

[47] For an article about British 'appeasement' in the West German magazine *Spiegel*, see for example, PRO: PREM 11/3806, Bonn telegram no. 778, 13/9/1962.

Of particular importance for the improvement of the GDR's international reputation was East Berlin's signing of the 1963 Test Ban Treaty. Accession to this international treaty was meant to be possible for any state which wished to join, but West Germany protested vehemently when the GDR, as a non-recognized state, was allowed to accede to it.[48] However, both President Kennedy and Prime Minister Macmillan were keen to de-escalate the international arms race, and, as negotiating the treaty with the Soviet Union had been difficult enough, they intended to avoid all unnecessary complications. Moreover, in order to make the Test Ban Treaty effective, both Washington and London desired 'to see the Treaty as widely applied as possible and to avoid any action which restricted its scope'.[49] Therefore they refused to heed Bonn's wishes to exclude the East German regime from signing it. Although the British Foreign Office was convinced that the West Germans were vastly exaggerating when they pointed to the danger that the GDR's signing of the Test Ban Treaty would improve the international standing of Ulbricht's regime, London made great efforts to diminish Bonn's apprehensions. But it was unlikely that the West Germans would adopt the proverbial British stiff-upper-lip attitude and 'grin and bear it'.[50] It was quickly recognized that the mere assurance that Britain would 'avoid any actions which might be construed as an act of recognition of the D.D.R.' was not sufficient to satisfy them.[51] Indeed, West German Foreign Minister Gerhard Schröder went so far as to ask Lord Home to make London's private reassurances public by writing in this vein 'to all states of the world not having diplomatic relations with the Soviet-occupied Zone'. Bonn hoped above all that both Britain and the United States would 'make it known unambiguously' that despite the signing of the Test Ban Treaty by unrecognized states, 'no treaty-like relations come into existence between them and territories they have not recognised as states'.[52]

---

[48] PRO: FO 371/169 212/CG 1075/3, 26/7/1963. The West German government based its request on a resolution passed by the Council of the Western European Union on 31 October 1962.

[49] Ibid., 1/8/1963.

[50] This advice was given a year later during similar West German concerns regarding the GDR's activities. PRO: FO 371/177 904/RG 1023/8, 17/9/1964.

[51] PRO: FO 371/169 212/CG 1075/3, 30/7/1963.

[52] Ibid., CG 1075/8, letter Schröder to Home, c.5/8/1963, unofficial translation.

In spite of misgivings about inflated West German sensitivities, London and Washington agreed to Schröder's request. Only the Federal Republic's desire to see the GDR excluded from any conference convened under the Treaty was not accepted, as Moscow 'would never agree to this'.[53] Although the Bonn government was grateful to the British for their readiness to make their views on the recognition question clear to the world, the West Germans still continued 'making a fuss over East German accession to the Nuclear Test Ban Treaty'.[54] Above all, Bonn feared the effect of the GDR's accession to the Treaty 'on a number of neutralist States' who might soon begin talking about East Berlin's 'national sovereignty'.[55] Still, there was not much else the British were prepared to do. The West Germans had to be content with the fact that the two Western powers would neither permit the East German signature on their copy of the treaty, nor be prepared to receive the instruments of ratification or accession from the GDR. They would, however, accept notification from the Soviet government that such instruments and the GDR signature had been obtained in Moscow. Moreover, London and Washington would assume that East Berlin had not entered into a treaty relationship with the West but was bound to observe the Test Ban Treaty because of its contractual relationship with the Soviet Union. It was generally concluded in London that the Ulbricht regime was so interested in signing this as well as other international agreements that it could be assumed that 'having purported to accede, they would presumably act accordingly in any event, in order to bolster their claim to appear as a responsible government'. After all, East Berlin would 'maintain that claim irrespective of whether we accept it or not'.[56]

Participation in the 1959 Geneva Conference and the signing of the Test Ban Treaty must both be regarded as important political victories for Ulbricht's recognition policy, and as severe defeats for the outgoing West German Chancellor Adenauer. Encouraged by these developments, the GDR from late 1963 embarked upon an

---

[53] PRO: FO 371/169 212/ CG 1075/3, 1/8/1963; /8, 6/8/1963; see also for example /3, FO telegrams nos. 194 and 195, 6/8/1963.

[54] PRO: FO 371/172 132/RG 1071/8, 3/11/1963.

[55] PRO: FO 371/169 212/CG 1075/15, 9/8/1963. The term 'neutralist' states tended to be used in Cold War terminology when referring to the 'non-aligned' world.

[56] PRO: FO 371/183 058/RG 1075/2, 8/4/1965. See also for example FO 371/169 212/CG 1075/3, 30/7/1963.

enhanced recognition campaign which continued to be character-ized by the three-pronged approach outlined above.[57] The East German regime was so confident of its newly gained international acceptance and the—as it seemed at the time—somewhat greater identification of the East German people with their state that it was prepared to enter into an agreement with the West Berlin Senate.[58] In late 1963, politicians from East and West Berlin suc-ceeded in working out a deal to issue cross-border passes which, for the first time since the erection of the Wall, would allow West Berliners to visit their relatives in the Eastern part of the city at Christmas 1963. Subsequently, agreements for 1964 and Easter 1965 and 1966 were also negotiated. Not surprisingly, Ulbricht did his best to proclaim these deals as yet another sign of the GDR's international recognition.[59] Neither the government in Bonn nor the British Foreign Office was entirely happy about this develop-ment. It looked as if the agreements negotiated between the West Berlin Senate, led by Willy Brandt, and the East Germans had been 'to the partial detriment' of West Germany's own 'strictly legal position' regarding non-recognition and the Hallstein Doctrine. They believed Ulbricht would be quick to exploit the sit-uation by 'talking in this way to some of the neutrals to persuade them that they also need not feel too inhibited by legal niceties of the "Hallstein Doctrine" '.[60] It might also strengthen the regime internally. Only a year later British diplomats perceived that the East Germans had successfully developed 'a national conscious-ness of their own'. It was concluded that there were 'bound to be increasing contacts' with the East Germans, in both the political and economic sphere.[61]

Indeed, throughout the 1960s the GDR leadership did not grow tired of attempting to intensify its trade contacts with the Western world. Improving the East German economy was, after all, the precondition for turning the GDR into a stable state. It was, there-fore, not surprising that East Berlin began waging a campaign to upgrade its trade missions, which had been established with most

[57] See PRO: FO 371/177 893/RG 1011/1, 7/2/1964.

[58] This agreement was most controversial within the Bonn government. See W. Brandt, *My Life in Politics* (New York: Viking, 1992), 67–71.

[59] See above all PRO: FO 371/172 199 (1963); also Peter Bender, *Neue Ostpolitik: Vom Mauerbau bis zum Moskauer Vertrag*, 2nd edn. (Munich: dtv, 1989), 126–9, 222–8.

[60] PRO: FO 371/177 942/RG 1076/6, 29/2/1964.

[61] PRO: FO 371/177 920, 16/10/1964.

Western countries during the 1950s, to consular or even ambassadorial status.[62] As early as February 1962, only a few months after the building of the Wall, East Berlin proposed setting up consular offices in West European capitals; an idea which was, however, angrily rejected.[63]

For Western states to enter into private or even semi-official trade relations with the GDR appeared to be a cautious movement towards *de facto* recognition of the GDR. These developments were certainly a far cry from the British Foreign Office's conviction as expressed in a 1949 memorandum that Britain should not 'allow the new [East German] government to establish itself too strongly'. For this would only deepen 'the present administrative division' and 'make the eventual task of winning over the whole of Germany' to the West 'much more difficult'.[64] The dilution of the original non-recognition doctrine was closely observed in East Berlin. Accordingly, in the 1960s Ulbricht believed that the GDR's endeavours to overcome its international isolation were most likely to succeed with Britain, a country whose post-war economic situation was less than satisfactory.[65] This mirrored the British government's belief that it was regarded as a soft target for East German propaganda. The GDR appeared to have embarked on increased propaganda activities in Britain in order to obtain 'popular recognition as a means of pressure for ultimate official recognition'.[66]

[62] For example, by 1955 trade missions which had no diplomatic status had been established with France, Austria, Belgium, the Netherlands, Italy, and the Scandinavian nations. However, Finland insisted on putting its relations with both German states on the basis of trade missions. As far as the Western world was concerned, initially the GDR attempted above all to enter into closer relations with France and the Scandinavian countries. In 1957 it had already encouraged closer co-operation among the Baltic Sea countries by means of bi- and multilateral commercial and cultural agreements to ensure that the Baltic Sea would remain an 'ocean of peace'. Ulbricht wished to obtain indications of recognition from as many states as possible. See Thomas, *Modell DDR*, 126–7; also Friedrich Eymelt, *Die Tätigkeit der DDR in den nichtkommunistischen Ländern*, ii: *Die Nordischen Staaten* (Bonn: DGfA, 1970), 4 ff.

[63] See Becker, *DDR und Großbritannien*, 139.

[64] PRO: FO 371/76 617/C 8047, undated, *c.*18/10/1949.

[65] However, France was equally interested in intensifying its trade relationship and—because of de Gaulle's striving for greater independence from Washington—its political relations with East Berlin. See for a good overview, Walter Schütze, 'Westeuropa: Frankreich', in Hans-Adolf Jacobson *et al.* (eds.), *Drei Jahrzehnte Außenpolitik der DDR: Bestimmungsfaktoren, Instrumente, Aktionsfelder* (Munich: Oldenbourg, 1979), 489–500.

[66] PRO: FO 371/163 695/WG 1052/17, 17/11/1960; see also already FO 371/76 618/C 8496, copy of article in GDR paper *Neue Zeit*, 4/11/1949.

The Foreign Office was convinced that 'a combination of circumstances' made Britain a 'particularly favourable ground' for the effectiveness of East German propaganda. There existed a 'deep-seated mistrust of a strong Germany in general and of the Federal Republic in particular'; British industry was keen to trade with the GDR; and there were close contacts between some British Members of Parliament 'on both sides of the House' and representatives of the East German regime. It was also believed without undue modesty that the 'liberality of our rules regarding the admission of foreigners' played into the hands of the GDR.[67]

The GDR leadership indeed had reason to believe that it might be possible to exploit the resentment which existed in London against a booming West Germany and its economic miracle. After all, throughout the decade a number of British parliamentarians of all political persuasions kept reminding the government of the day of the huge difference in trade volume with the GDR between West Germany and Britain. They also tended to indicate their agreement with East German propaganda by expressing themselves in favour of recognizing the GDR to boost British–East German trade relations.[68]

Although the assumption that recognition would lead to improved trade relations was disputed by the Foreign Office,[69] during the 1960s British politicians and officials were tempted to exploit the GDR's economic difficulties for the benefit of their own country. In particular, this was the case in the early to mid 1960s when East Berlin found it difficult to obtain large credits from Moscow and Bonn to purchase coal, chemicals, and other urgently required raw materials. Furthermore, it proved impossible for the GDR to replace West German raw materials with Soviet or

[67] Ibid. This document also contains a list of UK organizations keen to promote the GDR as well as a list of East Berlin's cultural activities in the UK. In particular, the UK authorities disliked the distribution of East German propaganda material which largely consisted of either books and pamphlets or films. Also the display of the GDR flag, the playing of East Berlin's national anthem, and the use of the title 'GDR' during sporting events and trade exhibitions was resented. See PRO: FO 371/183 049/RG 1054/8, 21, 23, 28 (Feb.–May 1965).

[68] See David Childs, 'British Labour and Ulbricht's State: The Fight for Recognition', in Adolf M. Birke and Günther Heydemann (eds.), *Britain and East Germany since 1918* (Munich: K. G. Saur, 1992), 95 ff. However, despite the impression created by this article, several Labour as well as Conservative MPs argued on behalf of the GDR.

[69] The FO's scepticism was largely confirmed in the course of the 1970s. See Klaus Larres, 'Britain and the GDR: Political and Economic Relations, 1949–1989', in Larres with Meehan (eds.), *Uneasy Allies*, 63–98.

Eastern European products.[70] Despite its intensive inter-zonal trade with Bonn, severe food shortages still existed in East Germany. There were also major industrial difficulties in areas such as fuel and power, engineering and building.[71] The Foreign Office concluded: 'In other words, for the East Germans, the first objective was not the cold war, nor a peace treaty, but to set their house in order.' It appeared that this assumption was confirmed by Ulbricht 'when he said that "The essential precondition for new successes . . . was the strengthening of the economic foundations of the D.D.R." '[72] Thus, not without a little wishful thinking, it was believed in London that there was scope 'to win some of the orders at present going to West Germany'.[73] British politicians and officials were not prepared to let the erection of the Wall influence trade relations with the GDR in an overly negative way. Indeed, one Treasury official concluded that the 'greater austerity' which the GDR regime could enforce on its people since the building of the Wall 'made East Germany a better business risk'.[74]

The Foreign Office, however, was fully aware of the potential conflict of interest between adherence to the non-recognition doctrine and the establishment of more intensive trade links with East Berlin. In view of the GDR's apparent eagerness to strengthen its trade with Western countries other than West Germany, the Board of Trade (BOT) and the Treasury interpreted the non-recognition doctrine in a much more liberal spirit. The BOT emphasized Britain's economic self-interest and the financial benefits resulting from entering into closer trade relations with the East German regime; consequently it frequently clashed with the more restrained Foreign Office view. Yet Britain's trade policy with the GDR was not always characterized by a battle between the Foreign Office and the Board of Trade. On occasion it developed

[70] This was one of the reasons why it was generally believed in London that during the Berlin Crisis it had only been the threat to halt the GDR's important inter-zonal trade with West Germany which had been responsible for 'curbing East German attempts at harassment on the access routes' to Berlin. PRO: PREM 11/3805, Brief no. 1 by E. Shuckburgh, 20/6/1962. For an overview of the GDR's foreign economic relations, see e.g. Maria Haendecke-Hoppe, 'Die Aussenwirtschaftlichen Beziehungen der DDR', in Gernot Gutmann and Maria Haendecke-Hoppe (eds.), *Die Außenbeziehungen der DDR* (Heidelberg: Edition Meyn, 1980), 61 ff.

[71] See e.g. PRO: FO 371/169 263/CG 1154/1, Feb./Mar. 1963.

[72] PRO: PREM 11/3805, Brief no. 1 by E. Shuckburgh, 20/6/1962.

[73] PRO: FO 371/177 949/RG 1102/5, 24/3/1964.

[74] PRO: FO 371/169 263/CG 1154/1, 28/2/1963.

into a severe clash of views between officials in both departments (often including the President of the Board of Trade) and the political leadership responsible for the country's foreign relations, above all, the Secretary of State and the Prime Minister. In such a situation the officials tended to emphasize the potential economic benefits accruing from a more intensive trade relationship with East Germany while, more often than not, Britain's political leadership tended to downplay the importance of these economic advantages. Both the Conservative administrations under Harold Macmillan and Alec Douglas-Home, and Harold Wilson's Labour government reasoned that it was vitally important for the UK's international standing to remain loyal to the policy of the Western alliance and to maintain friendly relations with Bonn and Washington. On the whole, the changes of government in October 1963 and October 1964 do not appear to have substantially altered Britain's relationship with the GDR.

A good case in point supporting the contention that British officials from the Foreign Office and the Board of Trade were often keen on trading with the GDR was the question of Western participation in the Leipzig Spring Fair in March 1962, the first such event after the building of the Berlin Wall. As London did not recognize the GDR there was naturally 'no question of official participation'. The Board of Trade argued, however, that the British government should not deter the FBI and British firms from attending the Fair. Such economic countermeasures were not justified and could be defended only if 'the West Germans themselves were taking action not merely to discourage but to prevent German businessmen from participating'.[75] Instead, it soon became apparent that Bonn was not planning 'to reduce inter-zonal trade at all'.[76] There was much sympathy for the BOT's attitude among Foreign Office officials. It was argued that the government would be 'ill-advised' suddenly to 'embark upon acts of economic warfare' against the GDR.[77] The British attitude was regarded as 'logically sound'. It would be regrettable 'if we were left in an isolated position in NATO', but 'so long as we are

[75] PRO: FO 371/163 702/CG 1861/1, 16/1/1962.
[76] Ibid., 18/1/1962. Bonn did not think that the West Germans were legally entitled to breach the inter-zonal trade agreement; moreover it would only lead to the GDR making difficulties over access to West Berlin.
[77] Ibid., 18/1/1962.

prepared to trade with East Germany it is in our interest to do so efficiently. We must ensure that our goods are known and a trade fair is one of the best ways of achieving this.'[78] Moreover, the FBI had just been authorized by the government to continue its discussions with East Berlin regarding British–East German trade arrangements. 'It would be inconsistent to tell them at the same time to advise U.K. firms to stay away from the Fair.'[79] This would only help Communist and fellow-travelling companies attending the Fair to claim that they were representing British industry in the absence of 'the more respectable firms'.[80] It was clear that the British government faced a dilemma: 'although it is in the United Kingdom's interest to trade with East Germany it is contrary to our interest to take any action which will help the regime to bolster their prestige.'[81]

On the whole, most Foreign Office officials believed that the former was more important. Moreover, the British government had no power to prevent British companies or, indeed, MPs from attending the Leipzig Fair. Thus, firms should not be discouraged from attending the Leipzig Fair, but should merely be asked to review 'the scale of representation' and whether 'commercial considerations' really required participation in the Fair.[82] The British embassy in Bonn, however, pointed out that this attitude would 'cause resentment and dismay' in Bonn and Washington. 'What we want to avoid is getting into an argument with the Germans and Americans as to what is or is not provocative. If we do so we shall find ourselves battling again on the old ground of our supposed weak attitude.'[83]

Although the discussion among British officials and within NATO continued throughout February 1962, as early as 2 February Foreign Secretary Lord Home came down on the side of caution in a long memorandum to Frederick Erroll, the President of the Board of Trade; it was also copied to the Prime Minister and the Chancellor of the Exchequer. In view of the government's much criticized attitude and activities in the Berlin Crisis, Home realized that Britain could not afford to remain 'virtually isolated' within the Political Committee of NATO. Thus 'flouting the principle of NATO solidarity' was inadvisable. It would 'be a great mistake to

---

[78] PRO: FO 371/163 702/CG 1861/1, 19/1/1962. [79] Ibid., 16/1/1962.
[80] Ibid., 16/1/1962; also 18/1/1962. [81] Ibid., 19/1/1962.
[82] Ibid., 3/1/1962. [83] Ibid., 19/1/1962.

oppose the [NATO] resolution' which called on Western firms to boycott the Leipzig Fair. He concluded that Britain had no alternative but to accept the resolution. 'The political advantages of not doing so will far outweigh any economic or commercial benefits we may hope to achieve.' London would 'be accused of acting disingenuously'. Home therefore believed that the British government ought to 'take some positive step to discourage the participation of British firms at Leipzig'. The FBI 'should be asked to abandon the arrangements they are making to organise a pavilion, so that we may avoid the embarrassment of having a *quasi* official British pavilion in Leipzig staffed as in the past by representatives of the F.B.I. and (if the truth were known) paid for with the tax-payers' money'.[84]

Above all, Home emphasized that 'behind this difference of opinion between ourselves and our Allies over Leipzig there lies the important political question of our attitude towards the D.D.R. and towards the whole question of Berlin'. He argued that there was a great danger that 'our attitude towards the Leipzig Fair will be regarded, by our friends and our enemies alike, as a test of our intentions over Berlin'. The Foreign Secretary made it unambiguously clear that it was not British policy 'to give Ulbricht's regime any assistance in surmounting its difficulties, or in improving its image towards its people or the world at large. . . . The last thing we want to do is to contribute to an impression in the Russians' minds that we think that the East Germans can stand on their own feet as an independent country and that a major Western power is willing to help them along this road.'[85] In fact, in spring 1962 few British or other Western companies attended the GDR's trade fair in Leipzig. However, the boycott of the fair could not be sustained. By 1964 Western firms had once again begun to attend regularly, and Britain had become the second largest Western exhibitor after France. In view of the country's economic troubles the Board of Trade had largely prevailed with its argument that 'the Zone represents a good potential market for British exports, and that the Leipzig Fair is one of the best leads into that market'.[86] In the course of the 1960s the British frequently found themselves in

---

[84] He explained that 'it would be most unfortunate if we were to find ourselves in a situation in which British businessmen and the F.B.I., alone of all the NATO allies, flock to the Leipzig Fair'. Ibid., letter Home, 3/2/1962.

[85] Ibid.

[86] PRO: FO 371/189 308/RG 1861/9, 4/8/1966; also /5, letter Gibbs, 23/2/1966.

similar dilemmas. It hardly ever seemed possible to benefit from trading with the GDR without antagonizing Bonn or Washington.

Despite considerable improvements in private British–East German economic relations, throughout the 1960s the BOT and the FBI/CBI were rarely satisfied with the development of the export trade with East Germany. While the GDR embarked on an intensified campaign to improve its trade with the Western world in 1963–4 and continued to be more than keen to send its own products to Britain, East Berlin often proved to be unable or unwilling to fulfil its arranged quotas of purchasing British goods. This frequently led to the temporary cancellation of the KfA's import licences and to a considerable reduction in the export quotas negotiated with the KfA. The GDR was only interested in certain products like machinery, while the British were particularly keen to sell products to the GDR which they found difficult to offer to other countries.[87] The announcement in June 1963 of the GDR's new market-orientated economic policy (the New Economic System of Planning and Management, NES)— reformed in 1967 and finally abolished in September 1970—only confirmed the continuation of the GDR's policy of being rather selective in their trade with Britain and other countries.[88] Under these circumstances, the GDR's attempts to conclude three-year instead of merely annual trade agreements in the mid-1960s were not viewed favourably by the British authorities.[89]

In 1964, the Foreign Office under R. A. Butler firmly rejected an application to grant a ten-year credit guarantee for the export of an oxygen steel plant, a continuous casting plant, and a fertilizer plant to the GDR. Apart from the unsatisfactory trade balance with the

---

[87] PRO: FO 371/172 171/RG 1154/5, 2/11/1963; also FO 371/163 649/CG 1154/11, 6/4/1962; FO 371/163 650/CG 1154/25 (C), 3/12/1962. See also Bell, *Britain and East Germany*, 165 ff. See also the interesting papers by the Bank of England on the GDR's economic situation, in FO 371/177 949/RG 1102/5, 9/3/1964; and FO 371/189 250/RG 1154/26, 20/4/1966; RG 1154/10, Memorandum on Anglo-German Economic Committee Meeting, 16–18/2/1966.

[88] See e.g. PRO: FO 371/172 171/RG 1154/5, 2/11/1963. For the NES and the GDR's economic performance in the 1960s, see McCauley, *The German Democratic Republic*, 107–16; Dietrich Staritz, *Geschichte der DDR 1949–1990*, expanded edn. (Darmstadt: WBG, 1996), 206 ff.; also Jeffrey Kopstein, *The Politics of Economic Decline in East Germany, 1945–1989* (Chapel Hill: University of North Carolina Press, 1997), 41–72.

[89] PRO: FO 371/163 650/CG 1154/25 (B) (C), 30/11/1962, 3/12/1962; FO 371/163 649/CG 1154/3, 5, 15, Jan., Feb. and June 1962. In 1966 the CBI unexpectedly supported the GDR's desire but it was given short shrift by the Foreign Office. See FO 371/189 250/RG 1154/26, 20/4/1966.

GDR, it was once again the likely point of view of Britain's NATO allies which decisively influenced this decision. While the British Export Credits Guarantee Department believed that the export of these large plants to the GDR had great commercial merit, the Foreign Office argued that this would lead to 'serious difficulties' if not to a 'serious row' with Britain's allies, including the United States. Britain would be 'completely isolated over this'.[90] In particular, the entire issue was a 'highly emotional question for all Germans' and 'such good friends of ours as the Chancellor and the Foreign Minister . . . would be horrified at the mere idea of our, as they would see it, strengthening Ulbricht and the East German system in this way'. Both Butler and Prime Minister Douglas-Home agreed that East Germany was 'a special case among *bloc* countries'. The UK ought not to be the first Western country offering longer-term credit with regard to trade with East Berlin. After all, this would in effect mean that Britain 'expected the separate East German regime to continue in existence for another 10 or 15 years'.[91] This view was, however, tenaciously challenged by Edward Heath, the President of the Board of Trade. Heath argued that Britain's industry needed these orders and that the GDR 'should not be placed in a different category from other bloc countries'. Yet in the end Heath had to give in to the forceful political arguments. It was clear that despite Britain's delicate economic situation, the Prime Minister and the Foreign Secretary were not prepared to sacrifice the country's friendly relations with the West German Erhard government and the American Johnson administration for the sake of greater trade with the GDR.[92]

This was even more the case after the change of government in October 1964. There had been 'deep suspicions' in Bonn regarding the intentions of the new Labour administration. After all, in opposition Harold Wilson had expressed understanding for the recognition of the GDR and for the continued division of Germany. Bonn had also been annoyed about a recent

[90] PRO: FO 371/177 963/RG 1154/15, 13/5/1964.

[91] PRO: FO 371/177 963/RG 1154/5, 15, 23/3/1964, 13/5/1964, 22/5/1964, 28/5/1964, 9/6/1964; RG 1154/22, 30/6/1964.

[92] Foreign Secretary Douglas-Home commented on Lord Carrington's memorandum in mid-May 1963: 'I think we should not agree to these long term credits. We do not recognise East Germany and that, I think, puts them in a different category to any other country in Eastern Europe.' PRO: FO 371/177 963/RG 1154/15, 13/5/1964; see also 9/6/1964, 18/6/1964, 15/7/1964, 17/7/1964.

parliamentary speech by the new Prime Minister which seemed to favour 'some form of disengagement'.[93] However, Britain's new government had been more than grateful for West German assistance in the recent sterling crisis and it also hoped to arrive at 'a satisfactory arrangement' with Bonn about NATO's nuclear policy. Even more importantly, the Wilson government needed to negotiate a deal with the West Germans about how to share the financial burden of paying for the costs of the British Rhine Army.[94] Thus, it appeared to be rather unwise to provoke a crisis with Bonn over long-term credits to the GDR. They continued to be denied to East Berlin for another five years.

Although British–East German trade relations improved somewhat in the late 1960s, the political crisis over the 1968 Warsaw Pact invasion of the CSSR also had some negative repercussions as far as trade with the GDR was concerned.[95] A year later these difficulties were, however, overcome and the GDR again began campaigning for the conclusion of a long-term trade agreement. Yet the Foreign Office was sceptical. It was no longer convinced that there was as much potential to expand trade with the GDR as was still claimed by the Board of Trade and by East Berlin, as well as by some British MPs and entrepreneurs. The GDR's weak economy and its great dependence on trade with the FRG and the COMECON countries did not suggest otherwise. London also still hesitated to enter into any long-term agreements for fear that this would undermine the policy of Western non-recognition, although France, the Netherlands, and Denmark had already concluded five-year trade agreements with East Berlin. Eventually, in November 1969, under the influence of West Germany's new *Ostpolitik*, the British government gave its blessing to a long-term three-year trade agreement between the CBI and the KfA Ltd. This indeed led to an improvement in British–East German trade relations and encouraged further co-operation.[96] The creation of a 'UK Section' within the KfA in East Berlin and the establishment of so-called 'GDR Committees' within the CBI and the London Chamber of Commerce occurred in the summer of 1970. The first official CBI office was opened in East Berlin a year later.

---

[93] PRO: FO 371/177 963/RG 1154/22, 30/6/1964.   [94] Ibid.
[95] See Sodaro, *Moscow, Germany and the West*, 111–34; Becker, *DDR und Großbritannien*, 145, 226–7.
[96] See Bell, *Britain and East Germany*, 42–5.

The GDR's attempt to obtain a declaration from the British government as the basis for this agreement was, however, still rejected. Despite the great improvements in British–East German trade contacts, until the signing of the German–German treaty in late 1972 Britain was still unable to resolve the dilemma inherent in its relations with the GDR. The British government felt obliged to adhere to the West's non-recognition doctrine as much as possible; at the same time it did not wish to damage Britain's trade relations with East Berlin.[97] In general, the Foreign Office welcomed West German Foreign Minister Schröder's more 'pragmatic view of German relations with Eastern Europe', which seemed to represent the beginning of the FRG's normalization of relations with the Warsaw Pact countries. Thus London noted with great relief the 'wind of change' which was 'beginning to blow in Bonn now that the Adenauer era is drawing towards a close'.[98]

In particular during the 1960s the Ulbricht regime was also highly active in the non-aligned and developing world.[99] There was naturally relatively little understanding of, and a distinct lack of interest in, the complicated German question in these countries thousands of miles away from Europe. Thus it was concluded in East Berlin that there might well be less resistance to the diplomatic recognition of the GDR than in the rest of the world. Internally, the British Foreign Office agreed with this assessment.[100] Moreover, East Berlin was convinced that its economic aid and the expertise of East German engineers, scientists, economists, and other experts would be most appreciated in these regions. The GDR effectively attempted to purchase recognition.[101] However, the West German government made great efforts to use its already considerable economic power as well as its growing political influence to undermine the GDR's endeavours to obtain a foothold in the developing world. For example, as far as

---

[97] See Becker, *DDR und Großbritannien*, 226–32; also Bell, *Britain and East Germany*, 47.

[98] PRO: FO 371/169 215/CG 1081/4, 4/4/1963. For the limits of Schröder's 'wind of change' policy and the continuation of Bonn's thinking within the old non-recognition framework, see e.g. FO 371/163 559/CG 1051/5, Record of Conversation, 12/3/1962.

[99] See, above all, Alexander Troche, *Ulbricht und die Dritte Welt: Ost-Berlins 'Kampf' gegen die Bonner 'Alleinvertretung'* (Jena: Palm & Enke, 1996). The book concentrates on the years after 1965 but also represents a valuable general study of the theme and contains a detailed account of the literature on the topic.

[100] PRO: FO 371/177 933/RG 1062/16, 3/4/1964.

[101] See Spanger, *The GDR in East–West Relations*, 12; see also Osten, *Außenpolitik der DDR*, 78–87.

India was concerned, the British Foreign Office concluded that 'the substantial West German aid to India is a powerful check on any leftward leanings which the Indians may secretly have'.[102]

On more than one occasion the West German government appealed to the British government to intervene with its former African or Asian colonies to prevent the deliberate or inadvertent recognition of the GDR by one of the new members of the Commonwealth. And more often than not, Britain attempted to be helpful. In September 1963 London, for instance, successfully managed to dissuade the Kenyan government from inviting 'people from East Germany' on a 'purely personal basis' to the forthcoming independence celebrations. The British government argued that 'any person so invited would doubtless claim that he was his country's official representative'. It could be expected that in such a case the GDR would subsequently use the event to assert that the Ulbricht regime had been recognized by President Kenyatta.[103]

Part of East Berlin's fight for diplomatic recognition was also the attempt to be accepted by international organizations. Although by the mid 1960s the GDR had managed to join a large number of organizations and associations, these were generally considered of only minor importance. The Ulbricht regime was above all keen to join the United Nations as the UN admitted only sovereign states. Thus, during the 1950s and 1960s, the GDR made several attempts to become a member of the United Nations' fourteen sub-organizations.[104] Year after year the West, however, succeeded

---

[102] PRO: 371/177 904/RG 1023/3, 19/3/1964. Similarly, when the Foreign Office considered the repercussions on the German question of the attempts by North Korea and North Vietnam to gain recognition in the neutralist world, it was argued that, unlike South Korea and South Vietnam, West Germany was now 'a major power who can use effective sanctions, particularly aid, to support their stand'. PRO: FO 371/172 139/RG 1076/1, 14/10/1963. See in general also Winrow, *The Foreign Policy of the GDR*, 42–3; Troche, *Ulbricht und die Dritte Welt*, 34–5. For the international dimension of the German–German conflict and the search for recognition, see also the interesting but rather abstract book by Heinrich End, *Zweimal deutsche Außenpolitik: Die internationale Dimension des innerdeutschen Konflikts 1949–1972* (Cologne: Verlag Wissenschaft und Politik, 1973).

[103] PRO: FO 371/172 131/RG 1062/1, 13/9, 18/9/1963. For the GDR's African policy, see Ulf Engel, *Die beiden deutschen Staaten in Afrika: Zwischen Konkurrenz und Koexistenz* (Hamburg: Insitut für Afrika-Kunde, 1998); also Bettina Husemann, *Die Afrikapolitik der DDR: Eine Titeldokumentation von Akten des Politbüro-Sekretäriats des Zentralkomitees der SED, 1949–1989* (Hamburg: Übersee-Institut, 1994).

[104] See Thomas, *Modell DDR*, 127; Osten, *Die Außenpolitik der DDR*, 87–91; and Wilhelm Bruns, *Die UNO-Politik der DDR* (Stuttgart: Verlag Bonn Aktuell, 1978). In 1954 and 1955 the GDR also applied for membership of the International Labour Organization (ILO) and UNESCO.

ILLUSTRATIONS

ILLUSTRATION 1. 'One Fatherland'
Peter Brookes (*The Spectator*, 24 Feb. 1990)

Brookes makes use of a classic form of caricature in the manner of James Gillray's cartoons of the Napoleonic wars. West Germany personified as Chancellor Kohl swallows East Germany.

ILLUSTRATION 2. 'Ve vill occupy ze sunbeds here at precisely 5. a.m. . . . !'
Bernard Cookson (*Sun*, London, 7 Apr. 1987)

Cookson's was one of the first cartoons about German holidaymakers. He has drawn them in a way that makes them easily identifiable as Nazis. The fact that they intend to begin their occupation at 5 a.m. sharp refers to a newspaper report that sunbeds were being reserved with beach towels as early as midnight.

ILLUSTRATION 3. 'At least there's a guaranteed sunbed.'
Bill Caldwell (*Daily Star*, 5 June 1992)

Britain's oldest travel firm, Thomas Cook, is purchased by Germany's biggest charter airline, LTU. Caldwell predicts that British holidaymakers will now enjoy German amenities, even if they have to put up with German drill.

ILLUSTRATION 4. 'Please don't get so excited Mein Fuhrer—it's only a game of football.'

Bill Caldwell (*Daily Star*, 4 July 1990)

Adolf Hitler is still alive and from his South American hideaway the centenarian follows the fortunes of modern Germany. The faithful old guard stands by, but their uniforms are showing signs of wear. The image of the *Führer* continues to be used by British cartoonists during major competitions between the two countries.

ILLUSTRATION 5. *Private Eye*, cover, 'Anglo-German Relations'
(No. 90, 28 May 1965)

This *Private Eye* cover refers to the first State visit to the Federal Republic by Her Majesty, the Queen, in May 1965. Public records show that the Queen feared anti-German public opinion could be exploited by a xenophobic British press. Her own, and her husband's, German family connections could form an embarrassment.

in preventing this by arguing that the GDR was not a sovereign and internationally recognized state and as such could not join a global organization consisting of sovereign states. These were also the main arguments successfully used when East Berlin applied for full membership of the United Nations in late February 1966.[105] The decision of the International Olympic Committee (IOC) in October 1965 that from 1968 two German teams would be free to participate in the Olympic Games was one of the GDR's rare successes in obtaining some degree of official international recognition. The IOC's decision had been taken despite strong West German protestations and British efforts to interfere behind the scenes on behalf of Bonn.[106]

Despite the Ulbricht regime's strenuous efforts, the GDR was not accepted as an equal partner in the world before the Basic Treaty between Bonn and East Berlin was concluded in late 1972. The imminent changes in German–German relations with the advent of *Ostpolitik* in 1969–70, however, contributed to the fact that ever more states proclaimed their intention to enter into diplomatic relations with East Berlin. Although a considerable number of countries had already recognized the GDR by 1969–70,[107] an avalanche of recognition would only occur after November/December 1972. Bonn's request to delay the recognition of the GDR until the Basic Treaty had fully taken shape (the Scheel Doctrine) was largely observed. The British Heath government did not officially communicate with the GDR authorities before this event.[108] Between November 1972 and May 1973, the UK and more than fifty other states recognized the East German republic and the GDR was soon able to join a large number of important international organizations.

---

[105] See PRO: FO 371/189 318/RG 2251/8–21 (Mar. 1966); also e.g. Becker, *DDR und Großbritannien*, 140–1.

[106] The West German protests may well have been counterproductive as they caused considerable resentment among the IOC members. See PRO: FO 371/183 165/RG 1801/7 (Apr. 1965), 13 (June 1965), 20, 21 (Oct. 1965), and, in particular, 10 (May 1965), 14, 15 (July 1965), 24 (Nov. 1965). See also in general Walter Schulz, *Die Stellung der Kultur- und Sportpolitik im System der auswärtigen Politik der DDR . . .* (Ph.D. thesis, University of Bonn, 1976).

[107] 1969: Cambodia, Sudan, South Vietnam, Congo, Somalia, the Central African Republic, Algeria, and the Maldives; 1970: Ceylon and Guinea, and a general consulate was established in India. See Thomas, *Modell DDR*, 126; see also the list limited to African countries in Winrow, *The Foreign Policy of the GDR*, 73, and 72–84.

[108] See Colin Munro, 'The Acceptance of a Second German State', in Birke and Heydemann (eds.), *Britain and East Germany*, 121 ff.

Conclusion

In the last resort, British governments of all political persuasions fully realized that their relationships with West Germany, the United States, and indeed the entire NATO alliance were much more important than any advantageous export deals with the GDR which violated the letter or the spirit of the West's non-recognition policy as agreed in late 1949. The Macmillan government's readiness to extend *de facto* recognition to the Ulbricht regime in the course of the long Berlin Crisis of 1958–63 appears to have been an exception rather than the rule. British motives for not recognizing the GDR differed from the West German or even the American rationale. While for a long time Bonn and Washington believed that there was a certain chance to eliminate the Ulbricht regime and consequently to bring about German unification, most British decision-makers did not strongly object to the continued division of Germany. On the whole, British decision-makers were opposed to recognizing the GDR for largely ideological and humanitarian reasons, but not because they desired to overcome the division of Germany. Yet Britain did not regard the GDR as a sovereign country before the development of West German *Ostpolitik* in the early 1970s. In fact, the British authorities went out of their way to support West Germany's battle against the recognition of the GDR in the non-aligned world by not hesitating to intercede with Britain's former colonies. Most non-aligned states had no interest in the German question but did not mind obtaining aid from both Bonn and East Berlin. On more than one occasion Bonn had appealed to the British government to intervene with its former African or Asian colonies to prevent the deliberate or inadvertent recognition of the GDR by one of the new members of the Commonwealth. And more often than not Britain had tried to be helpful. The government also did its best to buttress Bonn's policy to prevent the GDR's admission to international organizations. Like the United States, London was also, though often somewhat hesitantly, prepared to take Bonn's keen sensibilities into consideration as far as the improvement of East–West relations in Europe were concerned. It is much less clear whether the West German authorities always fully appreciated Britain's endeavours in this regard. Although they often expressed their gratitude for certain activities on their behalf, on the whole both Bonn and East Berlin appear to have believed that Britain was the weak link in the West's non-recognition policy. This impression may have been encouraged by Macmillan's activities in the Berlin Crisis and by some wavering as far as trade temptations were concerned. On the whole, however, this view does not seem to have done justice to Britain's fairly consistent adherence to the non-recognition of the GDR throughout the 1960s.

10

Great Britain and German Unification

SIR JULIAN BULLARD

The calendar of events reminds us of what happened, and of how quickly it happened. One of several excellent books about it is by Chancellor Kohl's foreign policy adviser, Horst Teltschik, who chooses the title *329 Tage*.[1] Written in diary form, it conveys better than works of hindsight the distinctive quality of this episode, which is the acceleration factor and the sense that events, rather than governments or individuals, were in charge, setting the direction and the pace too, in those 329 days from the collapse of the Wall to the Treaty of Unification.

Was any of this foreseen in Bonn, where I was serving until the spring of 1988? The broad answer is No. On my last day I could have gone the rounds of the political establishment in Bonn, or the industrial establishment in Düsseldorf or Stuttgart, or the financial establishment in Frankfurt, putting the question: 'Do you expect German unification, and if so, when?', and I should have got the same answers from one end of the political spectrum to the other: not in my lifetime, not in this century, perhaps my children will live to see it, and so forth.

There was in Bonn, and not in Bonn alone, a presumption, supported by a lot of respectable evidence, that the Soviet national interest required in 1988, as in 1948, the division of Germany and the inclusion of the GDR in the Soviet defence and industrial system. There was a huge Western investment in this assumption in the form of troops, bases, stores, equipment, staffs—and plans for every contingency, except the one that was about to happen. Those concerned were better prepared for a second Berlin blockade than for unification: later, it was to take Berlin many months to burn, consume, eat down, drink up, or otherwise dispose of the mountains and lakes of

---

[1] Horst Teltschik, *329 Tage: Innenansichten der Einigung* (Berlin: Siedler, 1991).

supplies stockpiled in the city. The truth is that, although unification was the official objective of the Federal Republic, to be seen acting as if you expected it and wanted it soon was to invite accusations of waking sleeping dogs, getting the Federal Republic a bad name, destabilizing the East–West relationship.

Am I saying that nobody in the West foresaw what was to happen in the following year? Not quite. There was General Vernon Walters; and Dominique Moisi; and a few academics and politicians; these were rewarded for their prescience by the labels 'visionary' or 'revanchist', depending on the speaker. The media in Germany slept through the opening phase. This applies to most of the British media too.

Let us look in turn at three criticisms which have been levelled at us: that Britain failed to foresee German unification; that Britain tried to prevent it; and that Britain's role in the whole business was insignificant.

True, in that summer of 1989, as the evidence mounted that the GDR had sprung a terminal leak, observers in London were visibly unprepared. With Parliament in recess until October, there was no need for instant comment from official sources. The media, however, could not evade the issue, and to look through British press cuttings from the summer of 1989 onwards is to be reminded how difficult it was even to read the course of current events, let alone to foresee what would happen next. Assumptions built up over four decades could not easily or quickly be abandoned. That the regime in the GDR had the population in a firm grip; that the Soviet Union would seek to prevent German unification at all costs; that a heavy price would have to be paid; that German unity could only come gradually, at the end of a long process, in the context of European unity—such things had been said so often, and for so long, and by so many political leaders and with such conviction, that evidence to the contrary was often ignored or dismissed. Where a commentator did brace himself to question the received wisdom, his mental leap was usually far too cautious. One of the best experts in one of the best British newspapers needed some courage to write in late September 1989: 'The future period during which German unity could be regarded as feasible has suddenly shrunk from a matter of decades to perhaps only 10 or 15 years.'[2]

---

[2] David Marsh in the *Financial Times*, 30 Sept. 1989.

Throughout that autumn and winter, and well into the spring and summer of the following year, editorial columns in the British press can be seen clinging to positions which events were already leaving far behind: on the likely duration of the GDR, for example, and on German membership of NATO.[3] Columnists, as distinct from leader-writers, were sometimes closer to the truth, sometimes even further from it.[4] The same can be said of readers' letters.[5]

The second charge was that Britain was opposed to German unification. This was certainly true of some people, for example, in the media; in both houses of Parliament; Eurosceptics; atavistic Germanophobes—and the Prime Minister. Her memoirs speak for themselves.[6] She describes how she quickly saw that the consequences of German unification might include some that would not be in the British interest as she defined it; and how she tried first Mitterrand and then Gorbachev in the hope of putting together an anti-unification front; and how she failed in this—a failure she calls the biggest foreign policy reverse of her whole career. But her words and actions were naturally noted, especially in West Germany, and they are still remembered. On 3 December 1989, when Kohl remarked to Bush that the British seemed reserved about German unification, Bush's reply was that this was the understatement of the year.[7]

Mrs Thatcher clung to her position for a long time after that. She did not repudiate Britain's commitment (1955) to support the unification of Germany, nor did she deny that the German people had the right of self-determination. But she qualified these things in such a way as to imply that she did not entirely trust the Germans. Did the famous Chequers Seminar of 30 March 1990 remove her fears? Apparently not, for she continued to say what to the Germans could only be wounding things. Some of Britain's best friends in Germany took these things very much to heart, and some of them felt that the Prime Minister was undoing the work of decades in the Anglo-German field. As late as 1993 Lady Thatcher was still unrepentant.[8] And she had her followers. Mr David

---

[3] e.g. the *Guardian* editorial, 10 May 1990.
[4] e.g. Conor Cruise O'Brien, 31 Oct. 1989 (and later) in *The Times*.
[5] e.g. D. Cameron Watt in the *Daily Telegraph*, 6 Sept. and 16 Nov. 1989.
[6] Margaret Thatcher, *The Downing Street Years* (London: HarperCollins, 1993).
[7] Teltschik, *329 Tage*, 64.   [8] *Der Spiegel*, 43/1993.

Howell, the Chairman of the Foreign Affairs Committee of the House of Commons, said afterwards:

There was a feeling in this country that the FRG had been the most successful political democracy, and of course the most successful economic democracy, in the postwar world. And I think there must have been a feeling around that here was a highly successful operation—was it wise to tamper with it? Was it wise to change it? or in the Americanism: if it ain't broke, don't fix it. So I think there was unease. There was unease that unification might tarnish and create new problems for what has been a very very spectacular and successful and really wonderful postwar society.[9]

As the direction of events became clearer, the implications for Britain began to be discussed, both in broad terms and in detail. A fear which surfaced very early in the process was that of 'destabilization'. The word is not entirely appropriate, since the risk perceived was that the rapid and encouraging march of events in Central and Eastern Europe—the shift from one-party government to pluralist democracy, the replacement of the command economy by the social market principle, the revival of positive nationalism, the collapse of the Soviet Empire, and the end of the Cold War—that this 'benign destabilization', so to speak, might be slowed down, sidetracked, or even brought to a halt. German unification, argued many in Britain, should not, or not necessarily, take priority over everything else.

The point at which the term 'destabilization' did apply was in regard to the leadership in Moscow. The governments in Bonn and London were at one in their belief that the positive trend of events in East–West relations, and especially in Europe, depended crucially on the person of the President of the USSR, Mikhail Gorbachev. But whereas Germans drew the conclusion that unification must be pressed through to completion while Gorbachev and, to a lesser degree, his Foreign Minister Shevardnadze were still there to assist it, a common feeling in some quarters in Britain was that any attempt to force the pace of unification might strengthen the position of Gorbachev's enemies in Moscow and perhaps put into their hands the issue which they needed to oust him. Subsequent events have tended to reinforce the German

---

[9] Interview with Hessische Rundfunk, 3 Oct. 1993.

rather than the British view, but the latter was a respectable intellectual position, not merely an instinctive prejudice.

Yet both instinct and prejudice did play a part in the nation-wide British reaction. The phrase 'eine atavistische Germanophobie', used by one German correspondent in London,[10] cannot stand as a blanket description of British attitudes, but it is certainly true of some individuals, including some in the government of the day. What is significant about the 'Ridley Affair' is not that a man of Mr Nicholas Ridley's age and background held such views on Germany, but that as a Cabinet Minister he felt free to express them publicly—not in an off-the-cuff remark, but at some length in an interview with a serious weekly magazine—and that his resignation did not occur immediately, but only forty-eight hours later. Likewise the 'Chequers Affair': what is open to criticism is not that the British Prime Minister consulted a group of academics about Germany, or that she and they expressed themselves very freely, or that a Private Secretary summarized the proceedings succinctly and with no little humour, but that the record was printed in a Sunday newspaper four months later—in the same week as Mr Ridley's resignation. It is hard to resist the conclusion that Mr Ridley's general attitude towards Germany was shared by others in high places in London. He knew that, and she knew it and he knew that she knew it . . . Such people are old enough to have experienced the Second World War, but not old enough to have taken an active part in it. As teenagers they had been vividly conscious of the simplicities of the year 1940 when Germany was the brutal foe, France the perfidious ally, Western Europe a collection of mere pawns on the chessboard, the United States the only real (but distant) friend.

But two things need to be said on the other side. First, the questions Mrs Thatcher was asking in that period were very much to the point:

What would unification cost, and who would pick up the bills?
What about the EC aspect?
What about QRR (Quadripartite Rights and Responsibilities)?
What would be done about the matters left over from the War? (Claims, etc.)
What would happen in Berlin?

---

[10] Gina Thomas of the *Frankfurter Allgemeine Zeitung*.

What would be the frontiers of the united Germany?
How would security be preserved in Central Europe?

These were seven extremely pertinent questions. At the time nobody in Germany was asking them, still less offering any answers. NATO, for example, was not mentioned anywhere in Kohl's Ten Points.[11] This was another of those occasions on which Mrs Thatcher was quicker in the uptake and on the draw than most others. As it was, her seven points, with others, became the Agenda for the EC and the 2 plus 4 group. The creation of the second of these groups in particular had a reassuring effect: it gave a signal that somebody was in charge, that things were being co-ordinated, that events were not in free fall. Yet this was a group which at Ministerial level held only four meetings, of which the first was largely procedural, the fourth ceremonial, and the third mainly devoted to the question of the German–Polish frontier. It was the officials of the six (really five) countries who did the spade-work, at and between their meetings.

Second, this was not a case where British policy was made by the Prime Minister alone. The lead Department was the FCO, and one of the Ministers at the FCO at the material time was Mr William Waldegrave. Questioned by a German radio station afterwards as to what British policy had been in 1989–90, he gave the reply:

The FO took the view, first of all, that it was right that Germany should be reunified. It would have made a mockery of all our policy since the War if we did not welcome it. And second, just at a lower level of prag-matism: since it was going to happen, it was better to join German rejoic-ing instead of sounding sour and thereby having German resentment.

FCO Ministers did their best to use words which did not directly contradict what the PM was saying. This must have been uncom-fortable sometimes, for example, when Mr Hurd had to ask in mid-November: 'Who's talking about unification?'; or on 6 February, in Berlin too, to stress the need for reasonable periods of transition. Mrs Thatcher did not change her mind, and probably she still has not and will not: so we saw and read and heard her comments to the German Ambassador at a conference in Cambridge; the gath-ering of academics at Chequers; the Nicholas Ridley affair; and

[11] Speech to the Bundestag, 28 Nov. 1989.

several speeches and newspaper interviews during that spring and summer, some in Britain and others in the USA, all carrying the message that the British Prime Minister for her part did not like the prospect of a united Germany 'dominating Europe'. But at the working level, after a slow and confused start, and following another (internal) seminar at Chequers at the end of January, the organs of British government marched to a different drum, a drum beaten by Mr Douglas Hurd.

What is the explanation for Mrs Thatcher's attitude? Here is the answer to that question from Sir Charles Powell, as reported by Teltschik, when they met secretly for three hours in Bonn on 9 February 1990:

She belonged to another generation than his own [Powell's], and she was still marked by the period when there had been a 'cultural gap' between Great Britain and Germany. She felt uneasy at the thought of a large and powerful Germany. The decisive thing for her was therefore the *consequences* of the unification of Germany.[12]

And Powell explains that this means especially the consequences for Gorbachev and the Soviet Union, and for NATO.

The third indictment was that Britain was ineffective, without influence on the course of events. If we did not wield the same influence as the USA or the FRG or the USSR, we certainly wielded as much as did France—but with a difference. French views made themselves felt chiefly on the special Paris–Bonn channel; British views mainly in the multilateral groupings and organizations where the product of the countless bilateral meetings was brought together, formalized, and put into words that all could accept and which would stand the test of time. What groups? The 2 plus 4, the 3 plus 1, NATO, the CSCE, and the EC. In all these negotiations, I have been assured, and have no reason to doubt, that the British role was very considerable. The device of 'suspending' QRR until they were terminated on the entry into force of the 2 plus 4 Treaty—this was a British idea.

Now in the negotiations there was certainly a 'Hurry Up' school and a 'Steady On' school. It would be wrong to imagine that those in favour of a more deliberate pace of advance were just trying to put off unification as long as possible. There was a genuine difference of opinion on a matter of judgement. The West Germans,

---

[12] Teltschik, *329 Tage*, 134.

supported by the USA, saw the whole situation as a 'window of opportunity'. How long could we be sure that Gorbachev would hold his place and his powers in Moscow? And what about Shevardnadze? From the answers to these questions the Germans and Americans drew the conclusion that the right course was to press on as fast as possible, keeping up the momentum and leaving details and difficulties to be picked up later. On the other side, some in the British chain of command also saw Gorbachev as a key player, but drew a different conclusion. Given that he had opponents as well as supporters, should we not be careful to avoid giving ammunition to his enemies? The East–West scene was developing very satisfactorily for the West, so why risk destabilizing it for the sake of a few months? If we rushed ahead we should be bound to drop stitches in the negotiations. How much better to tackle the questions in an orderly manner, slow enough to ensure accuracy and precision and to meet all the requirements of international law. The Quadripartite Agreement on Berlin of 1971, a much less significant document than those on the table in 1990, had taken many months to negotiate, and Germany could be unified just as well in 1991 as in 1990. This was for a time the British view, and one or two of the German officials rather agreed with it, as Teltschik records.

But with the line-up as it took shape, Washington and Bonn v. London and Paris, there could be only one outcome, and the British and French had to accept it with the best grace they could muster. Events bore out the US–German instinct, because serious legal slips were not made, and the two key Soviet leaders were indeed moved on, Shevardnadze at the end of 1990, Gorbachev a year later. The Western legal advisers prepared for more arguments with the Soviet Union than in fact took place: Moscow did not even try to assert its long-standing view of the status of West Berlin in relation to the rest of Germany.

As to Britain's role, therefore, I conclude that at government level we were neither so short-sighted, nor so hostile, nor so ineffective, as has sometimes been supposed.

In conclusion, I will offer a number of general reflections.

Money talked, and talked loudly, and with a strong German accent. Wherever there was a bill to pay, it was usually the West Germans who picked it up. Everything from the thousands of millions of DM paid to Moscow in respect of the Soviet troops permitted to remain in Germany until the autumn of 1994: their stationing costs; the installations and equipment which they left behind; their transport from Germany back to Russia; their retraining for civilian jobs; their accommodation in Russia when they finally got there—everything from these huge items, plus the very large costs of absorbing the GDR into the EC, right down to the expenses of those elections in the GDR in March 1990, including (Teltschik tells us) the cost of supplying and setting up specially enormous loudspeakers in Dresden so that Kohl could be sure that the sea of faces in the square in front of him could hear what he wanted to say—all this and much else was paid for, could only have been paid for, by the West German taxpayer, who in some degree can be said to have bought unification. Luckily, the Germany which had (and is still having) to find all this money was a Germany which had been living through a period of sustained economic prosperity and growth. Teltschik records Kohl as asking a CDU meeting in East Berlin in August 1990: 'When if not now could German unity be financed?'[13]

Looking back now, ten years later, one can perhaps say that all of the principal parties achieved what they wanted, though not without a price. Germany was united and recovered its full sovereignty, at a tremendous financial and social cost, but exactly in the form envisaged in the Relations Convention of 1955: 'The Signatory States will cooperate to achieve, by peaceful means, their common aim of a re-unified Germany enjoying a liberal-democratic constitution, like that of the Federal Republic, and integrated within the European community' (Article 7.2).

The USSR extricated itself from an over-exposed position in Central Europe and forged a new kind of partnership with Germany, but at the cost of publicly surrendering what had seemed the priceless and irreversible triumphs of the Red Army in the war.

The USA came perhaps closest to achieving a cost-free dividend. Bush was the hero of the diplomatic process, he was able to put some flesh on the slogan 'Partnership in Leadership', and he earned the everlasting gratitude of the German people—an asset which he found himself having to cash, literally, perhaps sooner than he expected, after the Iraqis invaded Kuwait at the end of

---

[13] *Tage*, 351: 'Wann, wenn nicht jetzt, könnte die deutsche Einheit finanziert werden?'

August 1990. Those who enjoy 'virtual history' may like to ask themselves: what if Saddam Hussein had made his move, say, two or three months earlier? Could the White House have sustained the necessary degree of attention to the cause of German unification while preparing and mounting Operation Desert Storm? But the domestic electoral dividend which Bush must also have hoped for eluded him in 1992.

France was able to preserve the Franco-German special relationship, but in a somewhat damaged condition, and had to face the fact of a united Germany in which the French post-war position, as one of the four powers with special responsibility for Berlin and Germany as a whole, had to go.

This last phrase applies also to Britain, which could be satisfied with a watertight set of agreements etc., but which did, indeed, become, as Mrs Thatcher had foreseen, relatively weaker, and which attracted more unpopularity than she perhaps realized, mainly by reason of words which she herself had spoken or chosen not to speak.

The serious difficulties which arose were not always those which had been foreseen and provided for. The legal documentation; Germany's Eastern frontiers; the constitutional process of attaching the GDR to the FRG; the EC aspects; full membership in NATO for the united Germany—under all these headings the tussle was expected to be tough and protracted, but in most cases this was not the case. Why not? Evidently because Gorbachev had decided that nothing really mattered except that Germany should be unified and satisfied and on the closest of terms with Russia.

By contrast, the economic and social costs of unification for the (West) German government and taxpayer have proved and are still proving vastly greater than had been calculated, even allowing for an element of electioneering—to the point where one might ask (1) suppose it had been a case of 16 million Germans having to absorb 60 million, instead of the other way round? and (2) suppose the division of Germany had lasted for 55 or 60 years instead of 45? Suppose this pair of pistols had been differently loaded? But such questions are best left to the Might-Have-Been department.

And lastly, back to Britain. What German unification required from Britain was alertness, insight, imagination, political instinct, diplomatic skills, and a kind of all-round professionalism in the civilian field to match the military professionalism which the

British armed services were called upon to show shortly afterwards in the Gulf War. Mrs Thatcher was at the head of Britain's affairs for only the first few months of the Gulf crisis, but she was in charge throughout the German unification process, which makes it difficult to compare her performance in these two contexts. To me she looked happier on the Gulf than on the German stage. Few would want to argue that the Gulf crisis played any part in Mrs Thatcher's fall from power in November 1990. But perhaps I am not alone in thinking that her prompt, critical, and persistent reaction to the opening moves on Germany illustrated the qualities which, as shown on a wide range of other issues, from European integration to the Poll Tax, persuaded her Party colleagues in the House of Commons that with her at No. 10 Downing Street the Conservatives would risk losing the next election. So in a subsidiary way and indirectly, at least, these German events may have contributed to her downfall.

Part IV

ECONOMIC AND FINANCIAL LINKS

11

Anglo-German Post-War Economic Relations and Comparative Performance

JENS HÖLSCHER and HENRY LOEWENDAHL

1. Introduction

The post-war period has been one of growing affluence for Germany and the UK. Both economies have experienced continuous growth of annual Gross Domestic Product (GDP) and per capita incomes have steadily increased.

Economic prosperity has been driven by several key factors: first, growth in the world economy as a whole has been pivotal, providing the markets for a rapid growth in exports; second, in both economies increasing labour and capital productivity has ensured international competitiveness; and, third, this has been achieved through constant investment in the fixed capital stock, in human capital, and in technological advance.

Interdependence between the German and UK economies has correspondingly intensified, as both countries took advantage of the trade and investment opportunities in each other's market.

While the overall picture for both economies is positive, the comparative performance of Germany and the UK has diverged for much of the post-war period, with Germany making relative gains over the UK, as seen in Section 2.1. Germany became the industrial centre of Europe. However, it was not until the 1970s that Germany overtook the UK in terms of economic size.

Since the 1970s, Germany has ensured continued economic leadership over the UK through greater economic stability, sustained capital investment, and higher research and development (R&D) expenditure, as seen in Section 2.3. The case study of cross-border activity in the automotive sector given in Section 3 underlines Germany's international competitiveness. Section 3.1 examines the changing fortunes of UK and German industry and trade relations, and 3.2 concentrates on Germany's advantage in R&D. Recent acquisitions in the auto sector are analysed in Section 3.3 before the essay concludes in Section 4.

2. A Statistical Overview of the Comparative Economic Performance of the German and UK Economies

This study will be divided into three sections: first, a comparison of key domestic economic parameters—GDP, per capita GDP, productivity, and capital investment; second, a comparison of international factors—export volume, export growth, per capita exports, and Anglo-German trade and investment; and, third, a more detailed look at Anglo-German trade and indicators of Germany's advantage—inflation, exchange rates, savings and investment.[1]

Comparisons with the other leading world economies (United States, France, Japan, and China) are given in the tables, although generally they are not discussed in the text.

2.1. Post-war key domestic economic parameters

In terms of the absolute level of GDP, between 1950 and 1997 a total transformation occurred, as can be seen in Table 11.1. In 1950 the German economy was 60 per cent the size of the UK economy, but in 1997 the UK economy was 60 per cent the size of Germany's. The faster relative growth of the German economy can be seen in Table 11.2. German economic growth exceeded UK levels in all periods, although the gap has progressively narrowed. However, the absolute size of the economy does not provide a useful indica-

---

[1] Data for Tables 1–11, 14, 15, and 22 are derived primarily from A. Maddison, 'Explaining the Economic Performance of Nations', *Journal of Economic Literature*, 25 (June 1987); id., *The World Economy in the Twentieth Century* (Paris: OECD, 1989); and id., *Explaining the Economic Performance of Nations: Essays in Time and Space* (Aldershot: Edward Elgar, 1995). Maddison provides extensive data covering the period from 1870 to the end of the 1980s. Other key sources were several OECD publications: OECD, *OECD Economies at a Glance: Structural Indicators* (Paris: OECD, 1996); OECD, *The OECD in Figures: Statistics on the Member Countries* (Paris: OECD, 1998); OECD, *Main Economic Indicators*, 212 (Paris: OECD, June/July 1998), and various *Country Surveys*; and World Bank publications: World Bank, *World Tables* (London: Johns Hopkins University Press, 1995), and World Bank, *Economic and Social Survey of Asia and the Pacific* (Washington: World Bank, 1998). Bank of America, *Country Data Forecasts* (World Information Services, Bank of America, March 1998) was also used, and various issues of *The Economist* (5 Feb. 1994, 27 Apr.–3 May 1996) were used to calculate GDP and GDP per capita and manufacturing productivity.

TABLE 11.1. Total Gross Domestic Product (international $US billions)

	Germany	UK	France	USA	Japan	China
1950	125.4	210	123.1	1019.7	93.3	184.9
1973	470.7	416.7	388.9	2326.2	719.5	682.6
1987	606.4	520.3	527.6	3308.4	1198.9	1869.9
1997	2115.4	1278.4	1393.8	7819.3	4223.4	3720

TABLE 11.2. Average annual compound growth rates in GDP 1950–1996

	Germany	UK	France	USA	Japan	China
1950–73	5.9	3	5.1	3.7	9.4	5.8
1973–87	1.8	1.6	2.2	2.5	3.7	7.5
1987–96	2.2	2.1	2.3	2.4	3.1	9.7

tor of the wealth of a country. Gross Domestic Product per capita is perhaps the key measure of a country's wealth, and this is given in Table 11.3. In 1950, German per capita income was 60 per cent of the UK level; by 1996 it was 12 per cent bigger. In the post-war period, the per capita income of all the major economies, with the exception of China, has converged to broadly similar levels. This has only been possible with a faster growth in per capita income in Germany, France, and Japan, relative to the UK and USA. From 1950 to 1987 the rate of growth in per capita real GDP in Germany was almost 3.8 per cent annually and in the UK 2.1 per cent.[2]

TABLE 11.3. Gross Domestic Product per capita, 1950–1996 (international $US)

	Germany	UK	France	USA	Japan	China
1950	2508	4171	2941	6697	1116	338
1973	7595	7413	7462	10077	6622	774
1987	9964	9178	9475	13550	9756	1748
1996	21200	18636	20533	27821	23235	3100

[2] It should be noted, however, that in the most recent period, 1992–7, UK growth has outstripped that of Germany by a factor of nearly 2 : 1.

Looking now at labour productivity, Table 11.4 tells an almost identical story, with Germany, France, and Japan closing the gap with US levels, and catching up and then exceeding UK productivity. In manufacturing the same results are found, as shown in Table 11.5. From the early 1970s to the late 1980s German productivity rapidly passed UK levels and was seemingly on a trend to exceed US levels. However, during the 1990s comparative UK productivity levels rose, and the apparent catch-up of Germany, France, and Japan with US manufacturing productivity began to reverse itself.[3]

TABLE 11.4. Comparative levels of labour productivity 1950–1989 (GDP per worker hour)

	USA	UK	France	Germany	Japan
1950	100	58.6	45	33.6	13.9
1973	100	68.8	74.7	72.8	43.8
1984	100	80.6	97.5	90.5	55.6
1989	100	81	95	89	65

TABLE 11.5. Comparative levels of manufacturing productivity 1950–1995 (output per hour)

	USA	UK	Germany	Japan
1950	100	40	39	18
1973	100	52	75	56
1989	100	61	80	80
1995	100	70	81	73

Note: Only the 1995 statistics for France were available—a comparative productivity of 85.

[3] From 1979 to 1992 the growth in manufacturing labour productivity in descending order was as follows: Japan 4%, UK 3.7%, US 2.5%, France 2.3%, and Germany 1.2%. N. Hood and S. Young, 'The United Kingdom', in J. H. Dunning (ed.), *Governments, Globalisation and International Business* (Oxford: Oxford University Press, 1997), 254. It should be noted, though, that in the aftermath of German unification there was a major problem of low productivity in East Germany. J. Hölscher and S. F. Frowen, *The German Currency Union of 1990: A Critical Assessment* (London and New York: Macmillan Press, St Martin's Press, 1997), and J. Hölscher and A. Hochberg (eds.), *East Germany's Economic Development: Domestic and Global Aspects* (London and New York: Macmillan Press, St Martin's Press, 1998).

TABLE 11.6. Labour productivity growth 1960–1996 (value added per employed person)

	Germany	UK	France	USA	Japan
1960–73	4.5	3.9	5.3	2.2	8.3
1973–79	3.1	1.5	2.9	0	−2.9
1979–96	1.8	2	2.1	0.8	2.4

From Table 11.6, the strong and consistent productivity growth of Germany (and France) stands out, as does the recent improvement in UK performance.

Labour productivity growth can arise from greater investment in fixed capital stock or by improved utilization of labour. Table 11.7 depicts the growth of investment in fixed capital stock, providing important insights into the nature of German and UK productivity growth. Growth in German fixed capital stock exceeds that of the UK markedly in all periods. While UK labour productivity growth is higher than Germany's in the most recent period, as shown in Tables 11.5 and 11.6, there is no similar trend for growth of fixed capital stock.

The strong relative performance of Germany in all periods in terms of capital investment suggests that the recent revival in UK labour productivity growth is caused by changes in labour-related variables. A more effective and intensified use of labour in the UK is likely to have underpinned UK productivity growth—rather than capital investment.[4] The persistently higher levels of German

TABLE 11.7. Rate of growth of fixed capital stock 1950–1996

	Germany	UK	France	USA	Japan
1950–73	5.35	3.28	3.62	3.38	7.98
1973–84	3.39	2.51	4	2.79	3.41
1984–96	3.1	2.2	1.5	4	4.7

[4] This conclusion is supported by the OECD, *The OECD in Figures*: 'Stronger labour productivity growth has not been linked to capital investment, which, in fact, has remained lower relative to GDP than in other recovery periods. Rather it seems linked to changes in

investment in R&D relative to the UK (see Table 11.22) also accounts for the lower levels of UK productivity.

2.2. Post-war key international economic parameters

Exports are a key indicator of the international competitiveness of an economy's production. As can be seen in Table 11.8, both Germany and the UK have achieved a huge rise in their volume of exports in the post-war period. The volume of German exports rose from just over one-quarter the level of UK exports in 1950 to two-thirds greater than the UK volume in 1997. In fact, Germany was the world's leading exporter in the mid-1980s, despite the fact that the German economy was over five times *smaller* than the US economy at the time. German growth rate in exports has greatly surpassed that of the UK for most of the post-war period, as Table 11.9 shows. In the boom years of 1950 to 1973 German exports increased by almost 300 per cent. The UK's increased by only 94 per cent in comparison. However, from the the mid-1980s to mid-1990s UK exports outstripped Germany's, and US exports

TABLE 11.8. Volume of exports 1950–1997 (1980s prices; 1997 at current prices; $US billions)

	Germany	UK	France	USA	Japan	China
1950	9.7	35.1	13.7	37	2.6	5.4
1973	142.7	84.8	84.7	150.1	70.4	10
1986	248.8	136.6	130	193.7	182.6	36
1997	569.6	340.7	368.6	844.5	456.9	166.3

TABLE 11.9. Annual average compound growth rate in export volume 1950–1996

	Germany	UK	France	USA	Japan	China
1950–73	12.4	3.9	8.2	6.3	15.4	2.7
1973–86	4.4	3.7	3.3	1.7	7.6	10.4
1986–96	2.5	4.7	5.1	8.8	4.6	15.3

work organisation with inflexible and outdated job demarcation giving way to more rational job allocation' (cited in J. Tomaney, 'The Reality of Workplace Flexibility', *Capital & Class*, 40 (Spring 1990), 29–60, 45–6).

surged by 8.8 per cent annually, making the USA again the world's largest exporter.

If we look at exports per capita, however (Table 11.10), Germany regains its position as the world's leading exporter. In 1950 Germany's exports per capita were less than one-third of the UK's. By 1986 Germany's were over twice the level of the UK. In 1995 German per capita exports were still over double those of the USA.

TABLE 11.10. Exports per capita 1950–1995 (current prices and exchange rates $US)

	Germany	UK	France	USA	Japan	China
1950	39.9	125.6	73.7	67.5	10	1
1973	1090	527	703	337	341	7
1986	3984	1885	2256	899	1603	30
1995	6957	5796	6314	3180	3630	138

If we look at trade between Germany and the UK (Figure 11.1), for almost all of the post-war period German exports have exceeded its imports from the UK, with the gap widening from 1980.

Exports and imports are clearly closely connected, and both are on an upward trend. Furthermore, the increase in two-way Anglo-German exports has exceeded the growth of total German and UK exports to the rest of the world, as seen in Table 11.11. Until the mid-1980s the UK and Germany became more important to each other as export markets relative to the rest of the world. However, from the mid-1980s two-way exports reduced in relative importance. This was probably due to the opening up of the Eastern European market and rapid growth in Asia-Pacific.

TABLE 11.11. The relative importance of bilateral Anglo-German exports

	Germany		UK	
	Total export growth (%)	Export growth to UK (%)	Total export growth (%)	Export growth to Germany (%)
1950–73	1470	2100	240	1040
1973–86	170	530	160	570
1986–97	230	150	250	170

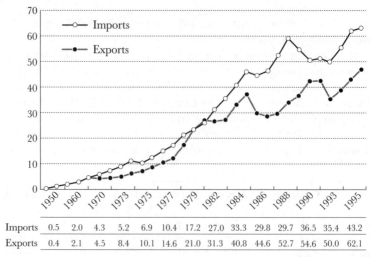

| Imports | 0.5 | 2.0 | 4.3 | 5.2 | 6.9 | 10.4 | 17.2 | 27.0 | 33.3 | 29.8 | 29.7 | 36.5 | 35.4 | 43.2 |
| Exports | 0.4 | 2.1 | 4.5 | 8.4 | 10.1 | 14.6 | 21.0 | 31.3 | 40.8 | 44.6 | 52.7 | 54.6 | 50.0 | 62.1 |

FIGURE 11.1. German imports from and exports to the UK 1950–1996 (DM billions)
Source: OECD (various) Germany Economic Survey, Paris: OECD.

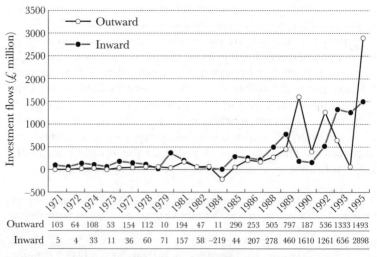

| Outward | 103 | 64 | 108 | 53 | 154 | 112 | 10 | 194 | 47 | 11 | 290 | 253 | 505 | 797 | 187 | 536 | 1333 | 1493 |
| Inward | 5 | 4 | 33 | 11 | 36 | 60 | 71 | 157 | 58 | −219 | 44 | 207 | 278 | 460 | 1610 | 1261 | 656 | 2898 |

FIGURE 11.2. UK outward direct investment flows to Germany and German inward flows to the UK 1981–1995*
* Net Investment.
Source: Business Monitor, *Overseas Transactions MA4* (London: HMSO, 1977); Business Monitor, *Overseas Transactions MA4* (London: DTI, 1985); Business Monitor, *Overseas Direct Investment MA4* (London, ONS, 1995a).

As with trade relations, an analysis of investment flows between Germany and the UK reveals that bilateral flows are on an upward path. This is particularly marked in the period since 1985, as can be seen in Figure 11.2.

For the whole of the 1970s and 1980s UK investment in Germany exceeded German investment in the UK, whereas in the 1990s there was almost twice as much German investment in the UK as UK investment in Germany. The investment flows in the 1990s were also far greater than those in previous decades.

Overall, investment flows are nearly in balance. From 1971 to 1995 the UK invested £8.6 billion in Germany while Germany invested £8.4 billion in the UK.

From Table 11.12 we can see that the UK is relatively more important for Germany than Germany is for the UK. A total of 7.8 per cent of German inward investment comes from the UK, whereas 6.0 per cent of UK inward investment comes from Germany. In terms of outward investment, 10 per cent of Germany's goes to the UK while 4.6 per cent of UK outward investment goes to Germany.

TABLE 11.12. Direct inward and outward investment stock in Germany and UK by major source and host countries as of end 1995

	German investment stocks		UK investment stocks	
	Inward % total	Outward % total	Inward % total	Outward % total
Australia	0.2	1.0	5.5	6.0
Belgium-Lux.	3.8	12.0	1.9	1.7
France	8.9	7.4	6.6	6.8
Germany			6.0	4.6
Japan	5.7	1.9	3.8	1.3
Netherlands	21.7	9.0	15.0	14.3
Switzerland	11.5	4.8	2.2	0.1
UK	7.8	10.0		
United States	25.8	19.5	42.2	31.5
Total ($USbn)	189.545	252.928	233.077	331.354

Source: Derived from OECD (1997) *International Direct Investment Statistics Yearbook*. Based on data using DM-denominated flows for Germany and sterling-denominated flows for UK.

For both countries the USA is the biggest source and host for investment, followed by the Netherlands. It is also clear that the German and UK investment stocks are biased toward German-speaking and English-speaking countries respectively.

However, if we look at investment flows from 1990 to 1995, (Table 11.13), we get a different picture. German inward investment in the UK as a proportion of total inward investment in the UK is 12.6 per cent, more than double the amount in terms of stock. The UK is now the biggest host for German outward investment in the world.

TABLE 11.13. German and UK investment flows by main source and host countries 1990–1995

	German investment flows		UK investment flows	
	Inward % total	Outward % total	Inward % total	Outward % total
Australia	0.2	0.5	5.0	6.9
Belgium-Lux.	10.5	11.7	1.7	0.4
France	20.1	9.0	8.7	4.9
Germany			12.6	5.4
Japan	9.7	1.3	3.7	0.6
Netherlands	14.2	10.3	14.7	16.5
Switzerland	0.6	4.2	5.9	−0.6
United Kingdom	18.2	13.6		
United States	0.4	11.6	49.4	28.7
Total ($USbn)	24.756	138.206	113.905	150.264

Source: Derived from OECD (1997) *International Direct Investment Statistics Yearbook*. Based on data using DM-denominated flows for Germany and sterling-denominated flows for UK.

The picture in terms of inward investment in Germany has also changed, with the UK accounting for 18.2 per cent of inward investment in Germany, the second largest source. During the 1990s, Germany and the UK became relatively more important to each other in terms of investment flows. However, the UK is still more important for German investment flows than Germany is for the UK.

2.3. Germany's advantage: economic stability and investment

According to the above economic indicators, Germany has caught up with and surpassed the UK. This is reflected in trade relations, where Germany has experienced a consistent trade surplus with the UK. At the same time, Germany and the UK have become more integrated with each other relative to the rest of the world in terms of trade and investment flows.

Germany's performance has been built on economic stability and sustained investment. A key indicator of stability is inflation, and, as shown in Table 11.14, Germany has achieved consistently low inflation. In contrast, the UK has proved unable to reduce inflation over time and to control inflation in times of crisis. This is particularly apparent in the period 1973–82.

TABLE 11.14. Annual average compound rate of increase in GDP deflator 1950–1997

	Germany	UK
1950–73	3.8	4.6
1973–82	4.7	15
1982–86	2.5	4.7
1986–97	2.8	4.7

The stability of the German economy is reflected in the sterling–Deutschmark exchange rate, with sterling continuously devaluing *vis-à-vis* the D-Mark, as can be seen in Figure 11.3.

Until the 1967 sterling crisis the exchange rate was relatively stable, with only one minor devaluation of sterling. The Bretton Woods System of exchange rates, with currencies pegged to the dollar at a fixed price of gold, provided stability.

However, with the growth of mobile offshore currency markets short-term capital flowed into 'hard' currencies. Germany had tighter monetary control and trade surpluses with the UK, and money flowed out of pounds into D-Marks. With the abolition of all exchange controls in the early 1970s, sterling went into free-fall against the D-Mark.

During the 1970s the value of the D-Mark more than doubled against sterling, with the oil-crisis and budget and trade deficits fuelling inflation in the UK and eroding confidence in sterling. From the start of the 1980s to the mid-1990s the D-Mark doubled again in value, with higher inflation and worsening UK trade deficits.

From the 1950s to the 1970s sterling devalued against the dollar, but since the 1980s the exchange rate has remained relatively stable. The rise of the D-Mark was not only representative of high relative inflation and trade deficits in the UK, but also of the underlying strength and stability of the German economy.

From a macro-economic point of view the exchange rate indicates the competitiveness of the whole national economy and shows a clear picture of both countries. One can even go a step further and claim that the continuing undervaluation of the D-Mark due to the monetary policy of the Bundesbank ensured the strength of the German economy.[5]

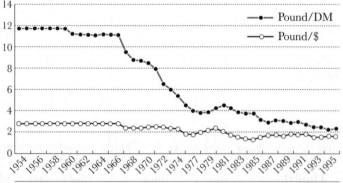

| Pound/DM | 11.73 11.71 11.72 11.71 11.22 11.1 11.17 9.555 8.736 7.975 6.049 4.051 3.888 4.556 3.87 3.784 2.941 3.079 2.925 2.483 2.26 |
| Pound/$ | 2.81 2.796 2.81 2.808 2.808 2.793 2.793 2.394 2.396 2.502 2.34 1.746 2.123 2.025 1.516 1.298 1.639 1.638 1.769 1.502 1.578 |

FIGURE 11.3. Sterling exchange rate against DM and $US 1954–1996
Source: Economic Trends (1997) Annual Supplement. London: ONS.

[5] J. Hölscher, *Entwicklungsmodell Westdeutschland: Aspekte der Akkumulation in der Geldwirtschaft* (Berlin: Duncker & Humblot, 1994); id., (ed.), *50 Years of the German Mark: Essays in Honour of Stephen F. Frowen* (Basingstoke: Palgrave, 2001).

As detailed in Table 11.15, Germany both saves more and invests more than the UK, and the gap between Germany and the UK widened further in the 1990s. With higher manufacturing productivity, faster growth rates of capital investment, and better export performance, it would be expected that Germany would have a trade surplus with the UK, and that manufactured goods would dominate German exports to the UK. As can be seen from Table 11.16, this is precisely the case.

Over 93 per cent of German exports to the UK in 1995 were manufactured goods. In fact Germany's manufactured exports to the UK exceeded the UK's total exports to Germany by almost one-fifth. The biggest component of Germany's manufactured exports was Machinery and Transport Equipment, which alone accounted for nearly the whole of Germany's £5.9 billion trade surplus with the UK.

At the same time, though, manufactured goods dominated UK exports to Germany, accounting for 87 per cent of total exports. Again Machinery and Transport Equipment was the biggest component of manufactures, and it is in this grouping that Germany enjoys its largest trade surplus. In all other classifications UK exports were more on a par with German levels.

From the Machinery and Transport Equipment classification, Road Vehicles has been highlighted. Trade in this product alone accounts for over £4.7 billion or 80 per cent of Germany's trade surplus with the UK. In this sense, trade in road vehicles is the key to understanding the comparative competitiveness of the German economy.

TABLE 11.15. Ratio of total gross savings and gross domestic investment to GDP 1950–1997

	Germany		UK	
	Savings/ GDP %	Investment/ GDP %	Savings/ GDP %	Investment/ GDP %
1950–73	24.1	27.5	16.6	17.9
1974–87	22.3	24	19.5	19.2
1990–98	20.0	22.2	16.4	13.3

Note: Figures for Investment/GDP are based on the average of: (1) 1950 and 1973 ratios; (2) 1973 and 1982 ratios; (3) 1982 and 1997 ratios.

TABLE 11.16. Anglo-German trade 1995 by SITC classification (£ million)

Product Classification	UK		Germany	
	Exports to Germany	% total exports to Germany	Exports to UK	% of total exports to UK
Food & Live Animals	573	2.9	762	3.0
Beverages & Tobacco	212	1.1	307	1.2
Crude Materials	238	1.2	313	1.2
Mineral Fuels & Lubricants & Related	1,502	7.5	154	0.6
Animal & Vegetable Oils, Fats & Waxes	26	0.1	32	0.1
Chemicals & Related Manufactures	2,418	12.1	3,373	13.1
Manufactured Goods— by Material	2,900	14.6	3,834	14.9
Machinery & Transport Equipment	9,743	48.9	14,871	57.7
Of which Road Vehicles	1,925	9.7	6,631	25.7
Miscellaneous Manufactured Articles	2,280	11.4	2,118	8.2
Commodities & Transactions not classified	29	0.1	23	0.1
Total Manufactures	17,342	87	24,196	93.8
Grand Total	19,922	100	25,787	100

Source: Derived from Business Monitor, *Overseas Trade Statistics of the United Kingdom with the World MA20* (London: HM Customs and Excise Tariff and Statistical Office, 1995b).

3. Comparative Advantage in the Automobile Industry

The automobile industry is of key importance not only for Germany and the UK but for Europe as a whole. It is the largest industry in Europe, accounting for 2 per cent of European Union added value and employing more than 11 million employees, directly or indirectly.[6] The following sections will discuss Anglo-German relations in the automobile industry in terms of production, trade, research and development, and acquisitions.

3.1. Changing fortunes

In the post-war era the comparative history of the UK and German auto industries has reflected that of their economies in general. While German production increased consistently, the UK's peaked at the start of the 1970s and fell almost every year for the next 15 years. In line with trends in the overall UK and German economies, in the 1990s UK auto production increased and Germany's levelled off. In 1956 UK total vehicle production was only 3 per cent less than Germany, by 1984 this figure was over 70 per cent, and in 1996 German production was still over 60 per cent higher.

The oft-cited causes of UK weakness in the auto industry, epitomizing the decline of UK industry in general, were bloated factories, arrogant workers and managers leading to unreliability, and bad quality. The Central Policy Review Staff study of *The Future of the British Car Industry* noted that: 'There are too many manufacturers with too many models, too many plants and too much

TABLE 11.17. German and UK vehicle production 1956–1996

	Germany		UK	
	Total Vehicles	Cars	Total Vehicles	Cars
1956	1,075,619	847,829	1,004,544	707,594
1972	3,815,982	3,166,021	2,329,430	1,921,311
1984	4,045,463	3,504,075	1,133,731	908,906
1990	4,976,552	4,197,434	1,565,957	1,295,611
1996*	4,842,909	3,800,065	1,924,448	1,686,134

*If we include vehicles assembled outside Germany by German firms using parts manufactured in Germany total vehicle production in 1996 would be 7,334,564 and car output 6,712,380.

Source: Derived from American Automobile Manufacturers Association (AAMA), *World Motor Vehicle Data* (Detroit: AAMA, 1998).

---

[6] European Commission/European Parliament, *Forum on the European Automobile Industry: Written Proceedings* (Luxembourg: European Commission, Mar. 1994).

capacity. Other severe weaknesses are poor quality, bad labour relations, unsatisfactory delivery record, low productivity and too much manpower.'[7]

From the mid-1980s UK output began to recover, largely due to Japanese inward investors. Almost three-quarters of the rise in UK production from 1991 to 1996 was accounted for by the output of the three Japanese producers.

However, the UK still suffered an enormous trade deficit in road vehicles. In 1997 the UK trade deficit in road vehicles was almost £6 billion, nearly 40 per cent of the total UK trade deficit. This was an increase on the previous two years, a period when the UK auto industry was growing at its fastest rate for a quarter of a century.

In 1995 the UK deficit in autos was almost £5.8 billion (see Table 11.16). Of this deficit in road vehicles over £4.7 billion was accounted for by the UK's deficit with Germany. In other words, over 81 per cent of the UK's trade deficit in road vehicles was with Germany. The UK's trade deficit in road vehicles with Germany accounted for one-third of the UK's total trade deficit in all goods with the whole world.

In contrast to the bumpy history of the UK car industry, German manufacturers achieved consistent success on world markets.

TABLE 11.18. UK passenger car production by manufacturer 1991–1996

Firm	1991	1992	1993	1994	1995	1996
Rover Group	395,624	378,797	406,804	462,614	473,951	473,217
Ford	339,271	302,146	271,793	269,058	273,896	328,028
Vauxhall	255,733	287,884	232,569	250,439	231,196	268,228
Peugeot/ Talbot	87,983	85,821	72,902	74,440	78,379	85,108
Honda	0	1,001	32,139	42,805	91,084	105,810
Nissan	124,666	179,009	246,281	204,944	215,346	231,627
Toyota	0	0	37,314	85,467	88,440	116,973
Total	1,236,900	1,291,880	1,375,524	1,466,823	1,532,084	1,686,134

Source: AAMA, *World Motor Vehicle Data* (Detroit: AAMA, 1998).

[7] Central Policy Review Staff, *The Future of the British Car Industry* (1975), p. v; cited in Hood and Young, 'The United Kingdom'.

German competitiveness has been built on high quality, high productivity, and continuous investment in the upgrading of production and technology. With intensifying price competition in the 1980s,[8] German auto producers moved up-market with models designed to meet individual customers' preferences. High-volume markets were not abandoned.[9]

By looking at the dependency of the 'national champions' of each country on their home market, we can see that the German automobile industry is the most internationally competitive in Europe, and the UK's the least. As noted above, one reason for the success of the German automobile industry is high productivity. In 1995 GM's German plant had the highest productivity in Europe, was over 2.5 times more productive than its sister plant in the UK, and over 3.5 times more productive than Rover's Longbridge plant. Other than Nissan, every producer in the UK had productivity below the European average.[10]

TABLE 11.19. Dependency of main 'national' auto manufacturers on home market 1994

Manufacturer	Dependency on home market sales (%)
Rover (UK)	80
Fiat (I)	62
Peugeot (F)	54
Renault (F)	54
Daimler-Benz (G)	47
Volkswagen (G)	38

Source: L. Moore, 'Developments in Trade and Trade Policy', in M. J. Artis and N. Lee (eds.), *The Economics of the European Union: Policy and Analysis* (Oxford: OUP, 1994), 315–16.

[8] e.g. in 1995 German manufacturing wages were the highest in the world. The average wage was $US32.10 for one hour of an employee's work ($US17.66 in wages), over double the UK remuneration of about $US14 ($US10 wages) (*The Economist*, 27 Apr.–3 May 1996).

[9] W. Streek, 'Successful Adjustment in Turbulent Markets: The Automobile Industry', in P. J. Katzenstein (ed.), *Industry and Politics in West Germany: Towards the Third Republic* (Ithaca: Cornell University Press, 1989); H.-G. Betz, 'German Model Reconsidered', *German Studies Review*, 19/2 (May 1996), 302–20; 309.

[10] It should be noted that a 1997 survey by the Economist Intelligence Unit found that three of the four most productive plants in Europe were Japanese producers in the UK. Nissan's Sunderland plant was most productive with 73.2 cars per worker followed by GM's Eisenach plant (IBB, 27 Aug. 1997).

TABLE 11.20. Productivity at major UK car plants compared to Germany and Europe, 1995

Manufacturer	Plant	Output per employee
Ford	Dagenham	36.5
Rover	Longbridge	19.4
Honda	Swindon	43.4
Nissan	Sunderland	50.1
Toyota	Derby	41.2
Vauxhall (GM)	Luton	27.2
Opel (GM)	**Eisenach (Germany)**	**71.9**
EU Average	All Europe	45

Source: R. Paisley, 'Toyota: A Case Study of Inward Investment in the UK', *British Economy Survey*, 26/2 (Spring 1997), 5–8, 6; United Nations Conference on Trade and Investment (UNCTAD), 'World Investment Report 1995: Transnational Corporations and Competitiveness', *Transnational Corporations*, 4/3 (Dec. 1995), 101–65, 136.

TABLE 11.21. Import penetration for new registrations of passenger cars 1968–1996

Year	Germany		UK		France	
	Units	Share %	Units	Share %	Units	Share %
1968	260,234	20.4	91,379	8.3	265,351	21.4
1972	562,069	26.2	384,946	23.5	338,062	20.6
1976	500,407	21.6	532,750	41.4	425,795	22.9
1980	638,682	26.3	858,319	56.7	428,516	22.9
1984	638,991	26.7	1,006,468	57.5	630,309	35.9
1988	816,892	29.1	1,249,691	56.4	816,848	36.8
1992	1,354,264	34.5	875,356	54.9	845,579	40.2
1996	1,144,229	32.7	1,256,364	63.0	939,101	44.1

Source: Derived from AAMA, *World Motor Vehicle Data* (Detroit: AAMA, 1998).

Higher productivity in German (and continental European) plants was a major reason for the increase in import penetration of the UK auto market from the rest of Europe. From 1968 to 1996 the UK went from having the lowest import penetration to the highest. The turning point was during the first half of the 1970s, when import penetration nearly tripled from 14.3 per cent in 1970 to 41.4 per cent in 1976. The year 1976 was the first when absolute

UK imports exceeded those of Germany, which has been the case for every year since 1976. In 1996 penetration in the UK market reached 63 per cent, a post-war high.

The rise in import penetration was to a large extent attributable to US assemblers increasing the proportion of their car sales in the UK from Europe—primarily from Germany. Ford and GM's combined figure for tied imports increased from 1 to 22 per cent from 1974 to 1984. They went from net exporters of 200,000 to net importers of around 350,000 cars. Ford and GM alone shed 28,000 jobs from 1969 to 1992. In 1993 Ford's net trade deficit from Britain reached £700 million and GM's £600 million.[11]

In contrast, Ford and GM produced almost 1.6 million passenger cars in Germany of which 60 per cent or nearly one million units were exported in 1996. They produced one million fewer cars in the UK, and exported only 250,000 in 1996.[12]

That US firms were a major reason for the UK's growing trade deficit is key to understanding Germany's competitive advantage over the UK. US auto firms have the most plants across Europe and are therefore best placed to compare countries. In fact, US firms in general are much more likely than German (or Japanese, French, and Italian) firms to have worldwide systems of performance evaluation.[13] In addition, US firms are not rooted to any one country in Europe in terms of national allegiances, and therefore provide the best indication of the relative location advantages of different sites.

3.2. Research and development

With US auto firms concentrating production in Germany rather than the UK, Germany offers key advantages, which overcome high relative labour costs. The comparison of GM's Luton and Eisenach plants showed the superior productivity of Germany, and

[11] A. Pike, 'Greenfields, Brownfields and Industrial Policy in the UK', *Regional Studies*, 30/1 (Feb. 1996), 69–77, 72; R. Church, *The Rise and Decline of the British Motor Industry* (Basingstoke: Macmillan, 1994), 109–11.

[12] Derived from American Automobile Manufacturers Association (AAMA), *World Motor Vehicle Data* (Detroit: AAMA, 1998); K. Eason, 'UK car-making resurgence driven by the Japanese', *The Times*, 3 Mar. 1997.

[13] A. Ferner, 'Country of Origin Effects and Human Resource Management in Multinational Companies', *Human Resource Management Journal*, 7/1 (1997), 19–37; A. Ferner and J. Quintanilla, 'Multinationals, National Business Systems, and the Management of HRM: The Enduring Influence of National Identity or a Process of "Anglo-Saxonisation" ', *International Journal of Human Resource Management, Special Issue* (1998), 7.

this is true for manufacturing in general. For example, US non-bank foreign-owned enterprises operating in Germany had a gross value added per head of 116.6 (average 1991–4, taking EU15 as 100). For US firms in the UK the figure was 87.3, the lowest in Europe, and nearly 30 per cent less than in Germany.[14]

However, productivity differences are not the only explanation for Germany's location advantages. In terms of research and development, Germany's lead over the UK is even more pronounced. Table 11.22 shows that UK expenditure on R&D is far below other major economies and, as Loewendahl argues,[15] the UK is experiencing an 'innovation deficit' which questions the long-term competitiveness of the UK economy. In fact, if the proportion of R&D associated with defence were subtracted, the gap between the UK and Germany would widen further—in 1996, 38 per cent of UK government R&D expenditure was on defence compared to only 10 per cent in Germany and only 6 per cent in Japan.[16]

In terms of patents, the contrast between the UK and Germany is more stark. In the UK, 45 per cent of US patents granted to large national firms were developed outside of the UK between 1985 and 1990. In Germany the figure was only 15 per cent.[17]

TABLE 11.22. Research and development expenditure as a percentage of GDP 1960–1997

	UK	Germany	Japan	USA	France
1960	2.5	1	1.4	2.7	1.3
1973	2.1	2.1	2	2.4	1.8
1985	2.29	2.71	2.81	2.77	2.3
1990	2.23	2.76	3.08	2.82	2.4
1995	2.02	2.3	2.98	2.61	2.3
1998	1.82	2.31	2.91	2.68	2.24

Source: H. B. Loewendahl, *Bargaining with Multinationals: The Investment of Siemens and Nissan in North East England* (Basingstoke: Palgrave, 2001).

[14] R. Barrell and N. Pain, 'Foreign Direct Investment, Technological Change, and Economic Growth within Europe', *Economic Journal*, 107/445 (Nov. 1997), 1770–86; 1776.

[15] H. B. Loewendahl, *Bargaining with Multinationals: The Investment of Siemens and Nissan in North East England* (Basingstoke: Palgrave, 2001).

[16] Ibid.

[17] R. Wade, 'Globalisation and its Limits: Reports of the Death of the National Economy are Greatly Exaggerated', in S. Berger and R. Dore (eds.), *National Diversity and Global Competition* (Ithaca: Cornell University Press, 1996), 83.

A study by Eurostat of high-tech and super-tech regions in Europe underlines Germany's strength. In terms of high-tech regions, out of the top ten regions six are in Germany and only one in the UK, as can be seen in Table 11.23. In these regions high-tech employment is dominated by the automobile industry. In terms of super-tech regions, again six out of the ten top regions are in Germany. Super-tech regions are characterized by employment in computers, office machinery, electronics and communication equipment, and pharmaceuticals. As with high-tech, the top two regions are in Germany. No super-tech regions are in the UK.

TABLE 11.23. Top ten high-tech regions, 1995

	People employed in high-tech	Those in high-tech as % of total employment
Baden-Württemberg (G)	820,000	17.3
Bayern (G)	713, 000	12.4
Nord Ovest (I)	282, 000	12.1
Rheinland-Pflaz (G)	203,000	12.0
Hessen (G)	313,000	11.8
Lombardia (I)	395,000	10.8
Est (F)	207,000	10.7
Niedersachsen (G)	338,000	10.3
West Midlands (UK)	232,000	9.9
Nordrhein-Westfalen (G)	693,000	9.5

Source: Eurostat, *Key Figures* (Belgium, June 1998).

TABLE 11.24. Top ten super-tech regions, 1995

	People employed in high-tech	Those in high-tech as % of total employment
Rheinland-Pflaz (G)	81,000	4.8
Hessen (G)	122,000	4.6
Vlaams Gewest (B)	96,000	4.1
Zuid (NL)	58,000	3.9
Lombardia (I)	137,000	3.8
Hamburg (G)	27,000	3.4
Baden-Württemberg (G)	162,000	3.4
Sachsen-Anhalt (G)	39,000	3.3
Nordrhein-Westfalen (G)	212,000	2.9
Ireland (whole country)	36,000	2.9

Source: Eurostat, *Key Figures* (Belgium, June 1998) .

If we look at US firms again, it is clear that Germany has the key location advantages for research and development activities. In 1992 US foreign-owned enterprises in the UK had three times as many assets as in Germany and in 1994 their gross product as percentage of host country GDP was 5.9 per cent for the UK compared to 2.9 per cent for Germany. But, in terms of R&D activity US firms carried out 40 per cent more in Germany than in the UK. In fact, the UK fared worse than all its competitors in terms of the research intensity of US affiliates.[18]

Therefore, while UK auto production has recovered again as the production of Japanese transplants came on stream, the UK has a continued weakness in this sector, especially when compared to Germany. This is revealed in terms of persistent trade deficits and in R&D.[19] For example, Nissan's second model to be produced in the UK, the Primera, was designed in Germany.

Low productivity, low R&D, and little appeal in international markets (Table 11.19) has not only led to a persistent trade deficit in autos but is also jeopardizing the future of the UK industry. In Europe there are 81 assembly plants and at present one-third of installed capacity in Europe is lying idle. It is likely that the UK will suffer most from rationalization, and by the end of 2000 BMW, Ford, and General Motors had all either pulled out of or announced major closures of their UK-based automotive assembly plants.

3.3. Cross-border takeovers

Anglo-German economic interaction in the automobile industry extends beyond trade relations. Just as two-way foreign investment has become a key feature of overall economic relations between Germany and the UK, in recent years foreign direct investment has played a major role in the automobile industry.

As with trade relations, the flows of direct investment in the auto industry are heavily biased, with Germany investing more in the UK

---

[18] Barrell and Pain, 'Foreign Direct Investment', 1776; R. Barrell and N. Pain, 'EU: An Attractive Investment', *New Economy*, 4/1 (Spring 1997), 50–4; 52; R. Barrell and N. Pain, 'The Growth of Foreign Direct Investment in Europe', *National Institute Economic Review* 2/160 (Apr. 1997), 63–75; 69.

[19] See Loewendahl, *Bargaining with Multinationals* for the incentives given by the UK government to attract inward investment by foreign firms, which prejudice high-value-added and research-intensive activities.

than the UK in Germany.[20] However, German direct investment in the UK has taken a different form to that of Japanese auto investment. Japanese investment has primarily involved the establishment of new or greenfield manufacturing plants.[21] In contrast, German investment has been concerned much more with the acquisition of indigenous firms. Therefore, while both German and Japanese inward investment in the UK is based on substantial capital flows, German investment has not involved capacity expansion.

Key to understanding these two forms of investment is that they both involve *control*; foreign control of the UK's automobile industry.

Similarly, both Japanese and German investment are representative of the weakness of indigenous UK industry. When Nissan, Honda, and Toyota invested in the UK in the 1980s, one of the key reasons why they chose the UK rather than Germany was the lack of competitive producers in the UK.[22] In 1994 Britain's biggest car producer and the only manufacturer in the UK with a full product range was acquired by BMW. One of the key reasons why BMW purchased Rover was the weakness of Rover at the time.

It has already been noted that one of the main weaknesses in the UK automobile industry (and UK industry in general) has been its management. One of BMW's specific ownership advantages over Rover was in middle-management structures.[23] These management structures are based upon better relations with workers to engender consensus and co-operation, and a long-term, and more internationalist perspective. In combination with BMW's famous engineering, design excellence, and marketing, BMW hoped it could raise the productivity of the workforce and competitiveness of output and market Rover globally.[24]

[20] For a discussion of Siemens' globalization strategy and semiconductor investment in the UK see H. B. Loewendahl, 'Siemens "Anglo-Saxon" Strategy: Is Globalising Business Enough?', *German Politics* (Apr. 1999).

[21] H. B. Loewendahl, 'Lean Production and Labour: Lessons from Japanese Investment in the UK', *Discussion Paper in German Studies* (University of Birmingham, Dec. 1998).

[22] Loewendahl, *Bargaining with Multinationals*, ch. 8.

[23] G. Bain, 'The UK's investment conundrum', *Financial Times*, 11 Aug. 1995.

[24] BMW's takeover of Rover would also give them access to sectors of the auto industry (in particular 4-wheel-drive and front-wheel-drive vehicles) in which BMW did not produce. Additionally, the acquisition was motivated by a desire to gain knowledge of the Japanese influence on Rover, through the Honda–Rover alliance, and of Rover's perceived engineering expertise (*The Economist*, 5 Feb. 1994; A. Pilkington, *Transforming Rover: Renewal Against the Odds 1981–1994* (Bristol: Bristol Academic Press, 1996), 1–22, 163–72).

After buying Rover from British Aerospace in 1994, BMW invested about £500 million a year to raise quality and productivity in a process that will eventually cost about £3 billion.[25] At the same time as counteracting previous under-investment at Rover, BMW also aimed to reintroduce the Rover marque to world markets, such as Latin America, compensating for the past management's failure to market globally.

Despite this much-needed new investment, Rover was still unprofitable. The main causes of Rover's unprofitability were threefold. The first was low productivity. The British Chancellor of the Exchequer, Mr Brown, said in response to job losses at Rover: 'unless we face up to the fact that we have a productivity gap with our competitors, then we will as a nation be failing to meet the challenges of the future.'[26] The second was the appreciation of sterling—a 30 per cent decrease in sterling's competitiveness since 1996, with the pound appreciating 13 per cent against the Mark since the acquisition,[27] and the third, poor quality and lacklustre products. In terms of quality, a recent study of 88,000 company cars found that Rover had the second worst reliability.[28] BMW was to be disappointed with both the quality of Rover's production and its engineering expertise. In terms of products, BMW quickly moved to close production of the 40,000 annual output of Rover 100s and later did the same for the badly selling Rover 400, 600, and 800 models. This led to a 26,000 cut in output and 1,500 job losses announced at the end of July 1998. By the time BMW's new flagship Rover 75 rolled out of the production line Rover's losses were more than BMW and its shareholders were willing to accept, and when the UK government's aid plan for upgrading Rover's Longbridge plant was rejected by the European Commission BMW made it clear that Rover was for sale. Rover was eventually sold in May 2000 for a symbolic £10 to the Phoenix Consortium

[25] H. Simonian, 'BMW's record with Rover augurs well for Rolls-Royce', *Financial Times*, 30 Apr. 1998.

[26] Cited in J. Jowit and R. Peston, 'Brown blasts Rover productivity: Chancellor blames carmaker for job losses in attempt to downplay influence of government economic policy', *Financial Times*, 24 July 1998.

[27] J. Griffiths, 'Rover to cut its output by 26,000 vehicles', *Financial Times*, 28 July 1998; *Financial Times*, 25 July 1998.

[28] J. Griffiths, 'Imported Japanese cars "more reliable": Toyota and Nissan Challenge fleet-rental data', *Financial Times*, 6 Feb. 1998.

made up of British business executives. Land Rover was subsequently sold to Ford and BMW will retain ownership of the new Mini.

Four years after BMW's acquisition of Rover, Volkswagen acquired Rolls-Royce in 1998 for £479 million and Vickers' Cosworth engineering subsidiary for an extra £120 million.[29] As part of the deal, BMW paid £40 million for the right to use the Rolls-Royce marque on cars. Volkswagen will retain the Crewe plant and the Bentley brand, while BMW will make Rolls-Royces at a separate site at Goodwood in south-east England from 2003 (BMW already supplies about 30 per cent of Rolls-Royce components).[30] After the sale of Rover, the UK's largest and its most prestigious producers came under German control.

A concluding comment by the *Financial Times* aptly summarizes post-war Anglo-German relations:

The contrasting fortunes of Rolls-Royce and VW are indicative of what has happened to industry in Britain and Germany since the war. Rolls-Royce is now a marginalised manufacturer of cars few can afford and which risk undermining the company's reputation for superior quality. VW is Europe's biggest carmaker.[31]

4. Conclusion

The statistical overview of German–British economic relations has revealed three key trends.

First, and most widely known, is Germany's rapid catch-up with the UK in all economic fields in the post-war period. This catch-up

---

[29] Like BMW when it acquired Rover, Volkswagen thought it could improve the competitiveness of Rolls-Royce through better management and greater investment and that it would have direct access to the luxury end of the market.

[30] H. Simonian, 'R-R cars head set to go despite last-ditch VW effort', *Financial Times*, 1 Aug. 1, 1998; J. Griffiths, 'The Silver Lady is captivated by BMW's charms', *Financial Times*, 29 July 1998; G. Bowley, H. Simonian, and R. Taylor, 'VW may try to top BMW offer for R-R motor cars', *Financial Times*, 1 Apr. 1998. BMW's tactics are to have car models spanning every segment of the market: the main luxury brands, the slightly downmarket Rover in the UK, and a presence at the pinnacle of the luxury car segment through Rolls-Royce (G. Bowley, 'Cruising the autobahn in style: FT interview Bernd Pischetsrieder: BMW won the battle for Rolls-Royce Motors, but its boss thinks the industry is in the grip of merger mania', *Financial Times*, 31 July 1998).

[31] R. Taylor, 'Patriotism is out of place in sale of Rolls-Royce: sentiment is in fact part of the reason it is now being sold', *Financial Times*, 15 May 1998.

was transformed into economic leadership from the 1970s, as Germany surpassed the UK in absolute as well as in relative terms.

Second, and a subject of increasing debate in academic and policy circles, is the resurgence of the UK economy from the late 1980s to the mid-1990s. We have seen that the UK has out-performed Germany in terms of many key economic indicators, such as productivity and export growth.

However, a more detailed comparison of Germany and the UK revealed that Germany's key sources of comparative advantage over the UK remain as strong, if not stronger, than in earlier periods. In terms of capital investment, economic stability, and research and development there has been no UK catch-up with Germany.

The improved UK performance relative to Germany since the late 1980s has been led by labour-related productivity increases. Long-term growth in productivity requires high levels of sustained capital investment. Given Germany's greater commitment to capital investment and the environment supporting it, the UK's relatively better economic performance is unlikely to continue in the long term.

Third, German–UK economic relations have been character-ized by increasing economic integration both in absolute terms and relative to their relations with the rest of the world. Until the mid-1980s this integration was primarily trade-led. However, since the mid-1980s, and especially in the 1990s, economic integration has been driven by foreign direct investment flows.

Since 1990, the UK has been the biggest host for German out-ward investment and the UK is the second biggest investor in Germany. In fact, this shift from trade to investment integration reflects trends in the world economy as a whole, where investment flows have exceeded trade flows since 1989.

The case study of Anglo-German economic relations in the auto industry reinforces the three conclusions given above. Until the early 1970s the UK auto industry grew, but from the 1970s to mid-1980s the industry collapsed. In contrast, the German auto indus-try grew throughout this period. From the mid-1980s the UK auto industry revived whilst Germany's stabilized. UK productivity, output, and exports grew rapidly.

However, German productivity still exceeded UK levels and Germany's advantage in terms of research and development remained as strong as ever. As a consequence, the UK experienced growing trade deficits in motor vehicles, even from 1995 to 1997 when UK auto production was rising rapidly. Germany was the biggest source of this deficit. A telling statistic is that in 1995 Germany's trade surplus with the UK in motor vehicles accounted for one-third of the UK's overall trade deficit with the whole world.

Trends in the auto industry have closely mirrored those of overall Anglo-German economic relations in the post-war period. Germany continues to have an underlying economic advantage over the UK, based on greater capital investment, greater research and development, and greater economic stability.

In the first two years after the introduction of the Single Currency in 1999, Germany's competitive advantage over the UK has strengthened as sterling appreciated against a weak Euro.[32] However, this will not necessarily be the scenario for the twenty-first century. Germany has lost the exchange rate instrument to ensure external competitiveness, and in the long term without a strong D-Mark the economic stability of the post-war period may not continue post-century. It also remains to be seen whether UK shareholder capitalism with an economy highly open to takeovers and a streamlined welfare state will become more competitive than German stakeholder capitalism.

---

[32] The strength of sterling *vis-à-vis* the Euro has made German exports to the UK more competitive, but has also had the effect of making German assets cheaper, facilitating UK acquisitions of German companies and greater integration of the German and UK economies. The most significant example is Vodafone's $163 billion acquisition of Germany's Mannesmann in 2000, which is the world's largest ever cross-border acquisition.

12

Banks and Bankers

Benedikt Koehler

In 1949 financial relations between Britain and Germany were at their nadir. At first glance, this comes as a surprise. Cross-fertilization between Germany and Britain in the sphere of finance had existed for many centuries, but two military contests in living memory had altogether obliterated this tradition. Even though Germany and Britain look back on centuries of thriving relationships in commerce and finance, by 1949 their common heritage had been all but destroyed. For this reason, it is worthwhile to review this background. Eventually, in the last quarter of the twentieth century, these historical ties reasserted themselves once more.

In Britain today there is widespread reluctance to join a supranational European currency, to give up the pound sterling divided into pence in favour of the Euro divided into cents. How could the adoption of a supranational currency, propagated by Germany, reliably support Britain's national sovereignty? There is some irony to this question, inasmuch as probably the first and undoubtedly the most lasting contribution which continental Europe made to Britain's financial system, during the ninth century AD, was monetary reform.

The regulation of coinage conventions was one of the reforms of the Carolingian Empire. It was common custom to designate units of currency by their weight, and even today in countries such as Turkey and Italy the terms for national currencies reflect their derivation from the Latin measure, 'libra'. Britain's own traditional division of the pound into twenty shillings, and of each shilling into twelve pence, was the result of the adoption of a Carolingian model developed on the European continent. Throughout the Middle Ages Britain's coinage continued to be cast in a Germanic mould. For the sake of differentiating the English pound as a measure of money from alternative weights, merchants of the Hanseatic League propagated their distinct weight for the pound. Hanseatic merchants had been doing business in London and all over England throughout the Middle Ages, and local merchants perceived them as coming from the 'East'. Hence, the pound of the Hanseatic merchants gave rise to the abbreviated designation 'pound sterling'. This term remains in use to this day and is vigorously defended against replacement by the Euro.

In modern times, a second lasting contribution to Britain's finance and commerce emanating from Germany was not in the field of monetary reform, but in the emergence of international banking. The eighteenth and nineteenth centuries witnessed the migration to England of talented financial entrepreneurs from Germany. Banking families such as Baring, Schroder, and Rothschild are notable examples of a large community. Other constituents of Germany's financial community followed. Deutsche Bank, for example, when it was floated on the Berlin Stock Exchange in 1870, stated in its business plan the express purpose to establish as soon as possible a foothold in the City of London.[1] Deutsche Bank duly opened for business in the City in 1873.[2] Other major German banks, foremost among them Dresdner Bank, soon followed suit. German banks in the City prospered. By 1914, the Acceptance Business of newcomers to the City such as Deutsche Bank, Dresdner Bank, and Disconto Gesellschaft almost equalled the turnover of earlier arrivals and current market leaders such as Kleinwort and Schroder. The decades preceding the First World War were the heyday of German banking in the City, and its market position at that time has never been matched since.

Until this time, the influx of banks and bankers across the Channel had been virtually a one-way traffic. Germans were obviously keen to do business in the City, but this movement was not reciprocated by their English counterparts. The reason lay in the relative position of the two countries' respective financial centres. There was simply no apparent commercial necessity for British Houses to seek out a presence in Germany, when without bothering to venture across the Channel British banks could do business with Germans on their doorstep in the City. This era ended

[1] Manfred Pohl and Kathleen Burk, *Die Deutsche Bank in London 1873–1998* (Munich: Piper, 1998).

[2] Lothar Gall *et al.*, *The Deutsche Bank 1870–1995* (London: Weidenfeld & Nicolson, 1995).

abruptly with the outbreak of the First World War. The calamities of the Great War brought the progress of German banks to a halt and German-owned assets in Britain were confiscated.[3] German commerce in the City practically disappeared. To all intents and purposes, Anglo-German financial relations ended in August 1914—not in 1929, 1933, 1939, or any of the other dates marking a step on the road towards financial decline or the military conflict that erupted in the Second World War.

By 1949, the common heritage of Anglo-German monetary and financial innovation was of no discernible significance, and one would have been hard-pressed to identify vestiges of the influence of generations of cosmopolitan, Continental bankers who had been so notable in an earlier era of peace and prosperity. Anyone with memories of this period would have retired many years before. One descendant of an important German banking family, Siegmund Warburg, was at that point, however, just beginning to assert himself in the City.[4] When he started his trading company, it would have been difficult to predict whether his contribution might be different from that of many other hardworking, cosmopolitan refugees from Europe, and whether he might create a link to a new generation and style of Anglo-German banking. From 1949 onwards, things began to change and the time had come for a new beginning.

Since 1949 Anglo-German financial relations have been marked by alternative responses to two key challenges: monetary reform and financial innovation. During this period of forty years important changes occurred in the two countries' respective positions, and their relationship to one another. Germany, at the outset of this period, was a debtor in international finance, whereas Britain, on the other hand, was a major international creditor. At a time when the Federal Republic of Germany was not yet established as an issuer of debt, even in its own domestic capital markets, and the Deutsche Mark was not convertible, Britain's pound sterling served as reserve currency, second in importance only to the United States dollar. Financially as much as politically, Britain and Germany were poles apart. Forty years later, the roles were

---

[3] Paul Emden, *Money Powers of Europe in the Nineteenth and Twentieth Centuries* (London: Sampson Low & Co., 1937), 222–4.

[4] Jacques Attali, *Un homme d'influence: Sir Siegmund Warburg (1902–1982)* (Paris: Fayard, 1985).

reversed, and by and large the pound had been replaced as a reserve currency by the Deutsche Mark. Although Germany's credit rating has improved steadily, there has been one immutable constant throughout this period: the City of London has remained a pivot of financial relations between the two countries. Indeed, one of the most interesting questions for a study of this period is how, irrespective of the unforeseen changes in the two countries' relative economic development, the City of London was able not only to defend, but also to consolidate this position as a hub of Anglo-German finance. This outcome was determined, in large part, by how the two countries addressed the challenges of financial innovation.

The Post-War Period

In effect, the financial constitutions of Germany and Britain have rarely had so much in common as since the Second World War. Both countries had sacrificed their store of economic wealth during the war years; both managed to reconstruct their economies only after the inflow of US assistance in the form of the Marshall Plan.[5] Even then, they succeeded only with difficulty.

The immediate aftermath of the Second World War brought irreversible changes to Britain's financial markets. In Germany's case, problems were compounded by the absence of a national currency, and by the legacy of war debt resulting from the First World War. The two countries pursued radically different economic policies. In Britain, the Labour Government brought the Bank of England into public ownership in 1946 and embarked on a wideranging programme of social reforms. Britain's public finances were soon stretched, and in 1949 the country experienced its first post-war devaluation.[6] Germany, in contrast to the interventionist economic policy of the Attlee administration, accompanied the introduction of a new national currency, the Deutsche Mark, with

[5] Michael J. Hogan, *The Marshall Plan: America, Britain and the Reconstruction of Western Europe* (Cambridge: Cambridge University Press, 1987); Knut Borchardt and Christoph Buchheim, 'Die Wirkung der Marshallplan-Hilfe in Schlüsselbranchen der deutschen Wirtschaft', *Vierteljahrshefte für Zeitgeschichte*, 35 (1987), 317–48; Gerd Hardach, *Der Marshall-Plan* (Munich: Deutscher Taschenbuch Verlag, 1994).

[6] Alec Cairncross, *Sterling in Decline: The Devaluations of 1931, 1949 and 1967* (Oxford: Blackwell, 1983).

a policy of tax reduction and economic deregulation.[7] Policy-makers in Britain opted for interventionism; Germany favoured deregulation. In Britain, interventionist social reforms were widely applauded, whereas economic and monetary reforms in Germany at the time were highly controversial and had a shaky start.

At this time, it was of key importance to reach agreement on an issue bequeathed to Germany by its military defeat: the question of Germany's war debt.[8] The complexity of these issues was compounded because international diplomacy had failed to resolve them in the 1920s, and many contentious issues were carried over from previous negotiations. One of the principal issues was the debt of Germany's public sector to foreign creditors, including rescheduled loans extended to Germany in the 1920s under the terms of the Dawes and Young Plans. Another issue was the confiscation of international property owned by Germans. In March 1951 the German government assumed responsibility for Germany's international debt in its entirety, and this step had far-reaching political as well as financial ramifications. The government in Bonn asserted its claim to be treated as the sole representative of the German people, and by implication thus asserted the indivisibility of Germany. In 1952, a conference to negotiate reparation claims convened in London.

Considering the complexity and extent of the issues involved—Germany, after all, was debtor to no fewer than 65 countries—it is astonishing how quickly an accord was reached. Perhaps the experience of the 1920s, when disagreement and acrimony between financial diplomats poisoned international affairs, had been a salutary lesson. Hermann Abs, who led the German delegation at the London conference, in his recollections noted the stance of Sir Edward Reid of Baring Brothers, who argued in favour of offsetting the value of confiscated German assets against foreign claims against Germany. Reid reasoned that it would be unfair to make a debtor pay twice for the same claim. Looking back years later Hermann Abs quipped that one way to tell how successful the London conference had been was by the fact that only few people remember it.[9] The London debt accord was

[7] Anthony J. Nicholls, *The Bonn Republic: West German Democracy 1945–1990* (London: Longman, 1997), 64–6.

[8] Alec Cairncross, *The Price of War: British Policy on German Reparations 1941–1949* (Oxford: Blackwell, 1986).

[9] Hermann J. Abs, *Entscheidungen 1949–1953: Die Entstehung des Londoner Schuldenabkommens* (Stuttgart: von Hase & Koehler, 1991).

signed in February 1953. The London conference not only ratified Germany's acknowledgement of responsibility to repay the principal of its debt in its entirety—even more importantly, through this acknowledgement, Germany achieved recognition as a creditworthy borrower and as a responsible and respectable partner in international public finance. The first and possibly most controversial issue between Britain and Germany this century had been concluded. From then on, both countries were preoccupied with domestic issues and for many years there was scarce incentive to resurrect contacts which had been lying fallow since 1914.

The 1960s

Anglo-German financial relations in the 1950s were marked by the need to emerge from the problems wrought by a previous decade, and were shaped by changing circumstances outside the realm of finance. The success story of the City of London in this period is all the more surprising considering that the linchpin of Britain's historic role in international finance had traditionally been its political status as a world power. By the end of the 1950s, this underpinning of the City's role had almost vanished, but since then the City has arguably become more important than ever before. To some extent, the 1960s were similarly determined by developments beyond the reach of European financiers. Once again, like the Marshall Plan, this impetus emanated from the United States. The chief difference was that this time the effect was altogether unforeseen and in all likelihood unintended. Its outcome was the creation of the Eurodollar and the Eurobond Markets, the largest financial market-place in the world today. The catalyst of this process was an arcane item of banking legislation passed in the United States many years before, termed innocuously Regulation Q.

Regulation Q had been introduced in the United States during the Great Depression as a means to define a ceiling on interest paid on savings deposits.[10] The original intention had been to shore up America's ailing banking sector. Twenty years later, Regulation Q served a different policy objective. It was hoped that the amount of

[10] 'Regulation Q', in *The New Palgrave Dictionary of Money and Finance* (London: Macmillan, 1992), iii. 326–7.

deposits available to bankers would be curtailed, thereby reining back credit growth. What America's Central Bank failed to foresee was the effect of convertible currencies and unimpeded money flows across borders. For, quite understandably, depositors seeking to improve their return on deposits simply transferred their dollar deposits out of America to banks outside US jurisdiction. Regulation Q brought forth first a trickle, then a flood, of US dollars heading towards the London market. Although there are many offshore banking centres, the pioneering role of banks in London in the creation of this market is reflected in the very term for such offshore deposits, Eurodollars. Why did this business come to London, rather than to any other centre?

The Eurodollar Market owed much to the ingenuity of London bankers, but also to the willingness of UK authorities who provided a favourable environment for innovation. In 1957, in response to that year's sterling crisis, British authorities withdrew the right of British banks to advance loans to foreign borrowers, unless they were denominated in foreign currency and funded by deposits of non-residents. Institutions such as the Bank of London and South America thus came to build an offshore banking business. British banks seized the opportunity afforded by changes in their regulatory environment to create a new market in financial services. Bankers from the United States followed suit, seeking to escape constraints placed on their domestic business.

For example, US banks operating at home were subject to US minimum reserve requirements. In London, on the other hand, no such constraint applied. In 1963, the effect of Regulation Q on American financial markets was compounded by the introduction of the Interest Equalisation Tax, a measure raising the costs to foreigners of issuing bonds in the United States. Regulation Q and Interest Equalization Tax put in place the precondition for a thriving financial market, where offshore dollars were deployed for the purpose of investing in offshore bonds. While the Eurodollar Market was strictly a market in bank loans and deposits, mostly short-term (up to one year) until the 1970s, a related market emerged in medium-term foreign-currency bonds sold to non-bank investors. This was the Eurobond Market, pioneered, as it happens, by the émigré German banker Siegmund Warburg, who built the reputation of his bank on arranging offshore debt for borrowers around the world. Today, the Eurobond Market is the largest single debt market in the world. Depending on one's point of view, it is a nightmare of unbridled competitiveness, or a supreme achievement made possible by the absence of national jurisdiction. The Annual Report of the Bank for International Settlements gives an idea of the size of the market-place. In 1989, the stock of international bond financing was at $US 1,085 billion. This compares with a US GDP for that year of $US 4,874 billion. The Euromarkets have come a long way since Siegmund Warburg issued the first Eurobond in an amount of 15 million dollars in 1963.

It is worth noting that when the Euromarket began, British and German financiers had little interest in one another. Before the First World War the most conspicuous groups of foreign bankers in the City were from France and Germany, but in the 1950s and 1960s their place was taken by bankers from the United States and from Japan. Even after the emergence of the Eurodollar Market, it was many years before German banks appeared in the City in significant numbers. In fact, when the growth of the Eurocurrency markets made it mandatory for German banks to establish a presence outside their own country, their preferred choice initially was not London but Luxembourg. Dresdner Bank, for example, returned to the London market in 1967; Commerzbank and Deutsche Bank followed in 1973. From 1963 to 1974, the number of American branches in the City increased from 11 to 125. By comparison, even by 1983, the number of German banks in the City did not exceed a dozen.

Whilst German and British bankers kept their distance from one another, another exogenous factor in financial markets spurred a new boom in the City. The fuel for this boom was the flow of Petrodollars looking for investments. Once again, the most important catalyst for the development of financial markets was politics, and the long memory of depositors. The newly enriched OPEC states of the 1970s were prone to antagonism towards the United States, and by implication preferred to avoid its financial market. No doubt they remembered that during the Suez Crisis, US authorities had blocked the deposits held in New York by certain Middle Eastern customers. It made sense, then, to channel Petrodollar balances to London, where the need to invest these deposits created vast opportunities for lending and investment. From then on, banks looking to increase their balance sheets and find lucrative lending opportunities found the right set of circumstances in the City. The conditions for attracting banks from Germany were now in place.

The 1970s

What makes the 1970s different from previous decades is the fact that key developments in financial markets were henceforth shaped by developments in the markets themselves, rather than by external factors. Since the 1970s, financial markets have increasingly integrated around the world. This trend has brought German and British banking into unprecedented proximity. The point of no return occurred in 1974, although once again this was not obvious at the time, when bank regulators were called in to clean up what appeared to be a local difficulty in a small town in Germany. Their perception changed drastically within twenty-four hours, and international banking had entered a new era.

The trigger for developments was at first sight comparatively innocuous. A long-established but comparatively small bank, in Cologne, had overextended itself with speculative positions in the foreign exchange markets and found itself unable to honour its commitments. What had happened was not unprecedented. Liquidation proved to be the only option.[11] What mattered in this case, however, was not that Herstatt Bank closed its doors; what shocked the financial community in Germany was the effect of that collapse on banks around the globe. Once again, an apparently minor banking technicality had vast repercussions.

Herstatt Bank had been active in foreign exchange markets, and when liquidators moved in to close the head office in Cologne, banks in New York were not yet open for business. When bankers in New York arrived at their desks, foreign exchange contracts with Herstatt had yet to settle. Herstatt Bank was no longer in a position to fulfil its previous commitments. By noon, they realized in dismay that whilst they had credited the accounts of Herstatt Bank with their part of foreign exchange transactions, no balancing payment was forthcoming from their counterpart in Germany. Appeals to the liquidator of Herstatt Bank to retrieve earlier payments were of

---

[11] *The New Palgrave Dictionary of Money and Finance* (London: Macmillan, 1992), ii. 303–4.

no avail, since all credit balances had been blocked with immediate effect. The fact that Herstatt's failure could cause reverberations beyond Germany's borders made bankers and regulators around the world sit up. Cross-border financial flows had become the main growth area for banks around the world, and it was clear that the clock could not be turned back. Clearly, if international banking had become a key growth area, then bank supervision, too, had to adjust to a new set of circumstances.

A committee to address this challenge was established in Basle in 1974. Delegates from the Bank of England chaired the Basle Committee; first George Blunden, then from 1977 Peter Cooke, by whose name the committee is still sometimes known.[12] For three reasons, the work of the Cooke Committee can be regarded as the most influential determinant of the banking industry in the last quarter-century. Bank supervisors for the first time agreed to exchange information between individual countries. Moreover, the Cooke Committee laid the groundwork for defining minimum standards of capital adequacy of international banks. Finally, it issued recommendations regarding concentration of credit risks. One can infer how complicated the issues concerning the Cooke Committee were by the fact that some of its recommendations were issued as late as 1988, fourteen years after its inception. This duration reflects anything but inertia in the work of a standing committee drawn from diverse sectors and interest groups. On the contrary, the Cooke Committee has had considerable success in creating a level playing field for banking around the world.

The 1980s

By the early 1980s London's position as Europe's leading financial centre was clearly no longer under serious threat from rivals such as Zurich or Luxembourg. From now on, much bigger issues than reciprocal banking relations between Germany and Britain were at stake. Financial markets needed to integrate across borders to compete around the world, and around the clock. Whereas previous developments had been sparked by political developments, this latest phase was an after-effect of technological progress, specifically

---

[12] *The New Palgrave Dictionary of Money and Finance* (London: Macmillan, 1992), i. 184–7.

in telecommunications. Liberalized financial markets have been a necessary condition for global competition in banking, but it is the instantaneous availability of news around the world which makes a global financial network a necessity rather than a luxury. The linkage between financial markets has meant that Europe's premier financial centre has become the testing ground, and the sharp end of competition, for financial institutions across Europe. When Germany's leading financial institution, Deutsche Bank, acquired a leading British merchant bank, Morgan Grenfell, it acknowledged the irreversible integration of German and British banking by inviting Grenfell's senior banker, John Craven, to join its own Board of Management. Never before had a foreign national been admitted to a position of such seniority in either Britain or Germany. John Craven's admittance to the Board of Management of Deutsche Bank was an acknowledgement that financial markets in Britain and Germany had by now become inseparable. Supervisors and practitioners now realized the need to promote a new framework for competition. These reforms culminated in a series of measures in 1986 aimed at promoting financial deregulation which were commonly referred to as London's Big Bang.[13]

The very term Big Bang illustrates that the financial community had begun to see itself in a new light. The vocabulary and language of bankers had hitherto been the epitome of understatement and reticence, but from now on, metaphors borrowed from the field of astronomy were used to project a new image of limitless aspiration. Finance had become a brazen and pioneering growth industry. The City's Big Bang began with a simple change to the market practice of securities traders: the abolition of fixed commission for individual securities purchases. This initial measure sparked off a chain reaction in the City. Fixed commissions for securities trading had been the prop for the stability of financial institutions. Big Bang knocked away this underpinning, and the struggle for survival became more intense. An old order lost its traditional source of income, and a scramble ensued to stake out new means of buying market share and revenue. Larger risks were taken, and this required a substantially larger equity base. One by

---

[13] Guy Galletly and Nicholas Ritchie, *The Big Bang: The Financial Revolution in the City of London and what it Means for You after the Crash* (Plymouth: Northcote House, 1988); Adrian Hamilton, *The Financial Revolution: The Big Bang Worldwide* (Harmondsworth: Viking, 1986); *Palgrave Dictionary of Money and Finance*, i. 202–6.

one the demarcation lines which separated brokers and jobbers, merchant banks and commercial banks were swept away. Within a very brief span of time, all but a few of the City's ancient merchant banks and broking houses married their skills to suitors who provided either the necessary capital, or a new and international client base, or, ideally, both of these qualities. Big Bang resulted in unexpected job creation and prosperity for the City, and finance has become one of Europe's leading growth industries over the last ten years. To put this in context: according to some estimates, Germany's GNP would increase by 5 per cent if the country had a financial centre of comparable stature to the City of London.[14]

The pace of change in financial markets and in supervisory practice owes much to initiatives emanating from Britain. Reciprocal repercussions on the British market emanating from Germany have been in the field of monetary policy and Central Banking.

The story of Germany's impact on Britain's financial system is to a large extent the success story of the Deutsche Mark and of the Deutsche Bundesbank.[15] Their successes have depended on each other, for by legal statute the Bundesbank is obliged to protect the value of the currency. In order to equip the Bundesbank with the necessary powers to carry out this mandate, its directors are authorized to take whatever steps are necessary without fear of intervention or interference by political authorities. The Bank of England, on the other hand, was until 1997 obliged to conduct interest rate policy along guidelines laid down by the Treasury.

How well has the Bundesbank fulfilled its mandate? Average inflation at 2.7 per cent in Germany from 1950 to 1988, however favourable compared to other countries, still implies a decrease of about two-thirds in the purchasing power of the Deutsche Mark during its first forty years. Comparing the exchange rate of the Deutsche Mark against the pound from 1950 to 1988, for example, one can see that in terms of the Deutsche Mark the pound's value was reduced to 27 per cent of its 1950 exchange rate.

Germany's inflation record made the DM the world's second most important reserve currency, after the US dollar. The track record of the Bundesbank, coupled with the importance to Europe

[14] Statistical information on trends in financial services is updated regularly by British Invisibles.

[15] David Marsh, *The Bundesbank: The Bank that Rules Europe* (London: Heinemann, 1992).

of Germany's economy, meant that if monetary systems within Europe were to converge, the German model would serve as the European benchmark.

Given the attention devoted to the alleged rivalry between Frankfurt and London as Europe's premier financial centre, it is somewhat surprising that until relatively recently, German and British finance followed quite distinct paths. It is also surprising that the two seminal factors acting as catalysts for banking in Britain and in Germany, the Eurodollar Market and the Cooke Committee, came about in response to market requirements, rather than political guidance. Regulation Q and Herstatt Bank's collapse had far-reaching implications, which were impossible to foresee at the time. It is doubtful whether the key event in the City of London's recent history, Big Bang, would have restructured business the way it has without the concurrent revolution in telecommunications. The extent of London's globalization over the last decade owes as much to the advances in telecommunications as to Big Bang. The integration of the Anglo-German financial industry has resulted from global rather than bilateral developments.

The turn of events for British and German banking during the last decade of the twentieth century would have taken even the most ambitious forecaster by surprise. Germany entered the decade on a wave of political and economic euphoria after the fall of the Berlin Wall, and the pent-up spending power of East Germans fuelled an upsurge in consumer spending.[16] The obsolescence of most of East Germany's industrial stock only gradually became apparent, and by then it was too late to reverse earlier commitments to align the standards of living and employment of those Germans who had lived and worked in the German Democratic Republic as quickly as possible with those of their cousins in the West. Within a short span of time many East German products were priced out of the market, and Germany found itself burdened with substantial subsidies to sustain jobs and welfare in East Germany.

At the same time, steps towards further European integration continued and received further impetus under the terms of the Treaty of Maastricht. By the end of the decade, eleven European

---

[16] 'Die Währungsunion mit der Deutschen Demokratischen Republik', *Monatsberichte der Deutschen Bundesbank*, 7 (1990).

countries had introduced the Euro, a common currency whose interest rates are set by a supranational, independent European Central Bank domiciled in Frankfurt. Britain chose to stay outside the common European currency and to postpone a decision on membership pending a referendum at an unspecified point in the future.

The City of London, meanwhile, has gone from strength to strength, attracting an ever-larger number of financial institutions from around the globe, creating wealth for bankers with highly prized skills and for the country as a whole. At the end of the 1990s Britain's financial sector employs over one million people, and two hundred thousand professionals work in the Square Mile. Britain's trade balance from financial services has outdistanced all rivals. In 1997, Britain's surplus was $US 11.7 billion, a multiple of the $US 1.4 billion registered by Germany. London has far surpassed

TABLE 12.1. German Banks in the City in 1997

Bank name, status (S = Subsidiary B = Branch R = Representative U = UK incorporated)	Year est.	Staff
Bankgesellschaft Berlin AG (B)	1995	n.a.
Bayerische Hypotheken- und Wechsel-Bank (B)	1980	110
Bayerische Landesbank (B)	1978	120
Bayerische Vereinsbank (B)	1978	150
Berliner Bank (B)	1980	30
BfG Bank (B)	1975	17
BHF Bank (B)	1986	90
Commerzbank (B)	1973	280
DePfa-Bank (R)	1993	6
Deutsche Bank/Deutsche Morgan Grenfell (B+S)	1976	5,000
Deutsche Schiffsbank (R)	1984	3
DG Bank (B)	1981	90
Dresdner Kleinwort Benson (S+B)	1961	2,500
Eurohypo (UK) (U)	1993	5
Hamburgische Landesbank (B)	1989	51
Landesbank Berlin (B)	1993	n.a.
Landesbank Hessen-Thüringen (B)	1980	150
Norddeutsche Landesbank (B)	1984	40
Rheinische Hypothekenbank (R)	1994	3
Sal. Oppenheim Jr. & Cie. Securities (S)	n.a.	n.a.
Südwestdeutsche Landesbank (B)	1978	40
West Merchant Bank (U)	1964	536
Westdeutsche Landesbank (B)	1973	240

Frankfurt not only as a financial centre, but as a commercial centre as well. Of Europe's five hundred largest companies, no fewer than 118 have their headquarters in London, compared to nine in Frankfurt. Inevitably, the price of progress has been a steady erosion of traditional ways of doing business. Many of the most venerable City names, independent firms such as Warburg, Kleinwort, or Baring, have begun a new chapter of their history as one by one they have been absorbed into larger organizations with head offices in Zurich, Amsterdam, or Frankfurt. The City of the 1990s has once again demonstrated its ability to survive and prosper in the face of unexpected change, and irrespective of Britain's decision on the Euro, its position as a global entrepôt of world finance remains intact. To look ahead, the world of Anglo-German finance may, conceivably, soon follow the pattern set in the days of Charlemagne: institutions in Britain have taken the lead in the development of market practice, whilst the overall framework for a monetary system is based on a German model.

Part V

MUTUAL PERCEPTIONS AND CULTURAL LINKS

13

The British-German State Visits
of 1958 and 1965
From Occupation to Normalization

ANTHONY GLEES

1. Introduction

In the growing literature on British–German relations after 1945, scant regard has been paid to the phenomenon of the various British–German State Visits, either as political events worth analysis in their own right, or more theoretically as indicators of sound relations between two States who plainly seek to co-operate on various matters, bilaterally and within international and European frameworks. There are probably several reasons for this. The Queen, although Head of the British State, is, like her German counterpart, the Federal President, not regarded as a *political* actor in relations which are, at their core, political transactions between the Governments of Britain and the Federal Republic. Even though the term *political* should never be confused with the term *party political*, it is not hard to see why State Visits which appear to be non-controversial and 'unpolitical' do not attract much scholarly attention. On the other hand, those always recognized as *political* actors in British–German relations, namely the Prime Minister of the United Kingdom and the Federal Chancellor, are, of course, not Heads of State and therefore not the subjects of State Visits and perhaps for this reason not particularly taken with the practice. Since they may lack interest in them, scholars drawing on Government papers and seeking to write about bilateral relations

Thanks are due to the Haus der deutschen Geschichte, Bonn, the Stiftung Bundeskanzler-Adenauer-Haus, the Landkreis Rhein-Sieg for inviting me to Bonn on 21 September 1999 to give the paper on which this essay is based, and to Jonathan Wright for his help in producing it.

may simply ignore State Visits for this reason and no other. Vernon Bogdanor's key analysis of the British monarchy, surprisingly, makes no mention of State Visits whatsoever.[1]

Furthermore, precisely because State Visits do not primarily involve Heads of Governments, memoirs produced by them, another vital source for researchers in this field, also invariably ignore them.[2] Finally, although many British Government papers relating to the Prime Minister's role are usually released under the Thirty Year rule, the papers of the Queen, or the Crown, are subject to a standard Hundred Year rule, although some of them may be released at the conclusion of a sovereign's reign or, from time to time, in collections of Prime Ministerial papers (the chief source for this particular study). Yet the Queen *is* a political actor. State Visits are more than meaningless public relations exercises. Even if it is chiefly the relations of Governments that must be scrutinized in examining British–German relations, there is also an important element of State relations surrounding them. Indeed, it might be said that it is the broad framework of relations between the two States which defines the limit and the opportunities of the relations between miscellaneous Governments.

Nowhere can this be seen more clearly than in the issues surrounding the first Federal German State Visit to the United Kingdom in 1958 (the first visit by a German Head of State since that by the Kaiser in 1907) and the first British State Visit to the Federal Republic of Germany in 1965. Far from being non-controversial and 'unpolitical', both these Visits were without doubt significant political events. The first caused controversy in both Britain and the Federal Republic, and, whilst the second was a major success, its planning and publicizing proved extremely contorted for British domestic political reasons. In the great

---

[1] Vernon Bogdanor, *The Monarchy and the Constitution* (Oxford: Clarendon Press, 1995). In eleven chapters, State Visits are not discussed or analysed, nor is there, as a consequence, any discussion of any advice, anecdotal or otherwise, which her Prime Ministers or advisers may have given the Queen on the question of visits to countries outside the Commonwealth, let alone Germany. There are no references to Germany, or any German Head of State in the index.

[2] Heuss, in his letters to a friend, which were edited and published as a diary, does mention his State Visits, and throws some light on his State Visit to Britain in 1958; HRH Prince Philip had the custom of writing internal reports on his State Visits but these have never found their way into the public record. Theodor Heuss, *Tagebuchbriefe 1955–63*, 3rd edn. (Tübingen: Wunderlich Verlag, 1970), 354–7; PREM 13 571 note for 10.06.65.

process of Britain's move from Occupying Power in western Germany (and, after 1949, in the Federal Republic of Germany), to becoming the European partner of West Germany, the complex of deliberations and strategies surrounding these State Visits forms a key part. It seems perfectly fair to argue that it was not until the process of reciprocal 'Visiting' had been concluded in 1965 that Britain fully regarded the Federal Republic as a genuine partner, nor (every bit as important) that the Federal Republic regarded itself as equal in political value to the United Kingdom.

Reciprocity was indeed of the essence. Both British and West German political leaders, the Queen and various German Presidents, knew only too well that the friendship engendered by State Visits between democracies has major political implications. In the case of Germany, there were few better ways of bestowing legitimacy on the fledgling Republic of Bonn than the acceptance of its hospitality by the Head of State of what was widely regarded as the oldest constitutional democracy in the world. It is therefore not surprising that following the State Visit of President Heuss to the UK in 1958, West German enquiries as to the agreement of the Queen to a corresponding visit to the Federal Republic in order to seal the relationship became increasingly urgent. They were motivated by more than mere politeness. In the event, much to German unhappiness and the subsequent clouding of British–German relations in the late 1950s and early 1960s (which Heuss's visit had not been able to dispel), it would be another seven years before that visit could be made to materialize.

An examination of the two State Visits sheds light on the British–German relationship after almost virtual sovereignty had been achieved in 1955 but prior to the visit of the Queen on 18 May 1965, a decade later. As we know, from the moment the Queen's plane landed at Wahn, her visit turned into a runaway success. It is no exaggeration to say that the public recognition, especially by British public opinion, that the Federal Republic was indeed a new Germany began on that day. West German support for Britain's entry into the European Community after 1965 (which before then had at best been only half-heartedly expressed) was one very tangible result of the Queen's visit to West Germany, and of her stay on the Petersberg. Had that visit taken place seven years earlier, Britain's first attempt at entry into the Community which ended in failure in January 1963 might well have met with success.[3] Whilst it is perfectly true that the main, and possibly immutable, obstacle was General de Gaulle and not Adenauer, the documentary record shows that had Adenauer been more confident of Britain's friendship towards the Federal Republic, it is not inconceivable that he might have worked more strongly on de Gaulle to lift his opposition.[4]

The Visit to the Federal Republic, therefore, as the *reciprocated visit* by Britain, may be said to mark the effective end of an inferior status for West Germany for successive British Governments—a status which emerged from defeat and occupation, through partial sovereignty, further refined (but by no means resolved) by President Heuss's visit to Britain. It does not seem exaggerated to claim that the period *from* 1965 until unification in 1990 (which changed many things) was the most productive period for constructive British–German relations since 1945 and more broadly represents a high-water mark in relations between the two States in the twentieth century as a whole—and that ultimately it was the Queen's State Visit that gave external form and context to this. 'Ultimately' because as the representative of the victor nation, it was her going to the Federal Republic that concluded this transition.

This interpretation is given weight not merely by the success of that Visit in comparison to what was at best the very limited success of Heuss's visit in 1958, as outlined below, but the choice of the Petersberg as the first key site for the Queen's stay in West Germany. For the Petersberg had been the location of Chamberlain's disastrous visit to Hitler after Munich in 1938 and, every bit as resonant, the seat of West Germany's Military Governors and the place where almost exactly eleven years later, on 21 September 1949, Adenauer was handed the Occupation Statute.[5] It was in part, at least, a site which signified the defeat of

---

[3] See Hans-Peter Schwarz (editor-in-chief), *Akten zur Auswärtigen Politik der Bundesrepublik Deutschland, 1963*, ed. by the Institut für Zeitgeschichte for the Auswärtiges Amt, 3 vols. (Munich: R. Oldenbourg Verlag, 1994). Also Hans-Peter Schwarz, *Adenauer: Der Staatsmann, 1952–1967* (Stuttgart: Deutsche Verlags-Anstalt, 1991), and the revealing memoir by Horst Osterheld, *'Ich gehe nicht leichten Herzens'*, Veröffentlichungen der Kommission für Zeitgeschichte, Reihe B: Forschungen, 44 (Mainz: Grünwald, 1986).

[4] Rainer A. Blasius (ed.), *Akten zur Auswärtigen Politik der Bundesrepublik Deutschland, 1963*, ed. by the Institut für Zeitgeschichte for the Auswärtiges Amt, 3 vols. (Munich: R. Oldenbourg Verlag, 1994), reviewed by Anthony Glees in *Bulletin of the German Historical Institute London*, 16/3 (Nov. 1994), 37–48.

[5] Anthony Glees, *Reinventing Germany: German Political Development Since 1945* (Oxford: Berg, 1996), 102. Adenauer refused to be photographed with the Statute; he passed the original to

the old Germany, and its submission to the wishes of the three great Western democracies. What the Occupation Statute set in motion was the beginning of the *ending* of occupation, not its continuation, and the *beginning* of real self-government for Germany, not its continued domination. The Federal Republic became a semi-sovereign State, and its Western Governors became High Commissioners. By lodging the Queen at the Petersberg for her time in Bonn, the Federal Government was making a point.

The very choice of the words ('Occupation Statute') to disguise the meaning of the text illuminated what was to become the central paradigm in British–German relations before 1965, already apparent in 1949: that it was dangerous for the Western powers to be seen to be transforming West Germany too quickly into a state equal to their own. This remained the general view of various British Governments (and their Heads) as well as Buckingham Palace well into the 1960s (by which time the United States and France had watered down their anxieties considerably), and it was one which the West Germans were obliged to accept when dealing with Britain. It was based on the belief that even if the Federal Republic prior to 1965 was in most ways the political equal of the United Kingdom, and a useful ally in Europe, British public opinion, fuelled by various MPs (and party prejudices) together with the British press, would under no circumstances accept any formal statement to this effect without raising a potentially damaging political storm. Fear of the consequences of going against public opinion was sufficiently great to make both Downing Street and Buckingham Palace extremely wary of publicly recognizing West Germany for what it had become. Far from diminishing such fears, the events surrounding Heuss's visit in 1958 strengthened them.

Pre-1965 British policy on how the formal relationship with the Federal Republic was to be expressed was constrained by British public opinion; the actual beliefs of British leaders, expressed in the paperwork of the British–German relationship, were publicly distorted in order to make Britain's dominance over West Germany appear crystal clear to a doubtful and potentially hostile electorate. This was as much the case in 1949 as it was throughout the 1950s, fading only in the afterburn of President de Gaulle's first

Heinrich von Brentano who then apparently mislaid it. Following a tip-off, it was discovered by Professor Rudolf Morsey in private hands fifty years later. Memories of the Versailles peace process may have motivated the Chancellor.

veto on British membership of the European Community, which, if it showed anything to ordinary Britons, showed that France was more of a threat to them than West Germany, that Britain's capacity to be dominant in Europe had slipped away—and that Britain needed friends in Europe.

2. Heads of State and State Visits

2.1. The context of British–German relations before 1949

British policy towards Germany before 1949 went through three different stages: first punitive, then constructive, and finally one which was to lead to the genuine partnership of the 1960s and beyond.[6] At the same time, it most certainly *was* a British aim to 'develop' democracy in Germany and the British and their Western Allies were determined to ensure that the new German democracy should be entirely Western in its practices and ends— that, after all, was the reason for seeking to initiate German political activity at a regional level less than six months after the capitulation of Nazi Germany. The British dealt with the tasks that confronted them with efficiency, even if individual Britons did not always find this easy.[7] Other leading figures took a more thoughtful view, even enjoying the job in hand, or aspects of it.[8]

---

[6] Glees, *Reinventing Germany*, 26–7; id., 'The British and the Germans: From Enemies to Partners', in C. Soe and D. Verheyen (eds.), *The Germans and their Neighbors* (Boulder, Colo.: Westview Press, 1993).

[7] The British Foreign Secretary, Ernest Bevin, was himself no friend of the Germans. Ivone Kirkpatrick wrote that 'one thing which left its mark upon him was the bellicose attitude of the German Social Democrats in 1914 for which he never forgave them. He felt betrayed and it made him more anti-German than anything else the Germans ever did.' Sir Ivone Kirkpatrick, *The Inner Circle* (London: Macmillan, 1959), 205.

[8] In January 1949 General Sir Brian Robertson set down on paper the first formal verdict on Britain's Occupation in Germany as a prelude to the Petersberg meeting with Adenauer and his Cabinet which was now in sight. He wrote that what he and his colleagues were doing 'had eased as part of the effort to effect a transition from ex-Enemy to a member of the Western community of nations'. He accepted that 'the process of converting Germany from the status of an ex-Enemy to becoming a member of the European Comity of nations' could be 'neither easy nor quick . . . [but] I am confident' that the prerequisites do exist for Western Germany to be fully incorporated as a useful member of Western Europe'. FO 371 76697 22.02.49. Noel Annan and his chief, Sir Christopher ('Kit') Steel, the first head of the Zonal Political Division, are good examples of British occupiers keen to build bridges to the new Germany. See Noel Annan, *Changing Enemies: The Defeat and Regeneration of Germany* (London: HarperCollins, 1995).

2.2. The King and Germany

King George VI was sent regular reports about the Federal Republic and its move towards statehood. It was the first involvement of the British Head of State in West German affairs. He was—if he wished to be—extremely well informed about them. This royal interest was, of course, an expression of the state interest of the United Kingdom in German affairs and the development of post-war Germany.[9] As the fifties progressed, British Governments felt increasingly confident that the West German experiment was going to be a decisive success. This raised the issue of the recognition of this success by accepting, at the highest level of government, that the Federal Republic was in almost all respects the equal of the United Kingdom and that the practice of reciprocal State Visits should be initiated.

2.3. The State Visit of President Heuss to the UK in 1958

Adenauer's sweeping election victory in 1957 concentrated British minds on the potential advantages of forging a strong relationship with him and the Federal Republic at governmental level. On 16 September 1957 Macmillan sent him a particularly cordial message claiming that: 'Your great victory will give comfort and encouragement to all who wish to work for a close relations between our two countries and for the unity and happiness of Europe.'[10] He was hoping now to get the Germans to revalue the DM and increase the payment they made for the stationing of British forces in Germany. Adenauer was so pleased with this letter that he asked whether it might be released to the press. This was immediately refused by a cautious British Foreign Office. All he was permitted to say was that what had been sent was 'simply a private message of good wishes'. Behind the scenes, however, Macmillan was pleased with this response, and minuted: 'Good. We must strike whilst the iron is hot.'

It was decided that both Adenauer and the Federal President, Theodor Heuss, should be invited to visit the UK.[11] Adenauer's

[9] FO 371 76768 *Reports on Germany for HM The King*, Mar. 1949.

[10] PREM 11 2341. The Federal Chancellor was plainly delighted and wrote back: 'Ich danke Ihnen sehr für Ihr liebenswürdiges Schreiben . . . Ihre freundschaftlichen und warmen Worte haben mich sehr ermutigt.'

[11] Harold Macmillan, *Riding the Storm: 1956–1959* (London: Macmillan, 1971), 452, mentions a visit to Heuss in Germany. His visit to the UK is not mentioned. Lord Home makes

visit was planned to take place in December, Heuss's in the autumn of 1958. In the event, Adenauer was ill and he did not come until 16 April 1958. It is interesting, however, that the very first draft plans for this visit included a formal reception for Adenauer given by the Queen. In order to prepare the British Prime Minister for the talks, the German Minister in London, Dr Ritter, briefed Macmillan's Private Secretary, Philip de Zulueta, at the West German Embassy. Things did not look too good, and the main cause for this was the Chancellor's anxiety about British anti-German sentiment. Adenauer, he was told, 'seems to be in a very suspicious mood' and had 'complaints about the anti-German campaign in the British press and wireless'. The Chancellor believed (wrongly but dangerously) that this was 'inspired' by the British Government. Another issue was the future of British politics. He had, the Prime Minister's Private Secretary was told, 'another pre-occupation with the future of the Conservative Government'. Although Adenauer had 'conceived great respect' for Macmillan and the Foreign Secretary, 'he detests Mr Bevan and Mr Gaitskell is anathema to him as a result of his disengagement plan'. Despite these difficulties, the meeting (or 'summit' as it was called at the time) went well. The problem of the British forces in Germany was 'settled', a high and expanding level of trade was targeted by both leaders, and Macmillan was assured that the Germans attached 'great significance' to EFTA. Adenauer's request to renew his acquaintance with Churchill was, however, forgotten, rather to the embarrassment of the British Government.

Matters were now considered sufficiently settled for the State Visit of the German President to be expedited and formal plans were drawn up in July 1958.[12] The blueprint used was the State Visit of President Giovanni Gronchi of Italy the previous year, which proved, inadvertently, to be a cause of two major behind-the-scenes difficulties before Heuss even arrived. The first relatively minor one simply concerned protocol but it caused considerable friction between Sir

---

no mention of either State Visit in his memoirs. Lord Home, *The Way the Wind Blows* (London: Collins, 1976).

[12] FO 371 137392 20.07.58.

Christopher Steel, the British Ambassador in Bonn, and the Queen's Household.[13]

What was much more serious was that Gronchi had been favoured with an honorary degree from Cambridge and thus the question of an honorary degree, this time from Oxford, was begged in respect of the German President. It was not, however, in the gift of the Government to realize this. On 20 July 1958 Clive Rose, the Foreign Office official dealing with the visit, minuted, 'Lord Scarbrough has recently mentioned the matter of an honorary degree from Oxford to the Vice-Chancellor designate, Mr Tom Boase.[14] The Government very much hoped that though they could, of course, not dictate to Oxford, it might be possible to give the President a degree.' Rose added that Oxford were 'more difficult about these awards than Cambridge' and had already expressed reluctance to follow suit. He recommended that the Foreign Secretary, Selwyn Lloyd, write direct to Boase, which he did, with great, even excessive, humility, three days later.

'I do not know what arrangements you have in mind for President Heuss's programme in Oxford. But I should like to say from the Foreign Office point of view that we very much hope it may be possible to consider giving him an honorary degree. Such an honour would be looked upon in Germany as a generous tribute to the character and ability of the President. From the point of view of Anglo-German relations it would not fail to have a beneficial effect. I am sure it is not necessary for me to recall Professor

---

[13] Gronchi had come with his wife but Heuss, a widower, had decided to travel alone. This meant that none of Heuss's suite were able to bring their wives. Steel, however, insisted his wife accompany him because his wife was well-known to the President who would wonder at her absence. Sir Christopher was told by Sir Terence Nugent, Comptroller of the Lord Chamberlain's Office, who was organizing the Royal end of the Visit, that if he insisted on bringing his wife, he would not only have to pay her costs himself but also in no circumstances would she be permitted to stay with her husband and the rest of the President's suite at the hotel the Queen had chosen (quaintly called 'The Goring'). When Steel questioned the sense of such archaic protocol, he was told very firmly that the Queen would not pay Lady Steel's bill even though it was accepted that her husband was in London at the Queen's request. Nor would he be entitled to ask the Foreign Office to pay for her. Furthermore, since a wife 'could only come as a lady-in-waiting to another lady', and since Heuss had no lady, that was that: it would, he was told, be 'highly improper for a lady to be in attendance on a gentleman' (which Lady Steel's membership of Heuss's suite would imply). FO 371 137392 03.09.58.

[14] Clive Rose (now Sir Clive Rose GCMG) had served in the Bonn Embassy until 1955; he worked in London until 1959 and ended a distinguished career as Ambassador and Permanent Representative to the North Atlantic Council.

[*sic*] Heuss's literary and academic achievements. Throughout his political career, he has remained pre-eminently a liberal in the traditional sense of the word . . . and during the Nazi era has suffered severe privations as a result of his liberal views and staunch anti-Nazi stand. The forthcoming State Visit is to take place shortly before the end of his second and last period of office. One point I should mention since it is not irrelevant from the Foreign Office point of view is that President Gronchi, the President of Italy, received an honorary degree during his State Visit last May.'

Boase replied to the Lord Chamberlain's Office on 25 July to say that no decision could be taken until 14 October, but five days later he wrote to Selwyn Lloyd from Magdalen College that he 'warmly welcomed Professor Heuss's visit, the more so as his academic and political record is well-known in Oxford'. He added, ominously, that the question of an honorary degree was a rather more difficult one, and 'not entirely technical', but that a proposal could be put to Convocation on 14 October and that he would write to him again after that date.

Since the State Visit was due to begin on 20 October this did not leave the British Government with much time to consider an alternative. Greater urgency in the matter was given by the President's intention to present Oxford with a very generously endowed 'Theodor Heuss Fellowship', open only to members of Oxford University, to fund postgraduate research in Germany. (He was also coming with a cheque for five thousand pounds towards the final cost of the Great Window at Coventry Cathedral.)

Meanwhile, all other arrangements were set in motion. Heuss was to take tea with the Queen Mother, visit the Grave of the Unknown Soldier (and lay a wreath), and an invitation to the State Dinner was sent to Churchill ('bearing in mind the difficulty and embarrassment we had on his invitation to the Queen's lunch for Adenauer'). On 22 August Steel prepared confidential notes on the President and his entourage for the Queen. It was vital, he said, 'to dwell a little on the great services which Heuss has rendered the budding Federal Government' since 'Adenauer, of course, has stolen the limelight'.[15] In all this, Steel stated, 'Heuss's position as

---

[15] Steel added that it should not be forgotten that the Chancellor was a 'highly controversial figure' and that it was 'one of the less admirable features of the local scene that polemics and intolerance play too large a part in political life' in Bonn—something for which 'the Socialists are by no means alone to blame'.

a genuinely respected and extremely popular figure has been of great value'. He warned that Heuss could be rather 'long-winded and "professorial" ' but that he 'exuded homeliness and paternalism', though he could 'not stand still for any length of time'. He added that he could read English but that 'in conversation he is at home only in German which he speaks with a deep guttural voice'. He had first visited England in 1911 and knew Kurt Hahn of Salem and Gordonstoun (thus providing a useful point of contact to the Duke of Edinburgh). Steel concluded that he thought it 'would be well to press the European Idea and particularly our association with it' rather than a 'too direct insistence' on Anglo-German relations. Von Brentano, the German Foreign Minister, was, Steel wrote, likely to 'give the impression of being somewhat aloof due to a certain shyness and reserve'. He was 'strictly honest'—and a chain-smoker. Bott, the President's personal assistant, was 'loud and opinionated' if well-meaning, Hecker 'small, undistinguished and a man of no great intelligence'. It is hard to imagine that these notes would have caused the Queen to anticipate the Visit with huge enthusiasm.

Much effort was given to the composition of the Queen's speech, to be delivered at the State Banquet. The various drafts, in particular the Queen's own changes, illustrate plainly the considerable policy difficulties that Heuss's visit was thought to engender.[16] We cannot say whether all these changes (which ended up by being major ones) were changes made by the Queen herself, but there is good reason to believe that they were.[17] The Government draft, and the suggestions made by Steel, all pulled in one direction; the texts coming from Buckingham Palace and Balmoral pulled in another, and there is no record or indeed suggestion of any Government advice to the Queen which would indicate that the changes were Government-led ones. Indeed, it is implausible to believe that having passed two drafts to the Queen, the

[16] FO 371 137393 22.09.58.

[17] Sir Clive Rose has stated that he believes all the changes that appear to have been made by the Queen were indeed made by her, but emphasizes that 'it is out of the question that on such an important and politically sensitive occasion as this undoubtedly was, any alterations would have been made by the Palace without full consultation and agreement with No. 10'. Letter from Sir Clive Rose GCMG, 05.12.99. He notes, too, that the links between the Foreign Office, Downing Street, the German Embassy and the Palace were strong and that as this was *before* the Franco-German entente came into being, high hopes hung on the future of the British–German relationship even if the British public had little idea of this.

Government would then produce a third draft in an entirely different spirit from either of them. It is therefore not unreasonable to assume that these changes were indeed the product of the Queen's own 'statecraft', although this is not to say that Palace officials may not have had their own input.

The first draft was completed by Clive Rose in the Foreign Office on 22 September. He noted that it consisted of 418 words, which, he said, compared most favourably with the 417 he had produced for President Gronchi. In addition to the usual niceties, it contained the following passage: 'My country takes great pride in the part it played in the unification of the three western zones. No one can fail to be impressed by the outstanding respect in which you are held . . . [despite] the tragic errors of the past . . . To me our links have an especially personal significance. My family connexions with Germany go back many generations . . . little more than one hundred years ago this connexion was strengthened by the marriage of Prince Albert to my great-Grandmother Queen Victoria. Relations between our two countries are as close now as they were at that time.'

The draft returned from Buckingham Palace showed that the Queen's first changes were to remove the 'great' in 'great pride' and the 'outstanding' in 'respect'; she changed 'errors' to 'events' and, for the time being, left the implication standing that she was more closely related to her 'English' great-grandmother than to her great-grandfather, the German Prince Albert. But, as the Queen's Private Secretary, Adeane, told the Foreign Office, in general she liked the draft 'and reacted favourably to it . . . It is unlikely that there will be any changes of substance.' In fact, he could not have been more wrong. However, on 10 October 1958 the German Ambassador H. H. Herwarth was shown a copy of this first draft and greeted it with enthusiasm: 'he particularly welcomed the reference to the Queen's family connexions with Germany.'[18]

Meanwhile, however (and unbeknown to Herwarth), Sir Christopher Steel told the Foreign Office that he was dissatisfied with the draft as it 'lacked warmth'. Rose then produced a new substantive paragraph which read: 'the tragic events of the past in relations between our two countries are part of history. But I am happy to say they are united in close bonds of alliance and association with

---

[18] FO 371 137394.

one another and with the other countries of the West.' This section was sent to Balmoral on 7 October. At this stage, it seems clear, the Queen decided to make substantial changes both to this passage and to the earlier draft, each of which was designed to make her words sound more, rather than less, cool to the Germans. The end result was that her speech was transformed from a statement proclaiming warm reconciliation, equality, and friendship, to what could have been taken as a declaration of Germany's continued inferior status. The existence of cordial relations with Germany now became conditional on the Germans' readiness to learn from their recent past and not the outcome of any wish the people of Britain might have. The Queen did, however, alter the phrasing about Queen Victoria so that she was as much the great-granddaughter of Albert as of Victoria.

Instead of the words which began with the phrase 'I am happy to say . . .', the Queen now wrote: 'We must now look to the future and through our alliance and our association with each other and with other countries of the west we must forge anew the bonds of amity and peace. Our common duty to Europe and our mutual interests demand no less than this.' As for the passage about her own family ties to Germany, the Queen now substituted: 'to me these links have an especially personal significance. My family connexions with the old Germany [*sic*] go back for many generations. One hundred and twenty years ago Queen Victoria married Prince Albert and both my husband and I are direct descendants of that union. It gives us both great pleasure to think that the relations between our two countries have been restored to something like what they were in those days. This visit is a sign that our friendship can prosper once again' (the Queen, it seems, had deleted the words 'relations are as close now as they were at that time' and inserted the phrase 'relations have been restored to something like what they were . . .'—clear, if hardly elegant prose).

Yet further and more severe changes were made, also, it appears, at the Queen's own insistence, which added harshness to the new coolness, and removed any trace of friendship. To make the implication entirely clear, she seems to have added a history lesson, one completely missing from the first draft, yet—on the day—validated by using Heuss's own expressions of deep regret about Germany's wicked past (of which she probably had prior warning). It might be an exaggeration to claim she used his sense of remorse against him, but her revised remarks seem much more closely in tune with perceived British public opinion and the attitudes to be found in much of Fleet Street once Heuss had departed, though whether the Queen helped, in part, to form these attitudes cannot be stated with any certainty.

The Queen's concluding remarks now read: ' . . . Our common duty to Europe and our mutual interest demand no less than this. My country has shown as has yours that it is ready to strengthen this association. No one can make history stand still. Events and situations change with startling speed. There were occasions in the past when our two countries were closely allied. Indeed the connexions between my Family and the old States of Germany go back many generations . . . As you yourself said, nothing can ever erase from the record certain deeds and events perpetrated in Europe within our memories. But their most important significance today is as a warning and as an example to the whole world of what happens when democracy breaks down. It is in that spirit that we are working together to rebuild true friendship . . . this visit will prove to be an important step to that end.'

Whilst the Queen was considering her speech at Balmoral, the news came from Oxford that the Government's request to grant Heuss an honorary degree had been turned down. Boase wrote to Selwyn Lloyd: 'Hebdomadal Council has asked me to inform you that while welcoming the visit of the President of the West German Federal Republic [*sic*] to Oxford on 22 October they are not, after much consideration, recommending to Convocation the conferment of an honorary degree on this occasion.'

Sir Frederick Hoyer-Millar, the Permanent Under-Secretary, replied on behalf of Selwyn Lloyd, who was ill, to say that he was 'naturally most disappointed that in spite of the considerations advanced in his letter of 23 July Hebdomadal Council are not recommending a degree'. He added that the Germans ('quite correctly') had not requested such a degree but 'it is clear that the President had hopes, if not expectations, that one would be conferred'. Understanding, however, that a decision from Oxford was not going to be overturned to suit anyone, including the British Government, he raised the question of an explanation: 'The Foreign Secretary would be very glad to know whether there are any reasons for the Council's decision which could be given to the German Ambassador. If they are such that they would not be suitable for transmission to Germany, the Foreign Secretary hopes he may at least be given them for his confidential information.'

Boase replied on 9 October that 'any debate is, of course, highly confidential'. He noted that the time given to him to 'obtain a majority in Council' meant 'normal procedures' would have been subject to 'short circuiting' and this had 'weighed with some'. However, he concluded with more bluntness than diplomacy, 'it was clear that there was strong feeling—in no way personal— against a degree being given to the representative of Germany' and that 'had the proposal reached Convocation it would have been opposed in open debate'. The Foreign Office decided, not surprisingly, to tell Herwarth that 'technical difficulties' prevented a degree being awarded; Oxford agreed to this, and Herwarth (who was said to have 'swallowed' this excuse) made no recorded comment to Heuss. In fact Heuss's visit to Oxford was very short and mainly taken up with a lunch (which he called a dinner) at All Souls.[19] It seems plain that he knew nothing about a degree for him and had no inkling of the hostility that some senior members bore him. He was, however, aware of the 'unfriendliness' of A. J. P. Taylor.[20]

It was noted, however, and subsequently widely reported in the German press, that Oxford undergraduates had 'greeted' the President in silence 'with their hands thrust deep in their pockets'. Steel wrote in his post-visit report that this was taken by the German media as a 'calculated insult'.[21] There is no doubt that anti-German feeling had been at the root of Heuss's treatment by Oxford and that the failure to differentiate between the old Germany, and the new, and those who were committed Nazis, and those who were not, was somewhat unfortunate to put it mildly.

Heuss did not deserve such treatment. Apart from the intention and generosity towards Oxford that underlay the idea of the Heuss Fellowship, he had not drawn any veils over the past. He had gone out of his way to visit the Wiener Library and pay tribute to the work of Dr Wiener for which he himself had arranged funding.[22] In his Mansion House speech he had bitten the bullet: 'No one will

---

[19] Heuss wrote: 'The nicest part [of the whole State Visit] was my visit to Oxford; I met Lord Halifax, the Chancellor, saw a bit, not too much, and had dinner; admittedly time was so short that I could not discover whether your friend Roberts [J. M. Roberts of Merton College] had been invited.' Heuss, *Tagebuchbriefe*, 355.

[20] Ibid. 354.   [21] Report 12.11.58.   [22] Heuss, *Tagebuchbriefe*, 356.

dream of belittling the terrible things that happened during the last war. I see in this hall more than one old acquaintance or friend who for political or so-called "racial" reasons was driven out of the country of his fathers. We are grateful to Britain for having given these unfortunate people the opportunity to find a living. We are aware, too, of our duty to make amends for the wrong that was done', and he singled out Victor Gollancz for special praise.[23] Heuss himself seems to have enjoyed his visit, which he said was 'completely normal', although he accepted fully that of those people who had turned out to see him 'eighty per cent had wanted to see the Queen, ten per cent her horses and ten per cent me'. [24]

The general reaction to Heuss's State Visit was, however, mixed at best and hostile at worst. Heuss himself had some inkling of this. He wrote to his friend that the papers 'were talking about whether the visit was a success, or premature, whether the British had been cool'. In fact, he insisted, the tabloids had been most taken by the Queen's remarks about the German origins of her family, or part of it, and he added: 'the Queen and not I was the object of criticism . . . Bevan told Herwarth that the reason he was so friendly towards me was because he wanted to assist the Queen. The German origins of the Royal Family had not been talked about since 1917 when they took the name of Windsor . . .' [25] The Foreign Office papers certainly include letters written by enraged members of the public all too easily capable of being used as proof that the visit had taken place too soon. The West German public was, according to the Embassy in Bonn, more taken up with the reception by Oxford undergraduates than any other aspect (it was just as well that the matter of the honorary degree remained secret). The East German Communist daily *Neues Deutschland*, gloating, called the visit 'a fiasco' and explained that 'the population and press of Great Britain have given an exceedingly unfriendly reception' to Heuss;

[23] FO 317 137395.

[24] Heuss, *Tagebuchbriefe*, 354–7. He had enjoyed meeting the Queen whom he found 'not at all shy, as I had been led to believe', and was flattered that she had read some of his works to prepare herself. Prince Philip had been 'totally relaxed' and attentive, and enjoyed 'family chatter' (Heuss knew his three sisters and their husbands). They both showed him their art collection. On being told by him that he was hoping to see her Holbeins, the Queen arranged for them to be sent over from Windsor where they were kept the next day. He found the Queen Mother 'harmless and simple' but also very friendly. He was amused by his apparent popularity amongst those on the left of British politics. Gaitskell told him it was because he had said he was not a hunter.

[25] Ibid. 357.

the US press said that the 'British public had been extremely restrained'. As for the British press, tabloid coverage included fierce anti-German comments from Cassandra (in the *Daily Mirror*), from A. J. P. Taylor (in the *Express*) which the Foreign Office described as 'vulgar', but more positive if hardly cheering words from Aneurin Bevan ('let us hope that from mutual wounds will come a mutual declaration that it shall never happen again' in the *News of the World*), while the *Daily Telegraph* spoke of a 'warm if restrained welcome'—a welcome contrast to the *Express*'s 'uncanny silence'. The *Daily Sketch* was taken as providing the best story under its headline 'OK Fritz, you're out of the Dog House'. Not surprisingly, press questions about the date of a return visit to the Federal Republic were answered with the unambiguous statement that the Queen's diary was already full to the end of 1960.

In his final sober report on the visit, Steel made it clear that a beginning to better relations had been made, even if it had fallen far short of the hopes that had originally been raised, and the warmth he himself had called for had not materialized. 'The visit', he wrote, 'was successful in achieving the aims of giving a lead to public opinion and clearing the way to a friendly Anglo-German relationship within the framework of the Western European and Atlantic Alliances. It jolted Germans out of some of their facile and complacent illusions. I hope it also broke down some of the more refractory British prejudices. It was salutary for the Germans to be reminded that their Nazi past is not forgotten in England; after a period of annoyance, it will lead them to pay more attention to Anglo-German problems and not take our friendship for granted. But the real significance is that it proves the determination of the present British Government to establish an Anglo-German relationship which, whilst not ignoring the past, would be firmly based on friendship, cooperation and alliance in the future.'[26]

The Queen's final words insisted that 'new bonds of friendship had been created by the Visit'. This was certainly the case (and she and Prince Philip had plainly been extremely kind to the old German at a personal level), but it would be wrong to argue that these 'new' bonds between the two states were strong ones. Rather than look to a new friendship based on an earlier one, it was plain that the new friendship was going to have to be a prospective one.

[26] FO 371 13796.

Public opinion in the UK, as expressed in letters from the public, by the tabloids, and by the dons and students of Oxford, showed that the public line taken by the Queen was more closely in tune with the feelings of the country than the line taken by the Foreign Office and the Prime Minister. Indeed, there must have been some fear that by mentioning her German antecedents, however blandly, the Queen had gone too far. Whilst plainly not a disaster, the visit was not much more than a very qualified success. Had Heuss realized precisely how the Queen or her advisers had toned down her comments, and how Oxford had refused to grant him an honorary degree, the private feelings of the Germans, and possibly the public feelings, might have been very different and less positive. At the end of the day, however, Heuss knew he was obliged—for reasons of state—to accept with gratitude whatever was meted out to him.

3. A British State Visit to the Federal Republic?

Despite the clear, and early, steps towards regarding the Federal Republic as a partner and not an inferior of the United Kingdom, an observer of British–German relations in the late 1950s and early 1960s might have been forgiven for believing that the return State Visit which would set the seal on this new relationship was destined to be the State Visit that could never take place. The reason for this was that prior to 1965 it *had* not taken place. Neither Downing Street nor Buckingham Palace was anxious to risk further alienation of a British public which they believed was seriously anti-German and had only just managed to stomach the German President's visit to the UK. It can be demonstrated that fear of public opinion in Britain took precedence over the belief, obviously shared by various Prime Ministers and the Queen, that such a Visit was in the best interests of the British nation.

Nor should their viewpoint be ridiculed out of hand. Public opinion, in any democracy, is a vital factor, always to be treated with respect. It would be quite unhistorical to deny that throughout the 1950s British public opinion, rooted in the history of the recent past, but often fanned by a strange alliance of a right-wing and nationalistic press and by some left-wing politicians, regarded the Federal Republic with considerable hostility. Because public opinion mattered, it impacted directly on British–German relations. When in the early 1950s the British Council sought to promote British contacts with West Germany, it was frequently attacked in the press who queried the use of public money to fund them. On 16 October 1952, to give but one example, under the headline 'British serenade the Germans', Lord Beaverbrook's *Daily Express* alleged that English madrigal singers had currently been 'wooing beefy Bavarians' during a Council-funded visit to Stuttgart [*sic*]. Anti-German feeling was repeatedly, and quite cynically, exploited 'to make the British Council appear misguided and unpatriotic as well as extravagant'. In fact, the Germans had paid for this particular occasion themselves.[27]

In March 1959 Konrad Adenauer took the unprecedented step of asking to speak privately to the British Prime Minister, Harold Macmillan, to express his deep anxiety at the prevalence of anti-German feeling in Britain, which he believed lacked any justification.[28] Although he did not spell this out, the implication was that it could hardly help Britain's application to join the European Community. This obviously made a deep impression on Macmillan, who pursued the matter on his return to Downing Street and clearly discussed it with the Queen.

Macmillan was plainly unsure whether a visit would prove risky at home. On the one hand, he thought it would now be right to ask the Queen to go to West Germany but on the other he was fearful of the risk involved. He asked the Foreign Office to generate a paper, presumably to help reach a decision. This paper (of which the first page is missing) was a bizarre mixture of factual reporting and pseudo-psychological theorizing designed to have things both ways. It provided evidence to support anti-German feeling whilst at the same time arguing that the Bonn Republic was not Weimar still less the Third Reich. Yet it contained enough potentially explosive material on how Germany could be viewed, to cause the Prime Minister to back off the idea of a visit. The paper noted that there were over four million Nazi party members and that it was 'not to be supposed they have all suffered [*sic*] a change of heart'. Ex-Nazis could be found in government. The recent outbreak of anti-Semitism in Germany was a reality. It had, however, 'had

[27] J. M. Mitchell, *International Cultural Relations* (London: Macmillan, published in association with the British Council, 1986), 108–9.

[28] PREM 11 3358 16.03.59.

compensating aspects. It will force the Germans to face the fact of their disgraceful past. The German people have suffered from psychopathic hysteria and when an individual psychopath has a shock which has the effect of making him forget the events leading up to the shock, the obvious treatment is to administer a reminder in small doses until such time as he becomes accustomed to what has happened, and faces reality as a normal person.' The Prime Minister was warned that: 'We shall certainly find the Germans saying that many of the recent incidents have been instigated by Communist agents from East Germany. There may be some truth in this.'[29]

Macmillan seems to have decided that the failure of the West Germans to purge former Nazis from the civil service provided the best grounds for keeping the Queen away from Germany. 'Nobody', he minuted personally, 'knows how many ex-Nazis are in fact employed either in the [West German] army, the civil service or the judiciary', adding that 'the revival of Krupp is not very popular here'. In order to gain further ammunition for this stance he approached senior Cabinet colleagues. Writing on 16 December 1959 he asked for their views of the Germans: 'Apart from the newspapers which specialise in working up anti-German feeling, there is, I think, genuine apprehension about the Germans.' He also wished to know how seriously they rated anti-German feeling in Britain, and whether they harboured fears of a 'revival of Hitlerism' themselves (set in the context of swastika daubing and gravestone desecrations currently, and quite reasonably, making headlines in Britain—and the Federal Republic).

The responses of Lord Home (then Commonwealth Secretary) and Selwyn Lloyd (then Foreign Secretary) were recorded.[30] Home (who as Lord Dunglass had been Chamberlain's Private Secretary in 1938) replied that even though some Germans were 'inclined to be tiresome and oversensitive', the British 'saw eye to eye' with them and thus the British Government should be as 'friendly as possible' to the new Germans. Selwyn Lloyd said 'there was a great deal of anti-German feeling in Britain and there always has been'. At the same time, the British had 'a great deal of common sense and a general acceptance that West Germany be tied as tightly as possible—economically, politically and militarily—to

[29] Ditto.
[30] PREM 11 3358 16.12.59. See Alistair Horne, *Macmillan, 1957–86* (London, 1989).

Western Europe'. He concluded: 'we must treat them always as allies not enemies.' From this it followed, he believed, that public opinion could become less hostile, and permit a more normal relationship.

These relatively reassuring words did not stiffen Macmillan's resolve but rather the reverse. He decided not to pursue the idea of a Visit in 1960. But the issue surfaced again almost as soon as he thought it had been killed. On 16 November 1960 Downing Street was formally informed that President Luebke and Dr Adenauer 'were again going to stress the desirability of the Queen visiting Germany in the summer of 1961'. It would not be possible for the Queen to come after the German elections. Equally, she could obviously not come just before the elections because, as Oliver (later Sir Oliver) Wright in Downing Street wrote on 22 November 1960: 'The Foreign Secretary considers it very undesirable for the Queen to visit Germany . . . it would risk being regarded almost as electioneering.' He added that the Queen ought to go to Ethiopia (to which she had also been invited) first in any case but that it had been decided 'not to make this point to Dr Adenauer'.[31]

Buckingham Palace, however, was by now wondering if Macmillan's advice was quite as sound as it had seemed. Sir Michael Adeane wrote to Downing Street that: 'A visit to Bonn would be more important than any other visit that the Queen could pay to a so far unvisited European country', although the suggestion was that it was 'sensible not to suggest such a visit, far less to plan or announce it, until the common market issue is decided'.[32]

A formal request was indeed made by the Germans again in 1961 but brusquely turned down after Macmillan and the Foreign Office agreed yet again that it was too risky. Adenauer was told that 'more time was necessary for public opinion in this country to develop with regard to closer Anglo-German relations'. Curiously, but not unimportantly, in order to justify this decision emphasis was put on the fact that even though the Germans' invitation was now six years old, it was no older than a similar invitation, from an

---

[31] PREM 11 5057.

[32] Ditto. Ben Pimlott quotes from these papers in his relatively brief account of the 1965 State Visit to Germany (although he misspells the name of the German Chancellor at the time). Ben Pimlott, *The Queen: A Biography of Elizabeth II* (London: HarperCollins, 1997), 355–7.

old ally of Britain, Haile Selassie, Emperor of Ethiopia.[33] This was intended by the Foreign Office to imply that the Queen was rather busy with one thing and another, and that the decision not to come to West Germany had absolutely nothing to do with its being West Germany. At the same time, it was obvious to everyone, including the West Germans, that there was plainly a political importance in visiting the Federal Republic which did not exist in the case of Ethiopia. It is not difficult to imagine that this may have added insult to injury.

In January 1962 Macmillan discussed the issue once again. He wrote: 'I suppose the question of the Queen's visit to Germany will have to be faced sooner or later.' What was more, in a radical departure from protocol, President Luebke of Germany had now decided to get personally involved. He told Sir Christopher (Kit) Steel that he really wanted to pay a private visit to the UK but felt he could not since the Queen had never repaid Heuss's visit to Britain. Steel minuted the Prime Minister that he himself thought that Luebke was, in fact, pointing out his serious concern that the Germans were feeling slighted over the delay to their request. To make matters worse, a leading Labour MP, Marcus Lipton, got wind of these—top secret—deliberations.[34]

Lipton decided to question Macmillan in Parliament about them. On 15 February 1962 he asked whether there was any truth in the rumour that the Queen might actually visit the Federal Republic since 'many of her subjects would view such a visit with serious misgivings'. Macmillan, rattled, immediately (and inaccurately) denied it—and sent the matter back to the Foreign Office. The Foreign Office was, of course, chiefly taken up with Britain's first application to join the European Community. It was precisely for this reason that at the beginning of 1963 the Foreign Office decided a different approach might now be asked for. It suggested that the Queen should probably (*sic*) be asked if she would be prepared to visit the Federal Republic. In other words, the Visit was now seen as worth the risk.[35]

But by the time the proposal reached the Palace, and the Queen's attention had been gained, the political landscape had changed yet again. General de Gaulle had said 'non' and for this reason and others, no more happy, but certainly less lofty, Macmillan's

---

[33] PREM 13 571 30.01.62.   [34] PREM 13 571.   [35] Ibid.

Government began to totter.[36] On one level, this removed the immediate rationale for the Visit (West German support for Britain's entry into Europe) which might justify its perceived danger. On another, however, it could be argued that the Visit was now more vital than ever: with France now seen as hostile, Britain needed all the allies it could muster. Even so, Macmillan took some time to see the point. Although he was told on 9 April 1963 by Sir Michael Adeane that the Queen, responding to the Foreign Office's views, 'would be prepared to go to Germany if you would like her to', Macmillan saw no reason not to continue dithering, although he took note that the Queen, plainly an international relations realist to the core, accepted that things would have to change in respect of British attitudes towards Germany.[37] The Queen said that she had now decided that in future when members of the British Royal Family visited Germany privately (to visit relations, or British regiments) they would 'exchange the normal courtesies with German civilian authorities'. Until then these civic worthies had been ignominiously ignored by the Royals in Germany. Buckingham Palace said the refusal to speak to Germans on these occasions was simply a 'curious hangover' of Occupation.

Macmillan could not be encouraged to act. Responding to the Queen's changed line he minuted: 'This [the visit to Germany] is a large political issue. The Cabinet should decide it.' On 29 April 1963 the Cabinet decided that it was politically far too risky and, once again, the visit to Germany was scrapped.[38]

On 15 January 1964, a new British Government and a new Prime Minister, Lord Home, visited the new German Chancellor Ludwig Erhard. Much to the surprise of the British team, Erhard's 'first question was about the Queen's visit'. The issue was clearly spiralling out of control. Home, however, had a ready response although it was not one that could hold for very long. The Germans were told that 'in view of The Queen's domestic situation' (Her Majesty was pregnant) the Government did not wish to trouble her with this matter, but would raise it with her in 1965. Home realized that in fact Britain no longer had any option. If West Germany was to become an equal partner the Visit would have to take place. No Visit would mean that West Germany might cease to help Britain enter the European Community.[39]

---

[36] Horne, *Macmillan*, 447, and chs. 16 and 17.   [37] PREM 13 571.   [38] Ibid.
[39] Ibid.

Significantly, however, the Palace did not want to seem over-enthusiastic. On 27 April 1964 the Palace suggested that the Queen's visit to West Germany be announced together with the Visit to Ethiopia and both take place in May 1965. A further minute dealt with one very sensitive point (which had caused such difficulty in 1958, as is discussed above): 'On the German visit Adeane asks that the Government's support for it should be publicly emphasized so as to counter possible suggestions that the Royal Family are going to Germany because of their strong private family ties and relationships. Adeane suggests that this support might be most conveniently given by a Question and Answer in the House of Commons.'[40]

Details were fleshed out at a meeting between Home's Office and Commander Colville on behalf of the Queen in May 1964. It was agreed that an announcement that the Queen would visit Germany would be made in 1965, forty-eight hours *before* one was to be made that she would also visit Ethiopia. In this way, it was hoped the Germans would forgive the seven-year hiatus and appreciate they were more important to Britain than the Ethiopians. Oddly enough, however, almost certainly at the personal wish of the Queen, her Secretary insisted the order of the announcements be reversed—the visit *to Ethiopia* was announced *first*, thus taking precedence over the planned visit to the Federal Republic. Even so, as the British Ambassador reported back to London, the announcement gave Anglo-German relations (no pun was intended) an 'immediate fillip'.[41]

The visit was now planned to take place from 18 to 28 May 1965, by which time Britain once again had changed Governments—and on this occasion governing parties as well. Harold Wilson, the Labour leader, was now Prime Minister. He had hopes that the SPD might soon join the Bonn government. Indeed, the Queen (and her Prime Minister) were said to have been delighted that Fritz Erler, a leading Social Democrat, had sent a personal message to the Queen on behalf of the SPD on 17 May to say her stay on the Petersberg 'was more than an act of representation. It was the hope that relations between the UK and the continent would become increasingly close' against the backdrop of 'the traditional and friendly relations between the SPD and the Labour Party'. It

---

[40] PREM 13 571.   [41] Ibid. 25 01.06.65.

was an auspicious prelude, but to maintain balance, the Queen, who had been told he was too ill to visit her, sent Konrad Adenauer a large bunch of (red) roses even though she knew the Petersberg was not far from his home in Rhoendorf and a suspicion existed, perhaps, that the illness was only diplomatic in origin.[42]

In the event, all political fears about the reaction of the British public melted away when British television recorded the quite rapturous welcome given to the Queen and the obvious delight and interest of the Queen in seeing—for the first time in her life—the new Germany in the west.

The royal party arrived at the Petersberg on 18 May and stayed for two nights. It was from the Petersberg that the visit to Bonn was conducted which set the tone magnificently whilst paying due regard to history. From the word go, everything exceeded everyone's expectations. Massive crowds chanted 'Eliz-a-beth—Eliz-a-beth' (a call her Majesty had almost certainly never been required to hear before, but one she seemed from her expression to find highly amusing).[43] In his formal report to Prime Minister Wilson at the end of the Visit, Sir Frank Roberts, the British Ambassador in Bonn (a man given neither to enthusiasm nor exaggeration), waxed lyrical. He began by stating that no one could have ignored 'the phenomenally warm welcome' German crowds had given the royal couple.[44] Things had gone from good to excellent. The Queen had made ten speeches, a far greater number than was usual, and her frankness in speaking about the past, and the need to build the future on a basis of understanding and close co-operation, was well-received in all quarters. Her visit to West Berlin went well (the Royal Car drove alongside the Wall to the delight of Berliners) and emphasized, he said, Britain's commitment to the liberty of the city.

Even the thorny question of the Queen's German relatives, in which Prince Philip acted for the Queen in order to put some distance between the British and the German royals, was most

---

[42] See H.-P. Schwarz, *Adenauer: The Statesman* (Providence and Oxford: Berghahn Books, 1997), 738. Schwarz writes that Adenauer had received a 'slight shock' after a train accident, and required three weeks' rest, so missing the Queen's Visit, but had been 'delighted' at the roses.

[43] Pimlott believes very plausibly that the Queen was, in fact, made rather anxious by these chants which may have reminded her of Nazi rallies. She did, however, write to Lord Longford that the visit was 'of absorbing interest'. Pimlott, *The Queen*, 357.

[44] PREM 13 571 28.05.65.

amicably resolved. Prince Philip had written and spoken personally to Sir Frank to ensure nothing untoward happened and to
inform him that Her Majesty was not anxious to be photographed
together with her relatives. The Queen, however, did refer to 'family ties with Germany', which Roberts declared was appreciated in
Germany (although it was probably intended more as a reference
to Prince Philip's family than, as the Germans seemed to take it, to
her own), and a strictly private dinner for her cousins, aunts, and
so on was quietly arranged in Wiesbaden.[45] In short, the Queen in
Germany could do no wrong. Even the British tabloids, Roberts
insisted, had dropped their hostile anti-German stance. 'The
Queen's smile has become a by-word in Germany', Roberts concluded, and said Springer's *Bild Zeitung* had summed it all up bril-
liantly in its final headline at the end of the visit: 'Your
Majesty—You were wonderful!' With the memory of *Britannia*
steaming gracefully out of Hamburg towards the North Sea,
accompanied by farewell roars, Roberts insisted that 'the reception
given was one the Royal Couple *personally* evoked'.

Oddly enough, the Queen's huge success in Germany seems to
have upset her Prime Minister back home. He not only refused to
meet her on her return to the UK, but also declined to add his own
good wishes to the ailing Adenauer. And when it was suggested he
might ask Prince Philip for a copy of his personal report on
Germany (the Prince was well-known for his 'very stimulating
reports on the various parts of the world he has visited'), he refused
to do this as well.[46]

[45] Information from the late Sir Frank Roberts GMG.
[46] PREM 13 571 09.06.65. Bizarrely, in the prologue to his memoirs, Wilson writes of
his affection for the Queen in almost excessive terms: 'I have been most fortunate in my
relationship with the Monarch. Perhaps something very different in my background
helped. As a result we were on easy conversational terms from the very start. She was fas-
cinated at the account I was able to give of what life was like in the "back to back" houses
she had seen in Leeds . . . She was always full of information about her tours . . . and particularly the impressions formed on her foreign visits.' Harold Wilson, *Memoirs: The Making
of a Prime Minister 1916–64* (London: Weidenfeld & Nicolson, 1986), 2. Adenauer does not
receive a mention in these memoirs. Philip Ziegler wrote of Wilson's relationship with the
Queen: 'Almost the only person with whom Wilson felt he could properly discuss matters
of high policy and who was clearly not after his job was the Queen. In awe of the monarchy as an institution, he soon felt affection and respect for her . . . When he resigned she
sent him a photograph of the pair of them . . . which he thereafter carried in his wallet.'
Philip Ziegler, *Wilson: The Authorized Life* (London: HarperCollins, 1995), 214. One might be
forgiven for believing that the public record, for whatever reason, did not correspond to the
private recollection.

More seriously, the 1965 State Visit to Germany represented the real beginning of the move to partnership with West Germany. As Roberts wrote: 'Before it, warmth was missing from the relationship although the countries worked together as allies. In Germany there was a widespread feeling that Britain was reserved and it was not understood why British memories should be longer than in other European countries which had suffered even more from Hitler's Reich. Yet Germans put aside the feeling that the return of Heuss's visit had been overlong delayed. It reminded the Germans that France was not their only ally and it was a reassertion of British interest in Germany.'[47]

It is therefore no exaggeration to claim that the Queen's 1965 visit to Germany initiated the most fruitful period in British–German relations in the twentieth century. What became of this relationship in the changed circumstances of the 1990s is not so much a reflection on the work done by British and German Governments, and British and German Heads of State before 1990, but rather on fears of the power of a united Germany developed by Margaret Thatcher. Oddly enough, these fears seem at once to have reflected public opinion and reinforced it, much as had happened thirty years earlier, even if 'fear of Germany' was by now interchangeable with 'fear of Europe'. Whether justified or not (and they certainly preceded any evidence of a new German danger), they possessed a political use in giving form to her Government's growing disaffection with Britain's membership of the European Union. What is more, they demonstrated the important truth that ultimately it was British Heads of Government rather than the Queen who determined the condition of Britain's relations with its partners.

[47] PREM 13 571.

14

The Academic Community
Modern and Contemporary Historians

A. J. NICHOLLS

Before 1914, there was no great institutional intimacy between the historical professions of the two countries, both being rather insular in their outlook. This did not mean that individual scholars did not pay attention to the work of their colleagues on either side of the North Sea; scholarly journals and the biographies of individuals testify to the fact that, if anything, intellectual contacts were more strongly developed before the First World War than thereafter.[1] This was especially true in the fields of classical studies, philology, and medieval history. There was, however, a perceived inferiority on the British side of the Channel, since German universities had a very high reputation for scholarship, whereas English universities (and this did not apply to the Scots) were as much social experiences for the national élite as intellectual powerhouses sponsoring research. British scholars who wanted to progress in their profession often studied at German universities; the reverse was less common, although the Rhodes scholarships at Oxford had created a small bridgehead for Germans who fulfilled Rhodes's criteria of aptitude for worldly success.

---

[1] The first issue of the the *English Historical Review* in January 1886 began with an article by Lord Acton describing the development of different schools in German history. Although professing respect for the pioneering work of German historians, especially in the history of ideas, Acton was unenthusiastic about German historical method and remarked: 'Probably there is no considerable group less in harmony with our sentiments in approaching the study of history than that which is mainly represented by Sybel, Droysen and Treitschke, with Mommsen and Gneist, Bernhardi and Duncker on the flank. Up to this moment it is the best found and most energetic of all; and as there is no symptom of declining favour and authority, it is important to understand along what lines of reasoning men so eminent, so quick to enquire into every new thing, have adhered to maxims which it has cost the world so much effort to reverse' (Lord Acton, 'German Schools of History', *English Historical Review*, 1 (1886), 7–42).

Even those British men who tried to improve themselves by experiencing the academic freedom practised in great German research universities did not always react with warmth to the experience. The great figures of the historical school of Ranke, Treitschke, and Meinecke did not seem overly interested in Britain, despite Ranke's history of England, which was not his greatest work. In the Wilhelmine Empire the academic view of Britain was not particularly favourable. Austen Chamberlain, who attended Treitschke's lectures in 1887, complained to his family that these had revealed to him a new side to the German character, 'a narrow-minded, proud, intolerant Prussian *chauvinism*'. This was not altogether surprising, since Treitschke had jettisoned an earlier liberal admiration for British institutions. Instead he adopted the view that Britain was continuously hostile to Germany, and that British naval supremacy, in particular, would have to be destroyed. He raged against the 'dreadful English hypocrites' whose Empire was based upon an 'abundance of sins and outrages'. Even a trip to Britain shortly before his death only confirmed these views; he referred to London as being like 'the dream of a drunken devil', and told his students that he hoped 'this English air bubble so called the English state, would eventually burst'.[2]

The outbreak of the First World War did not help matters; historians on both sides of the conflict entered with zeal into what we might now consider to be the public relations battle to demonstrate that their own side was the innocent victim of aggression and that Prussian militarism, on the one hand, or materialistic British capitalism, on the other, bore full responsibility for the outbreak of hostilities. For the first but not the last time, Rhodes scholarships were suspended for Germans. In the aftermath of the war liberal historians of what might be loosely termed the Fisher/Trevelyan school stressed the difference between a good liberal unification movement in Italy—somewhat tarnished, to be sure, by the arrival of Mussolini—and the unfortunate state-worshipping, jackbooted variety in Germany.[3] The German historical profession, for its

---

[2] Peter Winzen, 'Treitschke's Influence on the Rise of Imperialist and Anti-British Nationalism in Germany', in Paul Kennedy and Anthony Nicholls (eds.), *Nationalist and Racialist Movements in Britain and Germany before 1914* (London: Macmillan, 1981), 157–9.

[3] Trevelyan contrasted the British achievement of the 'sovereignty of the people' in the 1832 Reform Act with the fate of the Germans: 'The people did not become sovereign in Germany when Bismarck granted limited popular rights, because those rights had not been won by the action of the nation itself, as the first Reform Bill had been won.' He later

part, was greatly engaged in the battle against the so-called war guilt lie associated with the Treaty of Versailles, which had the spin-off effect of producing that admirable series of volumes of German diplomatic documents, *Die Große Politik der europäischen Kabinette*. These were considered by the German academic establishment, and by many neutral observers, to provide overwhelming proof of Germany's innocence in the outbreak of the First World War.[4] It is perhaps worth noting here that Professor Medlicott, in his inaugural lecture as Stevenson Professor of International History at the London School of Economics in May 1955, argued that if the aim of the publication had been to destroy the simplicity of the original war guilt thesis, it had succeeded, but 'if it hoped for a positive academic judgment helpful to German aspirations in the nineteen twenties it surely failed'.[5] There were of course, exceptions to this apologetic tendency in Germany, but perhaps the best known, Friedrich Meinecke's pupil Eckart Kehr, was really only to become famous after the Second World War, when his work was taken up with enthusiasm by a school of critical German historians in the mid-1960s. In neither Britain nor Germany was the historical study of the other country well represented at university level during the inter-war period.

On the British side, it might be remarked that the establishment of the discipline of International Relations as a subject for serious academic study in such places as the London School of Economics, Oxford University, and, above all, in the Royal Institute of

referred to Bismarck's rule as 'a new type of despotism'. George Macaulay Trevelyan, *British History in the Nineteenth Century (1782–1901)* (London: Longmans, 1922), 242 and 360. Fisher wrote: 'In Italy the triumph of nationalism was associated with the establishment of Parliamentary government on the English plan; in Germany with its decisive defeat.' He did, however, note that 'at regular intervals the cleansing tides of universal suffrage swept through the Reichstag and enabled fresh formations of opinion to make themselves felt in the political life of the country'. His appreciation of Mussolini and Hitler was only marginally more favourable to the former, but he regarded the acceptance of Nazi philosophy by the Germans as a 'note of that lack of balance and moderation which goes with the character of this remarkable people, at once the most virile and enthusiastic, the most industrious and submissive, the most methodical and sentimental in the world.' H. A. L. Fisher, *A History of Europe* (London: Edward Arnold, 1936), 980–1 and 1206.

[4] Albrecht Mendelssohn Bartholdy, Johannes Lepsius, and Friedrich Thimme (eds.), *Die Große Politik der Europäischen Kabinette 1871–1914: Sammlung der diplomatischen Akten des Auswärtigen Amts* (Berlin: Deutsche Verlagsgesellschaft für Politik und Geschichte, 1925–7). See also Immanuel Geiss, 'The Outbreak of the First World War and German War Aims', *Journal of Contemporary History*, vol. 1, no. 3 (1966).

[5] A. N. Medlicott, 'The Scope and Study of International History', Inaugural Lecture, 16 May 1955, *International Affairs*, 31 (1955), 413–26, at 421.

International Affairs at Chatham House created an ongoing interest in Anglo-German relations. This was furthered by the work of one of the Institute's earliest staff members, John Wheeler-Bennett, who went to live in Germany during the Weimar period and stayed there until shortly after the Röhm purge, in which he narrowly escaped the murderous attentions of the SS. He pioneered a type of contemporary historical investigation using a combination of published materials and in-depth interviews which informed such books as *Brest-Litovsk: The Forgotten Peace*; *Hindenburg: The Wooden Titan*; and later his controversial but influential book on the German army in politics, *The Nemesis of Power*, for which he was able to supplement personal knowledge of the *dramatis personae* with documents from captured German archives. Wheeler-Bennett's books aroused criticism in Germany, but in Britain they helped to stimulate interest amongst a generation of younger historians, a generation which included William Deakin, author of the definitive study of Hitler's relationship with Mussolini, *The Brutal Friendship*; James Joll, whose writings on Rathenau and on the Second International introduced many British scholars to the complexities of German intellectual life and revolutionary movements, and who was later to fill the chair of International History at LSE held by Professor Medlicott; and Alan Bullock, whose biographical studies of Hitler were long unsurpassed.[6] Also influential in this context was another Oxford historian, A. J. P. Taylor. Taylor's biography of Bismarck and his study of German history, concentrating on the nineteenth and twentieth centuries, were certainly not friendly to Germany, but they were nevertheless valuable as lively introductions to the subject for British students.[7] I would avoid referring to these scholars as a 'school' since their political viewpoints, methodological approaches, and intellectual interests were by no means uniform. Some of them, like Hugh Trevor-Roper, who made important contributions to controversies over Hitler's last days in power, his war aims and the nature of

    [6] Alan Bullock, *Hitler: A Study in Tyranny* (London: Odhams Press, 1952); id., *Hitler and Stalin: Parallel Lives* (London: HarperCollins, 1991). F. W. Deakin, *The Brutal Friendship: Mussolini, Hitler and the Fall of Italian Fascism* (London:Weidenfeld & Nicolson, 1962). James Joll, *The Second International, 1889–1914* (London: Weidenfeld & Nicolson, 1955); id., *Intellectuals in Politics: Three Biographical Essays* (London: Weidenfeld & Nicolson, 1960). J. W. Wheeler-Bennett, *Hindenburg: The Wooden Titan* (London: Macmillan, 1936); id., *Brest-Litovsk: The Forgotten Peace, March 1918* (London: Macmillan, 1938) and id., *The Nemesis of Power: The German Army in Politics, 1918–1945* (London: Macmillan, 1953).
    [7] A. J. P. Taylor, *The Course of German History* (London: Hamish Hamilton, 1945); id., *Bismarck: The Man and the Statesman* (London: Hamish Hamilton, 1955).

National Socialism, wrote mainly on issues other than Germany.[8] They did, however, create a dialogue with German historians which was to continue and intensify from the end of the Second World War.

These scholars were all to a greater or lesser degree affected by the experience of appeasement before 1939 and the total war which followed it, which meant that initially they were unlikely to be too sympathetic towards the historical establishment in West Germany. Anglo-Saxon scholarship, in general, tended to stress the elements of continuity it perceived between the illiberal characteristics of the Wilhelmine Empire and the Nazi dictatorship. I say Anglo-Saxon because, of course, one should remember that American scholars such as Gordon Craig, or German expatriates in US universities, like Hajo Holborn or Hans Rosenberg, also tended to present a more critical view of the Bismarck legacy at a time when the pre-1914 Empire was perceived, in West Germany at least, to have been something of a Golden Age. We should also remember the contribution within Britain itself of a very distinguished list of refugee historians from Germany, although it was not until the mid-1950s that the work of such important figures as Francis Carsten began to make an impact on British historiography.[9]

It could hence be argued that at the beginning of the 1950s the academic élites in these two countries held quite different perceptions of Germany's political and even social development in the nineteenth and twentieth centuries, and of the reasons for difficult Anglo-German relations during the period from roughly 1890 until 1945. The leading figures in the German historical profession, the *Zunft* as it was sometimes unkindly called, included men like Gerhard Ritter, Karl Dietrich Erdmann, and Hans Rothfels who, whilst unequivocally condemning the Third Reich, tended to take a more benign view of Germany's role in the pre-First World War period, to stress the weaknesses of the Weimar Republic and the

---

[8] H. R. Trevor-Roper, *The Last Days of Hitler*, 2nd edn. (London: Macmillan, 1950), and 'The Mind of Adolf Hitler', the introduction to *Hitler's Table Talk, 1941–4* (London: Weidenfeld & Nicolson, 1953).

[9] Francis L. Carsten, *The Origins of Prussia* (Oxford: Clarendon Press, 1954). This book was based on his Oxford University research thesis, completed in 1942, and it was not well received in Germany owing to its stress on social and economic factors. See Francis L. Carsten, 'From Revolutionary Socialism to German History', in Peter Alter (ed.), *Out of the Third Reich: Refugee Historians in Post-War Britain* (London: Tauris, 1998), 25–39.

external pressures upon it from rapacious neighbours and Soviet Communists, and to emphasize the importance of German resistance against Hitler, whilst noting that it had not been very well supported from London before or during the war. Their interpretation of the Third Reich also tended to stress the malign influence of Hitler himself and some of his more extreme followers—such as Himmler, Alfred Rosenberg, or Goebbels—and to gloss over the extent to which there had been widespread support for the Nazi movement, not least amongst members of the historical profession.

British historical élites nearly always adopted the opposite point of view. They explained National Socialism with reference to inherited traditions of an anti-Semitic or anti-democratic character. So far as German interpretations of British history were concerned, these were cautiously positive, but usually stressed that Britain had enjoyed the great advantage of well-established institutions operating behind safe island frontiers, a happy security which lasted at least until the Zeppelin raids in the First World War.

It was obvious, however, that the question which was bound to loom large in Anglo-German historiography was that of the responsibility for what had happened in the period between 1933 and 1945. It should be remembered that, whatever continuity there may have been between the historical élites in Germany before and after 1945—and this is an issue which has raised its head again recently[10]—the German historical profession did turn its scholarly attention at a very early stage to the problem of *Die Bewältigung der Vergangenheit* or overcoming the past. One of the earliest research institutions established in the Federal Republic was the Institut für Zeitgeschichte in Munich, under the direction of Paul Kluke, Helmut Krausnick, and later Martin Broszat. It organized research into the Third Reich, achieving an admirable level of scholarship and transforming our understanding of the Nazi dictatorship. The journal of the Institute in Munich, the *Vierteljahrshefte für Zeitgeschichte*, the first volume of which appeared in 1953, is still the most prestigious periodical dealing with contemporary German history. It is worth remembering that many of the figures who are

[10] See e.g. Götz Aly, 'Rückwärtsgewandte Propheten: Willige Historiker—Bemerkung in eigener Sache', in id., *Macht Geist Wahn: Kontinuitäten deutschen Denkens* (Berlin: Argon-Verlag, 1997), 153–83.

now regarded in some quarters as conservative members of the *Zunft*, Werner Conze, Karl Dietrich Erdmann, Theodor Schieder, and Hans Rothfels, were members of the supervisory board of the Institute or the editorial board of the journal. It is also interesting to note that from the beginning political scientists were represented in this venture—most notably Theodor Eschenburg. Indeed, one of the most important works of historical scholarship to appear in Germany in the 1950s was also that of a political scientist—using the term in its German rather than American sense—Karl Dietrich Bracher's *Die Auflösung der Weimarer Republik* (Stuttgart and Düsseldorf: Ring Verlag, 1955). Bracher eschewed any sort of nationalist apologia for Weimar's demise and made clear the importance of structural weaknesses in the German political system. These included the lack of an effective parliamentary tradition, the inappropriate behaviour of political parties, the uncooperative nature of the bureaucracy, the ideological presuppositions of national élites, the damaging influence of economic pressure groups, the fateful powers of the Presidency under the Weimar constitution, and the damaging influence of the *Reichswehr*. If I were to choose a single book which has had the most influence on the historical reassessment of Germany in the twentieth century I would pick that one. It was, of course, followed by important works from Bracher on the National Socialist seizure of power and the German dictatorship itself.

Far more sensational, however, was the impact of a work which came later and dealt with a rather more well trodden theme, namely the German involvement in the outbreak of the First World War. This was Fritz Fischer's *Griff nach der Weltmacht: Deutsche Kriegsziele 1914–1918*, which came out in 1961. It is now rather difficult to imagine why this book aroused such deep passions, but the fact that it did is itself not without significance. It should be remembered that as late as October 1963 the first full Ambassador to Britain after the Second World War, Hans Heinrich Herwarth von Bittenfeld, published an article in which he started by pointing out that many people in Britain still believed, and I quote, 'wrongly as it is now acknowledged', that Germany had been chiefly responsible for the outbreak of the First World War. This assumption of German innocence of responsibility for the War in 1914 illustrates the gulf which still existed between historical élites in Britain and Germany, since by that time most British undergraduates were being brought up on the work of the Italian historical journalist, Albertini, whose work *The Origins of the War of 1914* took a rather different view.[11]

Therefore, it was something quite new for a prestigious German historian to announce that the German authorities had in fact entered the war fully expecting to get something out of it, and that they continued to harbour grandiose plans for territorial expansion throughout most of its duration. A ferocious row broke out within the German historical profession, which spilled over into other countries, including Britain. Many of Fischer's senior historical colleagues in Germany either accused him of fouling his own nest, or of presenting his case in an over-simplified fashion. Fischer was supported mainly by his own pupils, such as Imanuel Geiß, whose documentation of the July crisis in 1914 was possibly even more damaging to conventional German views than the work of his professor.[12] British historians were, with one or two exceptions, sympathetic to Fischer, and he also received a great deal of support from scholars in the United States. James Joll, though not uncritical of Fischer, wrote an introduction to the British edition of *Griff nach der Weltmacht*. One of the important features of the Fischer controversy was that it involved German and British academics in wide-ranging discussions on the whole issue of causes and objectives in the First World War, something which was part of an international debate, reflected not least in the International Historical Congress at Vienna in 1965. It became evident that historical discussion did not need to be viewed from a confrontational and 'patriotic' position. Differences of opinion could run across national boundaries, and this was a healthy development which could bring with it benefits for scholarship. The fact was that, thanks to support from a number of organizations, including the British Council and the Deutscher Akademischer Austauschdienst, British and German academics and graduate students were able to make contact with each other on a much more regular basis than had been possible in the past. On the German side the establishment of the Volkswagen Foundation as the result of the privatization of the Volkswagen Works in 1961

[11] To be fair to Herwarth, his article was followed by another by the British Ambassador in Bonn, Christopher Steel, which put the blame on Austria and Russia. See H. H. Herwarth, 'Anglo-German Relations: A German View', *International Relations*, vol. 39, no. 4 (Oct. 1963), 511. For Steel's contribution, see 'A British View', ibid. 521.

[12] Imanuel Geiss (ed.) *Julikrise und Kriegsausbruch 1914: Eine Dokumentation*, 2 vols. (Hanover: Verlag für Literatur und Zeitgeschehen, 1963–4).

meant that academic research could now hope for adequate funding, especially if it showed itself interested in scientific enquiry which reached out beyond West Germany's frontiers.

On the British side, reforms in higher education funding meant that graduate students whose interests had been aroused by the Anglo-German controversies of the 1950s and early 1960s were able to obtain with relative ease scholarships to work in Germany, and found themselves in German archives, universities, and institutes where they were assisted by German researchers and archivists. Often they made close friendships, if not with the most senior professors then, even more helpfully, with their chief assistants.

The Fischer controversy was in some ways a genteel prologue to the more prolonged convulsion which shook German universities after 1968 and which is sometimes misleadingly referred to as the student revolution. It should not be forgotten that besides the wilder and more telegenic forms of student protest, a considerable intellectual ferment was going on in the German historical profession, both in terms of method and politics. Many younger German historians—and here the names of Hans-Ulrich Wehler, Jürgen Kocka, Hans and Wolfgang Mommsen come to mind—were approaching their subject in a critical fashion, being determined to jolt Germany out of what they perceived to be parochial attitudes, and to subject received ideas to rigorous criticism. Sometimes, but by no means always, this criticism used a neo-Marxist frame of reference. Although Fischer's work had been more of a moral crusade than a socio-economic analysis of the Wilhelmine Empire, many of those who sympathized with him began to question the belief in the primacy of foreign policy. This concept had informed much German historical writing in the eighty years after the foundation of the German Empire by Bismarck, and indeed it could be noticed in the assumptions underlying the works of many British diplomatic historians, Professor Medlicott himself not entirely excepted. Having earlier espoused a more critical assessment of Bismarck's Empire, British historians found themselves being overtaken by a rush of young Germans in a hurry, arguing that domestic politics, industrialization, and class conflict were the motive forces which had driven nineteenth-century Germany. They announced *der Primat der Innenpolitik*—the message of Eckart Kehr, whose essays were reissued by Hans-Ulrich Wehler in

1965.[13] This is not to suggest that the Kehrite School, as it was sometimes rather misleadingly called, had it all its own way in Germany during the late 1960s and 1970s, but it did help to create a new atmosphere of multipolarity in debate which encouraged British historians to involve themselves more closely with their German colleagues.

The expansion of universities in both Britain and Germany in the 1960s and early 1970s meant that there were more opportunities for ambitious and innovative historians in both countries. In West Germany many of the new generation had spent extended periods as graduate students or visiting fellows in the United States of America—particularly at the great graduate schools, such as Harvard, Princeton, or Stanford—and could speak fluent English. They had also come into contact with different approaches to history from those current in post-war Germany, especially in the field of social and economic history. For their part, the British were experimenting with new forms of university syllabus; in particular the concept of interdisciplinary European Studies—a combination of language, history, literature, and politics of European countries—was successfully developed in universities like Sussex and East Anglia. Anglo-German exchanges and colloquia became a common feature of historical scholarship, enriching the academic life of both countries. At the University of Sussex, for example, there was established an exchange of senior historical staff with the University of Freiburg. From 1968 Edgar Feuchtwanger, a historian of both Britain and Germany, started a link between the Universities of Southampton and Frankfurt (Main), and from 1978 until 1986 Richard Evans, whose own doctoral research had been devoted to the then almost untilled field of German feminism, ran a series of seminars at the University of East Anglia to which he invited groups of Germans working on social history, which was still relatively underdeveloped in the Federal Republic. They discussed with their British colleagues subjects such as the history of the family, the peasantry, crime, religion, health and medicine, and

[13] Eckart Kehr, *Der Primat der Innenpolitik: Gesammelte Aufsätze zur preußisch-deutschen Sozialgeschichte im 19. und 20. Jahrhundert*, ed. and with an introduction by Hans-Ulrich Wehler (Berlin: Walter de Gruyter, 1965). For discussions of the 'critical school' of German historians see Gerhard A. Ritter, *The New Social History in the Federal Republic of Germany* (London: German Historical Institute London, 1991), 21–37, and Stefan Berger, *The Search for Normality: National Identity and Historical Consciousness in Germany since 1800* (Providence and Oxford: Berghahn Books, 1997), ch. 4.

unemployment. It is worth noting that this admirable effort was funded at first by the British Social Science Research Council and then, when government cuts hit that body's budget, by the Nuffield Foundation and the University of East Anglia.[14] The commitment to a new form of social history, looking at society from the bottom up rather than from the top down, was a feature of British historical writing in the 1960s and 1970s. It had led to the foundation of the History Workshop, and owed a considerable amount to the influence of Marxist and neo-Marxist scholars such as E. P. Thompson and T. W. Mason, and of the French Annales School, which had been relatively unimportant in West German historiography. Thus influences were certainly moving in both directions, and stimulating debate at various levels.

There is no doubt that the 1960s and 1970s saw an unparalleled increase in academic contacts between Britain and West Germany—the German Democratic Republic being if anything rather more isolated from the West than some other Soviet bloc communities. To draw on my own experience, at St Antony's College in Oxford in 1965 there was established a programme of Visiting Fellowships for German historians which came to be affectionately referred to as the 'Volkswagen Professorship' because it was supported for the first eleven years by the Volkswagen Foundation. It brought a series of distinguished German professors to Britain, where they gave unstintingly of their expertise, not only in St Antony's but in lectures all round the country. Those who contributed especially to British understanding of German scholarship and who also took back to Germany insights which they gained in Britain included Gerhard A. Ritter of Münster and later of Munich University, K. D. Bracher, Martin Broszat, Fritz Fischer himself, Wolfgang Mommsen, Werner Conze, Lothar Gall, Thomas Nipperdey, and Hans-Peter Schwarz.[15]

One of the most impressive and important examples of Anglo-German co-operation in the field of Modern History during this period was the establishment of the German Historical Institute in

---

[14] Richard J. Evans, *Rethinking German History: Nineteenth Century Germany and the Origins of the Third Reich* (London: Allen & Unwin, 1987), 8–9.

[15] The Visiting Fellowship was later supported by the Leverhulme Trust, the German Academic Exchange Service, and the Stifterverband für die Deutsche Wissenschaft, with special funding from C & A Mode, Düsseldorf. For a list of the Professors until 1995, see A. J. Nicholls and Reiner Pommerin, *30 Years of German Visiting Fellows at St Antony's College 1965–1995* (Oxford: St Antony's College, 1996).

London. It must be said at the outset that this was very much a German initiative and that the substantial funding required for it came from the Federal Republic. Once again that admirable organization, the Stiftung Volkswagenwerk (today the Volkswagen Stiftung), played a key role in it, but the initiative for its establishment came from an academic, Dr Carl Haase, Keeper of the Archives of Lower Saxony, who, having visited the German Historical Institute in Rome in 1967, was struck by the thought that there ought to be a similar institution in London.

He was particularly keen that archivists from Lower Saxony should be able to work in London, given the close historical links between Hanover and the United Kingdom. The problems of a divided Germany also played a role here, because Dr Haase was an enthusiastic board member of the Hansischer Geschichtsverein. This learned society for the historical investigation of the Hanseatic ports covered both German states, but it was clear that such collaboration would soon cease and that then most of the Baltic would be effectively closed to Western researchers. He felt that Anglo-German relations would be a fruitful field in which archivists and historians could work over a lengthy historical sweep. Haase wrote to Dr Gambke, the head of the Volkswagen Foundation, and to a senior official in the Ministry of Education and Science, and began to mobilize support for what was clearly going to be a major new historical venture. He approached a number of historians interested in Britain, in particular Professor Paul Kluke of Frankfurt University, who had been one of the founders of the Institut für Zeitgeschichte in Munich. By February 1969 the Deutsch-Britischer Historikerkreis had been established at Frankfurt am Main, consisting of seven German and seven British historians. The most influential of the latter was the Director of the Institute of Historical Research in the University of London, Professor Geoffrey Dickens, a specialist in the History of the Reformation with a strong interest in Germany. On 5 December a Verein zur Förderung des Britisch-Deutschen Historikerkreises was set up, significantly enough being registered at the Headquarters of the Volkswagen Foundation in Hanover. Haase and Kluke were the leading members on the German side, but sadly Dr Haase became ill. His place on the committee was taken over by Professor Gerhard A. Ritter of Münster, who had been the first Visiting Volkswagen Fellow at St Antony's in Oxford and whose interest in British history went back to the 1950s, when as a graduate student in Oxford he had written a B.Litt. thesis on the British labour movement and the Bolshevik Revolution. Also very important at that time was the Treasurer of the Verein, Dr Wolfgang Mommsen, President of the Federal Archives, not to be confused with Professor Wolfgang J. Mommsen of the University of Düsseldorf, who was to become the director of the German Historical Institute in August 1977. Before that, however, the institute itself had to be founded. In January 1972 the Verein opened a small office in Chancery Lane, run by Lothar Kettenacker, where it began to organize conferences and grant scholarships to British and German Ph.D. candidates. Finally, on 4 November 1976 the German Historical Institute, funded by the Federal Ministry for Research and Technology, opened with Professor Kluke as Director and Lothar Kettenacker as his deputy. It was ideally situated near the British Library and the then Public Record Office as well as the central buildings of London University. However, its quarters were very cramped and on a temporary lease. When this lease fell in it appeared that the Institute might have to move into suburbia, thus losing its uniquely advantageous position for visiting researchers from either Germany or Britain. It was thanks to the energy and imagination of the second director, Professor Wolfgang J. Mommsen, that a dilapidated but beautiful building at 17 Bloomsbury Square, which had been occupied by the British Pharmaceutical Society and which the building officials of the relevant Federal German ministry regarded as far too risky for public purchase, was acquired and transformed into what must surely be one of the most attractive academic institutes anywhere in Europe. In this enterprise Professor Mommsen was helped by the far-sighted policy of the Volkswagen Foundation, which was prepared to buy and renovate the building, the origins of which date back to the seventeenth century, and rent it to the Institute. It was formally opened on 2 December 1982 in the presence of the Duke of Gloucester.[16]

The Institute has played a very important role in forging links between British and German communities of historians, but it has also stimulated interest in the history of the United Kingdom and

---

[16] German Historical Institute London, *German Historical Institute London, 1976–1986* (London: German Historical Insititute London, 1986), 9–16.

the British Empire amongst German historians, and in particular amongst doctoral and post-doctoral scholars. The list of publications under the auspices of the Institute since 1977 illustrates this well. To take only a limited number of examples, in 1976 Marie-Luise Recker, now a professor at the University of Frankfurt, published *England und der Donauraum, 1919–1929: Probleme einer europäischen Nachkriegsordnung* (Stuttgart, 1976); Hans-Christoph Junge produced a study of the Cromwellian Navy, *Flottenpolitik und Revolution: Die Entstehung der englischen Seemacht während der Herrschaft Cromwells* (Stuttgart, 1980); Hermann Wentker wrote about British aims in the Crimean War in *Zerstörung der Großmacht Rußland? Die britische Kriegsziele im Krimkrieg* (Göttingen, 1993). Nor has medieval history been neglected. In 1996, for example, Alfred Haverkamp and Hanna Vollrath edited a volume on *England and Germany in the High Middle Ages* (Oxford, 1996), and in 1997 Bärbel Brodt produced a study of urban development in East Anglia in the fourteenth century, *Städte ohne Mauern: Stadtentwicklung in East Anglia im 14. Jahrhundert* (Paderborn, 1997). Generally speaking, however, it can be said that the weight of publications has tended to lie in the nineteenth and twentieth centuries. Two themes particularly worth noting are the studies of British and German imperialism which Professor Mommsen certainly encouraged as a result of his own research expertise and which have continued to be a feature of the Institute's research agenda; and secondly the study of German exiles in Britain, especially those who were important for academic developments. Gerhard Hirschfeld's *Exil in Großbritannien: Zur Emigration aus dem nationalsozialistischen Deutschland* appeared in 1982 (with a British edition two years later), and in 1997 Peter Alter published *Out of the Third Reich: Refugee Historians in Postwar Britain.*

Under Mommsen's successor, Adolf M. Birke, the Institute embarked on an ambitious project in conjunction with the archives of Lower Saxony to publish a handbook listing and describing the documents held in the Public Record Office relating to the British occupation of Germany after the Second World War. This major research tool was published in 1993, edited by Adolf M. Birke, Hans Booms, and Otto Merker with the general title *Control Commission for Germany: British Element, Inventory.* Under the leadership of its next Director, Peter Wende, the Institute embarked on an innovative project for the publication of diplo-

matic reports from British embassies in Germany between the end
of the Napoleonic wars and the unification of Germany under
Bismarck.

In general, the Institute has provided a stimulus to Anglo-
German historical research in all areas of Modern History, broadly
defined. Its lectures, seminars, and workshops have been of great
assistance to those of us whose students are researching into
German topics at graduate level and its library is invaluable.

It has also given generous hospitality to the association of British
historians working on German and Austrian topics, the German
History Society. The founding of this society in 1977 reflected the
growing number of historians and graduate students in Britain
whose research interests were focused on Germany. The society
combined its Annual General Meeting every year with a conference in London, but was determined also to hold conferences
throughout Britain, and in the first five years of its existence
regional gatherings were held at the universities of Aston,
Leicester, Swansea, Manchester, Glasgow, and Dublin, an indication of the spread of interest in German history throughout British
universities. In the 1980s the Society flourished to such an exent
that its members decided to set up a journal, and in the autumn of
1984 the first edition of *German History*, edited by Richard Evans
and Mary Fulbrook, made its appearance, published at that time
at the university of East Anglia. Since then it has expanded greatly
and publication was taken over first by the Oxford University Press
and latterly by Arnold.

So far as the Political Scientists—using that term more in the
British than in the American sense—are concerned, here, too,
there has been a growth of interest in German politics, centring on
the development of democratic systems in West Germany, on the
success, and possibly decline, of *Volksparteien* like the CDU and the
SPD, and on the foreign policy of the Federal Republic with special
emphasis on *Ostpolitik*. Leading figures to be mentioned here—
though I should hasten to add this is by no means an exhaustive
list—would be Willy Paterson, who has analysed the SPD from various viewpoints and maintains a watching brief over contemporary
political developments; Stephen Padgett, who, with Eva Kolinsky,
was the first editor of the journal *German Politics*, which began in
April 1992; Peter Pulzer, whose recent account of West German
politics is a masterly summary of that country's constitution and

political culture;[17] Anthony Glees, who presented a challenging interpretation of Germany's recent history in *Reinventing Germany*; and Gordon Smith, who has produced some of the best evaluations of West German democracy.

It is a matter of great satisfaction that, once again with help from the German Academic Exchange Service, the Institute for German Studies has been established at the University of Birmingham as a centre for research and graduate teaching in the politics, inter-national relations, economics, and culture of contemporary Germany.

In Germany itself there has, so far as I know, been rather less institutional development of British History. This has been partly due to the relative meanness of British state authorities in funding equivalent facilities to the Visiting Professorships and the Institutes in the Federal Republic by comparison with the generosity and far-sightedness of German public authorities and Foundations. Nevertheless, the German Association for the Study of British History and Politics, in which Gustav Schmidt has played a lead-ing role, has an impressive list of publications. Mention should also be made of the Institute of British Studies attached to the Humboldt University in Berlin, in which political science and recent history are well represented. There have also been a num-ber of initiatives by German historians such as Gerhard A. Ritter when he was holding a Chair at Münster, Bernd-Jürgen Wendt in Hamburg, and Gustav Schmidt in Bochum, all of whom have attempted systematically to further the study of Britain in the nine-teenth and twentieth centuries. Ritter has been particularly prolific in looking at comparative social policy in the two countries; Bernd-Jürgen Wendt and Gustav Schmidt have worked extensively on British foreign policy in the twentieth century, with special atten-tion to the appeasement policies of the pre-1939 period, and Schmidt has more recently examined the British relationship with NATO and the European Community after 1945.[18]

---

[17] Peter Pulzer, *German Politics, 1945–1995* (Oxford: Oxford University Press, 1995); Anthony Glees, *Reinventing Germany: German Political Development since 1945* (Oxford: Berg, 1996).

[18] e.g. Gerhard A. Ritter, *Social Welfare in Germany and Britain: Origins and Development* (Leamington Spa: Berg, 1986); Bernd-Jürgen Wendt, *Economic Appeasement: Handel und Finanz in der britischen Deutschlandpolitik 1933–1939* (Düsseldorf: Bertelsmann Universitätsverlag, 1971); and Gustav Schmidt, *Zwischen Bündnissicherung und Priviligierte Partnerschaft: Die deutsch-britischen Beziehungen und die Vereinigten Staaten von Amerika, 1955–1963* (Bochum: Brockmeyer, 1995).

What is the conclusion to be drawn from this examination of the relationship between the academic study of Modern History and Politics at British and German universities? I think the most important is that the élites of both countries—and in Germany at least the professoriat still enjoys the status of an élite—are now accustomed to working together as part of a general academic discourse which transcends frontiers, and do not think of themselves as British or German. Many of the German colleagues I have mentioned in this chapter are as comfortable addressing academic audiences in the USA, France, or for that matter Australia, as they would be in Britain, and they do not see themselves, as many of their forerunners in the immediate post-war period would have done, as spokesmen for their country's national interests. The same is true for British historians. In the famous discussions which raged in the 1970s over the intentionalist and structuralist interpretations of Nazi Germany, for example, British and German scholars were to be found on both sides of the discussion and many took positions from which they could cheerfully open fire on either camp. Many of us remember vividly the conference held in 1977 at Cumberland Lodge near Windsor at which Tim Mason, Jürgen Kocka, Klaus Hildebrand, Martin Broszat, Michael Geyer, and many others argued over the importance of institutional Darwinism and class conflict as against anti-Semitic ideology in the development of the Third Reich. This is a subject which has not lost its interest, even in the 1990s.[19]

Similarly, the argument which dominated the 1980s about the meaning or validity of the so-called German *Sonderweg* saw historians from Britain like Geoff Ely and David Blackbourn letting fly at German colleagues who had apparently come to accept without question that the German bourgeoisie had feebly allowed itself to be feudalized by a dominant aristocratic élite instead of carrying out the democratic revolution which both neo-Marxism and modernization theory seemed to demand. They irritatingly pointed out that such a clear-cut bourgeois-democratic revolution had never occurred anywhere else, and so it was rather unfair to expect it of the Germans. Interestingly enough, their explosive joint work

---

[19] This is reflected in the controversy surrounding Daniel J. Goldhagen's *Hitler's Willing Executioners: Ordinary Germans and the Holocaust* (London: Little, Brown, 1996), which was critically received by scholars in Britain—see e.g. Brendan Simms, 'A Nation Minded to Murder?' in the *Times Higher Education Supplement*, 29 Mar. 1996, 20.

The Peculiarities of German History appeared in German as *Mythen deutscher Geschichtsschreibung: die gescheiterte Revolution von 1848* in 1980, four years before it was published by OUP in Britain. Their rejection of a German *Sonderweg* was by no means universally accepted, either in Britain or in Germany, but it clearly caused many German and British historians to reconsider some basic assumptions, and the influence of their critique can be detected in the nuanced *magnum opus* on German social history produced over recent years by Hans-Ulrich Wehler.[20]

In the other direction, German historians' views on British policy towards European integration after the Second World War have added a critical edge to the debate about Britain's attitudes towards its European neighbours during the 1950s and 1960s. Clemens Wurm and Gustav Schmidt, for example, have provided us with sympathetic, but ultimately critical accounts of British policy towards the EEC during its formative years, highlighting the strategic and economic reasons for British reluctance to commit the United Kingdom to supranational authority, and contrasting this with the more focused *dirigisme* of the French during the same period.[21]

In other areas, such as social or gender history, German and British collaboration has become an accepted aspect of the internationalization of these disciplines, and is taken for granted. In a recent collection of essays edited by Lynn Abrams and Elizabeth Harvey there are contributions by Claudia Schopmann, Regina Schulte, and Heide Wunder alongside those of American and British scholars of gender history.[22] It is also noteworthy that the journal *German History* now carries numerous articles by German

[20] Hans-Ulrich Wehler, *Deutsche Gesellschaftsgeschichte 1849–1914*, vol. iii: *Von der 'Deutschen Doppelrevolution' bis zum Beginn des Ersten Weltkrieges, 1849–1914* (Munich: Beck, 1995), See, in particular, ch. IVA, 848–1000. For my own views on the *Sonderweg*, see A. J. Nicholls, 'The Myth of the German *Sonderweg*', in Cyril Buffet and Beatrice Heuser (eds.), *Haunted by History: Myths in International Relations* (Providence and Oxford: Berghahn Books, 1998), 209–22.

[21] Clemens A. Wurm's views are accessible in English in 'Two Paths to Europe: Great Britain and France from a Comparative Perspective', in id. (ed.), *Western Europe and Germany: The Beginnings of European Integration 1945–1960* (Oxford: Berg, 1996), 175–200. See also id. (ed.), *Wege nach Europa: Wirtschaft und Außenpolitik Großbritanniens im 20. Jahrhundert* (Bochum: Brockmeyer, 1992), and Gustav Schmidt (ed.), *Großbritannien und Europa—Großbritannien in Europa: Sicherheitsbelange und Wirtschaftsfragen in der britischen Europapolitik nach dem zweiten Weltkrieg* (Bochum: Brockmeyer, 1989).

[22] Lynn Abrams and Elizabeth Harvey (eds.), *Gender Relations in German History: Power, Agency and Experience from the Sixteenth to the Twentieth Century* (London: UCL Press, 1997).

colleagues as well as those written by members of the British historical profession writing about Germany.

I should, however, end this fundamentally optimistic essay on a note of caution. As Richard Evans remarked in 1981: 'Historiography is a fragmented discipline; not only are there innumerable sub-disciplines and specialisms, but increasingly there are also competing theories and methodologies as well.'[23] Despite the eclipse of Marxism following the demise of the Cold War, this is still true of Modern History, and *a fortiori* of political science. There is always a danger that the fragmentation will weaken the academic élite and destroy its solidarity. In both our countries, the development of closer and more fruitful contacts at university level has been the result of enlightened policies by governments and foundations. Gifted researchers, teachers, and students are the backbone of such discourse, but they cannot operate without appropriate resources. During the last decades financial stringency has been cutting into universities and research, first of all in Britain but now increasingly in Germany too. It would be both tragic and ironic if, at a time when the European Union is supposedly bringing élites together, lack of funding for graduate students, senior researchers, academic conferences, and collaborative research projects should push us back into a parochialism from which we have not long escaped.

---

[23] Evans, *Rethinking German History*, 89.

15

Building Bridges
The Framework of Anglo-German Cultural Relations after 1945

PETER ALTER

Not so long ago diplomats and politicians considered cultural relations between states, nations, and societies to be of little or no immediate or urgent concern. On the contrary, in their view cultural contacts and institutionalized cultural transfers at whatever level and of whatever kind belonged entirely to the private sphere, depending on individual efforts and privately run institutions and organizations. For governments and states alike the whole complex was definitely an area not to get involved in, but better left to its own peculiar ways and rules. Only from the 1960s, at the height of the Cold War, when East and West were competing to convince other people, particularly in Third World countries, of the inherent value of their respective ideologies and societies, were cultural relations between nations suddenly declared the 'third pillar' of foreign policy, and considered almost on a par with diplomacy and economic affairs.

The quite unexpected lifting of cultural relations on to a more official level was accompanied by a broadening institutional framework to support them. It was, from now on, either directly inaugurated and run financially by governments or still left outwardly to private initiatives, but often sponsored by public funds, in various ways and with varying generosity. This new importance attached to cultural relations in the widest sense between states and nations as well as their institutional consolidation had early precursors, and among them Anglo-German cultural relations after 1945 are surely an excellent example. Moreover, it is a particularly interesting one because, at the end of the Second World War, cultural and academic ties between the two nations had, for obvious reasons, to be rebuilt completely from scratch. Nazism and the war had brought to an abrupt halt what little had existed between the two countries in the years prior to 1933 or 1939.

In the case of Britain and the Western zones of occupied Germany the renewal of cultural and academic contacts after 1945 got off to a flying start; goodwill, outstanding individual commitment, and strong official encouragement helped enormously to make good what had been missed in the past. When Sir Frank Roberts took up his post as British ambassador in Bonn early in 1963 his assessment of the situation at that point was impressive indeed. 'Anglo-German relations', Sir Frank later wrote in his memoirs,

were flourishing, particularly in the universities, despite the absence of any special arrangements on such an imposing scale as those under the Franco-German cultural agreements. We did benefit greatly from postwar institutions, which had grown from strength to strength, in particular from the Anglo-German Königswinter conferences, still inspired by their founder Lilo Milchsack, which provided and still provide 'Forty Years On' more intimate high-level and inter-disciplinary exchanges, covering all political parties, than any other similar international gatherings. Another has been Wilton Park. Originally established for the re-education of German prisoners of war selected as potential leaders of the new democratic Germany, it developed into an Anglo-German, then a European, and now a worldwide conference centre, but always with an Anglo-German core. The British Council had successfully taken over the work of the post-war 'Brücken' or 'Bridges' all over the British zone. It was a major tribute to their success that the headquarters of the British Council in Cologne remained in the offices of the Cologne 'Bridge', which were for many years placed at the disposal of the British Council by the Cologne authorities on the same favourable terms as in the more privileged occupation days.[1]

Anglo-German cultural relations after the war covered a broad area and were propelled by numerous new organizations, associations, and institutions. Among them, the Anglo-German Association (Deutsch-Englische Gesellschaft), which has organized the renowned Königswinter Conferences since 1950, was probably the most successful and influential. The annual conferences, to which Sir Frank refers in such glowing terms, in many respects

---

[1] Frank Roberts, *Dealing with Dictators: The Destruction and Revival of Europe 1930–70* (London: Weidenfeld & Nicolson, 1991), 239–40.

represent something totally new in political and cultural relations between two sovereign countries. With hindsight, half a century after their inauguration, it is clearer than ever just how innovative and creative they really were. Still a major event in the calendar of Anglo-German contacts during the year, the Königswinter Conferences demonstrate, perhaps more than anything else, that cultural, and political relations for that matter, between the two countries have never been so intense, so complex, and, one can safely say, so cordial as in the period since the end of the war.

The intensity of contacts between Britain and Germany or, to be more precise, between their governments, élites, and people in general from 1945 is unique and not at all comparable, say, with the years after the creation of the German nation-state in 1871, during the Wilhelmine era, when there were close family ties between the royal houses of England and Prussia, or the years of the Weimar Republic, let alone the Nazi period after 1933. This truly new quality in Anglo-German cultural and, of course, political relations after 1945 was created by the particular circumstances of that time. Against all the odds and the expectations of contemporaries at this, the nadir of Germany's political existence and moral standing, these circumstances turned out to be surprisingly advantageous to a new departure in the mutual perceptions of the two nations. The particular circumstances were, of course, the partitioning of Germany into zones of occupation, the ideological conflict between East and West and the Cold War of the 1950s and 1960s, the forging of the Western alliance, and the incipient integration of Western Europe under American tutelage.

In many ways, this was a strangely paradoxical development, to say the least, and hardly to be foreseen by either victors or vanquished in 1945. At precisely the moment when the German Reich disappeared from the mental map and the country faced catastrophe and disintegration, when the Germans lost political sovereignty and had to live, until 1990, in two separate states—at this very moment, cultural contacts between Britain and Germany, although at first heavily unbalanced and on a sort of one-way basis, intensified to a quite unprecedented degree. In other words, it might be argued that the Reich of 1871, which was more than fortunate to survive defeat in 1918, had actually been an obstacle in the path of closer cultural relations between Britain and Germany. Such relations had undoubtedly existed before 1871. The German

Reich, or rather, its leaders—for narrow-minded or nationalistic reasons, one can only speculate—neither encouraged greater activity in this field nor invited the alleged rival in trade and world politics, namely Britain, to ease and improve mutual relations by seeking closer contacts and a better understanding at the cultural level. The concept of a German cultural institute in Britain and a similar British institute in Germany, energetically aired by the Cambridge Germanist Karl Breul (1860–1932) on the eve of the Great War, was never really supported in earnest by the then Imperial government in Berlin.[2] Various other private initiatives which aimed to develop an active cultural policy abroad elicited lukewarm responses only. Politicians paid lip-service to a good idea, and pointed to problems of organization and funding.

On the other hand, Britain, before and after 1933, did not seem to have been too keen either to make a determined effort to put on a more formal and institutionalized basis what had been going on between the scholars, scientists, and artists of the two countries constantly since the late eighteenth century, and what may rightly be termed cultural exchange or cultural transfer. All these activities were clearly confined to private and individual initiatives, to individual interests and individual financing, most prominently the London-based British–German Friendship Society of 1912 with almost 600 members, and the Deutsches Institut für Ausländer, founded in Berlin in 1911.[3]

Soon after 1945, all this changed dramatically. Against the background of probably the lowest point in Anglo-German relations over the past two centuries, a relatively strong interest in more intimate contacts and co-operation in cultural matters seems to have emerged almost simultaneously on both sides. There were, of

[2] Karl Breul, 'A British Institute in Berlin and a German Institute in London', *Contemporary Review*, 99 (1911), 589–90; id., *Betrachtungen und Vorschläge betreffend die Gründung eines Reichsinstituts in London für Lehrer des Englischen* (Leipzig, 1900). For the pre-1914 period see Gerhard A. Ritter, 'Internationale Wissenschaftsbeziehungen und auswärtige Kulturpolitik im deutschen Kaiserreich', in Institut für Auslandsbeziehungen (ed.), *Interne Faktoren auswärtiger Kulturpolitik im 19. und 20. Jahrhundert*, xvi (Stuttgart, 1981), 5–16.

[3] For details see Paul M. Kennedy, *The Rise of the Anglo-German Antagonism 1860–1914* (London: Allen & Unwin, 1980); Percy Ernst Schramm, 'Englands Verhältnis zur deutschen Kultur zwischen der Reichsgründung und der Jahrhundertwende', in Werner Conze (ed.), *Deutschland und Europa: Historische Studien zur Völker- und Staatenordnung des Abendlandes: Festschrift für Hans Rothfels* (Düsseldorf: Droste, 1951), 135–75; Peter Alter, 'Science and the Anglo-German Antagonism', in T. R. Gourvish and Alan O'Day (eds.), *Later Victorian Britain 1867–1900* (London: Macmillan, 1988), 271–90.

course, different combinations of motives on the two sides, and it was not at all surprising that strong antipathy towards Germany was still widespread in Britain so soon after the war. Nevertheless, there was a growing conviction among the élites in both countries that a better understanding between Britain and Germany (or soon, to be more precise, West Germany) required greater knowledge of one another. Hitherto, this had simply been missing. If it had ever existed, it had been lost during the twentieth century in the aftermath of the naval rivalry prior to 1914, through the First World War, during the Nazi dictatorship, and, finally, the Second World War.

The surprising new attitude towards each other that developed quickly in both Britain and Germany after 1945 can be explained convincingly and plausibly in the German case. Twelve years of dictatorship and mental isolation from the outside world, of excessive nationalism, police terror, and, finally, war had prepared the ground for a cultural *rapprochement* with the West. And the British, for their part, had to take a close look at the former enemy after Germany's unconditional surrender. Taking control of their zone the British were faced with the task commonly termed 're-education', clearly a priority in their overall post-war planning for Germany.[4]

'Re-educating' the Germans, in a political as well as a cultural sense, was high on the political agenda of all the Allied powers once victory had been achieved and the occupation of the various zones successfully implemented. Consequently, Britain's willingness (one might call it a 'policy') to accept and be reconciled with its former enemy, in the form of far-reaching co-operation initially in the cultural field, was by no means unique. All four Allies, sooner or later, took the same stance, including the Soviets. This is often overlooked. In the climate of mounting ideological conflict between East and West the massive political and military presence of the Soviet Union in the Eastern zone of occupation and then its satellite, the German Democratic Republic, should, in Moscow's view, rest firmly on Soviet–German friendship and cultural co-operation. The French, as is well known, had the greatest qualms

[4] Lothar Kettenacker, 'The Planning for "Re-education" during the Second World War', in Nicholas Pronay and Keith Wilson (eds.), *The Political Re-education of Germany and her Allies After World War II* (London: Croom Helm, 1985), 59–81; Arthur Hearnden (ed.), *The British in Germany: Educational Reconstruction after 1945* (London: Hamish Hamilton, 1978). See also the eye-witness account by Noel Annan, *Changing Enemies: The Defeat and Regeneration of Germany* (London: HarperCollins, 1995).

and were the most reluctant to combine bilateral political co-operation with cultural exchange on what was supposed to be an equal basis, that is, to pursue a policy that was not merely a barely disguised attempt to impose French culture and allegedly superior French civilization on Germany in missionary fashion. In his book *Jahre der Besatzung 1945–1949*, published in 1983, the eminent political scientist and historian Theodor Eschenburg writes with much regret that French cultural policy in Germany in those formative years was solely intended to promote French civilization and, at the same time, to draw a veil over the severities of its occupation policy.[5]

However, even if one concedes that Britain's cultural policy in Germany broadly followed a line agreed upon by all the Allies, this policy had a special quality and was distinct from that of the other powers, even the United States, in two crucial respects.[6] First, British cultural policy in Germany started very early, and, in many ways, assumed a pioneering role in implementing what initially came under the auspices of 're-education' policy. Britain's essentially rather liberal cultural policy in Germany after 1945 could certainly not be taken for granted. In view of what had happened in the first half of the twentieth century, the British had no particular reason to inaugurate a policy which, at the time, gave the distinctly dubious impression of over-hasty reconciliation with the Germans and co-operation between equals. After all, it was hardly surprising that strong antipathy towards Germany and the Germans should be encountered in Britain, and politicians still had to take this into account, even if they themselves had a more impartial view of Germany and its future in the Western orbit. Against this background it must be said that the basically objective, unprejudiced, and even cordial attitude which members of the British Military Government and successive governments in London displayed towards Germany in the immediate post-war years was quite remarkable.

For the Germans, on the other hand, a policy of *rapprochement* with the British was more than welcome, for obvious reasons. They were desperately keen to grasp the helping hand that could lead

---

[5] Theodor Eschenburg, *Jahre der Besatzung 1945–1949* (Stuttgart and Wiesbaden: Deutsche Verlags-Anstalt, 1983), 97.

[6] See Hearnden (ed.), *The British in Germany*, and Alan Bance (ed.), *The Cultural Legacy of the British Occupation in Germany: The London Symposium* (Stuttgart: Heinz Verlag, 1997).

them out of misery, devastation, and dejection and seemed to promise hope in a most difficult situation. Moreover, in 1945, in 1950, in 1960, and today, cultural exchange between Britain and Germany could and can draw heavily on a reservoir of Anglophiles in Germany, certainly greater in number over the past two hundred years than the number of Germanophiles in Britain at any given time. Under the exceptional circumstances of post-war Germany, tentative moves on the part of the British to go ahead with bridge-building and to promote cultural contacts across a broad spectrum were met with enthusiasm in Germany.

All this may explain why rather close Anglo-German relations were established so soon after unconditional surrender at various levels. Shortly after the war, at Wilton Park, a prisoner-of-war camp in Buckinghamshire mentioned by Sir Frank Roberts above, the Foreign Office already supported courses for German prisoners in the democratic rebuilding of Germany. The British hoped that prisoners of war returning home from Britain would help in their modest way to break down the barriers of prejudice and resentment and to help integrate their country into the Western community of nations. From 1946 onwards Germans prominent in many walks of life were invited to Wilton Park, under the inspired leadership of German-born Heinz Koeppler, and shown British democracy and the British way of life mainly through discussions and lectures given by leading public figures. 'Few institutions', it was later said, 'have done more to acquaint German teachers with British life and customs and to break down the isolation in which so many of them had languished during the twelve years of the Hitler régime.'[7]

The exchange of British and German teachers and academics also got off to an early start. Helped by the Military Government and its officials at the Education Branch, British university teachers spent a few months at German universities, lecturing as well as debating with students and German colleagues alike. The distinguished historian, political scientist, and philosopher Sir Ernest Barker was one of the first to make the courageous move and face

[7] Edith Davies, 'British Policy and the Schools', in Hearnden (ed.), *The British in Germany*, 99; Dexter M. Keezer, *A Unique Contribution to International Relations: The Story of Wilton Park* (London: McGraw-Hill, 1973). Wilton Park was a manor house in Beaconsfield. 'When, late in 1950, its operations were moved south to Wiston House the name Wilton Park had come to mean so much to so many people that it was taken along. So now it is Wilton Park at Wiston House' (ibid. 4).

the hardships, but also the challenges of academic life in a country devastated both materially and morally.

Barker, then aged 73, went to Cologne for one semester to serve as Professor of Political Science in the autumn of 1947. In his memoirs he later gave a vivid description of living conditions in the city, four-fifths of which was rubble. About his students Barker wrote, mirroring in exemplary fashion a common experience at the time:

They wanted to learn what we English thought: I wanted to learn what young Germany was thinking; and we had thus a common eagerness. But I think there was also another thing which helped to make these 'colloquia' even more stimulating for me than my old discussion classes had been. These German students were passionate about intellectual and political ideas . . . The 'colloquia', in the course of our stay in Germany, became social parties as well as academic gatherings. My wife and I formed the habit of inviting the members to tea at our house in little groups . . . We were merely following an old Oxford and Cambridge practice in offering some small entertainment to students; but it was perhaps unusual in a German university, and it certainly bore happy fruits.[8]

Limited guest professorships like those taken by Sir Ernest Barker in 1947–8 and the philosopher Michael Foster[9] in 1948–50 at the University of Cologne were supplemented by bilateral conferences of specialists in Britain as soon as Germans were allowed to travel abroad again. Here Oxford University played a pioneering role as an academic venue. In the summer of 1949 economists from both countries met for two weeks and discussed problems of modern economic theory and the prospects of economic development in Western Europe. This was the very first meeting of its kind, still exclusively financed by the British hosts, in this case the organization known as German Educational Reconstruction (GER) under its chairman S. H. Wood, a former civil servant at the Ministry of Education. A few months later, in March 1950, historians from both countries met at a conference in Oxford along similar lines for the first time after the war, among them, on the British side, Geoffrey Barraclough, Sir Ernest Barker, E. H. Carr, A. J. P. Taylor, and Lionel Curtis, and, on the German side, Fritz

---

[8] Ernest Barker, *Age and Youth: Memories of Three Universities* (Oxford: Clarendon Press, 1953), 205–6.

[9] Michael Foster was a philosophy tutor at Christ Church, Oxford. After his early death in 1959 an exchange scholarship between West German universities and Oxford University was named after him in 1963.

Ernst, Richard Nürnberger, Otto Voßler, Fritz Fischer, and Hermann Heimpel.[10] Subsequent conferences were organized for experts on political science, industrial relations, social security, and old age welfare. Between conferences GER entertained and informed a stream of German visitors, from students and youth leaders to trade unionists and ministers of the new *Länder*. Their names, as a matter of fact, were often put forward by the officers attached to the reopened German universities by the Education Branch of the British Control Commission for Germany. By about 1950 these officers had increasingly turned into organizers of Anglo-German cultural exchanges for students and academics. It is not known whether they also helped to organize a meeting of British and German historians and schoolteachers in Brunswick. Between 21 and 28 June 1950 the participants discussed the representation of British and German history in textbooks for schools in both countries.[11] Many similar discussions were to follow, and these meetings eventually led to the founding of the Internationales Institut für Schulbuchverbesserung (now Georg-Eckert-Institut für Internationale Schulbuchforschung) in Brunswick in 1951.

However, the backbone for all these initiatives and the guarantor of continuous cultural work by the British in occupied Germany and later the Federal Republic was to be the British Council. It had made its debut in post-war Germany as early as 1946 by supporting the opening and later the running of rather makeshift information and education centres in the larger cities of the British zone of occupation and in Berlin, called, until their closure in 2001, 'Die Brücke'. By October 1946 there were already thirty-five such information centres in the British zone—all on a very modest scale, often offering no more than a few books and a selection of the British press.[12] They were undoubtedly used for propaganda or, if one prefers the term, publicity purposes. But, with the benefit of hindsight, it must be said that they also did,

[10] There are reports of the first two conferences in the weekly *Die Zeit* (9 June 1949, 7–8, and 20 Apr. 1950, 3). GER, founded in 1943 and dissolved in 1958, depended on private donations. On its work see Jane Anderson, ' "GER": A Voluntary Anglo-German Contribution', in Hearnden (ed.), *The British in Germany*, 253–67.

[11] Ingeborg Koza, *Deutsch-britische Begegnungen in Unterricht, Wissenschaft und Kunst 1949–1955* (Cologne and Vienna: Böhlau, 1988), 142–3.

[12] George Murray, 'The British Contribution', in Hearnden (ed.), *The British in Germany*, 89–94; David Phillips, 'The Rekindling of Cultural and Intellectual Life in the Universities of Occupied Germany with Particular Reference to the British Zone', in Gabriele Clemens (ed.), *Kulturpolitik im besetzten Deutschland 1945–1949* (Stuttgart: Franz Steiner, 1994), 115.

particularly in those early years, extremely useful pioneering work by presenting a broad spectrum of British culture, life, and politics to a wide audience. As the historian Gabriele Clemens points out in her study of British cultural policy in post-war Germany, the 'projection of Britain' or, put bluntly, the selling of Britain, was primarily intended to secure British influence in Germany.[13] However, financial constraints soon led to a reduction in the number of information centres, which stood at 64 around 1950. By the end of 1953 there were only twenty left and their number decreased further.[14] But in major West German cities and in Berlin 'Die Brücke' was, by the mid-1950s, synonymous with British cultural centres housing substantial libraries and offering language courses as well as seminars, films, lectures, theatre, and exhibitions. But, alas, by 1959 they had all disappeared, with the exception of the centres in Berlin and Cologne and a few 'regional offices' elsewhere.

Equivalent German institutions were established in Britain at a much later date, for fairly obvious political and financial reasons. It was not until 1958 that it was agreed, during a state visit by Federal President Theodor Heuss, the first after the war, to set up a Goethe Institute in London. It opened in 1962 and was followed by sister institutes in Manchester in 1967, in Glasgow in 1973, and, finally, in York in 1974. The German Academic Exchange Service (DAAD), which had already been represented in Britain between 1927 and 1939, was able to reopen its London office as early as 1952.[15] Its branch in Paris only started work eleven years later, in December 1963. The mid-1950s also saw the development of town twinning on a broad scale. However, in this field there were courageous forerunners, the most notable amongst them the cities of Bristol and Hanover. The two cities (a British initiative) twinned as early as 1947. Bonn and Oxford, Reading and Düsseldorf followed

[13] Gabriele Clemens, 'Die britische Kulturpolitik in Deutschland: Musik, Theater, Film und Literatur', in ead. (ed.), *Kulturpolitik*, 49–50; ead., *Britische Kulturpolitik in Deutschland 1945–1949* (Stuttgart: Franz Steiner, 1997), 16–17, 33–4; Anthony Glees, 'Britische Kulturpolitik in Deutschland in der unmittelbaren Nachkriegszeit', in Wolfgang J. Mommsen (ed.), *Die ungleichen Partner: Deutsch-britische Beziehungen im 19. und 20. Jahrhundert* (Stuttgart: Deutsche Verlags-Anstalt, 1999), 217–21.

[14] Clemens, *Britische Kultrpolitik*, 206.

[15] DAAD (ed.), *Deutscher Akademischer Austauschdienst/German Academic Exchange Service: London Office 1952–1977* (Bonn, 1977); Lothar Reinermann, 'Die Aussenstellen des DAAD in London und Kairo', in Peter Alter (ed.), *Der DAAD in der Zeit: Geschichte, Gegenwart und zukünftige Aufgaben—vierzehn Essays* (Cologne: Moeker Merkur, 2000), 164–95.

in 1949. By 1975 there were already 164 such links between Britain and West Germany, and 106 more were in the process of being negotiated.[16] The late 1960s was also the period when partnerships between schools and universities were forged in both countries in ever increasing numbers. As a footnote one could add that the German School in Petersham in south-west London opened in 1971.

It has become sufficiently clear so far that British cultural policy in post-war Germany was not solely inaugurated and funded by the state or state agencies. Right from the start a strong private element was involved. Individuals, associations, and private organizations played an active, often pioneering role. This was the second characteristic of British cultural activities in Germany in the early post-war years. An official British policy for occupied Germany, covering all aspects of cultural relations and based on binding directives, seems to have existed in outline only. Edward Heath, who was to become Prime Minister in 1970, recounts a telling anecdote from his days with the army in Hanover immediately after the end of the war. 'When my Brigade Commander', he remembers in his memoirs,

set me the task of organising the reconstruction of the city, he told me that we must set our priorities. This we could do alternately. 'What is your first priority?' I asked him. 'To get the racecourse rebuilt, so that my armoured regiments can get back to horses', he replied. 'What is yours?' he then asked. I announced at once, 'To rebuild the opera house at Herrenhausen on the edge of the city. My men must have culture'. Both projects were rapidly completed, and much relieved the daily monotony of the troops' lives. I was glad to be able to see Mozart's *Così fan tutte* as that house's first post-war production.[17]

Surely, Heath had his pleasure, and in his account there is no trace whatsoever of British detailed planning beyond the overall political concerns. This impression is confirmed by what *The Times* wrote in June 1964: 'It was no doubt the typically British approach that the links forged after the war with west German towns and

[16] A. E. C. Volle, 'Deutsch-britische Beziehungen. Eine Untersuchung des bilateralen Verhältnisses auf der staatlichen und nichtstaatlichen Ebene seit dem Zweiten Weltkrieg' (Ph.D. thesis, University of Bonn, 1976), 227.

[17] Edward Heath, *The Course of My Life: My Autobiography* (London: Weidenfeld & Nicolson, 1998), 102.

cities should have been the result of individual effort and not of government sponsoring.'[18]

One of the most prominent examples of the crucial role of individual initiative in Anglo-German relations after the war, particularly at the cultural and academic level, was the rescue of the prestigious Kaiser Wilhelm Society for the Promotion of Science. The British well knew, long before the war came to a virtual end, that German scientists no longer posed a threat to the Allies,[19] and they held no grudge against the Society because of its history since 1911. Unlike the Americans, therefore, they did not object to the continuation of the Kaiser Wilhelm Society, and some of its members and their work were highly appreciated in Britain. The integrity of Max Planck, who had been invited, as the only German scientist, to attend the postponed Newton tercentenary celebrations organized by the Royal Society in London in July 1946,[20] of Otto Hahn, Otto Warburg, and Max von Laue was never really in doubt.

Soon after Germany's unconditional surrender, when moves were initiated to rebuild German scientific organizations, scientists and scholars in the British Zone did not encounter much opposition from the occupying power. Moreover, the Germans were lucky in enlisting the dedicated support of Colonel Bertie Blount who was the officer of the British Military Government responsible for the reconstruction of research facilities in its zone. Blount, a chemist by trade who had obtained his Ph.D. from the University of Frankfurt in 1931, was determined to use all the freedom which the vagueness of his directives from London gave him. 'My wish was', he later wrote, 'to get German science on its feet again as quickly as I could; and I was naturally pleased to find that that was what I was instructed to do.'[21]

[18] *The Times*, 4 June 1964.

[19] R. V. Jones, *Most Secret War: British Scientific Intelligence 1939–1945* (London: Hamish Hamilton, 1978).

[20] Armin Hermann, *Max Planck mit Selbstzeugnissen und Bilddokumenten* (Reinbek: Rowohlt, 1984), 123–4.

[21] Quoted in Peter Alter, 'Die Kaiser-Wilhelm-Gesellschaft in den deutsch-britischen Wissenschaftsbeziehungen', in Rudolf Vierhaus and Bernhard vom Brocke (eds.), *Forschung im Spannungsfeld von Politik und Gesellschaft: Geschichte und Struktur der Kaiser-Wilhelm-/Max-Planck-Gesellschaft* (Stuttgart: Deutsche Verlags-Anstalt, 1990), 745. See also Otto Gerhard Oexle, *The British Roots of the Max-Planck-Gesellschaft* (London: A Publication of The German Historical Institute London, 1995); Anthony R. Michaelis, 'The Recovery of Science in Germany', *Interdisciplinary Science Reviews*, 6 (1981), 283–311.

As the Kaiser Wilhelm Society was still under threat of being dissolved by the Allied Control Council in Berlin, Blount suggested to his German counterparts that they found a 'Max-Planck-Gesellschaft' in the British Zone which could act, at least temporarily, as a trustee for the endangered Kaiser Wilhelm Society. The idea to name the new Society after the world-famous Max Planck came from Sir Henry Dale, then chairman of the Scientific Committee for Germany. On 11 September 1946 Britons and Germans acted together and founded the 'Max-Planck-Gesellschaft zur Förderung der Wissenschaften in der Britischen Zone' which eventually, on 8 July 1949, by dropping the words 'in der Britischen Zone', became the successor to the old Kaiser Wilhelm Society in the new democratic Federal Republic of Germany.

'Democratic' was a catchword in those years, and building a functioning democracy in Germany had been given top priority in Allied policies. Consequently, in the early post-war years there was undoubtedly always the assumption in the minds of those in charge that Britain should try to influence the Germans over the question of democracy in academic organization, education, and politics. Britain's cultural activities in its zone in Germany certainly centred on parading the 'British model', British experience, and British practice in all walks of life, and at times could not avoid a slightly patronizing tone. As a rule, the British initially took the active part and the Germans were the more or less grateful recipients. This clear-cut subordination gradually changed even before the founding of the Federal Republic in May 1949 and then, in the following years, it quickly turned into a partnership between equals.

In this amazing process the outstanding role of private individuals in triggering off a multifaceted Anglo-German cultural exchange so soon after the end of the war could also be observed on the German side. The weakness of responsible or authorized German state organs in the Zone up to 1949 and, when the Federal Republic had been established, a feeling of restraint meant that determined individuals had a unique opportunity to make an impact. They could now take the initiative and do something for Anglo-German co-operation which 'the state' had seemingly proved incapable of doing in all those decades before the Second World War. Seen in this light, the few years between 1945 and, say, 1955 were truly an exceptional period in Anglo-German relations, favoured by an unprecedented mood of reconciliation and willingness for new departures on both sides of the North Sea.[22]

The best-known brainchild of this seminal era after the war was the Deutsch-Englische Gesellschaft (Anglo-German Association) founded in Düsseldorf in March 1949 only a few weeks before the Federal Republic came into being. In retrospect it becomes ever clearer that the years around 1950 were of the greatest significance for the history of the whole of Western Europe. These years witnessed the launching of the Marshall Plan, the founding of the North Atlantic Pact, the early beginnings of European integration, and the incorporation of the Federal Republic into the Western camp. A deepening of Anglo-German relations was thus just another aspect of these formative years for the future of Europe. This was unmistakably the aim of the Deutsch-Englische Gesellschaft.[23] In the ensuing decades it became prominent, above all, through its highly successful Königswinter Conferences which started in 1950. With the Anglo-German Königswinter Conferences the Deutsch-Englische Gesellschaft really did enter new territory, essentially for two reasons. First, privately organized bilateral conferences, at first held only in West Germany at the small town of Königswinter on the Rhine, upriver near Bonn, but from 1974 onwards alternating between Germany and Britain, were a novelty in the history of relations between states and nations. Secondly, the Königswinter Conferences, the first of which, incidentally, lasted a full fortnight, created a conference style that the Germans had never experienced before. Thus, by their dedicated and enthusiastic involvement in the Königswinter Conferences right from the outset, the British helped to import a crucial element of their political culture into Germany.

[22] The 1970s and early 1980s witnessed a second wave of the establishing of institutes and associations to facilitate closer Anglo-German contacts. Most of them owed their existence to private initiatives. Among the new bodies were, for instance, the Anglo-German Foundation for the Study of Industrial Society in London/Bonn (1973), the German Historical Institute in London (1976), the Arbeitskreis Deutsche England-Forschung (1981), and the Prinz-Albert-Gesellschaft in Coburg (1981). The Volkswagen Visiting Professorship at St Antony's College, Oxford, was established in 1965.

[23] On the history of the Deutsch-Englische Gesellschaft see Roger Morgan, 'The History of Königswinter', in Frank Giles (ed.), *Forty Years On: Four Decades of the Königswinter Conference* (A Publication of the Deutsch-Englische Gesellschaft, 1990), 7–11. Ralph Uhlig, *Die Deutsch-Englische Gesellschaft 1949–1983: Der Beitrag ihrer 'Königswinter-Konferenzen' zur britisch-deutschen Verständigung* (Göttingen: Vandenhoeck & Ruprecht, 1986).

It was the explicit wish of the founders of the Deutsch-Englische Gesellschaft, amongst them most prominently Lilo Milchsack, the wife of a wealthy businessman from Düsseldorf, and Sir Robert Birley, Educational Adviser to the British Military Government from April 1947 and later headmaster of Eton,[24] that Germans and Britons interested in public affairs should get together once a year to discuss matters of particular substance and moment.[25] Each conference would start with a plenary session in which four so-called introducers would launch their topics, and the meeting would then break up into four working groups for detailed discussion. Since the early 1950s the topics have virtually chosen themselves. One group would discuss the current state of East–West relations and the German question; another the progress, or lack of it, in the European integration process. A third group would tackle the economic state of Europe and the world; while a fourth would go into a huddle over the social flavour of the year: communications, media, demography, the environment, social problems. There would then be a final plenary session in which the spokespersons for each group would report back and the conference as a whole would debate the great issues before departing.

When the Deutsch-Englische Gesellschaft celebrated the fortieth conference with a short history of its past meetings, a number of politicians, journalists, diplomats, trade unionists, and academics who had participated at the conferences at some time or another were asked to reminisce. Among those who did so was the late Lord Grimond, former leader of the Liberal Party. In his contribution he described the Königswinter Conferences as 'a stroke of genius' and went on as follows: 'The British and Germans needed to be brought together. The conferences discussed policy, but their chief contribution was to introduce and educate . . . [Königswinter] was a triumph of imagination and tact from which a great many people have gained what they could have got in no other way.'[26] The then President of the Federal Republic, Richard von Weizsäcker, himself a regular Königswinter participant, sent a message which said: 'One would look in vain for an association

---

[24] Lord Annan rightly called Birley 'the most famous of all the British educators in Germany' (Annan, *Changing Enemies*, 161). See also Arthur Hearnden, *Red Robert: A Life of Robert Birley* (London: Hamish Hamilton, 1984), and Robert Birley, 'British Policy in Retrospect', in Hearnden (ed.), *The British in Germany*, 46–63.

[25] For details see Uhlig, *Deutsch-Englische Gesellschaft*, esp. 16–26.

[26] Giles (ed.), *Forty Years On*, 26.

between states with as much continuous success as Königswinter. Time and again others model themselves on it. Even so, there is nothing to compare with it in the entire world. Königswinter will indeed remain unique.'[27] So, may we conclude that, since their modest beginnings in 1950, the Königswinter Conferences have been an unmitigated success in Anglo-German relations? Does the Königswinter story appear as something so self-evidently good that nobody could possibly disagree? In fact, this really seems to be the case, mainly for three reasons.

First, the Königswinter Conferences have always been given wide coverage in the media, both in Britain and Germany, and the reports, with only a very few exceptions, have always been extremely favourable. The *Daily Telegraph* summed it all up in 1996 when it called the conferences 'the annual check of Anglo-German health'.[28] This assessment accorded them a very high position indeed in bilateral relations, not because of the tangible results which they produced but rather because of the opportunities for communication and informal discussion which they provided. It therefore comes as no surprise that leading politicians in both countries have also praised the conferences in glowing terms. When the Königswinter Conference took place in Berlin for the first time in 1997 Klaus Kinkel, the Federal Minister for Foreign Affairs, called the institution 'a symbol of German–British reconciliation since 1945. It stands for sincerity and fairness in our dealings with each other. And it also signifies the strong desire of two European countries to walk together, as friends and partners, the road to [the] future.'[29] Kinkel's British counterpart Malcolm Rifkind spoke, on the same occasion and using similar rhetoric, of 'the strong relationship' between Germany and Britain which 'is particularly evident in the Königswinter Conference'.[30] However, in spite of all the public support and the messages from Presidents, Prime Ministers, Chancellors, and Foreign Secretaries, it is worthy of note that the so-called 'Königswinter experience' has not yet figured explicitly in the memoirs of any British or German politician.

Secondly, the exclusive Königswinter Conferences, as a strictly bilateral forum for members of the political and social élite in both

---

[27] Giles (ed.), *Forty Years On*, 1.   [28] *Daily Telegraph*, 29 Apr. 1996.
[29] *47. Deutsch-Englisches Gespräch/Königswinter Conference in Berlin, 13–15 March 1997* (A Publication of the Deutsch-Englische Gesellschaft, n.d.), 3.
[30] Ibid. 12.

countries, of 'opinion makers' in the widest sense, and as an annual ritual that conjures up the values of open dialogue and Anglo-German understanding, soon became a model for similar bilateral conferences—particularly German–American and German–French. None of them were anything like as successful as the Königswinter Conferences, for reasons which are not easy to identify. In recent years efforts have also been made to establish a German–Dutch, a German–Polish, an Anglo-Italian and other 'Königswinters'. It remains to be seen whether these efforts will turn out to be anything more than short-lived initiatives born out of either goodwill or a passing political crisis of confidence in the relations of the countries in question. However, all this emulation of Königswinter is ample proof of its lasting success.

Thirdly and finally, Königswinter's success is clearly manifested in its longevity. The conferences have now been thriving for more than half a century. At the gathering in Dresden in 1991, the first on German soil which was not held in the town of Königswinter, the political columnist Peter Jenkins asked: 'Has Königswinter worked itself out of a job? Are we, like other postwar institutions, the victim of our success?' His answer was a firm 'no'.[31]

Jenkins's assessment is shared by Vernon Bogdanor, the Oxford constitutional historian and political scientist. 'Attendance at these conferences has, for me,' he writes, 'reinforced the lesson, that, despite the homogenizing forces of modern technology, economics and mass culture, the differences between one country and another remain deep-seated and profound, the product of their own distinctive historical experience. Nowhere is this more true than in our respective attitudes to the European Community.' And he goes on:

It is in displaying our unlikeness to each other that the Königswinter Conferences make their most valuable contribution to international understanding. For it is only if we recognize and confront our differences that we can hope to transcend them. And does one not always admire the more those qualities one does not possess oneself?[32]

Whether this verdict explains Königswinter's lasting success remains an open issue.

[31] Peter Jenkins, 'Winding-Up Address', in *41. Deutsch-Englisches Gespräch/Königswinter Conference in Dresden, 14–17 March 1991* (A Publication of the Deutsch-Englische Gesellschaft, n.d.), 53.
[32] Vernon Bogdanor, 'Reminiscence', in Giles (ed.), *Forty Years On*, 51.

The political scientist Roger Morgan, a veteran of the conferences himself, has raised two equally important questions. 'Have the Königswinter conferences over the years', he asked in the *Festschrift* for the fortieth anniversary of the conferences, 'been essentially a meeting-place for German anglophiles and British friends of Germany, whose already positive feelings it has merely reinforced?' Morgan's answer is an unequivocal 'no'.

There has indeed been a lot of this, but the record shows that Königswinter has also attracted many public figures who felt scepticism or even mistrust towards the other country, and whose misgivings, while not deepened by the experience, have by no means been totally dispelled. Not even decades of Königswinter could make a Richard Crossman or a Peter Shore warm to the idea of joining Germany in the European Community, but their presence was illuminating, both for them and for their German interlocutors.[33]

Roger Morgan's second question touches directly upon a fundamental problem of this kind of conference in our day and age. He asks 'whether the . . . experience of a purely bilateral gathering like Königswinter justified itself in a world where London and Bonn constantly have to be aware not only of each other's concerns, but also the views of Washington, Moscow and Paris'. Morgan himself provides an answer to which practically nothing has to be added.

The answer to the recurrent suggestion that Königswinter should be 'multilateralised' has always been that, as long as individual nations remain the principal centres of decision in the world, there is a strong case for pairs of them—for instance the Anglo-German pair—to concentrate at times on systematically comparing notes about what is on their minds, and what influences their positions.[34]

Intimate bilateral contacts between nations, be it of a cultural or political nature or both, have surely not become redundant in a Europe which is heading for an unprecedented union. They are building-blocks of that great political edifice, begun in the 1950s and to be completed in the twenty-first century, because, in their peculiar and tested way, they bring the Europeans closer together. In the case of Britain and Germany this has been achieved with remarkable success over the past half century. 'Anglo-German relations', the historian Wolfgang J. Mommsen said in 1989,

---

[33] Roger Morgan, 'The History of Königswinter', ibid. 10.   [34] Ibid. 10–11.

have now emerged from the long shadow cast over them by a century of Anglo-German antagonism and two World Wars . . . Contacts between Germans and the English slowly developed at many levels, especially private contacts, supported by numerous social institutions. They in particular helped to lay the foundations for a new mutual understanding which also created the basis for a fresh start among the general public.[35]

There can be no doubt that bilateral contacts between Britain and Germany of a political, economic, and cultural nature have reached an extraordinarily high level. However, one cannot deny that, despite all the efforts and initiatives, there are still deficits and imbalances. German interest in Britain remains greater than British interest in Germany. Telling indicators of this are, for instance, the number of visitors to each other's country—the German contingent to Britain traditionally being much higher than vice versa—or the number of literary translations from one language into the other. Perhaps more than anything else student exchanges between the two countries mirror a situation which is not likely to redress itself fundamentally in the foreseeable future, for understandable, though regrettable reasons.

When the first Chancellor of the Federal Republic, Konrad Adenauer, visited London in December 1951 and met Winston Churchill he suggested that many more English students should go to Germany.[36] However, this was to remain unsatisfactory for many years to come. In 1989 there were 3,991 German students registered at British universities, but only 2,039 British students in Germany.[37] Since then the number of students participating in exchange programmes or studying with the help of private means in the other country has increased substantially. In 1996, for example, there were no less than 4,270 German students who benefited from the Erasmus programme alone, initiated and subsidized by the Commission of the European Union, but only 2,042 British

---

[35] Wolfgang J. Mommsen, 'From Wartime Adversary to Partner—Anglo-German Relations since World War II', *40 Years Deutsch-Englische Gesellschaft e. V. 1949–1989. Jubilee Meeting 7th June 1989, Industrie-Club Düsseldorf* (Bornheim: Deutsch-Englische Gesellschaft, 1989), 27 and 33.

[36] Konrad Adenauer, *Erinnerungen 1945–1953* (Stuttgart: Deutsche Verlags-Anstalt, 1965), 509.

[37] Deutscher Akademischer Austauschdienst, *Berichte der Außenstellen 1991* (Bonn: DAAD, 1992), 86.

students used it for a period of study in Germany.[38] There are clearly limits and imbalances in mutual perception which even governmental initiatives and publicly sponsored institutions are unable to overcome. They have to be accepted, now and in the future.

[38] Deutscher Akademischer Austauschdienst, *Berichte der Außenstellen 1996* (Bonn: DAAD, 1997), 86.

16

German—A Lost Cause?

Klaus Reichert

The other day I wanted to buy a box of cigarettes from a Frankfurt tobacconist. I specified: 'Die große Schachtel.' The girl did not understand. I tried again: 'Die große Schachtel', and now a knowing smile crossed her face: 'Ah, you mean de "bick bocks"—it sure means "große Schachtel" but we say "bick bocks".' All this was pronounced in the concise sharp Frankfurt dialect, and no Englishman would have recognized the words of his own tongue. 'Big box'—sure enough it was half as long as 'große Schachtel' and the alliteration made it memorable. Stepping out of the tobacconist I came across a huge clothes shop with a large advertisement in each of its twelve display windows. 'Need a change?' it asked. Next to this store another shop was offering 'lifestyle underwear' with a special eye-catcher: 'simply different'—it didn't say 'different from this or that', but 'simply different', difference apparently being a quality in itself without any need to differentiate between what was to be expected and what was not. Had I gone into this shop and asked for a 'body suit' the woman wouldn't have understood, or she would have asked: 'Is it a body, you mean?' Having grasped that 'body' was German-English for 'body suit' and that this was what I wanted, she would have gone on in the typical neo-German mixture of everyday language: 'Welche size?' As I didn't know I would have had to consult my wife by using what is called in German 'ein Handy'. It sounds English but isn't: it is an entirely made-up word. The English equivalent would be 'mobile phone', the American equivalent 'cellular phone', or 'cell'. In order to coin a word like 'handy' one makes use of two languages.

Trying to buy one of these phones I come across a poster depicting a man and a woman, each in a circle and apparently speaking

A shorter German version of this essay was published in *Börsenblatt für den Deutschen Buchhandel*, 21 (Mar. 1998).

to each other over the phone. In big letters the poster says underneath: 'It's so easy.' In somewhat smaller letters under this we read: 'to fall in love', and underneath this, in slightly smaller letters again, but now in German: 'Das neue Siemens S 6.' Next to it and smaller again we read: 'Easy to use. Siemens Mobiltelefone.' Simple as these expressions are, they presuppose, in order to be understood, a process of decoding which is not so simple: English—German—English—German; then there is the double meaning of 'easy' which in the first instance leads you into the trap of falling in love and which must then be emended to refer to a product which offers a special quality. 'Das neue S 6' makes you remember an 'old S 6', perhaps, but at the same time is associated with the double meaning of the number '6', which functions only in German (sex), but would not have been possible without the English phrases; and this is preceded by the two pictures. All of this entails shifting ground and changing one's reference systems quickly, something which we should bear in mind when speaking of the Anglicization or rather Americanization of German, which is, of course, deeply regrettable for the sake of the purity of the language, whatever that means. In this essay I maintain that this question has two sides. There are losses and gains, and they encroach upon German on two different planes, as I demonstrate in this essay.

It is a fact—'Es ist ein Fakt', as we would say in our New German—that English is increasingly flooding into German, into other European languages, and into the languages of the rest of the world, although to a lesser degree. There are many reasons for this and they are well known: first internationalization, then the globalization of industry and finance, commerce and transport, computer technology and the armed forces. Rapid development in these fields necessitated a means of communication that was easy to acquire, precise and succinct in its significations (denotations rather than connotations), flexible in its forms, and, moreover, a world language. All of these conditions were given in English, more than in any of the other world languages, Spanish or Portuguese, Chinese or Japanese. The advantages of English include its simple word formation, its uninflected nouns and verbs, and its fairly simple grammar and syntax in comparison to any other language. English also has a large number of one-syllable words because it is an uninflected language, and this practically predestines it to be used for computer commands. And, as tourism demonstrates, anyone who has even the rudiments can make himself understood to some extent all over the world. Added to this is the fact that English belongs to two Indo-European language families, which confers a certain lexical advantage on the Romance languages from the start.

It is possible to acquire fairly comprehensible, usable English in a relatively short time, shorter, at least, than is necessary for any other language. This is one of its advantages. It must be added, however, that at the same time English is an extremely difficult language which is hardly ever mastered by foreigners because of the immense richness of its vocabulary, its idioms, and the nuances of its use. The complexity of usage compensates for the lack of rules. The construction of a sentence may be grammatically correct, but a native English-speaker shakes his head and says: 'We wouldn't say that.' If an Englishman tells a foreigner that he speaks very good English it means that he is doing tolerably well; if the Englishman says nothing it means that the number of mistakes is within acceptable limits; if the Englishman corrects the foreigner, his chances of eventually growing into the language go up. But, as I have said, a foreigner never perfectly masters the language because, to exaggerate only slightly, English consists of exceptions and unique cases, rather like English law, which is not codified but consists of precedents. We are not speaking of great sophistication here. It begins at the level of discussing a novel, when the foreigner stumbles over the imponderabilities of the English language. None of this, of course, pertains to the fields of communication referred to above—transport, computers, technology, finance, etc. Either the language is a rudimentary form of English anyway, as in the case of air transport, or the semantic range is so narrow that equivalents can easily be substituted, as in finance or in the armed forces.

If the use of English could be restricted to these fields, nobody would be alarmed. But this is not the case. English has assumed an all-pervasive presence, which has transformed almost every aspect of everyday life, and not only in Germany. Every child's bedroom has a computer in it; the language used on radio and TV is English, or some form of it; and even 6-year-old Germans look forward to 'wenn der DeeJay Power gibt'. This, however, has little to do with the creeping Anglicization of the everyday life of Germans, seen as a threat. Rather, we are looking at the impact of

an entertainment industry which pervades all stages of life, starting
with childhood. In aeroplanes, supermarkets, hotel lobbies, lifts,
and restaurants—wherever we happen to be, a soft background
noise exhorts us to 'have fun!' While we can close our eyes, we
unfortunately cannot close our ears, and so we are permanently
exposed to this musical environmental pollution. It is said that we
live in an information society; in reality, we live in an entertainment society. Even a genuine information medium such as the
news is presented in an entertaining way. Bad news becomes titil-
lating and is quickly forgotten; catastrophes are made palatable
and easily digested. The transformation of serious, difficult, and
problematic issues into quick entertainment demands appropriate
language, consisting of short sentences without subordinate
clauses, and reduced to a vocabulary of three to four hundred
words. In Germany this has led to the almost complete extinction
of the subjunctive. Tenses are mixed up, cases and conjunctions
are used incorrectly, and inflections are dropped. German (like
Italian and French) is wasting away because the media provide the
standard for language today, not the academics or the universities
or the churches. English—especially American English—comes in
only in the wake of the media. This is the result not so much of the
Americanization of Western Europe after the war, as has been
claimed, but rather of the easy adaptability of English to any context.

Whatever the causes of Anglicization, the fact that English is
about to transform German cannot be disputed. And it seems to me
that English can only transform a language that is receptive. It is not
so much the influx of English or American words that must be
explained. New words always enrich a language, although for one
or two decades now they have been flooding into German as never
before. The real problem from a linguistic point of view is how these
words are taken over. Here we can observe that the whole structure
of German may be changed fundamentally in the long run. To give
one example. Does one use foreign words according to the rules of
word formation in one's own language? In this case one would speak
of the 'super coolen Outfits mit den trendigen Tops'.[1] This would be

---

[1] This and the following example are taken from a collection of essays which is highly
instructive for our topic: Dieter E. Zimmer, *Deutsch und anders* (Reinbek: Rowohlt, 1997), 29.
However, I take the argument in a different direction.

the traditional way of adopting foreign words to one's own linguistic system, but we now find a tendency to retain the original form of the word. A world-famous German fashion designer speaks in an interview about how she arrived from her 'hand-tailored-Geschichte' to her 'refined Qualitäten' and concludes: 'Man muss Sinn haben für das effortless, das magic meines Stils.' This sounds hopelessly mixed up—it isn't German, it isn't English—but it is a reality in present-day New German.

I do not want to decide which of these two ways of treating foreign words is better, but simply to demonstrate the possibilities. The Germans certainly have '*ge*surfed', not 'surf*ed*', '*ge*checkt', not 'check*ed*', and some have 'abgefackt', but hardly 'geabfackt', or even 'gefuckedup'. What about the verb 'to e-mail'? Have we 'ge-e-mailed' each other, or, more correctly when dealing with compound words, 'e-gemailed', by analogy with 'aufgeschrieben' and 'abgeknickt'? In this case the first form, 'ge-e-mailed', has probably established itself, despite the complications of writing it down, because it is no longer considered to be a compound word.

A special feature of the German language, which allows compound words to be formed (with or without a hyphen), is another problem. Words can be formed just by joining one noun to one or two or three or more others without any linguistic signs of partition. They range from the simple 'Geschichtsschreibung' (history writing) to very long words indeed, such as the grotesque 'Wiederbelebungsversuchsanstaltstürschlüsselversteck' (the place where the key to the resuscitation station is hidden). Thus 'a fragrant smell of flowers' would turn up in Goethe as 'Blumenwürzgeruch' or the 'coolness of the evening wind' would be, again in Goethe, 'Abendwindeskühle'. In English such compounds do not exist, and if one wants to join words together they have to be hyphenated. But the English hyphen, so I am told, was abandoned some years ago and words are left to stand on their own. In recent German we find a tendency to break up compounds. Thus a typically German characteristic is sacrificed, and even hyphenation is rejected. Readability is certainly enhanced if one word is placed next to the other without links, allowing us to read and learn only in bite-size chunks; on the other hand it diminishes an ability to grasp connections as the curve of the syntax is broken up.

We see here a kind of syntactical double structure: English word strings superimposed upon German compounds. One may deplore this—however, no one knows where it is going to lead. In the history of languages innovations have either been integrated or discarded, and nobody knows why. All that can be said is that innovations open up possibilities that can enrich a language. In the case of placing isolated words next to each other as in English, we must remember that this was common in German Baroque literature, where we read forms such as 'der schwere Mut' or 'die Liebes Pein'. Thus compound-building is a rather late development. To isolate words may be a resort to earlier possibilities, and represent a rejuvenation of the language by the revitalization of older, disused roots. Linguistic changes may entail the double process of progression and regression, and this may be one requisite for the adoption of innovations. Lost possibilities—we shall have to wait for the poets to show us whether this works or not. I should just like to stress that words freed from the band holding compounds together can be perceived more clearly. Paradoxically, this may allow us to become aware of the possibility of joining them up, however haltingly at first.

When we think about the influence of English upon German, two quite different aspects must be distinguished. On the one hand we see the dissemination of a mixed language which disregards the rules of at least two languages. It is a made-up language, neither German nor English, which is used by children and young people, in tourism, advertising, the entertainment industry, and in particular, in attempts to Germanize (or, perhaps, to de-Anglicize) computer language, to mention only a few especially fruitful instances. In Hesse, for example, 'motherboard' has been creatively turned into 'Massabord'. On the other hand the importance of English in schools, universities, and the sciences is increasing rapidly. These two aspects have little or nothing to do with each other. The first is a wild growth, under pressure of acceleration as in rap music. It is often witty and inventive, as if applying the slogan of the German fashion designer Hugo Boss: 'Innovate, don't imitate.' The other is a strategy administered from above. It is the result of deliberate language policy, adopted in recognition of the growing importance of English throughout the world. Of course, Germany is not alone in this. It was recently reported that France, which in many respects is Anglophobe and even created its own computer language, plans to introduce English as the main foreign language. And Switzerland, too, which since its existence has had one of the two main languages, French or German, as the first foreign language, is switching over to English. What reasons other than economic ones can there be for this? In Germany, English has almost completely outstripped French, Latin, or Russian as first foreign language. Nobody, of course, would deny the importance of English as a means of communication for Europe and the rest of the world. But within the wealth and range of the cultures of Europe, England and the English language, not to mention American English, have played only one role, and certainly not the most important one. (In passing, I should like to mention the philosopher Schopenhauer, who, in his work, quotes extensively from Greek, Latin, French, Italian, Spanish, and English authors. The only quotations he feels he needs to translate are the English ones.) What other reasons, apart from economic or technological or administrative ones, can we have?

To put it the other way round, the European cultures are relegated to playing the role of extras in Shakespeare's history plays. What we are heading for now, as Harald Weinrich recently warned in a keynote speech at a conference of German Romanists held in Jena, is a linguistic monoculture which promises efficiency and short-term success but entails irreparable damage. Weinrich said: 'It seems to me . . . that Anglophonism can also be interpreted as a monoculture. With all its undisputed advantages, it has the undoubted disadvantage of sending its stupidities around the globe as quickly as its judiciousness.'[2] And further: 'I could imagine a different cultural policy, one whose aim would be to maintain diversity of languages in our much too standardized world, and in particular, in Europe, whose variety is what makes it attractive. This would apply not only in everyday usage, but particularly in the state-regulated education sector.' Its poverty in terms of forms makes English easier to learn than any other language, and greater degree of success comes more quickly than in any other language. Its particular difficulties, the things that make English such a rich language, cannot be overcome anyway, and certainly not at school or university. What our official programmes and strategies achieve is at best pragmatic competence, but not the acquisition of another culture in its uniqueness and richness. As this is so, it would not be sensible to prescribe even more English at an even earlier stage. The scholar of Romance languages therefore suggests, and the

---

[2] Harald Weinrich, 'Von der schönen fremden Freiheit der Sprachen', contribution to the *Feuilleton* section of the *Süddeutsche Zeitung*, 4–5 October 1997.

scholar of English can only agree, that instruction in foreign languages should begin with a more difficult language, and certainly one with a greater diversity of forms, such as Latin, or French. The earlier the pathways in the brain are laid down by a complicated language system, the greater are the chances of building other, similarly complicated languages on the same foundations. This would, of course, take a great deal of time, and gratification is delayed, as success will not come quickly. But this is the only way to maintain a plurality of cultures.

In spite of the presence of English in everyday life and in our schools from an early age, it is becoming increasingly difficult to read, say, Shakespeare at school or even at university, something which was accepted as a matter of course thirty years ago when students started with Latin and Greek as first and second languages. That is to say, linguistic proficiency acquired under the demands of present-day requirements does not enable you to read the authors that we associate with English culture. To understand Shakespeare or Milton, the Romantics, or Joyce, cultural competence is required. That means taking into account the whole range of European cultures. Milton cannot be understood without a knowledge of his Latin, Greek, Hebrew, Italian, and French background.

In our universities there is a growing tendency now to teach certain subjects in English, in particular, the natural sciences, economics, and medicine. Most scholars in these fields publish in English in order to be read. This pays tribute to the fact that since the 1930s English has gradually become the lingua franca of the so-called hard sciences, assuming the role that Latin played in the Middle Ages and the Renaissance. (By comparison, in Japan or Denmark in the 1930s a student of medicine was required to have a good command of German.) Publication in English is of prime importance because it allows scholars to be mentioned in the notorious Citations Index. This is a list which enumerates who is quoted by whom, how often, and where. It is a means of measuring careers and pinning down the economic value of each scholar at a given time, if one happens to get on the list at all. There is no place any more for the kind of research that necessarily goes on for years, for hypotheses whose implications may take generations to grasp, until they do perhaps change the course of science—think of Copernicus, or Harvey, or even Newton. Judged by the principle of immediate success, such research will have no chance in the future.

However, it certainly is possible to use English in the sciences, medicine, and economics, because their contents are independent of the linguistic form in which they are expressed. But there is a tendency now to adopt English also in the humanities, where it represents a disastrous impoverishment. A growing number of scholars in the social sciences and in the humanities write and publish in English now, even in German journals or conference proceedings. Many conferences held in Germany—on history, art history, literature, philosophy, or sociology—are conducted in English, even if there are hardly any participants from English-speaking countries. German, French, Italian, and Spanish scholars will converse in English. Everybody knows, however, that more than easily convertible transmission of information is at stake in these disciplines. Thought works differently in each language. This is the result not only of certain traditions of thinking which have evolved their own particular styles, but also of the specific structure of each language. Each language implies its own world view, gives special orientations in time and space, and provides certain possibilities of thinking at the expense of others. The philosophies of Kant or Hegel, Fichte or Schelling, Benjamin, Rosenzweig, or Heidegger were only possible in German. They can, of course, be translated—that is, as a rule, one thread of thought can be isolated out of the complexity of meanings—and the translated texts may unfold their own history of reception in other cultures. But they will have lost what one would call in German their identity, the cultural context which gives them meaning and which they had in their original form of thinking, as a form or special expression of their language. Each culture has developed conditions of knowledge and understanding, and styles of thinking peculiar to their own language, which produce hypotheses and experiences and ideas which distinguish them from those of other cultures.

Anyone who has had to translate their own work from German into English, or vice versa, has found that texts have to be at least partially rethought and restructured in the other language, and that much cannot be translated at all. I once had to translate an essay[3] which prominently featured 'das erkennende Subjekt', that

[3] 'Christian Kabbalah in the Seventeenth Century', in Josef Dan (ed.), *The Christian Kabbalah* (Cambridge, Mass.: Harvard University Press, 1997).

dynamic, processual thing from the German philosophy of monism. In English, the 'correct' equivalent is 'the knowing subject', but this implies something different, namely, a subject that *already knows*, not one that is in the process of gaining knowledge. Here is another example, going in the other direction this time. In an English lecture about the old rhetorical technique of imagining places in a well-known setting, marking them with mnemonics, and then recalling them during a speech, thus composing the speech out of firmly located and illustrative elements, I had been able to use English words which expressed just this technique: 're-member', 're-collect', 're-mind', 're-call'. But all these words and the associated meanings do not exist in German, which has only the reflexive verb 'erinnern'.

This was a lesson for me about the cultural differences which exist in two such closely related languages. The complex of words around 'memory' in the English language retains an outside reference, whence it draws its nourishment; it is to some extent interactive. In German, the whole process has been internalized, something is 'er-innert'. Will such productive and identity-defining differences be a thing of the past in a future monoculture? To return to Harald Weinrich, after speaking of sending stupidities around the globe, he went on: 'Thus one can ask oneself, for example, whether the disregard for linguistic form as a condition of knowledge that is rampant in the current theory of science does not itself represent a stupidity virus which thrives in the nutrient solution of theories expressed exclusively in English and has long since become resistant to crises.'[4] Weinrich recommends (as I have already mentioned above) following a different cultural policy in order to combat this virus. 'Then', he says, 'different hypotheses could develop in the medium of differently structured languages, other experiences could be tried out, and other ideas could mature. Only such counteraction would create space for what I once called a "linguistically competent society".'

Dominance of English in school and at university, in the humanities and sciences, will in the long run lead to an extinction of other styles of thinking and other modes of seeing the world—and there is much to suggest that this process is irreversible. In the last resort this will also lead to a sclerosis of English, because languages as

---

[4] Weinrich, 'Von der schönen fremden Freiheit der Sprachen'.

well as cultures are kept alive only by exchange. This is one part of the picture, the self-sacrifice of German as the vehicle of a special tradition in the name of international competition, with language behaving like an economic commodity. But what about the other side, the Anglicization of everyday German? Critics speak of a catastrophe, and about the destruction of German.[5] I propose, more carefully, to speak about its changeability. Everybody knows that language is a living thing, that constant innovation is fundamental for its survival. If one wants to conserve language at a given point in history, it will mean if not its death, then at least its petrification.

It isn't even possible, except in an abstract way, to speak of *the* language, for German, French, English (*das Deutsche, das Französische, das Englische*) are fictions, conventions, agreements. They were more or less useful during the few centuries when the languages developed, but they did not have much to do with the reality of languages as they were spoken. In the Middle Ages there were only regional dialects on the one hand, and, on the other, Latin as a common language for the fairly small group of clerics. But the one common and, as it were, made-up language was not shut off against the many regional languages. The Latin of Hildegard von Bingen is interlaced with Old High German words where there were no Latin equivalents. In the most famous collection of popular songs, the *Carmina Burana*, we find Latin and Middle High German words and expressions next to each other and mixed up in a poetical hotchpotch, just as in today's German-English pop songs. In other countries we find similar examples throughout the Middle Ages. Dante, in an incredible act of creation, invented the Italian language. He declared that his Florentine Tuscan was the most flexible dialect, borrowed some elements from other dialects and from the Latin of the courts, the Church, and chancelleries, and added his own linguistic theory in which he justified his construct. Then he wrote his poem in this made-up language. If he had not been the poet that he was, and had not other great poets, such as Boccaccio and Petrarca, written in his idiom and developed it further, who knows whether Italian as a common language might not have come into being in a different place altogether—in polyglot Venice, for example, which would certainly have found a means of communication that bound people together useful.

---

[5] This is the main drift of Dieter E. Zimmer's arguments in his collection of essays, *Deutsch und anders*.

A particularly instructive example for my subject is the origin of what we today call English. The West Germanic dialect known as Anglo-Saxon was a highly developed and formally extremely rich language with a surprisingly varied literature. Alfred the Great, King of Western Saxony, had translated important works from Latin in the ninth century, using idiomatic expressions in the vernacular for which he is still famous. Thus he began a development that could have made Anglo-Saxon into one of the great Germanic languages of the Middle Ages, rather like Old Icelandic. But then there was the great rupture of the Norman conquest in 1066, with its influx of Norman French, which became the language of court and chancellery. French poets went to England, English poets went to France, and, as a consequence, authors wrote in two or three languages at the same time; literary forms were transported from one language to the other and back again. The process of amalgamation took more than three hundred years, resulting in the evolution of the mixed language which we call English. This hybridization is mainly characterized by two things. First, there was an enormous influx of foreign words, which, over the centuries, were no longer perceived as foreign. This accounts for the incomparable lexical richness of English; for almost every word of Germanic origin ('ground') there is also one from the Romance languages ('fundament' or 'basis'). And, secondly, English lost the old formal wealth which had allowed it to be flexible and to adopt foreign elements easily, a characteristic which it does not share with other languages and which makes it so attractive today.

The first great work written in this amalgamated idiom, in this 'Franglais', was Chaucer's *Canterbury Tales* (1400), in which we find words of different origins next to each other: 'natúre', 'coráge', 'aventúre', 'chivalrye', 'resoun', and 'vertú'. After more than a hundred years, a change of accent, and the loss of the umlaut from French, these words became genuine English words—'nature', 'courage', 'adventure', 'chivalry', 'reason', and 'virtue'. Nor does Chaucer differentiate between good and bad, high and low, courtly and vulgar words. His microcosm of English society around 1400 can accommodate every word. Pretty much the same is true of Shakespeare, two hundred years later, although the language has become more fixed in respect of an idiom familiar to us. Nothing is excluded. Rapid switches in register from the sublime and poetical to the everyday and obscene, often within one and the same metaphor; changes in the rhythm of verses which break all the rules when the drama calls for it; all these things reveal a great artist who had to entertain and keep the attention of a large audience (up to two thousand people of all classes, from the aristocracy to unemployed craftsmen, from ladies to prostitutes, and soldiers to pickpockets). Shakespeare was the first cultural entrepreneur on a grand scale, against tough competition, and he showed what popular culture can be. If, today, we no longer notice the garishness and sauciness, the indecencies and incongruities, this is a result of historical distance, the disappearance or change in meaning of many words, and intimidation by classicism, and in Germany, in particular, of the fact that Shakespeare has come down to us in the harmonized translations of Schlegel and the Tiecks.

These historical reminiscences are not intended to deflect us from our theme. I simply want to place it into a larger context, and to see it in a longer perspective. How did earlier ages react to the influx of foreign languages, and to the intermingling of levels? Luther, who founded the German used by Kant and Goethe, was much criticized by his contemporaries for the irreverent use of language in his translation of the Bible. He took words from wherever he could get them: the streets, the mother at the hearth, the common man in the market. 'You have to watch people's mouths, how they speak, and translate accordingly', as he said.[6] Luther took language as a living thing, he did not adhere to humanistic standards as his contemporaries wished him to do. He disregarded conventions and the language of the élite, and precisely by doing so he founded a language that could be understood by the majority of the German people. And Luther's German, despite its often dubious origins, became the yardstick of our language for centuries.

There are a number of reasons for Luther's success, not only the victory of Protestantism. More important, I believe, is that his work coincided with the emergence of the so-called national languages, which in their turn were the consequence of early modern nation-building, of the formation of what Benedict Anderson has called

---

[6] In his seminal 'Sendbrief vom Dolmetschen' (1530), in which he defends his translation of the Bible: 'Denn man muß nicht die Buchstaben in der lateinischen Sprach fragen, wie man soll Deutsch reden, wie diese Esel tun, sondern man muß die Mutter im Hause, die Kinder auf der Gassen, den gemeinen Mann auf dem Markt drum fragen, und denselbigen auf das Maul sehen, wie sie reden und darnach dolmetschen; da verstehen sie es denn und merken, daß man deutsch mit ihnen redet.' Quoted from Martin Luther, *An den christlichen Adel deutscher Nation und andere Schriften* (Stuttgart: Reclam, 1960), 175.

'imagined communities'.[7] A national language required unification, regulation, a distinction between right and wrong, customary
and unusual, and the marginalization of regional dialects. Another
distinction, added in the eighteenth and nineteenth centuries, was
that between proper and improper, which further reduced the
range of the language as a medium available to everybody.
National consciousness grew with the emergence of national languages, and only now was it possible to speak with national pride
or patriotism of *the* German language, or *the* English language.
This was soon extended to include national styles in art and music,
cooking and mentalities. It was now that the frontiers of language
began to close, and checks were set up to determine what was and
was not allowed in, and especially to establish how foreign words
were to be treated.

   This was not so much of a problem for English because of its dual
origins, but it was a big problem for German, and some people
believed that the overbearing influence of French had to be curbed.
Attempts were made, notably by Joachim Heinrich Campe, to
find German equivalents for French words.[8] He introduced
'Brüderlichkeit' and 'Minderheit' for 'fraternité' and 'minorité'
respectively, and invented 'Hochschule' for 'university'. In the latter case, as in many others, both forms have survived. Many words
were left untranslated but assimilated retaining their original grammatical form, gradually becoming regarded as German words
(*Friseur, Akademie*). A third group consisted of *Fremdwörter*, unassimi-
lated foreign words, which Adorno once called the Jews of language.[9] Some people argued for their retention; others were in
favour of rejecting them. It was a curious debate. The Brockhaus
dictionary of 1884, for example, states that the following words are
dispensable: 'Annonce, Bravour, Distanz, Engagement, Evidenz,
Legitimität, Portemonnaie, Situation', and that 'demonstrieren,
kommunizieren, absolvieren' should be completely avoided.[10] It
is difficult to predict the career of foreign words in one's own

   [7] Benedict Anderson, *Imagined Communities: Reflections on the Origin and Spread of Nationalism*
(London and New York: Verso, 1987).
   [8] Joachim Heinrich Campe, *Wörterbuch der Erklärung und Verdeutschung der unserer Sprache
aufgedrungenen fremden Ausdrücke* (Brunswick: Schulbuchhandlung, 1801; 2nd edn. 1813).
   [9] Theodor W. Adorno, 'Wörter aus der Fremde', in *Noten zu Literatur II* (Frankfurt:
Suhrkamp, 1961).
   [10] *Brockhaus' Conversations-Lexikon*, 13th edn. (Leipzig: Brockhaus, 1884), vii, entry:
'Fremdwörter'.

language. No one could do without them now, and hardly anybody still senses their foreign origins.

The question of syntax is of course different from the lexical one. Fifty years ago, Gottfried Benn identified this as an urgent issue.[11] English, or rather American, influence means that modern German contains many strings of words which are clearly un-German. But what does un-German mean? By what rules? The rules of yesterday's tradition; the rules of people over 50 with a university degree? What I want to say is that although there are conventions in syntax—agreements, customs, the norms of a national language, King's or Queen's English, the Chancellor's German, if you wish—there is no reason not to question them. Poets and writers have always known this, and those who use language in everyday life do so too. You cannot dictate normatively what a good sentence is like. You know it when you read it, and a good sentence may be formed according to the rules of convention or it may not be. And language is kept alive by the latter rather than the former. Literary history is full of innovation.

There have also been attempts to impose foreign structures artificially upon a codified language. Milton wrote *Paradise Lost*, as it were, multilingually: its vocabulary is English but its syntax is Latin, and it contains expressions modelled on Greek or Hebrew forms. The scope of his linguistic creativity, however, was not really perceived and exploited until the twentieth century, when the polyglot James Joyce took him as one of his most important models.[12] Post-modern literary scholarship has largely focused attention on Milton, and for the study of the blending of levels of language which is the topic of this essay, perhaps only Shakespeare is more fruitful. Similar attempts to change the spirit of the language by imposing foreign structures upon it were also made in Germany. Examples are Johann Heinrich Voß's version of Homer, and Hölderlin's translations of Pindar and Sophocles. Both tried, Hölderlin more radically than Voß, to write Greek using German words, and both attempts were roundly criticized. Voß's work, after much polishing, eventually established itself; Hölderlin's boldness was not discovered until the twentieth century, when it was realized what an impact he might have had on the German

---

[11] e.g. in his poem, 'Satzbau', available in Gottfried Benn, *Gedichte*, ed. C. Perels (Stuttgart: Reclam, 1988).

[12] In his *Ulysses*, as well as in his own great epic on the Fall, *Finnegans Wake*.

language. Instead, after Schiller, Uhland and Scheffel developed the German language in ballad style. In the 1920s, Franz Rosenzweig and Martin Buber made an even more ambitious attempt to imitate the complete grammatical system of Hebrew (tenses, word formation, syntax) in their translation of the Bible, using newly made-up or long obsolete, but always foreign-sounding, words.[13] Their intention was to create a language in which the Jewish youth of the future, with its dual identity, could learn German while being simultaneously introduced to Hebrew. It is at the other extreme of what happens with English in German now.

Admittedly, these historical examples come from above, and form no part of the reality of everyday language, at least so long as the fiction persists that there is such a thing as *the* German language. Yet they demonstrate that the homogeneity of a language is not a given, and that attempts have always been made, as the result of a non-identification with German, to make audible the foreign voice within and beneath one's own language. They also show that contamination is possible, and how it works. Today contamination comes from below, so to speak, and from all sides. It is omnipresent. Historical memory may serve to calm fears that the German language is being destroyed. Languages cannot be destroyed, they can only be changed. And even if it is a long-drawn-out process, it will not take as long in our time of accelerated change as English did to emerge in the Middle Ages. All we can say now is that we do not know where we are up to, but that the process cannot be held up.

That German, like most of the European languages, is open to an influx of English at all—apart from the need for a lingua franca, one which English is best suited to fulfil, as we have seen—is a result of the fact that languages have lost the role they once played as *national* languages. In the same way, the idea of nation has been revealed as the fiction, the 'imagined community' that it was from the start. However, it was able to conceal this behind self-assertions that precipitated catastrophes. And in the wake of the break-up of national languages, linguistic minorities and regional dialects have made a come-back. Britain has witnessed this phenomenon, as

---

[13] See my *Zeit ist's: Die Bibelübersetzung von Franz Rosenzweig und Martin Buber im Kontext* (Stuttgart: Steiner, 1993). A shorter English version is published in S. Budick and W. Iser (eds.), *The Translatability of Cultures: Figurations of the Space Between* (Stanford: Stanford University Press, 1996), 169–85.

have France, Belgium, Spain, and ex-Yugoslavia. Battles have often been waged in the name of suppressed languages against the imposition of a national language and associated demands for purity. Germans do not share this mentality which tries to protect diversity, but regional dialects in Germany are beginning to assert themselves, even in the entertainment industry, against both the lingua franca of their own national language and the contamination of everyday language around them. The effect is something like that of medieval dialects asserting themselves against Latin.

Although harbouring a certain well-founded scepticism about mixtures such as 'das effortless, das magic meines Stils', quoted above, I shall defend the contemporary tendency towards a double or mixed language. German has become wittier, more playful, more agile, has acquired characteristics which have not generally been associated with it, apart from the language of an Anglophile like Lichtenberg or a Francophile like Heine. The language of advertising is no longer a dull instrument to persuade you to buy. Sometimes one doesn't even know what is being advertised because behind each phrase in German, English, or both languages there usually is a witty idea which has to be deciphered before a relation to the product can be found. German has discovered the typically English device of punning which was looked down on for centuries. Most German pop bands sing in English, at last providing a counterbalance to the sentimental singing, popular since the war, which still dominates our TV shows. Rap groups have two or three so-called 'rimers' who, in their spoken songs, slip from one language to the other and back again, producing cascades of inventive and witty rhymes in breathless rapidity. Many of our more interesting younger writers, who have grown up quasi-bilingually, handle shifts in linguistic context with an ease which gives us a foretaste of a potential future German language: agile, open, inclusive rather than exclusive, associative, witty, fully awake. Have they learned this from rap, from advertising, from video clips, or perhaps from Arno Schmidt, whose German is unthinkable without English and deliberate Anglicisms?

In conclusion, I should like to point out that we all live simultaneously at different times and in different cultures today. Language has largely lost its role as a marker of cultural or social exclusion. If someone loves rap and its rhythms it does not mean that he has become deaf to the audacities of *Faust* part two, or Kafka. Is

German dying out? I think there will be several German languages, sometimes even in one and the same head, just as we have always spoken and written differently, depending on the situation. The difference is that today the instruments for determining what is good German and what is not have lost their credibility. (Writers have always ignored them anyway.) This has nothing to do with arbitrariness, a deplorable *laissez-faire, laissez-aller*, or a thoughtless 'anything goes'. Rather, it suggests a process of change which leads us out of the captivity of national languages and opens our minds to possibilities for which our language previously had no space. And as we constantly change language levels, we will become more aware of language. But ultimately, nobody can say what this will all amount to, neither those who predict catastrophe, nor those who are eternally curious about language.

17

Worthy Opponents
Football Rivalry as *Ersatzkrieg?*

Andreas Helle

In 1968 the popular historian, Arthur Hopcraft, looked back to the World Cup final of 1966 in the concluding remarks to his famous book *The Football Man.* Optimistically, he expressed the hope that in the not too distant future young Englishmen and Germans would no longer think of the war when their national teams play football against each other.[1] This hope has turned out to be somewhat over-optimistic, however. While Hopcraft sees international football primarily as an opportunity for friendly contact between peoples, recent events have revived interpretations of the game as a continuation of war with an admixture of different means. Thirty years on from 1966, the European Football Championships of 1996 witnessed the sad climax of the belligerent spirit Hopcraft had obviously attributed to bitter wartime memories. Rarely since 1945 have relations between Britons and Germans seemed as excited as during Euro '96. Yet to many observers this merely confirms the manipulative effects of professional sports on a mass audience.

International football, it seems, has an ambiguous impact. The game brings peoples into contact with each other, but at the same time it divides them into two potentially hostile camps of spectators. This is especially obvious in the case of English and German football fans. Friendly contact between fan clubs from the two countries is common and widespread; clubs or national selections meet each other regularly. Yet, on the whole, this does not seem to affect the intensity of football rivalry between the two countries. Although charismatic players such as Kevin Keegan, who led the

---

[1] A. Hopcraft, *The Football Man: People and Passions in Soccer,* 2nd edn. (Harmondsworth: Penguin, 1971) 190.

Hamburger SV to win the German League in 1979, or Jürgen Klinsmann, England's footballer of the year in 1995, have had some impact on the public perception of their native country, their appearance was largely seen against the background of familiar notions of a typically German or English national character.

A superficial glance at the mood and rhetoric of football coverage in the media supports the impression that the game is merely an *ersatz* for bloodier forms of competition. It sometimes seems as if the two wars between, amongst others, Britain and Germany in this century have only been transferred to another battlefield. Matches between German and English sides are exceptionally charged with emotion. Interestingly enough, this quality seems to derive not from differences but from a feeling of affinity. Rivalry has increased with the integration of the two countries into European institutions. Although both national teams play a similar style of football, and German and English players usually display similar attitudes to the game, there is a significant difference. Since 1966, when England became world champions for the first and, so far, only time at Wembley against West Germany, it has failed against German teams in a number of important matches. To judge from the media coverage of the 1996 European championship match between their teams, this series of epic clashes has affected the relationship between the two countries.

The disturbing experience of increased violence linked to international football matches has led pessimistic, usually well-educated, observers to describe football as an *ersatzkrieg*, a functional surrogate for war. Football matches are considered a safety valve that helps to regulate human aggressiveness, thereby keeping relations between countries relatively peaceful, yet hostile. Football's popularity is thus attributed to a basic need: the excitement sparked off by the game is interpreted as the result of an allegedly innate belligerent human spirit, or, sometimes, as the fulfilment of a basic need for excitement.[2] It is here that football and war are said to resemble one another. Other approaches focus on the fact that identification with one of the competing sides, and what they stand for, arouses football enthusiasm. Here the function of football is to separate one

[2] A detailed discussion in J. Huizinga, *Homo Ludens: Vom Ursprung der Kultur im Spiel*, 2nd edn. (Hamburg: RoRoRo, 1994), 9–12.

group of human beings from the other, and, at the same time, to stabilize collective identity.[3]

These approaches, however, are based on anthropological axioms rather than empirically convincing interpretations. The evidence gleaned from the examination of a sample of German and English newspapers is less clear-cut.[4] It reveals neither genuine aggressiveness against the other nation, nor, indeed, deeply entrenched positive national identities. The documents examined lack the solemnity, clarity, and unity one would expect from common arguments about the impact of international football matches.[5] This impression is supported by the style of press coverage in recent years. More and more newspapers are cultivating a pluralist style of news coverage. They do not publish just one article about an important match, but four on the day before, another four match reports, and finally one or two essays about the experience of seeing that particular match, or about its social meaning. Football matches apparently serve as a point of reference for competing analyses not only of the game, but also of society at large. Important matches spark off public debate about the collective self. Thus media coverage of football matches is moving away from a culture exclusively of sport experts, and is developing into a blend of social criticism, lifestyle essays, and society news.

England's Old Enemy

There is no simple answer to the question of what English papers write when they write about England, Englishness, and the reasons for the success, or, more typically, the failure of English national teams facing a German team. Football offers spectacular events for the media. Matches against German teams are certainly among the most dramatic. German national teams occupy a special position, and not only in tabloid papers, because encounters with them

---

[3] A recent example is J. Fauret, 'Nationalstaaten und Sport', in E. François, H. Siegrist, and J. Vogel (eds.), *Nation und Emotion: Deutschland und Frankreich im Vergleich: 19. und 20. Jahrhundert* (Göttingen: Vandenhoeck & Ruprecht, 1995).

[4] I looked at a total of five British and four German newspapers: the *Sun*, *Daily Mirror*, *Daily Mail*, *Daily Telegraph*, and *Guardian*, and on the German side *Bild-Zeitung*, *Frankfurter Allgemeine Zeitung* (henceforth cited as *FAZ*), *Frankfurter Rundschau*, and *Süddeutsche Zeitung*. Various collections of sports writing offered further material.

[5] See Fauret, 'Nationalstaaten', 323.

have coincided with turning points in the fortunes of the English game over the past thirty years. After all, an English team faced Germany at Wembley on 30 July 1966, when England won the World Cup. However, it is not only the climax of English football that is associated with a match against Germany. Folk wisdom has it that 14 June 1970, when a promising English team lost to Helmut Schön's side in the quarter-final of the World Cup in Mexico, marked the beginning of the deterioration of English football.[6] Ever since, it seems, German football teams have stood in the way of English attempts to gain another international football triumph. In 1972 England lost to a German team in the quarter-final of the European championships; in 1990, after nearly two decades in the wilderness, England lost on penalties to Germany in the World Cup semi-final in Italy. And finally, in 1996, penalties again decided the semi-final of Euro '96, the European championship hosted by the English Football Association. Reports of these matches form the bulk of the source material examined for this article.

A comparison between media coverage of the 1966 World Cup final and later matches reveals that Germany at the time was not considered a 'special' opponent. After June 1970, however, it was labelled the 'Old Enemy', an epithet it has carried ever since. This prominent position, formerly occupied by Scotland, was earned not only by a series of successes on the pitch. Different economic developments in Britain and Germany during these years did not help to ease English feelings about yet another German success. English comments about a defeat by German teams always reveal a strong feeling that the country is falling behind this potent neighbour who, after all, lost two world wars and one world cup to England, as a popular slogan claims.

While commentators do not agree about the reason for the alleged decline of English football, certain issues that are associated with the perceived progress of the Germans, both in the economy and in football, come up regularly in their articles. The most important one is the debate about England's long decline, and its alleged lack of modernity. A number of topics are linked to this subject. In particular, the British style of playing is constantly

---

[6] S. Kuper, 'Southgate, Philippa and the Buffaloes: A Diary of Euro 96', in id. (ed.), *Perfect Pitch. (1) Home Ground* (London: Review, 1997), 172–3; D. Thompson, *4—2* (London: Bloomsbury, 1996), 219.

at issue between those who support a so-called Continental style, and traditionalists. Even though the days of the English defender, reared on red beef, as one newspaper observed, are surely over, English journalists do not part easily with players like Terry Butcher or Tony Adams. The quintessentially British style of football has a lot to do with attitude, or heart. The modernization of football is consequently interpreted, somewhat sentimentally, as a loss of heart.

This question already subliminally dominated the coverage of the 1966 World Cup, which took place at a time of serious financial and economic crisis in Britain. Newspapers interpreted England's success in 1966 as evidence that things were not all that bad. From 1970 onwards, however, Germany was gradually turned into a model of modernity in the British newspapers. Especially their first success at Wembley in April 1972 helped to create this image. Virtually all English journalists agree that this match marked a difference in modernity, style, and youth. By 1990, the supposed modernization gap between Germany and England had become a firmly established *topos*, and was sometimes a cause for defeatist respect. The *Daily Telegraph* offers a good example on the day before the World Cup final of 1990, which Germany reached by beating England in the semi-final on penalties:

West Germany, it can be argued, has enough prestige already without winning the World Cup. We have voiced plenty of concern in these pages about the consequences of a united Germany. But tonight's team is from the old Federal Republic. That country has been a model of prosperity, industry, and atonement for past evil. The Federal Republic's virtues are embodied in its footballers, who show a sportsmanship historically associated with England. We hope they win tonight.[7]

Other elements come up regularly in this debate about Britain's modernity, or rather lack of it: hooligans, a phenomenon that, for reasons of space, I cannot adequately deal with here, and the sheer lack of success since 1966. English journalists offer various reasons for the supposed decline of England and its football players. In the *Daily Mirror*, for instance, Ken Jones blames a 'cultural decline' for repeated failure from the European Championship quarter-final against Germany in 1972 onwards. According to Jones's somewhat simplistic logic, 'decline' can be blamed on three factors: 'Big

---

[7] 'The case for Germany . . .', *Sunday Telegraph*, 8 July 1990.

wages, club envy and overpowering ambition has brought a scowl to the face of English football and inevitably it shows in the play of an England team.'[8]

The most common explanation for England's alleged decline—not only in football—is a lack of courage. For certain sections of the press, Sir Alf Ramsey embodied intransigence, stagnation, and aversion to innovation as long as he was England manager. However, many other elements figure in the debate on modernization in Britain, focused on, among other things, football. Even the notoriously belligerent language of many newspapers belongs in this category. The frequent allusion to 'England's finest hour' (in football writing, of course, the 'two finest hours' at Wembley 1966), the reference to 'dambusters', or the declaration of a football war against Germany—all these peculiar traits of football hysteria serve as a reminder of better, more successful days.

While there is wide agreement among journalists and sports writers about the lack of progress in England generally, and in English football in particular, there is no consensus on how to close the gap to competitors. Obviously, strategies advocated depend primarily on the political bias of the respective newspaper. The *Daily Mail*, for instance, usually calls for and fosters feelings of unity and patriotism. In a leader on 1 August 1966, the day after England won the World Cup, the paper attacked the Labour government for its alleged mishandling of Britain's economic turmoil in 1966:

We do not want to strain the sporting analogy. But let's have another look at the World Cup Final. The quality which won England the cup was the ability to work as a team. The differences and conflicting ideas of 11 men were submerged into one unified tactical force. What a contrast to the way Britain is now facing the 12 months of truth![9]

The *Guardian*, on the opposite side of the political spectrum, usually blames social inequality, youth unemployment, class differences, or simply the Tory government and its chauvinism for the shortcomings of English football. On occasion, when other sports sections have lamented a defeat against Germany, the *Guardian* has been more concerned with the social consequences triggered by that event. Matthew Engel, for instance, referring to riots in

---

[8] K. Jones, 'Ramsey's men are League fall-guys', *Daily Mirror*, 15 May 1972.
[9] 'Extra time', *Daily Mail*, 1 Aug. 1966.

Trafalgar Square after the 1996 semi-final against Germany, writes in the *Guardian*:

Maybe Scotland, Ireland and Wales can take defeat with more unanimous good grace. But these are countries with greater social cohesion. The blame [for rioting] should not be heaped on English football. In a country as large, as diverse and generally out of sorts with itself as England, it was probably impossible for a balloon that grew as big as this one to have been pricked with a smaller bang.[10]

However, many reflections on yet another failure against Germany go beyond the question of modernization. Giles Smith, for instance, blames the lack of success in penalty shoot-outs on certain English national characteristics: 'A penalty shoot-out enables the losers to walk away feeling they have won a moral victory—and you could mount a convincing and historically-sourced argument that the English in general relish a moral victory, with its comforting undertow of resentment, much more than they appreciate the real thing.'[11] Not only is losing *per se* considered typically English by some observers, but celebrating a victorious football match offers an opportunity to discover new and unexpected sides of an audience that transcend their mere Englishness: 'There is a peculiar intimacy in openly celebrating in front of complete strangers. You have to cast away your English reserve, and in my case, middle classness.'[12]

The picture of the Other, in this case Germany, is less complex. In general, the coverage of football matches against Germany does not include extensive information about the 'Old Enemy'. Rather, old stereotypes about German efficiency usually make up most of what is said about the opponent. Many journalists content themselves with some remarks about the attitude of German players, roughly along the lines of Eric Todd's observations in the *Guardian* in 1966: 'Method is a dominant trait of the German race, and on Saturday it was very much in evidence.'[13] We find a similar opinion about Germans in an article written by Alex Ferguson, manager of Manchester United, in June 1996: 'Attitude . . . can be

---

[10] M. Engel, 'The old lines are trotted out but the game really has changed', *Guardian*, 28 June 1996.

[11] G. Smith, 'Nowhere to hide on the last journey for England', *Daily Telegraph*, 29 June 1996.

[12] H. Thompson, 'Hope, glory and inevitable pig-sickness', *Guardian*, 28 June 1996.

[13] E. Todd, 'Moore's majesty emblazons England triumph', *Guardian*, 1 Aug. 1966.

as important as ability at this level, and Germany have that in abundance.'[14]

Seen from an English perspective, Germany has developed from an inferior opponent into a better version of England itself—in the game of football at least, and sometimes in other respects as well. This provokes different reactions, and sometimes even respect: 'The Germans now occupy that place in our culture (held in previous centuries by France and Spain) reserved for "worthy opponents". We look at what they do, and generally agree, at the moment, that they do it better, or, as we like to say in our down-putting way, more "efficiently".'[15]

Football matches against Germany have been considered unique occasions for assessing England's place in the world. Mark Wright, a former England international, who had his own hurtful experience of 1990, expressed this feeling in an article for the *Daily Telegraph* in June 1996, on the day before England was again to meet Germany in the semi-final of an important football competition: 'The whole country wants success over Germany because they are so successful and people gauge themselves against the Germans.'[16] During the 1990s in particular this competitive approach was salient because England's economic recovery, together with the so-called 'German disease', fostered the feeling that England finally deserved a success on the pitch. When England lost on penalties again at Wembley in 1996, this caused an outburst of disappointment in the newspapers. A particularly bitter comment was published in the *Daily Telegraph*:

The immovable object of German football held firm and England set off on the journey home . . . The history that English fans wanted to repeat itself was a certain day in 1966, when extra time produced a thrilling English victory . . . Thirty years have changed a lot. Germany have not lost a penalty competition in 20 years and have raced ahead to become the most dominant force in Europe.[17]

Another newspaper complained on the same occasion:

[14] A. Ferguson, 'Why Vogts' Germany are singular sensations', *Sunday Telegraph*, 23 June 1996.

[15] R. Davies, 'Why our gallant chaps will have the last laugh', *Daily Telegraph*, 4 July 1990.

[16] M. Wright, 'Confidence high six years on', *Daily Telegraph*, 26 June 1996.

[17] P. Hayward, 'Seconds out as Southgate plays the reluctant fall guy in sad echo of Turin', *Daily Telegraph*, 27 June 1996.

In our hearts many expected to lose. But once we had lost the pain was greater because of the vast symbolic importance of the thing. If it only had been the Czech Republic, or even France. It had to be Germany, and so we are left with the unanswered and unanswerable question: Why do they (nearly) always beat us?[18]

After the anticlimax at Wembley, Niall Ferguson writing in the *Daily Mail* suggested another way of escaping eternal inferiority:

We must regard last night's defeat as another sort of victory—not a moral victory, but a historical victory. For surely we British have achieved nothing more admirable this century than teaching the Germans how to beat us at our own game. . . . Nor is football the only thing we have taught the Germans this century. We have—after two great conflagrations—taught them economic liberalism and parliamentary democracy, too. Not bad going.[19]

The examined articles are not without envy of, or aversion to, Germans. Far from it. Football coverage reveals a widespread English uneasiness about an allegedly growing German dominance, a feeling that is apparently not eased by EU membership and greater economic co-operation. On the contrary, sometimes it seems that England feels increasingly uncertain in the face of a nation that stands for success, but certainly not for elegance. There is also, of course, outright anti-German feeling. The *Daily Mirror* in particular has displayed some fine examples in recent years.

Matches against German sides have gained a significance that cannot be explained only by their merits in the field of sport. Over the past thirty years, Germany has become synonymous with economic success, efficiency, and modernity. These qualities are not exclusive to sports performances. On the contrary, there is hardly any evidence that intimate knowledge of Germans has led commentators to this opinion. The notion of a particular German national character derives primarily from political analysis and historical writing. In sports sections of British papers any information about the other side that goes beyond football trivia is rare.

The analysis of recent football matches between German and English teams in English newspapers betrays common social anxieties rather than national pride and ethnic prejudice. The

---

[18] S. Glover, 'This patriotic passion should be turned to good account', *Daily Telegraph*, 28 June 1996.

[19] N. Ferguson, 'Cheer up, it's only a game . . .', *Daily Mail*, 27 June 1996.

characteristics ascribed to the opponent are significant only against the background of these anxieties. In the English case self-perception is structured by the debate about the alleged moral, political, and economic decline of the nation. Additionally, during the 1990s, the actual boundaries of the English nation become precarious. The replacement of the Union Jack by the St George's cross as the flag prevalent among fans, for instance, is frequently interpreted as the manifestation of a crisis of national identity.[20] Germany's image in British newspapers consequently appears like an inverse picture of England's problems and attractions. Only in those rare moments of success, or after a brilliant, tense match, does a kind of emotional agreement among spectators exist. It is only then that the collective 'us' is indeed an emotion, and not an abstract concept.

Germany: Nostalgia and Taboos

Compared to the belligerent language in British papers, the absence of such rhetoric in German newspapers is striking. Of course, the war does matter in the German coverage of football matches against England. However, it matters in an entirely different manner. German journalists, it seems, have agreed on a collective renunciation of belligerent language and open nationalism. Even the mass circulation German tabloid, the notorious *Bild-Zeitung*, is a model of impartiality compared to its English counterparts. German newspapers not only avoid belligerent language, they condemn its use in English papers as bad taste.

Additionally, the frequent successes of German teams against England have a major disadvantage. The examined papers contain much less reflection on national characteristics and give much less thought to the ups and downs of a complete society. Elements of an all too familiar debate about Germany's international reputation are discernible. The quality press, at least, regardless of its political bias, repeatedly emphasizes the negative aspects of the supposed national character. Although most German journalists

[20] M. Engel, 'Wembley cries "God for Terry, England St George" with the spirit of Dunkirk thrown in for good measure', *Guardian*, 23 June 1996; 'Football as it should be played', *Guardian*, 26 June 1996; T. Parsons, 'It's coming home to where the heart is', *Daily Mirror*, 24 June 1996.

would reject the notion of a national character, they none the less complain about behaviour which is seen as typically German. Editorials about the consequences of the bad conduct of German football supporters are common. In the *Frankfurter Allgemeine Zeitung*, for instance, Steffen Haffner describes the typical German fan in Mexico: 'The German supporters have thus completed the image of the German as such. The German in Mexico, foreigners say, not only behaves badly, drinks too much, and abuses women; even worse is his intolerance and aggressiveness.'[21]

After unification, this anxiety continues to be widespread in German papers. It is apparently fostered by a feeling that Germany is still under probation politically. In such a climate German journalists exercise a collective restraint that can develop into downright self-hatred among left-wing writers and journalists. This feeling is frequently expressed as a complaint about the lack of refinement among German players, about the ugly functionalism of German teams, and, above all, about a lack of emotion. The widespread desire to have a different and more beautiful—in a word, less German—style of football manifests itself in admiration for players like Franz Beckenbauer and Günter Netzer, who display unusual technical skill. And, finally, many sports writers lament the damage caused by the modernization of German football. This complaint is usually embedded in a comprehensive critique of modern times and the decline of contemporary culture.[22]

For the majority of observers who mourn the moral decay of German football, spoilt as it allegedly is by success and big money, England is still a model of traditionalism and authentic football values.[23] At the same time, many feel that the two countries are related, and not only on the pitch. Some characteristics are repeated again and again in German newspaper coverage and sports writing: the athletic character of English players, their honesty, and their professional solidarity. English players are considered to be tough but fair. They do not accept defeat until a match is definitely over, and so forth. In a nutshell, characteristics

[21] S. Haffner, 'In Leon sind alle Deutschen Fußballbrüder', *FAZ*, 15 June 1970 (all translations by Andreas Helle).

[22] Cf. H. Böttiger, *Kein Mann, kein Schuß, kein Tor: Das Drama des deutschen Fußballs* (Munich: Beck, 1993).

[23] H. Väth, *Profifußball: Zur Soziologie der Bundesliga* (Frankfurt: Campus, 1994), 130–4; J. Rollmann, *Beruf: Fußballprofi. Oder: Ein Leben zwischen Sein und Schein* (Berlin: Sportverlag, 1997), 167–71.

ascribed to English players mirror those attributed to German players in English papers, except, perhaps, for fairness and honesty. This image of honest, unspoiled traditionalism is usually symbolized by the most famous English football grounds: Wembley and Manchester's Old Trafford. These arenas are holy ground, as German journalists like to say. After the first German success at Wembley in 1972, for instance, *Bild-Zeitung* suggested that all Germany matches should henceforth be held at Wembley.[24] The paper obviously hoped to preserve the spirit of Wembley, not an accidental allusion to the spirit of Berne, where a German team won its first World Cup in 1954.

In spite of the widespread admiration for England's qualities in football, its national team has never been more than one arch-rival amongst others. Additionally, during the 1990s, a somewhat patronizing attitude has replaced much of the former respect for English teams. Today's pre-match reports resemble stereotyped commercials such as those for 'After Eight' chocolates. 'Odd' English habits such as cricket, five o'clock tea, or the monarchy are invariably mentioned, along with pseudo-expert notions such as 'kick-and-rush-football', a fake English term invented by German journalists. Most German papers offer revealing admiration for the allegedly simple patriotism and the national cohesion of the English. It is quite obvious that this admiration reflects the absence of such attitudes among Germans. There is a typical quotation from the *Frankfurter Allgemeine Zeitung* after the 1990 World Cup semi-final in Turin: 'The defeated Britons wallow in pain and pride tonight.—The Queen Mum, too, performed her national duty. . . . And indeed, it was a national duty to watch the match against the Germans, who are seen with a mixture of admiration and old prejudice.'[25]

In general, German sports journalists have a relaxed attitude to English football today. The common view is that the former teacher has now turned apprentice. This reversal of roles was a frequent subject in the Euro '96 coverage, stimulated by its motto 'Football's coming home'. Yet, as German journalists are restricted in their work by rules of sportsmanship and anti-nationalism, they are circumspect in using negative stereotypes. During the 1960s

---

[24] G. Pietsch, 'Keine Panzer mehr', *Bild-Zeitung*, 2 May 1972.
[25] 'Die geschlagenen Briten schwelgen in Schmerz und Stolz—Auch die Königinmutter gehorcht der nationalen Pflicht', *FAZ*, 6 July 1990.

and 1970s in particular, these limitations were manifest in the sports sections of all examined newspapers. A popular method for evading this self-restraint is to quote from foreign newspapers. In 1970 *Bild-Zeitung*, for instance, quoted unnamed Mexicans at length in order to highlight supposedly negative English characteristics. These included arrogance, contempt for foreigners, lack of respect for foreign teams during the World Cup in England, and racial prejudice which the Mexicans experienced in England in 1966.[26]

If the sports section is used as a platform for reflection about German society and its development at all, matches against England have obviously not sparked off such a debate recently. The reason is simple. Since 1970 Germany has not lost an important football match to England. Consequently, England is one among several countries with a well-respected national football team. Some of them, too, were among Germany's enemies in the last two wars.

Conclusion

As in the English case, German papers reflect anxieties and reservations widespread in Germany. From here, the Other, in this case England, is formed in accordance with one's own needs. The perception of English characteristics in German newspapers reflects what journalists and writers miss in their own culture. The result of their efforts cannot be called an informed and complex image of England. Coverage of particular matches is an opportunity to gather arguments about the collective self, and to support it with concrete evidence. Against this background it is likely that the envious rivalry with which the English perceive Germany sometimes does not stem from football matches, but from a contrast in the development of the two countries, which has coincidentally been reflected in the turn of fortunes in football since 1966. In Germany there is no comparable unease: peculiar habits and the much-quoted traditionalist behaviour of Englishmen are interpreted as evidence of a more fortunate history, and of a nation less at odds with itself than Germany.

[26] 'Ihr "England Haß" ist vier Jahre alt', *Bild-Zeitung*, 13 June 1970.

Football articles in English and German papers contain little information about the opponent beyond portraits of important players, and the usual trivia and clichés. It would be over hasty, though, to conclude that the game itself does not add much to cultural transfer between participating countries. Although international football matches reinforce existing national stereotypes because they foster an inverse perception of the Other, football fans also read other sections of their newspaper, and they probably travel more than the average citizen. The limits of interpretation of football matches depend on this knowledge, and sometimes prejudice, about the other side in the competition. Football offers an occasion for identification, and for comparison with others. The game reveals—and also affects to some extent—the interpretative context of the perception of others. Above all, however, it enables heterogeneous people to share the experience of genuine, though short-lived, unity without lengthy theoretical, political, or theological debate. In this, and not in the alleged roots of football in human aggressiveness, lies its resemblance to war.

Notes on Contributors and Editors

PETER ALTER is Professor of Modern History at the Gerhard Mercator University in Duisburg and writes on British, Irish, and German history. He was a Fellow and Deputy Director of the German Historical Institute London (1976–94), and Guest Fellow of Trinity Hall, Cambridge. His books include *The German Question and Europe* (2000), *Nationalism* (2nd edn. 1994), and *The Reluctant Patron: Science and the State in Britain 1850–1920* (1987). He is editor/co-editor of *Die Konstruktion der Nation gegen die Juden* (1999), *Out of the Third Reich: Refugee Historians in Post-War Britain* (1998), *Exilanten und andere Deutsche in Fontanes London* (1996), and *Nationalismus: Dokumente zur Geschichte und Gegenwart eines Phänomens* (1994).

SIR JULIAN BULLARD, Fellow of All Souls College, Oxford, and St Antony's College, Oxford, has held various diplomatic posts in Germany. He was the British Ambassador in Bonn from 1984 to 1988. He has published widely on Anglo-German relations.

ANTHONY GLEES is Reader in German Politics at Brunel University. His most recent book is *Reinventing Germany* (1996). His research is on contemporary German politics and British–German relations. He is currently examining the work of the former East German Ministry for State Security in the United Kingdom.

ANDREAS HELLE, as an academic at the University of Frankfurt am Main, has worked on the emergence of national movements and collective experiences in a media society. His book, *Ulster: Die blockierte Nation*, was published in 1999. He works in the Planning Department of the SPD Party Headquarters in Berlin.

BEATRICE HEUSER holds a D.Phil. from Oxford and a *Habilitation* from the Philipps University in Marburg/Lahn. She is Professor of International and Strategic Studies at King's College London. Her major publications include *NATO, Britain, France and the FRG: Nuclear Strategies and Forces for Europe 1949–2000* (1997) and *Nuclear Mentalities? Strategies and Beliefsystems in Britain, France and the FRG* (1998). With Cyril Buffet she has edited *Haunted by History: Myths in International Relations* (1998). Most recently, she has completed *Reading Clausewitz* (2002), and has edited a volume (with Anja Hartmann) entitled *Thinking War, Peace and World Orders*.

JENS HÖLSCHER is head of the research group 'Economics of Transition' at the University of Brighton. Previously he taught at the Universities of Berlin, Swansea, Birmingham, and Chemnitz. He held Visiting Professorships at the Universities of Halle (IWH), Bonn (ZEI), and Almaty (KIMEP). He is interested in monetary and transition economics, both areas in which he has published widely. He is co-editor of the book series *Studies in Economic Transition* and his most recent book is entitled (ed.), *50 Years of the German Mark: Essays in Honour of Stephen F. Frowen* (2001).

LOTHAR KETTENACKER is Deputy Director of the German Historical Institute London and Professor of History at the University of Frankfurt am Main. He has published on Nazi history and Anglo-German relations, and is the author of a study on British planning for Germany during the Second World War, *Krieg zur Friedenssicherung: Die Deutschlandplanung der britischen Regierung während des Zweiten Weltkrieges* (1989). His most recent publication is *Germany Since 1945* (1997).

BENEDIKT KOEHLER is a Manager at the World Gold Council in London. He was educated at Yale University and the University of Tübingen, and has been a professional banker since 1979. He is the author of a biography, *Ludwig Bamberger: Revolutionär und Bankier* (1999).

KLAUS LARRES is Reader in Politics and Jean Monnet Professor of European Foreign and Security Policy at the Queen's University of Belfast. He was educated at Cologne University and the London School of Economics, and his main fields of interest are the international history of the Cold War, European integration, and Anglo-German and Anglo-American relations in the twentieth century. Among his publications are the monograph *Politik der Illusionen: Churchill, Eisenhower und die deutsche Frage 1945–1955* (1995) and the edited volumes *Germany since Unification: The Development of the Berlin Republic* (1998, 2nd edn. 2001), and *Uneasy Allies: British–German Relations and European Integration since 1945* (2000). His book *Churchill's Cold War: The Power of Personal Diplomacy (1908–55)* will be published in May 2002.

HENRY B. LOEWENDAHL is a Senior Consultant in Pricewaterhouse-Coopers, Belgium. In 1999 he was awarded a doctorate from the Institute for German Studies, University of Birmingham, and his thesis, *Bargaining with Multinationals: The Investment of Siemens and Nissan in North East England*, is being published as a book by Palgrave. His main fields of interest are corporate globalization strategy, foreign direct investment, and economic development. Recent articles include 'Siemens' Anglo-Saxon Strategy', *German Politics* (April 1999) and 'Turkey's Foreign Direct Investment Performance', *Centre for European Policy Studies* (November 2000).

N. PIERS LUDLOW is a Lecturer in International History at the London School of Economics. His principal area of research is the history of European integration and Britain's troubled relationship with that process. He has published *Dealing With Britain: The Six and the First UK Application to the EEC* (1997) and numerous articles and chapters on the 1950s and 1960s.

ALAN S. MILWARD is Professor of the History of European Integration at the European University Institute. He is the author of *The Reconstruction of Western Europe (1945–51)* (1984) and *The European Rescue of the Nation-State* (1992) among other works. He is currently appointed as Official Historian to write a history of the United Kingdom's entry into the European Community.

TONY NICHOLLS is Professor of Modern German History at the University of Oxford and Fellow of St Antony's College, Oxford. He has conducted research on European, and particularly German, history in the twentieth century. His recent publications include 'Zusammenbruch und Wiederaufbau: Die Reichsbahn während der Besatzungszeit', in Lothar Gall and Manfred Pohl (eds.), *Die Eisenbahn in Deutschland: Von den Anfängen bis zur Gegenwart* (1999); *The Bonn Republic: West German Democracy 1945–1990* (1997); *Freedom with Responsibility: The Social Market Economy in Germany 1918–1963* (1994); and *Weimar and the Rise of Hitler*, 4th revised edn. (2000).

JEREMY NOAKES is Professor of History at the University of Exeter. His main field of research is Nazism and the Third Reich. His publications include *The Nazi Party in Lower Saxony 1921–1933* (1971), *Government, Party and People in Nazi Germany* (1980), and *Nazism 1919–1945*, 4 vols. (1983–98).

KLAUS REICHERT is Professor of English Literature and Director of the Centre for Research in Early Modern History, Culture and Science. His fields of interest include Renaissance and modernist literature, history and theory of translation, and history of science. Among his publications are *Fortuna oder die Beständigkeit des Wechsels* (1985), *Vielfacher Schriftsinn: Zu Finnegans Wake* (1989), and *Der fremde Shakespeare* (1998). Currently he is editing the German edition of the works of Virginia Woolf, nineteen volumes of which have so far been published. He is also a translator from English, Dutch, and Hebrew.

MARTIN P. C. SCHAAD is Assistant Director of the Einstein Forum in Potsdam, Germany. His work on the history and politics of the European Communities has been published in a number of learned journals and editions. His dissertation was awarded the Annual Prize of the German Historical Institute London in 1996 and has recently been published as *Bullying Bonn: Anglo-German Diplomacy on European Integration, 1955–61* (2000).

GUSTAV SCHMIDT is Professor of International Politics, Faculty of Social Sciences, and co-opted member of the Faculty of History, Ruhr University Bochum. He has been visiting professor at St Antony's College, Oxford; Emory University; University of Toronto; and Cornell University. His major publications include *The Politics and Economics of British Appeasement, 1930–1937* (1985; translation of *England in der Krise, 1981*); and *Der europäische Imperialismus* (1985). He has contributed to, and been guest editor of, two themed issues of the journal *Contemporary European History: Divided Germany in a Divided Europe* (vol. 3, part 2, July 1994) and *Changing Perspectives on European Security and NATO's Search for a New Role: From the 1960s to the Present* (vol. 7, part 3, November 1998). Other edited volumes include *Zwischen Bündnissicherung und privilegierter Partnerschaft: Die deutsch-britischen Beziehungen und die Vereinigten Staaten von Amerika, 1955–1963* (1995); (with Charles F. Doran) *Amerikas Option für Deutschland und Japan* (1996); and *A History of NATO: The First Fifty Years*, 3 vols. (2001).

PETER WENDE was Director of the German Historical Institute London and is Professor Emeritus of History at the University of Frankfurt am Main. He has published on German and British history. Among his publications are *Große Revolutionen der Geschichte: Von der Frühzeit bis zur Gegenwart* (ed., 2000), *British and German Historiography, 1750–1950* (ed. with Benedikt Stuchtey, 2000), *Rivalität und Partnerschaft: Studien zu den deutsch-britischen Beziehungen im 19. und 20. Jahrhundert: Festschrift für Anthony J. Nicholls* (ed. with Gerhard A. Ritter, 1999), *Reform in Great Britain and Germany, 1750–1850* (ed. with T. C. W. Blanning, 1999), *Englische Könige und Königinnen: Von Heinrich VII. bis Elisabeth II.* (ed., 1998), *Geschichte Englands* (2nd edn. 1995), and *Politische Reden* (ed., 3 vols., 1990–4).

JONATHAN WRIGHT is a Tutorial Fellow and University Lecturer in Politics at Christ Church, Oxford. His research interests are in German politics and foreign policy. His recent publications include 'The role of Britain in West German foreign policy since 1945', *German Politics*, 5 (1996), 26–42, and 'Stresemann's concept of international relations', in Adolf M. Birke, Magnus Brechtken, and Alaric Searle (eds.), *An Anglo-German Dialogue* (2000). He is co-editor of *Liberalism, Anti-Semitism and Democracy: Essays in Honour of Peter Pulzer* (2001), and has recently completed a long-standing project, *Gustav Stresemann: A Political Biography*.

CLEMENS A. WURM is Professor of West European History at the Humboldt University in Berlin. He has published on the history of France and Britain, on the history of international relations in the twentieth century, and on European integration. His books include *Industrielle Interessenpolitik und Staat: Internationale Kartelle in der britischen Außen- und Wirtschaftspolitik während der Zwischenkriegszeit* (1988) and *Business, Politics and*

International Relations: Steel, Cotton and International Cartels in British Politics 1924–1939, trans. by Patrick Salmon (1993). He has edited *Internationale Kartelle und Außenpolitik: Beiträge zur Zwischenkriegszeit. International Cartels and Foreign Policy: Contributions on the Interwar Period* (1989), *Wege nach Europa: Wirtschaft und Außenpolitik Großbritanniens im 20. Jahrhundert* (1992), and *Western Europe and Germany: The Beginnings of European Integration 1945–1960* (1995/1996).

Index